PLUTARCH'S LIVES

VOLUME FOUR

THE FORUM, TEMPLE OF SATURN

PLUTARCH'S LIVES

The Translation Called Dryden's

Corrected from the Greek and Revised by

A. H. CLOUGH

Sometime Fellow and Tutor of the Oriel College, Oxford, and Late Professor of the English Language and Literature at University College, London

With
Dr. William Smith's Historical Notes

IN FIVE VOLUMES

VOLUME FOUR

Illustrated

WILDSIDE PRESS

CONTENTS

Vol. IV

	PAGE
AGESILAUS	3
POMPEY	58
COMPARISON OF POMPEY WITH AGESILAUS	171
ALEXANDER	178
CÆSAR	286
PHOCION	366
CATO THE YOUNGER	413
AGIS	495
CLEOMENES	520
TIBERIUS AND CAIUS GRACCHUS	565
CAIUS GRACCHUS	594
COMPARISON OF TIBERIUS AND CAIUS GRACCHUS WITH AGIS AND CLEOMENES	619

ILLUSTRATIONS

Vol. IV

The Forum, Temple of Saturn,	*Frontispiece*
	FACING PAGE
The Return of the Ten Thousand Under Xenophon	12
Pompey the Great	50
Aristotle and His Pupil Alexander	182
Alexander at the Dead Body of Darius Codomanus	240
Cæsar Crossing the Rubicon	326

PLUTARCH'S LIVES

AGESILAUS[1]

Translated by W. Needham, M.D.

ARCHIDAMUS, the son of Zeuxidamus, having reigned gloriously over the Lacedæmonians, left behind him two sons, Agis the elder, begotten of Lampido, a noble lady, Agesilaus, much the younger, born of Eupolia, the daughter of Melesippidas. Now the succession belonging to Agis by law, Agesilaus, who in all probability was to be but a private man, was educated according to the usual discipline of the country, hard and severe, and meant to teach young men to obey their superiors. Whence it was that, men say, Simonides called Sparta " the tamer of men," because by early strictness of education, they, more than any nation, trained the citizens to obedience to the laws, and made them tractable and patient of subjection, as horses that are broken in while colts. The law did not impose this harsh rule on the heirs apparent of the kingdom. But Agesilaus, whose good fortune it was to be born a younger brother, was consequently bred to all the arts of obedience, and so the better fitted for the government, when it fell to his share; hence it was that he proved the most popular-tempered of the Spartan kings, his early life having added to his natural kingly and command-

---

[1] Agesilaus, son of Archidamus II., succeeded his half-brother Agis II., B.C. 398. He died in the winter of 361-360 B.C., after a life of above 80 years and a reign of 38 years. In his reign, indeed, Sparta's fall took place, but not through him, for he was one of the best citizens and generals that Sparta ever had.—DR. WILLIAM SMITH.

ing qualities the gentle and humane feelings of a citizen.

While he was yet a boy, bred up in one of what are called the *flocks,* or classes,[2] he attracted the attachment of Lysander, who was particularly struck with the orderly temper that he manifested. For though he was one of the highest spirits, emulous above any of his companions, ambitious of preëminence in every thing, and showed an impetuosity and fervor of mind which irresistibly carried him through all opposition or difficulty he could meet with; yet, on the other side, he was so easy and gentle in his nature, and so apt to yield to authority, that though he would do nothing on compulsion, upon ingenuous motives he would obey any commands, and was more hurt by the least rebuke or disgrace, than he was distressed by any toil or hardship.

He had one leg shorter than the other, but this deformity was little observed in the general beauty of his person in youth. And the easy way in which he bore it, (he being the first always to pass a jest upon himself,) went far to make it disregarded. And indeed his high spirit and eagerness to distinguish himself were all the more conspicuous by it, since he never let his lameness withhold him from any toil or any brave action. Neither his statue nor picture are extant, he never allowing them in his life, and utterly forbidding them to be made after his death. He is said to have been a little man, of a contemptible presence; but the goodness of his humor, and his constant cheerfulness and playfulness of temper, always free from any thing of moroseness or haughtiness, made him more attract-

---

[2] Into which the children were enrolled at the age of seven years, as he says in his life of Lycurgus. See Vol. I., p. 106.

ive, even to his old age, than the most beautiful and youthful men of the nation. Theophrastus writes, that the Ephors laid a fine upon Archidamus for marrying a little wife, "For" said they, "she will bring us a race of kinglets, instead of kings."

Whilst Agis, the elder brother reigned, Alcibiades, being then an exile from Athens, came from Sicily to Sparta; nor had he stayed long there, before his familiarity with Timæa, the king's wife, grew suspected, insomuch that Agis refused to own a child of hers, which, he said, was Alcibiades's, not his. Nor, if we may believe Duris, the historian, was Timæa much concerned at it, being herself forward enough to whisper among her helot maid-servants, that the infant's true name was Alcibiades, not Leotychides. Meanwhile it was believed, that the amour he had with her was not the effect of his love but of his ambition, that he might have Spartan kings of his posterity. This affair being grown public, it became needful for Alcibiades to withdraw from Sparta. But the child Leotychides had not the honors due to a legitimate son paid him, nor was he ever owned by Agis, till by his prayers and tears he prevailed with him to declare him his son before several witnesses upon his death-bed. But this did not avail to fix him in the throne of Agis, after whose death Lysander, who had lately achieved his conquest of Athens by sea, and was of the greatest power in Sparta, promoted Agesilaus, urging Leotychides's bastardy as a bar to his pretensions. Many of the other citizens, also, were favorable to Agesilaus and zealously joined his party, induced by the opinion they had of his merits, of which they themselves had been spectators, in the time that he had been bred up among them. But there was a man named Diopithes, at Sparta, who had a great knowledge of ancient oracles, and was thought particularly skilful and clever in all points of religion and divination. He alleged, that it was unlawful to make a lame man king of Lacedæmon, citing in the debate the following oracle:—

> Beware, great Sparta, lest there come of thee,
> Though sound thyself, an halting sovereignty;
> Troubles, both long and unexpected too,
> And storms of deadly warfare shall ensue.

But Lysander was not wanting with an evasion, alleging, that if the Spartans were really apprehensive of the oracle, they must have a care of Leotychides; for it was not the limping foot of a king that the gods cared about, but the purity of the Herculean family, into whose rights if a spurious issue were admitted, it would make the kingdom to halt indeed. Agesilaus likewise alleged, that the bastardy of Leotychides was witnessed to by Neptune, who threw Agis out of bed by a violent earthquake, after which time he ceased to visit his wife, yet Leotychides was born above ten months after this.

Agesilaus was upon these allegations declared king, and soon possessed himself of the private estate of Agis, as well as his throne, Leotychides being wholly rejected as a bastard. He now turned his attention to his kindred by the mother's side, persons of worth and virtue, but miserably poor. To them he gave half his brother's estate, and by this popular act gained general good-will and reputation, in the place of the envy and ill-feeling which the inheritance might otherwise have procured him. What Xenophon tells us of him, that by complying with, and, as it were, being ruled by his country, he grew into such great power with them, that he could do what he pleased, is meant to apply to the power he gained in the following manner with the Ephors and Elders. These were at that time of the greatest authority in the State; the former, officers annually chosen; the Elders, holding their places during life; both instituted, as already told in the life of Lycurgus, to restrain the power of the kings. Hence it was that there was always from generation to generation, a feud and contention between them and the kings. But Agesilaus took another course. Instead of contending with them, he courted them; in all proceedings he commenced by taking their advice, was always ready to go, nay almost run, when they called him; if he were upon his royal seat hearing causes and the Ephors came in, he rose to them; whenever any man was elected into the Council of Elders, he presented him with a gown and an ox. Thus, whilst he made show of deference to them, and of a desire to extend their authority, he secretly advanced his own, and enlarged the prerogatives of the kings by several liberties which their friendship to his person conceded.

To other citizens he so behaved himself, as to be less blamable in his enmities than in his friendships; for against his enemy he forbore to take any unjust advantage, but his friends he would assist, even in what was unjust. If an enemy had done any thing praiseworthy, he felt it shameful to detract from his due, but his friends he knew not how to reprove when they did ill, nay, he would eagerly join with them, and assist them in their misdeed, and thought all offices of friendship commendable, let the matter in which they were employed be what it would. Again, when any of his adversaries was overtaken in a fault, he would be the first to pity him, and be soon entreated to procure his pardon, by which he won the hearts of all men. Insomuch that his popularity grew at last suspected by the Ephors, who laid a fine on him, professing that he was appropriating the citizens to himself, who ought to be the common property of the State. For as it is the opinion of philosophers, that could you take away strife and opposition out of the universe, all the heavenly bodies would stand still, generation and motion would cease in the mutual concord and agreement of all things, so the Spartan legislator seems to have admitted ambition and emulation, among the ingredients of his Commonwealth, as the incentives of virtue, distinctly wishing that there should be some dispute and competition among his men of worth, and pronouncing the mere idle, uncontested, mutual compliance to unproved deserts to be but a false sort of concord. And some think Homer had an eye to this, when he introduces Agamemnon well pleased with the quarrel arising between Ulysses and Achilles,[3] and with the " terrible words " that passed between them, which he would never have done, unless he had thought emulations and dissensions between the noblest men to be of great public benefit. Yet this maxim is not simply to be

---

[3] After the feast was over, with which Alcinous entertained Ulysses, the song which the attendant harper first recited was " of a story, the fame of which then went to heaven, the quarrel of Ulysses, and Achilles the son of Peleus, how once they disputed, at the rich feast in honor of the gods, with terrible words; and the king of men, Agamemnon, rejoiced in his mind, because the noblest of the Achæans were disputing." Their dispute was, Athenæus and the scholiasts say, whether Troy should be taken by open war or by stratagem.—*Odyssey*, viii. 74.

AGESILAUS

granted, without restriction, for if animosities go too far, they are very dangerous to cities, and of most pernicious consequence.

When Agesilaus was newly entered upon the government, there came news from Asia, that the Persian king was making great naval preparations, resolving with a high hand to dispossess the Spartans of their maritime supremacy. Lysander was eager for the opportunity of going over and succoring his friends in Asia, whom he had there left governors and masters of the cities, whose mal-administration and tyrannical behavior was causing them to be driven out, and in some cases put to death. He therefore persuaded Agesilaus to claim the command of the expedition, and by carrying the war far from Greece into Persia, to anticipate the designs of the barbarian. He also wrote to his friends in Asia, that by embassy they should demand Agesilaus for their captain. Agesilaus, therefore, coming into public assembly, offered his service, upon condition that he might have thirty Spartans for captains and counsellors; two thousand chosen men of the newly enfranchised helots, and allies to the number of six thousand. Lysander's authority and assistance soon obtained his request, so that he was sent away with the thirty Spartans, of whom Lysander was at once the chief, not only because of his power and reputation, but also on account of his friendship with Agesilaus, who esteemed his procuring him this charge a greater obligation, than that of preferring him to the kingdom.

Whilst the army was collecting to the rendezvous at Geræstus, Agesilaus went with some of his friends to Aulis, where in a dream he saw a man approach him, and speak to him after this manner: "O king of the Lacedæmonians, you cannot but know that, before yourself, there hath been but one general captain of the whole of the Greeks, namely, Agamemnon; now, since you succeed him in the same office and command of the same men, since you war against the same enemies, and begin your expedition from the same place, you ought also to offer such a sacrifice, as he offered before he weighed anchor." Agesilaus at the same moment remembered that the sacrifice which Agamemnon offered was his own daughter, he being so directed by the oracle. Yet was he not at all disturbed at it, but as soon as he arose, he told his dream to his friends, adding, that he would propitiate the goddess with the sacrifices a goddess must delight in, and would not follow the ignorant example of his predecessor. He therefore ordered an hind to be crowned with chaplets, and bade his own soothsayer perform the rite, not the usual person whom the Bœotians, in ordinary course, appointed to that office. When the Bœotian magistrates understood it, they were much offended, and sent officers to Agesilaus, to forbid his sacrificing contrary to the laws of the country. These having delivered their message to him, immediately went to the altar, and threw down the quarters of the hind that lay upon it. Agesilaus took this very ill, and without further sacrifice immediately sailed away, highly displeased with the Bœotians, and much discouraged in his mind at the omen boding to himself an unsuccessful voyage, and an imperfect issue of the whole expedition.

When he came to Ephesus, he found the power and interest of Lysander, and the honors paid to him, insufferably great; all applications were made to him, crowds of suitors attended at his door, and followed upon his steps, as if nothing but the mere name of commander belonged, to satisfy the usage,

to Agesilaus, the whole power of it being devolved
upon Lysander. None of all the commanders that
had been sent into Asia was either so powerful or
so formidable as he; no one had rewarded his friends
better, or had been more severe against his enemies;
which things having been lately done, made the
greater impression on men's minds, especially when
they compared the simple and popular behavior of
Agesilaus, with the harsh and violent and brief-
spoken demeanor which Lysander still retained.
Universal deference was yielded to this, and little
regard shown to Agesilaus. This first occasioned
offence to the other Spartan captains, who resented
that they should rather seem the attendants of
Lysander, than the councillors of Agesilaus. And at
length Agesilaus himself, though not perhaps an
envious man in his nature, nor apt to be troubled
at the honors redounding upon other men, yet eager
for honor and jealous of his glory, began to apprehend that Lysander's greatness would carry away
from him the reputation of whatever great action
should happen. He therefore went this way to
work. He first opposed him in all his counsels;
whatever Lysander specially advised was rejected,
and other proposals followed. Then whoever made
any address to him, if he found him attached to
Lysander, certainly lost his suit. So also in judicial
cases, any one whom he spoke strongly against was
sure to come off with success, and any man whom he
was particularly solicitous to procure some benefit
for, might think it well if he got away without an
actual loss. These things being clearly not done by
chance, but constantly and of a set purpose,
Lysander was soon sensible of them, and hesitated
not to tell his friends, that they suffered for his sake,
bidding them apply themselves to the king, and such

as were more powerful with him than he was. Such sayings of his seeming to be designed purposely to excite ill feeling, Agesilaus went on to offer him a yet more open affront, appointing him his meat-carver; and would in public companies scornfully say, "Let them go now and pay their court to my carver." Lysander, no longer able to brook these indignities, complained at last to Agesilaus himself, telling him, that he knew very well how to humble his friends. Agesilaus answered, "I know certainly how to humble those who pretend to more power than myself." "That," replied Lysander, "is perhaps rather said by you, than done by me; I desire only, that you will assign me some office and place, in which I may serve you without incurring your displeasure."

Upon this Agesilaus sent him to the Hellespont, whence he procured Spithridates, a Persian of the province of Pharnabazus, to come to the assistance of the Greeks with two hundred horse, and a great supply of money. Yet his anger did not so come down, but he thenceforward pursued the design of wresting the kingdom out of the hands of the two families which then enjoyed it, and making it wholly elective; and it is thought that he would on account of this quarrel have excited a great commotion in Sparta, if he had not died in the Bœotian war. Thus ambitious spirits in a commonwealth, when they transgress their bounds, are apt to do more harm than good. For though Lysander's pride and assumption was most ill-timed and insufferable in its display, yet Agesilaus surely could have found some other way of setting him right, less offensive to a man of his reputation and ambitious temper. Indeed they were both blinded with the same passion, so as one not to recognize the authority of his

THE RETURN OF THE TEN THOUSAND UNDER XENOPHOR

superior, the other not to bear with the imperfections of his friend.

Tisaphernes being at first afraid of Agesilaus, treated with him about setting the Grecian cities at liberty, which was agreed on. But soon after finding a sufficient force drawn together, he resolved upon war, for which Agesilaus was not sorry. For the expectation of this expedition was great, and he did not think it for his honor, that Xenophon with ten thousand men should march through the heart of Asia to the sea, beating the Persian forces when and how he pleased, and that he at the head of the Spartans, then sovereigns both at sea and land, should not achieve some memorable action for Greece. And so to be even with Tisaphernes, he requites his perjury by a fair stratagem. He pretends to march into Caria, whither, when he had drawn Tisaphernes and his army, he suddenly turns back, and falls upon Phrygia, takes many of their cities, and carries away great booty, showing his allies, that to break a solemn league was a downright contempt of the gods, but the circumvention of an enemy in war was not only just but glorious, a gratification at once and an advantage.

Being weak in horse and discouraged by ill omens in the sacrifices, he retired to Ephesus, and there raised cavalry. He obliged the rich men, that were not inclined to serve in person, to find each of them a horseman armed and mounted; and there being many who preferred doing this, the army was quickly reinforced by a body, not of unwilling recruits for the infantry, but of brave and numerous horsemen. For those that were not good at fighting themselves, hired such as were more military in their inclinations, and such as loved not horse-service substituted in their places such as did. Agamemnon's example had been a good one, when he took the present of an excellent mare, to dismiss a rich coward from the army.[4]

When by Agesilaus's order the prisoners he had taken in Phrygia were exposed to sale, they were first stripped of their garments, and then sold naked. The clothes found many customers to buy them, but the bodies being, from the want of all exposure and exercise, white and tender-skinned, were derided and scorned as unserviceable. Agesilaus, who stood by at the auction, told his Greeks, " These are the men against whom ye fight, and these the things you will gain by it."

The season of the year being come, he boldly gave out that he would invade Lydia; and this plaindealing of his was now mistaken for a stratagem by Tisaphernes, who, by not believing Agesilaus, having been already deceived by him, overreached himself. He expected that he should have made choice of Caria, as a rough country, not fit for horse, in which he deemed Agesilaus to be weak, and directed his own marches accordingly. But when he found him to be as good as his word, and to have entered into the country of Sardis, he made great haste after him, and by great marches of his horse, overtaking the loose stragglers who were pillaging the country, he cut them off. Agesilaus

[4] Ætha, Agamemnon's mare, which was driven with one of his own by Menelaus in the race, Iliad XXIII., 295, had been given him by Echepōlus, son of Anchises, "as a gift, not to go with him to the windy Ilium, but that he might stay and enjoy himself at home; for Zeus had given him great wealth, and he lived in spacious Sicyon."

meanwhile, considering that the horse had outridden the foot, but that he himself had the whole body of his own army entire, made haste to engage them. He mingled his light-armed foot, carrying targets, with the horse, commanding them to advance at full speed and begin the battle, whilst he brought up the heavier-armed men in the rear. The success was answerable to the design; the barbarians were put to the rout, the Grecians pursued hard, took their camp, and put many of them to the sword. The consequence of this victory was very great; for they had not only the liberty of foraging the Persian country, and plundering at pleasure, but also saw Tisaphernes pay dearly for all the cruelty he had showed the Greeks, to whom he was a professed enemy. For the king of Persia sent Tithraustes, who took off his head, and presently dealt with Agesilaus about his return into Greece, sending to him ambassadors to that purpose, with commission to offer him great sums of money. Agesilaus's answer was, that the making of peace belonged to the Lacedæmonians, not to him; as for wealth, he had rather see it in his soldiers' hands than his own; that the Grecians thought it not honorable to enrich themselves with the bribes of their enemies, but with their spoils only. Yet, that he might gratify Tithraustes for the justice he had done upon Tisaphernes, the common enemy of the Greeks, he removed his quarters into Phrygia, accepting thirty talents for his expenses. Whilst he was upon his march, he received a *staff* from the government at Sparta, appointing him admiral as well as general. This was an honor which was never done to any but Agesilaus, who being now undoubtedly the greatest and most illustrious man of his time, still, as Theopompus has said, gave himself more occasion of glory in his own virtue and merit than was given him in this authority and power. Yet he committed a fault in preferring Pisander to the command of the navy, when there were others at hand both older and more experienced; in this not so much consulting the public good, as the gratification of his kindred, and especially his wife, whose brother Pisander was.

Having removed his camp into Pharnabazus's province, he not only met with great plenty of provisions, but also raised great sums of money, and marching on to the bounds of Paphlagonia, he soon drew Cotys, the king of it, into a league, to which he of his own accord inclined, out of the opinion he had of Agesilaus's honor and virtue. Spithridates, from the time of his abandoning Pharnabazus, constantly attended Agesilaus in the camp whithersoever he went. This Spithridates had a son, a very handsome boy, called Megabates, of whom Agesilaus was extremely fond, and also a very beautiful daughter, that was marriageable. Her Agesilaus matched to Cotys, and taking of him a thousand horse, with two thousand light-armed foot, he returned into Phrygia, and there pillaged the country of Pharnabazus, who durst not meet him in the field, nor yet trust to his garrisons, but getting his valuables together, got out of the way and moved about up and down with a flying army, till Spithridates joining with Herippidas the Spartan, took his camp, and all his property. Herippidas being too severe an inquirer into the plunder with which the barbarian soldiers had enriched themselves, and forcing them to deliver it up with too much strictness, so disobliged Spithridates with his questioning and examining, that he changed sides again, and went off with the Paphlagonians to Sardis. This was a very great vexation to Agesilaus, not only that he had lost the friendship of a valiant commander, and with him a considerable part of his army, but still more that it had been done with the disrepute of a sordid and petty covetousness, of which he always had made it a point of honor to keep both himself and his country clear. Besides these public causes, he had a private one, his excessive fondness for the son, which touched him to the quick, though he endeavored to master it, and, especially in presence of the boy, to suppress all appearance of it; so much so that when Megabates, for that was his name, came once to receive a kiss from him, he declined it. At which when the young boy blushed and drew back, and afterward saluted him at a more reserved distance, Agesilaus soon repenting his coldness, and changing his mind, pretended to wonder why he did not salute him with the same familiarity as formerly. His friends about him answered, "You are in the fault, who would not accept the kiss of the boy, but turned away in alarm; he would come to you again, if you would have the courage to let him do so." Upon this Agesilaus paused a while, and at length answered, "You need not encourage him to it; I think I had rather be master of myself in that refusal, than see all things that are now before my eyes turned into gold." Thus he demeaned himself to Megabates when present, but he had so great a passion for him in his absence, that it may be questioned whether if the boy had returned again, all the courage he had would have sustained him in such another refusal.

After this, Pharnabazus sought an opportunity of conferring with Agesilaus, which Apollophanes of Cyzicus, the common host of them both, procured for him. Agesilaus coming first to the appointed place, threw himself down upon the grass under a tree, lying there in expectation of Pharnabazus, who, bringing with him soft skins and wrought carpets to lie down upon, when he saw Agesilaus's posture grew ashamed of his luxuries and made no use of them, but laid himself down upon the grass also, without regard for his delicate and richly dyed clothing. Pharnabazus had matter enough of complaint against Agesilaus, and therefore, after the mutual civilities were over, he put him in mind of the great services he had done the Lacedæmonians in the Attic war, of which he thought it an ill recompense to have his country thus harassed and spoiled, by those men who owed so much to him. The Spartans that were present hung down their heads, as conscious of the wrong they had done to their ally. But Agesilaus said, "We, O Pharnabazus, when we were in amity with your master the king, behaved ourselves like friends, and now that we are at war with him, we behave ourselves as enemies. As for you, we must look upon you as a part of his property, and must do these outrages upon you, not intending the harm to you, but to him whom we wound through you. But whenever you will choose rather to be a friend to the Grecians, than a slave of the king of Persia, you may then reckon this army and navy to be all at your command, to defend both you, your country, and your liberties, without which there is nothing honorable, or indeed desirable among men." Upon this Pharnabazus discovered his mind, and answered, "If the king sends another governor in my room, I will certainly come over to you, but as long as he trusts me with the government, I shall be just to him, and not fail to do my utmost endeavors in opposing you." Agesilaus was taken with the answer, and shook hands with him; and rising, said,

"How much rather had I have so brave a man my friend than mine enemy."

Pharnabazus being gone off, his son, staying behind, ran up to Agesilaus, and smilingly said, "Agesilaus, I make you my guest;" and thereupon presented him with a javelin which he had in his hand. Agesilaus received it, and being much taken with the good mien and the courtesy of the youth, looked about to see if there were any thing in his train fit to offer him in return; and observing the horse of Idæus, the secretary, to have very fine trappings on, he took them off, and bestowed them upon the young gentleman. Nor did his kindness rest there, but he continued ever after to be mindful of him, so that when he was driven out of his country by his brothers, and lived an exile in Peloponnesus, he took great care of him, and condescended even to assist him in some love-matters. He had an attachment for a youth of Athenian birth, who was bred up as an athlete; and when at the Olympic games this boy, on account of his great size and general strong and full-grown appearance, was in some danger of not being admitted into the list,[5] the Persian betook himself to Agesilaus, and made use of his friendship. Agesilaus readily assisted him, and not without a great deal of difficulty effected his desires. He was in all other things a man of great and exact justice, but when the case concerned a friend, to be straitlaced in point of justice, he said, was only a colorable pretence of denying him. There is an epistle written to Idrieus, prince of Caria,

---

[5] Of not being allowed, that is, to join in the contests for the *boys'* prizes; as it could not be believed that he was not over the age. At the Olympic games, part of the first and the whole of the second day was taken up with the boys' contests.

that is ascribed to Agesilaus; it is this: "If Nicias be innocent, absolve him; if he be guilty, absolve him upon my account; however be sure to absolve him." This was his usual character in his deportment towards his friends. Yet his rule was not without exception; for sometimes he considered the necessity of his affairs more than his friend, of which he once gave an example, when upon a sudden and disorderly removal of his camp, he left a sick friend behind him, and when he called loudly after him, and implored his help, turned his back, and said it was hard to be compassionate and wise too. This story is related by Hieronymus, the philosopher.

Another year of the war being spent, Agesilaus's fame still increased, insomuch that the Persian king received daily information concerning his many virtues, and the great esteem the world had of his temperance, his plain living, and his moderation. When he made any journey, he would usually take up his lodging in a temple, and there make the gods witnesses of his most private actions, which others would scarce permit men to be acquainted with. In so great an army, you should scarce find a common soldier lie on a coarser mattress, than Agesilaus; he was so indifferent to the varieties of heat and cold, that all the seasons, as the gods sent them, seemed natural to him. The Greeks that inhabited Asia were much pleased to see the great lords and governors of Persia, with all the pride, cruelty, and luxury in which they lived, trembling and bowing before a man in a poor threadbare cloak, and at one laconic word out of his mouth, obsequiously deferring and changing their wishes and purposes. So that it brought to the minds of many the verses of Timotheus,

AGESILAUS

> Mars is the tyrant, gold Greece does not fear.[6]

Many parts of Asia now revolting from the Persians, Agesilaus restored order in the cities, and without bloodshed or banishment of any of their members, reëstablished the proper constitution in the governments, and now resolved to carry away the war from the seaside, and to march further up into the country, and to attack the king of Persia himself in his own home in Susa and Ecbatana; not willing to let the monarch sit idle in his chair, playing umpire in the conflicts of the Greeks, and bribing their popular leaders. But these great thoughts were interrupted by unhappy news from Sparta; Epicydidas is from thence sent to remand him home, to assist his own country, which was then involved in a great war;

> Greece to herself doth a barbarian grow,
> Others could not, she doth herself o'erthrow.

What better can we say of those jealousies, and that league and conspiracy of the Greeks for their own mischief, which arrested fortune in full career, and turned back arms that were already uplifted against the barbarians, to be used upon themselves, and recalled into Greece the war which had been banished out of her? I by no means assent to Demaratus of Corinth, who said, that those Greeks lost a great satisfaction, that did not live to see Alexander sit in the throne of Darius. That sight

[6] The two verses are those of the old translation, and express Plutarch's meaning. But in the original passage, *O Greeks, that have found out barbarian ills,* or, crimes such as only barbarians could be guilty of, is what Andromache says, when the herald, Talthybius, has announced to her, that her child, Astyanax, is to be put to death.—(*Eurip., Troades,* 759.)

should rather have drawn tears from them, when they considered, that they had left that glory to Alexander and the Macedonians, whilst they spent all their own great commanders in playing them against each other in the fields of Leuctra, Coronea, Corinth, and Arcadia.

Nothing was greater or nobler than the behavior of Agesilaus on this occasion, nor can a nobler instance be found in story, of a ready obedience and just deference to orders. Hannibal, though in a bad condition himself, and almost driven out of Italy, could scarcely be induced to obey, when he was called home to serve his country. Alexander made a jest of the battle between Agis and Antipater, laughing and saying, "So whilst we were conquering Darius in Asia, it seems there was a battle of mice in Arcadia." Happy Sparta, meanwhile, in the justice and modesty of Agesilaus, and in the deference he paid to the laws of his country; who, immediately upon receipt of his orders, though in the midst of his high fortune and power, and in full hope of great and glorious success, gave all up and instantly departed, "his object unachieved,"[7] leaving many regrets behind him among his allies in Asia, and proving by his example the falseness of that saying of Demostratus, the son of Phæax, "That

---

[7] The passage in the Iliad (IV., 175) from which the words *his object unachieved* are borrowed is the lament of Agamemnon over Menelaus's wound, when he had been shot by Pandarus,— *if he dies, the Achæans will at once cry out to go home; Helen the Argive will be left for Priam and the Trojans to boast of, while his bones shall rot in the soil, as he lies in Trojan earth, his object unachieved.* "Lying in Trojan earth, having failed in what he attempted," or, "without having done what he wanted," is the last line.

the Lacedæmonians were better in public, but the Athenians in private." For while approving himself an excellent king and general, he likewise showed himself in private an excellent friend, and a most agreeable companion.

The coin of Persia was stamped with the figure of an archer; Agesilaus said, That a thousand Persian archers had driven him out of Asia; meaning the money that had been laid out in bribing the demagogues and the orators in Thebes and Athens, and thus inciting those two States to hostility against Sparta.

Having passed the Hellespont, he marched by land through Thrace, not begging or entreating a passage anywhere, only he sent his messengers to them, to demand whether they would have him pass as a friend or as an enemy. All the rest received him as a friend, and assisted him on his journey. But the Trallians,[8] to whom Xerxes also is said to have given money, demanded a price of him, namely, one hundred talents of silver, and one hundred women. Agesilaus in scorn asked, Why they were not ready to receive them? He marched on and finding the Trallians in arms to oppose him, fought them, and slew great numbers of them. He sent the like embassy to the king of Macedonia, who replied, He would take time to deliberate: "Let him deliberate," said Agesilaus, "we will go forward

---

[8] The reading is uncertain. The Trallians are evidently not the people commonly called by this name, the inhabitants of the town of Tralles, in Asia Minor, still flourishing in Plutarch's time, but a tribe of wild Thracians. The name may perhaps be corrupt; but certain Trallians of Thrace are spoken of as having taken part in the foundation of the town in Asia which took their name.

in the mean time." The Macedonian, being surprised and daunted at the resolution of the Spartan, gave orders to let him pass as a friend. When he came into Thessaly, he wasted the country, because they were in league with the enemy. To Larissa, the chief city of Thessaly, he sent Xenocles and Scythes to treat of a peace, whom when the Larissæans had laid hold of, and put into custody, others were enraged, and advised the siege of the town; but he answered, That he valued either of those men at more than the whole country of Thessaly. He therefore made terms with them, and received his men again upon composition. Nor need we wonder at this saying of Agesilaus, since when he had news brought him from Sparta, of several great captains slain in a battle near Corinth, in which the slaughter fell upon other Greeks, and the Lacedæmonians obtained a great victory with small loss, he did not appear at all satisfied; but with a great sigh cried out, "O Greece, how many brave men hast thou destroyed; who, if they had been preserved to so good an use, had sufficed to have conquered all Persia!" Yet when the Pharsalians grew troublesome to him, by pressing upon his army, and incommoding his passage, he led out five hundred horse, and in person fought and routed them, setting up a trophy under the mount Narthacius. He valued himself very much upon that victory, that with so small a number of his own training, he had vanquished a body of men that thought themselves the best horsemen of Greece.

Here Diphridas, the Ephor, met him, and delivered his message from Sparta, which ordered him immediately to make an inroad into Bœotia; and though he thought this fitter to have been done at another time, and with greater force, he yet obeyed the magistrates. He thereupon told his soldiers that the day was come, on which they were to enter upon that employment, for the performance of which they were brought out of Asia. He sent for two divisions of the army near Corinth to his assistance. The Lacedæmonians at home, in honor to him, made proclamation for volunteers that would serve under the king, to come in and be enlisted. Finding all the young men in the city ready to offer themselves, they chose fifty of the strongest, and sent them.

Agesilaus having gained Thermopylæ, and passed quietly through Phocis, as soon as he had entered Bœotia, and pitched his camp near Chæronea, at once met with an eclipse of the sun, and with ill news from the navy, Pisander, the Spartan admiral, being beaten and slain at Cnidos, by Pharnabazus and Conon. He was much moved at it, both upon his own and the public account. Yet lest his army, being now near engaging, should meet with any discouragement, he ordered the messengers to give out, that the Spartans were the conquerors, and he himself putting on a garland, solemnly sacrificed for the good news, and sent portions of the sacrifices to his friends.

When he came near to Coronea, and was within view of the enemy, he drew up his army, and giving the left wing to the Orchomenians, he himself led the right. The Thebans took the right wing of their army, leaving the left to the Argives. Xenophon, who was present,[9] and fought on Agesilaus's

---

[9] *Xenophon, who was present*, calls it the *hardest-fought battle* of his time in the Hellenics (*IV.*, *3*, 16), referring evidently to the last struggle between Thebans and Spartans, when "they met shield against shield, pushing, fighting, killing, and falling;" to which he adds in his Agesilaus (*II.*, 12), "there was no war-

side, reports it to be the hardest fought battle that he had seen. The beginning of it was not so, for the Thebans soon put the Orchomenians to rout, as also did Agesilaus the Argives. But both parties having news of the misfortune of their left wings, they betook themselves to their relief. Here Agesilaus might have been sure of his victory, had he contented himself not to charge them in the front, but in the flank or rear; but being angry and heated in the fight, he would not wait the opportunity, but fell on at once, thinking to bear them down before him. The Thebans were not behind him in courage, so that the battle was fiercely carried on on both sides, especially near Agesilaus's person, whose new guard of fifty volunteers stood him in great stead that day, and saved his life. They fought with great valor, and interposed their bodies frequently between him and danger, yet could they not so preserve him, but

shout or cry, though not silence either, only the sort of utterance that comes of anger and fierce fighting." *The temple of Minerva the Itonian,* spoken of in the next page, standing *near the battle-field,* was a great sanctuary of the whole Bœotian people, founded by them when they first entered Bœotia, in the plain before Coronea; they called it after the name of that in their own late country in Thessaly. Here the feast of All Bœotians (the Pambœotia) was held, and the congress of the Bœotian towns met. There were in the temple brazen statues, made by Agoracritus, Phidias's scholar, of the Itonian Minerva, and Jupiter, or Pluto, who was worshipped here in some mystic connection with Minerva. See Pausanias (*IX.,* 24), and Strabo (*IX.,* 2, 29), and Col. Leake, Northern Greece (*Vol. II., chap. xii., pp.* 137-141.) The Thessalian *Minerva Itonis* is mentioned in the Life of Pyrrhus (*Vol. III., p.* 35); the little stream that ran by the temple, the Curalius, was also called by the name of that near the temple in Thessaly.

that he received many wounds through his armor with lances and swords, and was with much difficulty gotten off alive by their making a ring about him, and so guarding him, with the slaughter of many of the enemy and the loss of many of their own number. At length finding it too hard a task to break the front of the Theban troops, they opened their own files, and let the enemy march through them, (an artifice which in the beginning they scorned), watching in the mean time the posture of the enemy, who having passed through, grew careless, as esteeming themselves past danger; in which position they were immediately set upon by the Spartans. Yet were they not then put to rout, but marched on to Helicon, proud of what they had done, being able to say, that they themselves, as to their part of the army, were not worsted.

Agesilaus, sore wounded as he was, would not be borne to his tent, till he had been first carried about the field, and had seen the dead conveyed within his encampment. As many of his enemies as had taken sanctuary in the temple, he dismissed. For there stood near the battle-field, the temple of Minerva the Itonian, and before it a trophy erected by the Bœotians, for the victory which under the conduct of Sparton, their general, they obtained over the Athenians under Tolmides, who himself fell in the battle. And next morning early, to make trial of the Theban courage, whether they had any mind to a second encounter, he commanded his soldiers to put on garlands on their heads, and play with their flutes, and raise a trophy before their faces; but when they, instead of fighting, sent for leave to bury their dead, he gave it them; and having so assured himself of the victory, after this he went to

Delphi, to the Pythian games, which were then celebrating, at which feast he assisted, and there solemnly offered the tenth part of the spoils he had brought from Asia, which amounted to a hundred talents.

Thence he returned to his own country, where his way and habits of life quickly excited the affection and admiration of the Spartans; for, unlike other generals, he came home from foreign lands the same man that he went out, having not so learned the fashions of other countries as to forget his own, much less to dislike or despise them. He followed and respected all the Spartan customs, without any change either in the manner of his supping, or bathing, or his wife's apparel, as if he had never travelled over the river Eurotas. So also with his household furniture and his own armor; nay, the very gates of his house were so old, that they might well be thought of Aristodemus's setting up. His daughter's *Canathrum*, says Xenophon, was no richer than that of any one else. The Canathrum, as they call it, is a chair or chariot made of wood, in the shape of a griffin, or tragelaphus,[10] on which the children and young virgins are carried in processions. Xenophon has not left us the name of this daughter of Agesilaus; and Dicæarchus expresses some indignation, because we do not know, he says, the name of Agesilaus's daughter, nor of Epaminondas's mother. But in the records of Laconia, we ourselves found his wife's name to have been Cleora, and his two daughters to have been called Eupolia and Prolyta. And you may also to this day see Agesilaus's spear kept in Sparta, nothing differing from that of other men.

There was a vanity he observed among the

[10] Half goat, half deer.

Spartans, about keeping running horses for the Olympic games, upon which he found they much valued themselves. Agesilaus regarded it as a display not of any real virtue, but of wealth and expense; and to make this evident to the Greeks, induced his sister, Cynisca, to send a chariot into the course. He kept with him Xenophon, the philosopher, and made much of him, and proposed to him to send for his children, and educate them at Sparta, where they would be taught the best of all learning; how to obey, and how to command. Finding on Lysander's death a large faction formed, which he on his return from Asia had established against Agesilaus, he thought it advisable to expose both him and it, by showing what manner of a citizen he had been whilst he lived. To that end, finding among his writings an oration, composed by Cleon the Halicarnassean, but to have been spoken by Lysander in a public assembly, to excite the people to innovations and changes in the government, he resolved to publish it, as an evidence of Lysander's practices. But one of the Elders having the perusal of it, and finding it powerfully written, advised him to have a care of digging up Lysander again, and rather bury that oration in the grave with him; and this advice he wisely hearkened to, and hushed the whole thing up; and ever after forbore publicly to affront any of his adversaries, but took occasions of picking out the ringleaders, and sending them away upon foreign services. He thus had means for exposing the avarice and the injustice of many of them in their employments; and again when they were by others brought into question, he made it his business to bring them off, obliging them, by that means, of enemies to become his friends, and so by degrees left none remaining.

Agesipolis, his fellow king, was under the disadvantage of being born of an exiled father, and himself young, modest, and inactive, meddled not much in affairs. Agesilaus took a course of gaining him over, and making him entirely tractable. According to the custom of Sparta, the kings, if they were in town, always dined together. This was Agesilaus's opportunity of dealing with Agesipolis, whom he found quick, as he himself was, in forming attachments for young men, and accordingly talked with him always on such subjects, joining and aiding him, and acting as his confidant, such attachments in Sparta being entirely honorable, and attended always with lively feelings of modesty, love of virtue, and a noble emulation of which more is said in Lycurgus's life.

Having thus established his power in the city, he easily obtained that his half-brother Teleutias might be chosen admiral, and thereupon making an expedition against the Corinthians, he made himself master of the long walls by land, through the assistance of his brother at sea. Coming thus upon the Argives, who then held Corinth, in the midst of their Isthmian festival, he made them fly from the sacrifice they had just commenced, and leave all their festive provision behind them. The exiled Corinthians that were in the Spartan army, desired him to keep the feast, and to preside in the celebration of it. This he refused, but gave them leave to carry on the solemnity if they pleased, and he in the mean time stayed and guarded them. When Agesilaus marched off, the Argives returned and celebrated the games over again, when some who were victors before, became victors a second time, others lost the prizes which before they had gained. Agesilaus thus made it clear to everybody, that the Argives must in their own eyes have been guilty of great cowardice, since they set such a value on presiding at the games, and yet had not dared to fight for it. He himself was of opinion, that to keep a mean in such things was best; he assisted at the sports and dances usual in his own country, and was always ready and eager to be present at the exercises either of the young men, or of the girls, but things that many men used to be highly taken with, he seemed not at all concerned about. Callippides, the tragic actor, who had a great name in all Greece and was made much of, once met and saluted him; of which when he found no notice taken, he confidently thrust himself into his train, expecting that Agesilaus would pay him some attention. When all that failed, he boldly accosted him, and asked him, whether he did not remember him? Agesilaus turned, and looking him in the face, "Are you not," said he, "Callippides the showman?" Being invited once to hear a man who admirably imitated the nightingale, he declined, saying, he had heard the nightingale itself. Menecrates, the physician, having had great success in some desperate diseases, was by way of flattery called Jupiter; he was so vain as to take the name, and having occasion to write a letter to Agesilaus, thus addressed it: "Jupiter Menecrates to King Agesilaus, greeting." The king returned answer: "Agesilaus to Menecrates, health and a sound mind."

Whilst Agesilaus was in the Corinthian territories, having just taken the Heræum, he was looking on while his soldiers were carrying away the prisoners and the plunder, when ambassadors from Thebes came to him to treat of peace. Having a great aversion for that city, and thinking it then advantageous to his affairs publicly to slight them, he took the opportunity, and would not seem either to see them, or hear them speak. But as if on purpose to punish him in his pride, before they parted from him, messengers came with news of the complete slaughter of one of the Spartan divisions by Iphicrates, a greater disaster than had befallen them for many years; and that the more grievous, because it was a choice regiment of full-armed Lacedæmonians overthrown by a parcel of mere mercenary targeteers. Agesilaus leapt from his seat, to go at once to their rescue, but found it too late, the business being over. He therefore returned to the Heræum, and sent for the Theban ambassadors to give them audience. They now resolved to be even with him for the affront he gave them, and without speaking one word of the peace, only desired leave to go into Corinth. Agesilaus, irritated with this proposal, told them in scorn, that if they were anxious to go and see how proud their friends were of their success, they should do it to-morrow with safety. Next morning, taking the ambassadors with him, he ravaged the Corinthian territories, up to the very gates of the city, where having made a stand, and let the ambassadors see that the Corinthians durst not come out to defend themselves, he dismissed them. Then gathering up the small remainders of the shattered regiment, he marched homewards, always removing his camp before day, and always pitching his tents after night, that he might prevent their enemies among the Arcadians from taking any opportunity of insulting over their loss.

After this, at the request of the Achæans, he marched with them into Acarnania, and there collected great spoils, and defeated the Acarnanians in battle. The Achæans would have persuaded him to keep his winter quarters there, to hinder the Acarnanians from sowing their corn; but he was of the contrary opinion, alleging, that they would be more afraid of a war next summer, when their fields were sown, than they would be if they lay fallow. The event justified his opinion; for next summer, when the Achæans began their expedition again, the Acarnanians immediately made peace with them.

When Conon and Pharnabazus with the Persian navy were grown masters of the sea, and had not only infested the coast of Laconia, but also rebuilt the walls of Athens at the cost of Pharnabazus, the Lacedæmonians thought fit to treat of peace with the king of Persia. To that end, they sent Antalcidas to Tiribazus, basely and wickedly betraying the Asiatic Greeks, on whose behalf Agesilaus had made the war. But no part of this dishonor fell upon Agesilaus, the whole being transacted by Antalcidas, who was his bitter enemy, and was urgent for peace upon any terms, because war was sure to increase his power and reputation. Nevertheless once being told by way of reproach, that the Lacedæmonians had gone over to the Medes, he replied, " No, the Medes have come over to the Lacedæmonians." And when the Greeks were backward to submit to the agreement, he threatened them with war, unless they fulfilled the king of Persia's conditions, his particular end in this being to weaken the Thebans; for it was made one of the articles of peace, that the country of Bœotia should be left independent.[11] This feeling of his to Thebes appeared further afterwards,

---

[11] The smaller towns of Bœotia, that is, independent of Thebes; free from any obligation to form part of the Bœotian confederacy, which had hitherto existed, with Thebes at its head. The Cadmea is the citadel of Thebes.

when Phœbidas, in full peace, most unjustifiably seized upon the Cadmea. The thing was much resented by all Greece, and not well liked by the Lacedæmonians themselves; those especially who were enemies to Agesilaus, required an account of the action, and by whose authority it was done, laying the suspicion of it at his door. Agesilaus resolutely answered, on the behalf of Phœbidas, that the profitableness of the act was chiefly to be considered; if it were for the advantage of the commonwealth, it was no matter whether it were done with or without authority. This was the more remarkable in him, because in his ordinary language, he was always observed to be a great maintainer of justice, and would commend it as the chief of virtues, saying, that valor without justice was useless, and if all the world were just, there would be no need of valor. When any would say to him, the Great King will have it so; he would reply, "How is he greater than I, unless he be juster?" nobly and rightly taking, as a sort of royal measure of greatness, justice, and not force. And thus when, on the conclusion of the peace, the king of Persia wrote to Agesilaus, desiring a private friendship and relations of hospitality, he refused it, saying, that the public friendship was enough; whilst that lasted there was no need of private. Yet in his acts he was not constant to his doctrine, but sometimes out of ambition, and sometimes out of private pique, he let himself be carried away; and particularly in this case of the Thebans, he not only saved Phœbidas, but persuaded the Lacedæmonians to take the fault upon themselves, and to retain the Cadmea, putting a garrison into it, and to put the government of Thebes into the hands of Archias and Leontidas, who had been betrayers of the castle to them.

This excited strong suspicion that what Phœbidas did was by Agesilaus's order, which was corroborated by after occurrences. For when the Thebans had expelled the garrison, and asserted their liberty, he, accusing them of the murder of Archias and Leontidas, who indeed were tyrants, though in name holding the office of Polemarchs, made war upon them. He sent Cleombrotus on that errand, who was now his fellow king, in the place of Agesipolis, who was dead, excusing himself by reason of his age; for it was forty years since he had first borne arms, and he was consequently exempt by the law; meanwhile the true reason was, that he was ashamed, having so lately fought against tyranny in behalf of the Phliasians, to fight now in defence of a tyranny against the Thebans.

One Sphodrias, of Lacedæmon, of the contrary faction to Agesilaus, was governor in Thespiæ, a bold and enterprising man, though he had perhaps more of confidence than wisdom. This action of Phœbidas fired him, and incited his ambition to attempt some great enterprise, which might render him as famous as he perceived the taking of the Cadmea had made Phœbidas. He thought the sudden capture of the Piræus, and the cutting off thereby the Athenians from the sea, would be a matter of far more glory. It is said, too, that Pelopidas and Melon, the chief captains of Bœotia, put him upon it; that they privily sent men to him, pretending to be of the Spartan faction, who, highly commending Sphodrias, filled him with a great opinion of himself, protesting him to be the only man in the world, that was fit for so great an enterprise. Being thus stimulated, he could hold no longer, but hurried into an attempt as dishonorable and treacherous as that of the Cadmea, but executed with less valor and less success; for the day broke whilst he was yet in the Thriasian plain, whereas he designed the whole exploit to have been done in the night. As soon as the soldiers perceived the rays of light reflecting from the temples of Eleusis, upon the first rising of the sun, it is said that their hearts failed them; nay, he himself, when he saw that he could not have the benefit of the night, had not courage enough to go on with his enterprise; but, having pillaged the country, he returned with shame to Thespiæ. An embassy was upon this sent from Athens to Sparta, to complain of the breach of peace; but the ambassadors found their journey needless, Sphodrias being then under process by the magistrates of Sparta. Sphodrias durst not stay to expect judgment, which he found would be capital, the city being highly incensed against him, out of the shame they felt at the business, and their desire to appear in the eyes of the Athenians as fellow-sufferers in the wrong, rather than accomplices in its being done.

This Sphodrias had a son of great beauty named Cleonymus, to whom Archidamus, the son of Agesilaus, was extremely attached. Archidamus, as became him, was concerned for the danger of his friend's father, but yet he durst not do any thing openly for his assistance, he being one of the professed enemies of Agesilaus. But Cleonymus having solicited him with tears about it, as knowing Agesilaus to be of all his father's enemies the most formidable, the young man for two or three days followed after his father with such fear and confusion, that he durst not speak to him. At last, the day of sentence being at hand, he ventured to tell him, that Cleonymus had entreated him to intercede for his father. Agesilaus, though well aware of the love between the two young men, yet did not prohibit it, because Cleonymus from his earliest years had been looked upon as a youth of very great promise; yet he gave not his son any kind or hopeful answer in the case, but coldly told him, that he would consider what he could honestly and honorably do in it, and so dismissed him. Archidamus, being ashamed of his want of success, forbore the company of Cleonymus, whom he usually saw several times every day. This made the friends of Sphodrias to think his case desperate, till Etymocles, one of Agesilaus's friends, discovered to them the king's mind, namely, that he abhorred the fact, but yet he thought Sphodrias a gallant man, such as the commonwealth much wanted at that time. For Agesilaus used to talk thus concerning the cause, out of a desire to gratify his son. And now Cleonymus quickly understood, that Archidamus had been true to him, in using all his interest with his father; and Sphodrias's friends ventured to be forward in his defence. The truth is, that Agesilaus was excessively fond of his children; and it is to him the story belongs, that when they were little ones, he used to make a horse of a stick, and ride with them; and being caught at this sport by a friend, he desired him not to mention it, till he himself were the father of children.

Meanwhile, Sphodrias being acquitted, the Athenians betook themselves to arms, and Agesilaus fell into disgrace with the people; since to gratify the whims of a boy, he had been willing to pervert justice, and make the city accessory to the crimes of private men, whose most unjustifiable actions had broken the peace of Greece. He also found his colleague, Cleombrotus, little inclined to the Theban war; so that it became necessary for him to waive the privilege of his age, which he before had claimed, and to lead the army himself into Bœotia; which he did with variety of success, sometimes conquering, and sometimes conquered; insomuch that receiving a wound in a battle, he was reproached by Antalcidas, that the Thebans had paid him well for the lessons he had given them in fighting. And, indeed, they were now grown far better soldiers than ever they had been, being so continually kept in training, by the frequency of the Lacedæmonian expeditions against them. Out of the foresight of which it was, that anciently Lycurgus, in three several laws, forbade them to make many wars with the same nation, as this would be to instruct their enemies in the art of it. Meanwhile, the allies of Sparta were not a little discontented at Agesilaus, because this war was commenced not upon any fair public ground of quarrel, but merely out of his private hatred to the Thebans; and they complained with indignation, that they, being the majority of the army, should from year to year be thus exposed to danger and hardship here and there, at the will of a few persons. It was at this time, we are told, that Agesilaus, to obviate the objection, devised this expedient, to show the allies were not the greater number. He gave orders that all the allies, of whatever country, should sit down promiscuously on one side, and all the Lacedæmonians on the other: which being done, he commanded a herald to proclaim, that all the potters of both divisions should stand out; then all the blacksmiths; then all the masons; next the carpenters; and so he went through all the handicrafts. By this time almost all the allies were risen, but of the Lacedæmonians not a man, they being by law forbidden to learn any mechanical business; and now Agesilaus laughed and said, "You see, my friends, how many more soldiers we send out than you do."

When he brought back his army from Bœotia through Megara, as he was going up to the magistrate's office in the Acropolis, he was suddenly seized with pain and cramp in his sound leg, and great swelling and inflammation ensued. He was treated by a Syracusan physician, who let him blood below the ancle; this soon eased his pain, but then the blood could not be stopped, till the loss of it brought on fainting and swooning; at length, with much trouble, he stopped it. Agesilaus was carried home to Sparta in a very weak condition, and did not recover strength enough to appear in the field for a long time after.

Meanwhile, the Spartan fortune was but ill; they received many losses both by sea and land; but the greatest was that at Tegyræ,[12] when for the first time they were beaten by the Thebans in a set battle.

All the Greeks were, accordingly, disposed to a general peace, and to that end ambassadors came to Sparta. Among these was Epaminondas, the Theban, famous at that time for his philosophy and learning, but he had not yet given proof of his

---

[12] The site of *Tegyræ,* or Tegyra, *where the Spartans were beaten by the Thebans in a set battle,* more fully described in the life of Pelopidas, is placed above the marshes, on the heights that rise to the north of the lake. " In the time of Plutarch, all the part of Bœotia to the northward of the Lake Copais seems to have been no better inhabited than at present, for in one of his dialogues he introduces an assertion that about Tegyra and Mount Ptoum, two places formerly so much famed for their oracles, hardly a herdsman or shepherd was to be met with in a day's journey." (*Leake's Northern Greece, Vol. II., ch. xii., p.*

capacity as a general. He, seeing all the others crouch to Agesilaus, and court favor with him, alone maintained the dignity of an ambassador, and with that freedom that became his character, made a speech in behalf not of Thebes only, from whence he came, but of all Greece, remonstrating, that Sparta alone grew great by war, to the distress and suffering of all her neighbors. He urged, that a peace should be made upon just and equal terms, such as alone would be a lasting one, which could not otherwise be done, than by reducing all to equality. Agesilaus, perceiving all the other Greeks to give much attention to this discourse, and to be pleased with it, presently asked him, whether he thought it a part of this justice and equality that the Bœotian towns should enjoy their independence. Epaminondas instantly and without wavering asked him in return, whether he thought it just and equal that the Laconian towns should enjoy theirs. Agesilaus started from his seat and bade him once for all speak out and say whether or not Bœotia should be independent. And when Epaminondas replied once again with the same inquiry, whether Laconia should be so, Agesilaus was so enraged that, availing himself of the pretext he immediately struck the name of

159.) The passage referred to is in the Dialogue on the Cessation of Oracles, a phenomenon which one of the speakers, Ammonius the philosopher, explains by *the general depopulation which former wars and factions have occasioned in pretty nearly all the habitable world, and more particularly in Greece, the whole of which could now scarcely furnish the three thousand men-at-arms whom the single town of Megara sent to fight at Platæa. With so few to consult him in these days why should the deity keep up all his former oracles?* (De Defectu Oraculorum, 8.)

AGESILAUS

the Thebans out of the league, and declared war against them. With the rest of the Greeks he made a peace, and dismissed them with this saying, that what could be peaceably adjusted, should; what was otherwise incurable, must be committed to the success of war, it being a thing of too great difficulty to provide for all things by treaty.

The Ephors upon this despatched their orders to Cleombrotus, who was at that time in Phocis, to march directly into Bœotia, and at the same time sent to their allies for aid. The confederates were very tardy in the business, and unwilling to engage, but as yet they feared the Spartans too much to dare to refuse. And although many portents, and prodigies of ill presage, which I have mentioned in the life of Epaminondas,[13] had appeared; and though Prothous, the Laconian, did all he could to hinder it, yet Agesilaus would needs go forward, and prevailed so, that the war was decreed. He thought the present juncture of affairs very advantageous for their revenge, the rest of Greece being wholly free,[14] and the Thebans excluded from the peace. But that this war was undertaken more upon passion than judgment, the event may prove; for the treaty was finished but the fourteenth of Scirophorion, and the Lacedæmonians received their great overthrow at Leuctra, on the fifth of Hecatombæon, within twenty days. There fell at that time a thousand Spartans,

---

[13] The life of Epaminondas is lost.

[14] Or perhaps, omitting the word *free,* Greece being wholly with them, or the whole of Greece being with them. If the text should not be altered, it means, all the other Greek States being at this time independent, and therefore disunited, no league under any sovereign or predominant State (except Sparta) any longer existing.

and Cleombrotus their king, and around him the bravest men of the nation; particularly, the beautiful youth, Cleonymus, the son of Sphodrias, who was thrice struck down at the feet of the king, and as often rose, but was slain at the last.

This unexpected blow, which fell so heavy upon the Lacedæmonians, brought greater glory to Thebes than ever was acquired by any other of the Grecian republics, in their civil wars against each other. The behavior, notwithstanding, of the Spartans, though beaten, was as great, and as highly to be admired, as that of the Thebans. And indeed, if, as Xenophon says, in conversation good men even in their sports and at their wine let fall many sayings [15] that are worth the preserving; how much more worthy to be recorded, is an exemplary constancy of mind, as shown both in the words and in the acts of brave men, when they are pressed by adverse fortune! It happened that the Spartans were celebrating a solemn feast, at which many strangers were present from other countries, and the town full of them, when this news of the overthrow came. It was the gymnopædiæ, and the boys were dancing in the theatre, when the messengers arrived from Leuctra. The Ephors, though they were sufficiently aware that this blow had ruined the Spartan power, and that their primacy over the rest of Greece was gone forever, yet gave orders that the dances should not break off, nor any of the celebration of the festival abate; but privately sending the names of the slain to each family out of which they were lost, they continued the public spectacles. The next morning, when they had full intelligence concerning

---

[15] Xenophon's remark about the casual *sayings* of *good men* is in the beginning of his Banquet.

it, and everybody knew who were slain, and who survived, the fathers, relatives, and friends of the slain came out rejoicing in the market-place, saluting each other with a kind of exultation; on the contrary, the fathers of the survivors hid themselves at home among the women. If necessity drove any of them abroad, they went very dejectedly, with downcast looks, and sorrowful countenances. The women outdid the men in it; those whose sons were slain, openly rejoicing, cheerfully making visits to one another, and meeting triumphantly in the temples; they who expected their children home, being very silent, and much troubled.

But the people in general, when their allies now began to desert them, and Epaminondas, in all the confidence of victory, was expected with an invading army in Peloponnesus, began to think again of Agesilaus's lameness, and to entertain feelings of religious fear and despondency, as if their having rejected the soundfooted, and having chosen the halting king, which the oracle had specially warned them against, was the occasion of all their distresses. Yet the regard they had to the merit and reputation of Agesilaus, so far stilled this mumuring of the people, that notwithstanding it, they intrusted themselves to him in this distress, as the only man that was fit to heal the public malady, the arbiter of all their difficulties, whether relating to the affairs of war or peace. One great one was then before them, concerning the runaways (as their name is for them) that had fled out of the battle, who being many and powerful, it was feared that they might make some commotion in the republic, to prevent the execution of the law upon them for their cowardice. The law in that case was very severe; for they were not only to be debarred from all honors, but also it was a disgrace to intermarry with them; whoever met any of them in the streets, might beat him if he chose, nor was it lawful for him to resist; they in the meanwhile were obliged to go about unwashed and meanly dressed, with their clothes patched with divers colors, and to wear their beards half shaved, half unshaven. To execute so rigid a law as this, in a case where the offenders were so many, and many of them of such distinction, and that in a time when the commonwealth wanted soldiers so much as then it did, was of dangerous consequence. Therefore they chose Agesilaus as a sort of new lawgiver for the occasion. But he, without adding to or diminishing from or any way changing the law, came out into the public assembly, and said, that the law should sleep for to-day, but from this day forth be vigorously executed. By this means he at once preserved the law from abrogation, and the citizens from infamy; and that he might alleviate the despondency and self-distrust of the young men, he made an inroad into Arcadia, where carefully avoiding all fighting, he contented himself with spoiling the territory, and taking a small town belonging to the Mantineans, thus reviving the hearts of the people, letting them see that they were not everywhere unsuccessful.

Epaminondas now invaded Laconia, with an army of forty thousand, besides light-armed men and others that followed the camp only for plunder, so that in all they were at least seventy thousand. It was now six hundred years since the Dorians had possessed Laconia, and in all that time the face of an enemy had not been seen within their territories, no man daring to invade them; but now they made their entrance, and burnt and plundered without resistance the hitherto untouched and sacred territory, up to Eurotas, and the very suburbs of Sparta; for Agesilaus would not permit them to encounter so impetuous a torrent, as Theopompus calls it, of war. He contented himself with fortifying the chief parts of the city, and with placing guards in convenient places, enduring meanwhile the taunts of the Thebans, who reproached him by name as the kindler of the war, and the author of all that mischief to his country, bidding him defend himself if he could. But this was not all; he was equally disturbed at home with the tumults of the city, the outcries and running about of the old men, who were enraged at their present condition, and the women, yet worse, out of their senses with the clamors, and the fires of the enemy in the field. He was also himself afflicted by the sense of his lost glory; who having come to the throne of Sparta when it was in its most flourishing and powerful condition, now lived to see it laid low in esteem, and all its great vaunts cut down, even that which he himself had been accustomed to use, that the women of Sparta had never seen the smoke of the enemy's fire. As it is said, also, that when Antalcidas once being in dispute with an Athenian about the valor of the two nations, the Athenian boasted, that they had often driven the Spartans from the river Cephisus, "Yes," said Antalcidas, "but we never had occasion to drive you from Eurotas." And a common Spartan of less note, being in company with an Argive, who was bragging how many Spartans lay buried in the fields of Argos, replied, "None of you are buried in the country of Laconia." Yet now the case was so altered, that Antalcidas, being one of the Ephors, out of fear sent away his children privately to the island of Cythera.

When the enemy essayed to get over the river,

and thence to attack the town, Agesilaus, abandoning the rest, betook himself to the high places and strong-holds of it. But it happened, that Eurotas at that time was swollen to a great height with the snow that had fallen, and made the passage very difficult to the Thebans, not only by its depth, but much more by its extreme coldness. Whilst this was doing, Epaminondas was seen in the front of the phalanx, and was pointed out to Agesilaus, who looked long at him, and said but these words, "O, bold man!" But when he came to the city, and would have fain attempted something within the limits of it that might raise him a trophy there, he could not tempt Agesilaus out of his hold, but was forced to march off again, wasting the country as he went.

Meanwhile, a body of long discontented and bad citizens, about two hundred in number, having got into a strong part of the town called the Issorion, where the temple of Diana stands, seized and garrisoned it. The Spartans would have fallen upon them instantly; but Agesilaus, not knowing how far the sedition might reach, bade them forbear, and going himself in his ordinary dress, with but one servant, when he came near the rebels, called out, and told them, that they mistook their orders; this was not the right place; they were to go, one part of them thither, showing them another place in the city, and part to another, which he also showed. The conspirators gladly heard this, thinking themselves unsuspected of treason, and readily went off to the places which he showed them. Whereupon Agesilaus placed in their room a guard of his own; and of the conspirators he apprehended fifteen, and put them to death in the night. But after this, a much more dangerous conspiracy was discovered of

Spartan citizens, who had privately met in each other's houses, plotting a revolution. These were men whom it was equally dangerous to prosecute publicly according to law, and to connive at. Agesilaus took counsel with the Ephors, and put these also to death privately without process; a thing never before known in the case of any born Spartan.

At this time, also, many of the Helots and country people, who were in the army, ran away to the enemy, which was matter of great consternation to the city. He therefore caused some officers of his, every morning before day, to search the quarters of the soldiers, and where any man was gone, to hide his arms, that so the greatness of the number might not appear.

Historians differ about the cause of the Thebans' departure from Sparta. Some say, the winter forced them; as also that the Arcadian soldiers disbanding, made it necessary for the rest to retire. Others say, that they stayed there three months, till they had laid the whole country waste. Theopompus is the only author who says that when the Bœotian generals had already resolved upon the retreat, Phrixus, the Spartan, came to them, and offered them from Agesilaus ten talents to be gone, so hiring them to do what they were already doing of their own accord. How he alone should come to be aware of this, I know not; only in this all authors agree, that the saving of Sparta from ruin was wholly due to the wisdom of Agesilaus, who in this extremity of affairs quitted all his ambition and his haughtiness, and resolved to play a saving game. But all his wisdom and courage was not sufficient to recover the glory of it, and to raise it to its ancient greatness. For as we see in human bodies, long used to a very strict and too exquisitely regular diet, any single great disorder is usually fatal; so here one stroke overthrew the whole State's long prosperity. Nor can we be surprised at this. Lycurgus had formed a polity admirably designed for the peace, harmony, and virtuous life of the citizens; and their fall came from their assuming foreign dominion and arbitrary sway, things wholly undesirable, in the judgment of Lycurgus, for a well-conducted and happy State.

Agesilaus being now in years, gave over all military employments; but his son Archidamus, having received help from Dionysius of Sicily, gave a great defeat to the Arcadians, in the fight known by the name of the Tearless Battle, in which there was a great slaughter of the enemy, without the loss of one Spartan. Yet this victory, more than anything else, discovered the present weakness of Sparta; for heretofore victory was esteemed so usual a thing with them, that for their greatest successes, they merely sacrificed a cock to the gods. The soldiers never vaunted, nor did the citizens display any great joy at the news; even when the great victory, described by Thucydides, was obtained at Mantinea, the messenger that brought the news had no other reward than a piece of meat, sent by the magistrates from the common table. But at the news of this Arcadian victory, they were not able to contain themselves; Agesilaus went out in procession with tears of joy in his eyes, to meet and embrace his son, and all the magistrates and public officers attended him. The old men and the women marched out as far as the river Eurotas, lifting up their hands, and thanking the gods, that Sparta was now cleared again of the disgrace and indignity that had befallen her, and once more saw the light of day. Since before, they tell us, the Spartan men, out of

AGESILAUS

shame at their disasters, did not dare so much as to look their wives in the face.

When Epaminondas restored Messene, and recalled from all quarters the ancient citizens to inhabit it, they were not able to obstruct the design, being not in condition of appearing in the field against them. But it went greatly against Agesilaus in the minds of his countrymen, when they found so large a territory, equal to their own in compass, and for fertility the richest of all Greece, which they had enjoyed so long, taken from them in his reign. Therefore it was that the king broke off treaty with the Thebans, when they offered him peace, rather than set his hand to the passing away of that country, though it was already taken from him. Which point of honor had like to have cost him dear; for not long after he was overreached by a stratagem, which had almost amounted to the loss of Sparta. For when the Mantineans again revolted from Thebes to Sparta, and Epaminondas understood that Agesilaus was come to their assistance with a powerful army, he privately in the night quitted his quarters at Tegea, and unknown to the Mantineans, passing by Agesilaus, marched towards Sparta, insomuch that he failed very little of taking it empty and unarmed. Agesilaus had intelligence sent him by Euthynus, the Thespian, as Callisthenes says, but Xenophon says by a Cretan; and immediately despatched a horseman to Lacedæmon, to apprise them of it, and to let them know that he was hastening to them. Shortly after his arrival the Thebans crossed the Eurotas. They made an assault upon the town, and were received by Agesilaus with great courage, and with exertions beyond what was to be expected at his years. For he did not now fight with that caution and cunning which he formerly made use of, but put all upon a desperate push; which, though not his usual method, succeeded so well, that he rescued the city out of the very hands of Epaminondas, and forced him to retire, and, at the erection of a trophy, was able, in the presence of their wives and children, to declare that the Lacedæmonians had nobly paid their debt to their country, and particularly his son Archidamus, who had that day made himself illustrious, both by his courage and agility of body, rapidly passing about by the short lanes to every endangered point, and everywhere maintaining the town against the enemy with but few to help him. Isadas, however, the son of Phœbidas, must have been, I think, the admiration of the enemy as well as of his friends. He was a youth of remarkable beauty and stature, in the very flower of the most attractive time of life, when the boy is just rising into the man. He had no arms upon him, and scarcely clothes; he had just anointed himself at home, when upon the alarm, without further waiting, in that undress, he snatched a spear in one hand, and a sword in the other, and broke his way through the combatants to the enemies, striking at all he met. He received no wound, whether it were that a special divine care rewarded his valor with an extraordinary protection, or whether his shape being so large and beautiful, and his dress so unusual, they thought him more than a man. The Ephors gave him a garland; but as soon as they had done so, they fined him a thousand drachmas, for going out to battle unarmed.

A few days after this there was another battle fought near Mantinea, in which Epaminondas, having routed the van of the Lacedæmonians, was eager in the pursuit of them, when Anticrates, the Laconian, wounded him with a spear, says Dioscorides;

POMPEY THE GREAT

but the Spartans to this day call the posterity of this Anticrates, swordsmen,[16] because he wounded Epaminondas with a sword. They so dreaded Epaminondas when living, that the slayer of him was embraced and admired by all; they decreed honors and gifts to him, and an exemption from taxes to his posterity, a privilege enjoyed at this day by Callicrates, one of his descendants.

Epaminondas being slain, there was a general peace again concluded, from which Agesilaus's party excluded the Messenians, as men that had no city, and therefore would not let them swear to the league; to which when the rest of the Greeks admitted them, the Lacedæmonians broke off, and continued the war alone, in hopes of subduing the Messenians. In this Agesilaus was esteemed a stubborn and headstrong man, and insatiable of war, who took such pains to undermine the general peace, and to protract the war at a time when he had not money to carry it on with, but was forced to borrow of his friends and raise subscriptions, with much difficulty, while the city, above all things, needed repose. And all this to recover the one poor town of Messene, after he had lost so great an empire both by sea and land, as the Spartans were possessed of, when he began to reign.

But it added still more to his ill-repute when he put himself into the service of Tachos, the Egyptian. They thought it too unworthy of a man of his high station, who was then looked upon as the first commander in all Greece, who had filled all countries with his renown, to let himself out to hire to a barbarian, an Egyptian rebel, (for Tachos was no better) and to fight for pay, as captain only of a band of mercenaries. If, they said, at those years of

[16] Machæriones, from machæra, a sword.

eighty and odd, after his body had been worn out with age, and enfeebled with wounds, he had resumed that noble undertaking, the liberation of the Greeks from Persia, it had been worthy of some reproof. To make an action honorable, it ought to be agreeable to the age, and other circumstances of the person; since it is circumstance and proper measure that give an action its character, and make it either good or bad. But Agesilaus valued not other men's discourses; he thought no public employment dishonorable; the ignoblest thing in his esteem, was for a man to sit idle and useless at home, waiting for his death to come and take him. The money, therefore, that he received from Tachos, he laid out in raising men, with whom having filled his ships, he took also thirty Spartan counsellors with him, as formerly he had done in his Asiatic expedition, and set sail for Egypt.

As soon as he arrived in Egypt, all the great officers of the kingdom came to pay their compliments to him at his landing. His reputation being so great had raised the expectation of the whole country, and crowds flocked in to see him; but when they found, instead of the splendid prince whom they looked for, a little old man of contemptible appearance, without all ceremony lying down upon the grass, in coarse and threadbare clothes, they fell into laughter and scorn of him, crying out, that the old proverb was now made good, " The mountain had brought forth a mouse." They were yet more astonished at his stupidity, as they thought it, who when presents were made him of all sorts of provisions, took only the meal, the calves, and the geese, but rejected the sweetmeats, the confections and perfumes; and when they urged him to the acceptance of them, took them and

AGESILAUS

gave them to the helots in his army. Yet he was taken, Theophrastus tells us, with the garlands they made of the papyrus, because of their simplicity, and when he returned home, he demanded one of the king, which he carried with him.

When he joined with Tachos, he found his expectation of being general-in-chief disappointed. Tachos reserved that place for himself, making Agesilaus only captain of the mercenaries, and Chabrias, the Athenian, commander of the fleet. This was the first occasion of his discontent, but there followed others; he was compelled daily to submit to the insolence and vanity of this Egyptian, and was at length forced to attend him into Phœnicia, in a condition much below his character and dignity, which he bore and put up with for a time, till he had opportunity of showing his feelings. It was afforded him by Nectanabis, the cousin of Tachos, who commanded a large force under him, and shortly after deserted him, and was proclaimed king by the Egyptians. This man invited Agesilaus to join his party, and the like he did to Chabrias, offering great rewards to both. Tachos, suspecting it, immediately applied himself both to Agesilaus and Chabrias, with great humility beseeching their continuance in his friendship. Chabrias consented to it, and did what he could by persuasion and good words to keep Agesilaus with them. But he gave this short reply, " You, O Chabrias, came hither a volunteer, and may go and stay as you see cause; but I am the servant of Sparta, appointed to head the Egyptians, and therefore I cannot fight against those to whom I was sent as a friend, unless I am commanded to do so by my country." This being said, he despatched messengers to Sparta, who were sufficiently supplied with matter both for dispraise of Tachos, and commendation of Nectanabis. The two Egyptians also sent their ambassadors to Lacedæmon, the one to claim continuance of the league already made, the other to make great offers for the breaking of it, and making a new one. The Spartans having heard both sides, gave in their public answer, that they referred the whole matter to Agesilaus; but privately wrote to him, to act as he should find it best for the profit of the commonwealth. Upon receipt of his orders, he at once changed sides, carrying all the mercenaries with him to Nectanabis, covering with the plausible pretence of acting for the benefit of his country, a most questionable piece of conduct, which, stripped of that disguise, in real truth was no better than downright treachery. But the Lacedæmonians, who make it their first principle of action to serve their country's interest, know not any thing to be just or unjust by any measure but that.

Tachos, being thus deserted by the mercenaries, fled for it; upon which a new king of the Mendesian province was proclaimed his successor, and came against Nectanabis with an army of one hundred thousand men. Nectanabis, in his talk with Agesilaus, professed to despise them as newly raised men, who, though many in number, were of no skill in war, being most of them mechanics and tradesmen, never bred to war. To whom Agesilaus answered, that he did not fear their numbers, but did fear their ignorance, which gave no room for employing stratagem against them. Stratagem only avails with men who are alive to suspicion, and expecting to be assailed, expose themselves by their attempts at defence; but one who has no thought or expectation of any thing, gives as little

AGESILAUS

opportunity to the enemy, as he who stands stock-still does to a wrestler. The Mendesian was not wanting in solicitations of Agesilaus, insomuch that Nectanabis grew jealous. But when Agesilaus advised to fight the enemy at once, saying it was folly to protract the war and rely on time, in a contest with men who had no experience in fighting battles, but with their great numbers might be able to surround them, and cut off their communications by intrenchments, and anticipate them in many matters of advantage, this altogether confirmed him in his fears and suspicions. He took quite the contrary course, and retreated into a large and strongly fortified town. Agesilaus, finding himself mistrusted, took it very ill, and was full of indignation, yet was ashamed to change sides back again, or to go away without effecting any thing, so that he was forced to follow Nectanabis into the town.

When the enemy came up, and began to draw lines about the town, and to intrench, the Egyptian now resolved upon a battle, out of fear of a siege. And the Greeks were eager for it, provisions growing already scarce in the town. When Agesilaus opposed it, the Egyptians then suspected him much more, publicly calling him the betrayer of the king. But Agesilaus, being now satisfied within himself, bore these reproaches patiently, and followed the design which he had laid, of overreaching the enemy, which was this.

The enemy were forming a deep ditch and high wall, resolving to shut up the garrison and starve it. When the ditch was brought almost quite round, and the two ends had all but met, he took the advantage of the night, and armed all his Greeks. Then going to the Egyptian, "This, young man, is your opportunity," said he, " of saving yourself, which I all this while durst not announce lest discovery should prevent it; but now the enemy has, at his own cost, and the pains and labor of his own men, provided for our security. As much of this wall as is built will prevent them from surrounding us with their multitude, the gap yet left will be sufficient for us to sally out by; now play the man, and follow the example the Greeks will give you, and by fighting valiantly, save yourself and your army; their front will not be able to stand against us, and their rear we are sufficiently secured from, by a wall of their own making." Nectanabis, admiring the sagacity of Agesilaus, immediately placed himself in the middle of the Greek troops, and fought with them; and upon the first charge soon routed the enemy. Agesilaus having now gained credit with the king, proceeded to use, like a trick in wrestling, the same stratagem over again. He sometimes pretended a retreat, at other times advanced to attack their flanks, and by this means at last drew them into a place inclosed between two ditches that were very deep, and full of water. When he had them at this advantage, he soon charged them, drawing up the front of his battle equal to the space between the two ditches, so that they had no way of surrounding them, being inclosed themselves on both sides. They made but little resistance; many fell, others fled and were dispersed.

Nectanabis, being thus settled and fixed in his kingdom, with much kindness and affection invited Agesilaus to spend his winter in Egypt, but he made haste home to assist in the wars of his own country, which was he knew in want of money, and forced to hire mercenaries, whilst their own men

AGESILAUS

were fighting abroad. The king, therefore, dismissed him very honorably, and among other gifts presented him with two hundred and thirty talents of silver, toward the charge of the war. But the weather being tempestuous, his ships kept in shore, and passing along the coast of Africa he reached an uninhabited spot called the Port of Menelaus, and here, when his ships were just upon landing, he expired, being eighty-four years old, and having reigned in Lacedæmon forty-one. Thirty of which years he passed with the reputation of being the greatest and most powerful man of all Greece, and was looked upon as, in a manner, general and king of it, until the battle of Leuctra. It was the custom of the Spartans to bury their common dead in the place where they died, whatsoever country it was, but their kings they carried home. The followers of Agesilaus, for want of honey, inclosed his body in wax, and so conveyed him to Lacedæmon.

His son Archidamus succeeded him on his throne; so did his posterity successively to Agis, the fifth from Agesilaus; who was slain by Leonidas, while attempting to restore the ancient discipline of Sparta.

POMPEY[1]

Translated by W. Oldys, LL.D.

The people of Rome seem to have entertained for Pompey from his childhood, the same affection that Prometheus in the tragedy of Æschylus expresses for Hercules, speaking of him as the author of his deliverance in these words,

> Ah cruel Sire! how dear thy son to me!
> The generous offspring of my enemy![2]

For on the one hand, never did the Romans give such demonstrations of a vehement and fierce hatred against any of their generals, as they did against Strabo, the father of Pompey; during whose lifetime, it is true, they stood in awe of his military power, as indeed he was a formidable warrior, but immediately upon his death, which happened by a stroke of thunder, they treated him with the utmost contumely, dragging his corpse from the bier, as it

---

[1] Cn. Pompeius Magnus, the Triumvir, was born on the 30th of September B.C. 106, and was consequently a few months younger than Cicero, who was born on the 3rd of January in this year, and six years older than Cæsar. He was assassinated September 29th, 48 B.C. His head was brought to Cæsar when he arrived in Egypt soon afterwards, but he turned away from the sight, shed tears at the melancholy death of his rival, and put his murderers to death.—Dr. William Smith.

[2] *Ah, cruel Sire! how dear thy son to me!* is from the Prometheus Unbound, the lost play of Æschylus, where Hercules releases whom his father Jupiter had bound. Pompey's father was of course a Pompeius like himself, Cnæus Pompeius Strabo; but the name of Strabo made way in the son's case for that of Magnus.

was carried to his funeral. On the other side, never had any Roman the people's good-will and devotion more zealous throughout all the changes of fortune, more early in its first springing up, or more steadily rising with his prosperity, or more constant in his adversity, than Pompey had. In Strabo, there was one great cause of their hatred, his insatiable covetousness; in Pompey, there were many that helped to make him the object of their love; his temperance, his skill, and exercise in war, his eloquence of speech, integrity of mind, and affability in conversation and address; insomuch that no man ever asked a favor with less offence, or conferred one with a better grace. When he gave, it was without assumption, when he received, it was with dignity and honor.

In his youth, his countenance pleaded for him, seeming to anticipate his eloquence, and win upon the affections of the people before he spoke. His beauty even in his bloom of youth had something in it at once of gentleness and dignity; and when his prime of manhood came, the majesty and kingliness of his character at once became visible in it. His hair sat somewhat hollow or rising a little; and this, with the languishing motion of his eyes, seemed to form a resemblance in his face, though perhaps more talked of than really apparent, to the statues of king Alexander. And because many applied that name to him in his youth, Pompey himself did not decline it, insomuch that some called him so in derision. And Lucius Philippus, a man of consular dignity, when he was pleading in favor of him, thought it not unfit to say, that people could not be surprised if Philip was a lover of Alexander.

It is related of Flora, the courtesan, that when she was now pretty old, she took great delight in speaking of her early familiarity with Pompey, and was wont to say, that she could never part after being with him without a bite. She would further tell, that Gemininus, a companion of Pompey's fell in love with her, and made his court with great importunity; and on her refusing, and telling him, however her inclinations were, yet she could not gratify his desires for Pompey's sake, he therefore made his request to Pompey, and Pompey frankly gave his consent, but never afterwards would have any converse with her, notwithstanding that he seemed to have a great passion for her; and Flora, on this occasion, showed none of the levity that might have been expected of her, but languished for some time after under a sickness brought on by grief and desire. This Flora, we are told, was such a celebrated beauty, that Cæcilius Metellus, when he adorned the temple of Castor and Pollux with paintings and statues, among the rest dedicated hers for her singular beauty. In his conduct also to the wife of Demetrius, his freed servant, (who had great influence with him in his lifetime, and left an estate of four thousand talents,) Pompey acted contrary to his usual habits, not quite fairly or generously, fearing lest he should fall under the common censure of being enamoured and charmed with her beauty, which was irresistible, and became famous everywhere. Nevertheless, though he seemed to be so extremely circumspect and cautious, yet even in matters of this nature, he could not avoid the calumnies of his enemies, but upon the score of married women, they accused him, as if he had connived at many things, and embezzled the public revenue to gratify their luxury.

Of his easiness of temper and plainness, in what related to eating and drinking, the story is told, that once in a sickness, when his stomach nauseated common meats, his physician prescribed him a thrush to eat; but upon search, there was none to be bought, for they were not then in season, and one telling him they were to be had at Lucullus's, who kept them all the year round, "So then," said he, "if it were not for Lucullus's luxury, Pompey should not live;" and thereupon not minding the prescription of the physician, he contented himself with such meat as could easily be procured. But this was at a later time.

Being as yet a very young man, and upon an expedition in which his father was commanding against Cinna, he had in his tent with him one Lucius Terentius, as his companion and comrade, who, being corrupted by Cinna, entered into an engagement to kill Pompey, as others had done to set the general's tent on fire. This conspiracy being discovered to Pompey at supper, he showed no discomposure at it, but on the contrary drank more liberally than usual, and expressed great kindness to Terentius; but about bedtime, pretending to go to his repose, he stole away secretly out of the tent, and setting a guard about his father, quietly expected the event. Terentius, when he thought the proper time come, rose with his naked sword, and coming to Pompey's bedside, stabbed several strokes through the bedclothes, as if he were lying there. Immediately after this there was a great uproar throughout all the camp, arising from the hatred they bore to the general, and an universal movement of the soldiers to revolt, all tearing down their tents, and betaking themselves to their arms. The general himself all this while durst not venture out because of the tumult; but Pompey, going about in the midst of them, besought them with tears; and at last threw himself prostrate upon his face before the gate of the camp, and lay there in the passage at their feet, shedding tears, and bidding those that were marching off, if they would go, trample upon him. Upon which, none could help going back again, and all, except eight hundred, either through shame or compassion, repented, and were reconciled to the general.

Immediately upon the death of Strabo, there was an action commenced against Pompey, as his heir, for that his father had embezzled the public treasure. But Pompey, having traced the principal thefts, charged them upon one Alexander, a freed slave of his father's, and proved before the judges, that he had been the appropriator. But he himself was accused of having in his possession some hunting tackle, and books, that were taken at Asculum. To this he confessed thus far, that he received them from his father when he took Asculum, but pleaded further, that he had lost them since, upon Cinna's return to Rome, when his house was broken open and plundered by Cinna's guards. In this cause he had a great many preparatory pleadings against his accuser, in which he showed an activity and steadfastness beyond his years, and gained great reputation and favor; insomuch that Antistius, the prætor and judge of the cause, took a great liking to him, and offered him his daughter in marriage, having had some communications with his friends about it. Pompey accepted the proposal, and they were privately contracted; however, the secret was not so closely kept as to escape the multitude, but it was discernible enough, from the favor shown him by Antistius in his cause. And at last, when Antistius pronounced the absolutory sentence of the judges, the people, as if it had been upon a signal given, made the acclamation used according to ancient custom, at marriages, *Talasio*. The origin of which custom is related to be this. At the time when the daughters of the Sabines came to Rome, to see the shows and sports there, and were violently seized upon by the most distinguished and bravest of the Romans for wives, it happened that some goatswains and herdsmen of the meaner rank were carrying off a beautiful and tall maiden; and lest any of their betters should meet them, and take her away, as they ran, they cried out with one voice, *Talasio,* Talasius being a well-known and popular person among them, insomuch that all that heard the name, clapped their hands for joy, and joined with them in the shout, as applauding and congratulating the chance. Now, say they, because this proved a fortunate match to Talasius, hence it is that this acclamation is sportively used as a nuptial cry at all weddings. This is the most credible of the accounts that are given of the Talasio. And some few days after this judgment, Pompey married Antistia.

After this he went to Cinna's camp, where finding some false suggestions and calumnies prevailing against him, he began to be afraid, and presently withdrew himself secretly; which sudden disappearance occasioned great suspicion. And there went a rumor and speech through all the camp, that Cinna had murdered the young man; upon which all that had been anyways disobliged, and bore any malice to him, resolved to make an assault upon him. He, endeavoring to make his escape, was seized by a centurion, who pursued him with his naked sword. Cinna, in this distress, fell upon his knees, and offered him his seal-ring, of great value, for his ransom; but the centurion repulsed him insolently, saying, "I did not come to seal a covenant, but to be revenged upon a lawless and wicked tyrant;" and so despatched him immediately.

Thus Cinna being slain, Carbo, a tyrant yet more senseless than he, took the command and exercised it, while Sylla meantime was approaching, much to the joy and satisfaction of most people, who in their present evils were ready to find some comfort if it were but in the exchange of a master. For the city was brought to that pass by oppression and calamities, that being utterly in despair of liberty, men were only anxious for the mildest and most tolerable bondage. At that time Pompey was in Picenum in Italy, where he spent some time amusing himself, as he had estates in the country there, though the chief motive of his stay was the liking he felt for the towns of that district, which all regarded him with hereditary feelings of kindness and attachment. But when he now saw that the noblest and best of the city began to forsake their homes and property, and fly from all quarters to Sylla's camp, as to their haven, he likewise was desirous to go; not, however, as a fugitive, alone and with nothing to offer, but as a friend rather than a suppliant, in a way that would gain him honor, bringing help along with him, and at the head of a body of troops. Accordingly he solicited the Picentines for their assistance, who as cordially embraced his motion, and rejected the messengers sent from Carbo; insomuch that a certain Vindius taking upon him to say, that Pompey was come from the schoolroom to put himself at the head of the people, they were so incensed that they fell forthwith upon this Vindius and killed him. From henceforward Pompey, finding a spirit of government upon him, though not above twenty-three years of age, nor deriving an

authority by commission from any man, took the
privilege to grant himself full power, and causing a
tribunal to be erected in the market-place of Auxi-
mum, a populous city, expelled two of their principal men, brothers, of the name of Ventidius, who
were acting against him in Carbo's interest, commanding them by a public edict to depart the city;
and then proceeded to levy soldiers, issuing out
commissions to centurions, and other officers, according to the form of military discipline. And in this
manner he went round all the rest of the cities in
the district. So that those of Carbo's faction flying,
and all others cheerfully submitting to his command, in a little time he mustered three entire
legions, having supplied himself beside with all
manner of provisions, beasts of burden, carriages,
and other necessaries of war. And with this equipage he set forward on his march towards Sylla,
not as if he were in haste, or desirous of escaping
observation, but by small journeys, making several
halts upon the road, to distress and annoy the
enemy, and exerting himself to detach from Carbo's
interest every part of Italy that he passed through.

Three commanders of the enemy encountered
him at once, Carinna, Clœlius, and Brutus, and
drew up their forces, not all in the front, nor yet
together on any one part, but encamping three
several armies in a circle about him, they resolved
to encompass and overpower him. Pompey was no
way alarmed at this, but collecting all his troops into
one body, and placing his horse in the front of the
battle, where he himself was in person, he singled
out and bent all his forces against Brutus, and
when the Celtic horsemen from the enemy's side
rode out to meet him, Pompey himself encountering
hand to hand with the foremost and stoutest among

them, killed him with his spear. The rest seeing this turned their backs, and fled, and breaking the ranks of their own foot, presently caused a general rout; whereupon the commanders fell out among themselves, and marched off, some one way, some another, as their fortunes led them, and the towns round about came in and surrendered themselves to Pompey, concluding that the enemy was dispersed for fear. Next after these, Scipio, the consul, came to attack him, and with as little success; for before the armies could join, or be within the throw of their javelins, Scipio's soldiers saluted Pompey's, and came over to them, while Scipio made his escape by flight. Last of all, Carbo himself sent down several troops of horse against him by the river Arsis, which Pompey assailed with the same courage and success as before; and having routed and put them to flight, he forced them in the pursuit into difficult ground, unpassable for horse, where seeing no hopes of escape, they yielded themselves with their horses and armor, all to his mercy.[3]

Sylla was hitherto unacquainted with all these actions; and on the first intelligence he received of his movements was in great anxiety about him, fearing lest he should be cut off among so many and such experienced commanders of the enemy, and marched therefore with all speed to his aid. Now Pompey, having advice of his approach, sent out orders to his officers, to marshal and draw up all his forces in full array, that they might make the finest and noblest appearance before the commander-in-chief; for he expected indeed great honors from him, but met with even greater. For as soon

[3] Carinnas, Cœlius, not Clœlius, and Brutus, father of Marcus Brutus, were the generals. The river Arsis is the Æsis.

as Sylla saw him thus advancing, his army so well appointed, his men so young and strong, and their spirits so high and hopeful with their successes, he alighted from his horse, and being first, as was his due, saluted by them with the title of Imperator, he returned the salutation upon Pompey, in the same term and style of Imperator, which might well cause surprise, as none could have ever anticipated that he would have imparted, to one so young in years and not yet a senator, a title which was the object of contention between him and the Scipios and Marii. And indeed all the rest of his deportment was agreeable to this first compliment; whenever Pompey came into his presence, he paid some sort of respect to him, either in rising and being uncovered, or the like, which he was rarely seen to do to any one else, notwithstanding that there were many about him of great rank and honor. Yet Pompey was not puffed up at all, or exalted with these favors. And when Sylla would have sent him with all expedition into Gaul, a province in which it was thought Metellus who commanded in it had done nothing worthy of the large forces at his disposal, Pompey urged that it could not be fair or honorable for him, to take a province out of the hands of his senior in command and superior in reputation; however, if Metellus were willing, and should request his service, he should be very ready to accompany and assist him in the war. Which when Metellus came to understand, he approved of the proposal, and invited him over by letter. And on this Pompey fell immediately into Gaul, where he not only achieved wonderful exploits of himself, but also fired up and kindled again that bold and warlike spirit, which old age had in a manner extinguished in Metellus, into a new heat; just as molten copper, they say, when poured upon that which is cold and solid, will dissolve and melt it faster than fire itself. But as when a famous wrestler has gained the first place among men, and borne away the prizes at all the games, it is not usual to take account of his victories as a boy, or to enter them upon record among the rest; so with the exploits of Pompey in his youth, though they were extraordinary in themselves, yet because they were obscured and buried in the multitude and greatness of his later wars and conquests, I dare not be particular in them, lest, by trifling away time in the lesser moments of his youth, we should be driven to omit those greater actions and fortunes which best illustrate his character.

Now, when Sylla had brought all Italy under his dominion, and was proclaimed dictator, he began to reward the rest of his followers, by giving them wealth, appointing them to offices in the State, and granting them freely and without restriction any favors they asked for. But as for Pompey, admiring his valor and conduct, and thinking that he might prove a great stay and support to him hereafter in his affairs, he sought means to attach him to himself by some personal alliance, and his wife Metella joining in his wishes, they two persuaded Pompey to put away Antistia, and marry Æmilia, the step-daughter of Sylla, borne by Metella to Scaurus her former husband, she being at that very time the wife of another man, living with him, and with child by him. These were the very tyrannies of marriage, and much more agreeable to the times under Sylla, than to the nature and habits of Pompey; that Æmilia great with child should be, as it were, ravished from the embraces of another for him, and that Antistia should be divorced with dishonor and misery by him, for whose sake she had been but just before bereft of her father. For Antistius was murdered in the senate, because he was suspected to be a favorer of Sylla for Pompey's sake; and her mother, likewise, after she had seen all these indignities, made away with herself, a new calamity to be added to the tragic accompaniments of this marriage, and that there might be nothing wanting to complete them, Æmilia herself died, almost immediately after entering Pompey's house, in childbed.

About this time news came to Sylla, that Perpenna was fortifying himself in Sicily, that the island was now become a refuge and receptacle for the relics of the adverse party, that Carbo was hovering about those seas with a navy, that Domitius had fallen in upon Africa, and that many of the exiled men of note who had escaped from the proscriptions were daily flocking into those parts. Against these, therefore, Pompey was sent with a large force; and no sooner was he arrived in Sicily, but Perpenna immediately departed, leaving the whole island to him. Pompey received the distressed cities into favor, and treated all with great humanity, except the Mamertines in Messena; for when they protested against his court and jurisdiction, alleging their privilege and exemption founded upon an ancient charter or grant of the Romans, he replied sharply, "What! will you never cease prating of laws to us that have swords by our sides?" It was thought, likewise, that he showed some inhumanity to Carbo, seeming rather to insult over his misfortunes, than to chastise his crimes. For if there had been a necessity, as perhaps there was, that he should be taken off, that might have been done at first, as soon as he was taken prisoner, for then it would have been the act of him that commanded it. But here Pompey commanded a man that had been thrice consul of Rome, to be brought in fetters to stand at the bar, he himself sitting upon the bench in judgment, examining the cause with the formalities of law, to the offence and indignation of all that were present, and afterwards ordered him to be taken away and put to death. It is related, by the way, of Carbo, that as soon as he was brought to the place, and saw the sword drawn for execution, he was suddenly seized with a looseness or pain in his bowels, and desired a little respite of the executioner, and a convenient place to relieve himself. And yet further, Caius Oppius, the friend of Cæsar, tells us, that Pompey dealt cruelly with Quintus Valerius, a man of singular learning and science. For when he was brought to him, he walked aside, and drew him into conversation, and after putting a variety of questions to him, and receiving answers from him, he ordered his officers to take him away, and put him to death. But we must not be too credulous in the case of narratives told by Oppius, especially when he undertakes to relate any thing touching the friends or foes of Cæsar. This is certain, that there lay a necessity upon Pompey to be severe upon many of Sylla's enemies, those at least that were eminent persons in themselves, and notoriously known to be taken; but for the rest, he acted with all the clemency possible for him, conniving at the concealment of some, and himself being the instrument in the escape of others. So in the case of the Himeræans; for when Pompey had determined on severely punishing their city, as they had been abettors of the enemy, Sthenis, the leader of the people there, craving liberty of speech, told him, that what he was about to do was not at all consistent with justice, for that he would pass by the guilty, and destroy the innocent; and on Pompey demanding, who that guilty person was that would assume the offences of them all, Sthenis replied, it was himself, who had engaged his friends by persuasion to what they had done, and his enemies by force; whereupon Pompey being much taken with the frank speech and noble spirit of the man, first forgave his crime, and then pardoned all the rest of the Himeræans. Hearing, likewise, that his soldiers were very disorderly in their march, doing violence upon the roads, he ordered their swords to be sealed up in their scabbards, and whosoever kept them not so, were severely punished.

Whilst Pompey was thus busy in the affairs and government of Sicily, he received a decree of the senate, and a commission from Sylla, commanding him forthwith to sail into Africa, and make war upon Domitius with all his forces: for Domitius had rallied up a far greater army than Marius had had not long since, when he sailed out of Africa into Italy, and caused a revolution in Rome, and himself, of a fugitive outlaw, became a tyrant. Pompey, therefore, having prepared every thing with the utmost speed, left Memmius, his sister's husband, governor of Sicily, and set sail with one hundred and twenty galleys, and eight hundred other vessels laden with provisions, money, ammunition, and engines of battery. He arrived with his fleet, part at the port of Utica, part at Carthage; and no sooner was he landed, but seven thousand of the enemy revolted and came over to him, while his own forces that he brought with him consisted of six entire legions. Here they tell us of a pleasant incident that happened to him at his first arrival.

For some of his soldiers having by accident stumbled upon a treasure, by which they got a good sum of money, the rest of the army hearing this, began to fancy that the field was full of gold and silver, which had been hid there of old by the Carthaginians in the time of their calamities, and thereupon fell to work, so that the army was useless to Pompey for many days, being totally engaged in digging for the fancied treasure, he himself all the while walking up and down only, and laughing to see so many thousands together, digging and turning up the earth. Until at last, growing weary and hopeless, they came to themselves, and returned to their general, begging him to lead them where he pleased, for that they had already received the punishment of their folly. By this time Domitius had prepared himself, and drawn out his army in array against Pompey; but there was a watercourse betwixt them, craggy, and difficult to pass over; and this, together with a great storm of wind and rain pouring down even from break of day, seemed to leave but little possibility of their coming together, so that Domitius, not expecting any engagement that day, commanded his forces to draw off and retire to the camp. Now Pompey, who was watchful upon every occasion, making use of the opportunity, ordered a march forthwith, and having passed over the torrent, fell in immediately upon their quarters. The enemy was in a great disorder and tumult, and in that confusion attempted a resistance; but they neither were all there, nor supported one another; besides, the wind having veered about, beat the rain full in their faces. Neither indeed was the storm less troublesome to the Romans, for that they could not clearly discern one another, insomuch that even Pompey himself, being unknown, escaped narrowly; for when one of his soldiers demanded of him the word of battle, it happened that he was somewhat slow in his answer, which might have cost him his life.

The enemy being routed with a great slaughter, (for it is said, that of twenty thousand there escaped but three thousand,) the army saluted Pompey by the name of Imperator; but he declined it, telling them, that he could not by any means accept of that title, as long as he saw the camp of the enemy standing; but if they designed to make him worthy of the honor, they must first demolish that. The soldiers on hearing this, went at once and made an assault upon the works and trenches, and there Pompey fought without his helmet, in memory of his former danger, and to avoid the like. The camp was thus taken by storm, and among the rest, Domitius was slain. After that overthrow, the cities of the country thereabouts were all either secured by surrender, or taken by storm. King Iarbas, likewise, a confederate and auxiliary of Domitius, was taken prisoner, and his kingdom was given to Hiempsal.

Pompey could not rest here, but being ambitious to follow the good fortune and use the valor of his army entered Numidia; and marching forward many days' journey up into the country, he conquered all wherever he came. And having revived the terror of the Roman power, which was now almost obliterated among the barbarous nations, he said likewise, that the wild beasts of Africa ought not to be left without some experience of the courage and success of the Romans; and therefore he bestowed some few days in hunting lions and elephants. And it is said, that it was not above the space of forty days at the utmost, in which he gave a total overthrow to the enemy, reduced Africa, and established the affairs of the kings and kingdoms of all that country, being then in the twenty-fourth year of his age.

When Pompey returned back to the city of Utica, there were presented to him letters and orders from Sylla, commanding him to disband the rest of his army, and himself with one legion only to wait there the coming of another general, to succeed him in the government. This, inwardly, was extremely grievous to Pompey, though he made no show of it. But the army resented it openly, and when Pompey besought them to depart and go home before him, they began to revile Sylla, and declared broadly, that they were resolved not to forsake him, neither did they think it safe for him to trust the tyrant. Pompey at first endeavored to appease and pacify them by fair speeches; but when he saw that his persuasions were vain, he left the bench, and retired to his tent with tears in his eyes. But the soldiers followed him, and seizing upon him, by force brought him again, and placed him in his tribunal; where great part of that day was spent in dispute, they on their part persuading him to stay and command them, he, on the other side, pressing upon them obedience, and the danger of mutiny. At last, when they grew yet more importunate and clamorous, he swore that he would kill himself if they attempted to force him; and scarcely even thus appeased them. Nevertheless, the first tidings brought to Sylla were, that Pompey was up in rebellion; on which he remarked to some of his friends, "I see, then, it is my destiny to contend with children in my old age;" alluding at the same time to Marius,[4] who, being but a mere

[4] Marius the younger.

youth, had given him great trouble, and brought him into extreme danger. But being undeceived afterwards by better intelligence, and finding the whole city prepared to meet Pompey, and receive him with every display of kindness and honor, he resolved to exceed them all. And, therefore, going out foremost to meet him, and embracing him with great cordiality, he gave him his welcome aloud in the title of Magnus, or the Great, and bade all that were present call him by that name. Others say that he had this title first given him by a general acclamation of all the army in Africa, but that it was fixed upon him by this ratification of Sylla. It is certain that he himself was the last that owned the title; for it was a long time after, when he was sent proconsul into Spain against Sertorius, that he began to write himself in his letters and commissions by the name of Pompeius Magnus; common and familiar use having then worn off the invidiousness of the title. And one cannot but accord respect and admiration to the ancient Romans, who did not reward the success of action and conduct in war alone with such honorable titles, but adorned likewise the virtues and services of eminent men in civil government with the same distinctions and marks of honor. Two persons received from the people the name of Maximus, or the Greatest, Valerius, for reconciling the senate and people, and Fabius Rullus, because he put out of the senate certain sons of freed slaves who had been admitted into it because of their wealth.

Pompey now desired the honor of a triumph, which Sylla opposed, alleging that the law allowed that honor to none but consuls and prætors, and therefore Scipio the elder, who subdued the Carthaginians in Spain in far greater and nobler conflicts, never petitioned for a triumph, because he had never been consul or prætor; and if Pompey, who had scarcely yet fully grown a beard, and was not of age to be a senator, should enter the city in triumph, what a weight of envy would it bring, he said, at once upon his government and Pompey's honor. This was his language to Pompey, intimating that he could not by any means yield to his request, but if he would persist in his ambition, that he was resolved to interpose his power to humble him. Pompey, however, was not daunted; but bade Sylla recollect, that more worshipped the rising than the setting sun; as if to tell him that his power was increasing, and Sylla's in the wane. Sylla did not perfectly hear the words, but observing a sort of amazement and wonder in the looks and gestures of those that did hear them, he asked what it was that he said. When it was told him, he seemed astounded at Pompey's boldness, and cried out twice together, "Let him triumph," and when others began to show their disapprobation and offence at it, Pompey, it is said, to gall and vex them the more, designed to have his triumphant chariot drawn with four elephants, (having brought over several which belonged to the African kings,) but the gates of the city being too narrow, he was forced to desist from that project, and be content with horses. And when his soldiers, who had not received as large rewards as they had expected, began to clamor, and interrupt the triumph, Pompey regarded these as little as the rest, and plainly told them that he had rather lose the honor of his triumph, than flatter them. Upon which Servilius, a man of great distinction, and at first one of the chief opposers of Pompey's triumph, said, he now perceived that Pompey was truly great and worthy of a triumph. It is clear that he might easily have been a senator, also, if he had wished, but he did not sue for that, being ambitious, it seems, only of unusual honors. For what wonder had it been for Pompey, to sit in the senate before his time? But to triumph before he was in the senate, was really an excess of glory.

And moreover, it did not a little ingratiate him with the people; who were much pleased to see him after his triumph take his place again among the Roman knights. On the other side, it was no less distasteful to Sylla to see how fast he came on, and to what a height of glory and power he was advancing; yet being ashamed to hinder him, he kept quiet. But when, against his direct wishes, Pompey got Lepidus made consul, having openly joined in the canvass and, by the good-will the people felt for himself, conciliated their favor for Lepidus, Sylla could forbear no longer; but when he saw him coming away from the election through the forum with a great train after him, cried out to him, "Well, young man, I see you rejoice in your victory. And, indeed, is it not a most generous and worthy act, that the consulship should be given to Lepidus, the vilest of men, in preference to Catulus, the best and most deserving in the city, and all by your influence with the people? It will be well, however, for you to be wakeful and look to your interests; as you have been making your enemy stronger than yourself." But that which gave the clearest demonstration of Sylla's ill-will to Pompey, was his last will and testament; for whereas he had bequeathed several legacies to all the rest of his friends, and appointed some of them guardians to his son, he passed by Pompey without the least remembrance. However, Pompey bore this with great moderation and temper; and when Lepidus and others were disposed to obstruct his interment in the Campus Martius, and to prevent any public funeral taking place, came forward in support of it, and saw his obsequies performed with all honor and security.

Shortly after the death of Sylla, his prophetic words were fulfilled; and Lepidus proposing to be the successor to all his power and authority, without any ambiguities or pretences, immediately appeared in arms, rousing once more and gathering about him all the long dangerous remains of the old factions, which had escaped the hand of Sylla. Catulus, his colleague, who was followed by the sounder part of the senate and people, was a man of the greatest esteem among the Romans for wisdom and justice; but his talent lay in the government of the city rather than the camp, whereas the exigency required the skill of Pompey. Pompey, therefore, was not long in suspense which way to dispose of himself, but joining with the nobility, was presently appointed general of the army against Lepidus, who had already raised up war in great part of Italy, and held Cisalpine Gaul in subjection with an army under Brutus. As for the rest of his garrisons, Pompey subdued them with ease in his march, but Mutina in Gaul resisted in a formal siege, and he lay here a long time encamped against Brutus. In the mean time Lepidus marched in all haste against Rome, and sitting down before it with a crowd of followers, to the terror of those within, demanded a second consulship. But that fear quickly vanished upon letters sent from Pompey, announcing that he had ended the war without a battle; for Brutus, either betraying his army, or being betrayed by their revolt, surrendered himself to Pompey, and receiving a guard of horse, was conducted to a little town upon the river Po; where he was slain the next day by Geminius, in execution of Pompey's commands. And for this Pompey was much censured; for, having at the beginning of the revolt written to the senate that Brutus had voluntarily surrendered himself, immediately afterward he sent other letters, with matter of accusation against the man, after he was taken off. Brutus, who with Cassius slew Cæsar, was son to this Brutus; neither in war nor in his death like his father, as appears at large in his life. Lepidus upon this being driven out of Italy, fled to Sardinia, where he fell sick and died of sorrow, not for his public misfortunes, as they say, but, upon the discovery of a letter, proving his wife to have been unfaithful to him.

There yet remained Sertorius, a very different general from Lepidus, in possession of Spain, and making himself formidable to Rome; the final disease, as it were, in which the scattered evils of the civil wars had now collected. He had already cut off various inferior commanders, and was at this time coping with Metellus Pius, a man of repute and a good soldier, though perhaps he might now seem too slow, by reason of his age, to second and improve the happier moments of war, and might be sometimes wanting to those advantages which Sertorius by his quickness and dexterity would wrest out of his hands. For Sertorius was always hovering about, and coming upon him unawares, like a captain of thieves rather than soldiers, disturbing him perpetually with ambuscades and light skirmishes; whereas Metellus was accustomed to regular conduct, and fighting in battle array with full-armed soldiers. Pompey, therefore, keeping his army in readiness, made it his object to be sent in aid to Metellus; neither would he be induced to disband his forces, notwithstanding that Catulus called upon him to do so, but by some colorable device or other he still kept them in arms about the city, until the senate at last thought fit, upon the report of Lucius Philippus, to decree him that government. At that time, they say, one of the senators there expressing his wonder and demanding of Philippus whether his meaning was that Pompey should be sent into Spain as proconsul, "No," replied Philippus, "but as pro-*consuls*," as if both consuls for that year were in his opinion wholly useless.

When Pompey was arrived in Spain, as is usual upon the fame of a new leader, men began to be inspired with new hopes, and those nations that had not entered into a very strict alliance with Sertorius, began to waver and revolt; whereupon Sertorius uttered various arrogant and scornful speeches against Pompey, saying in derision, that he should want no other weapon but a ferula and rod to chastise this boy with, if he were not afraid of that old woman, meaning Metellus. Yet in deed and reality he stood in awe of Pompey, and kept on his guard against him, as appeared by his whole management of the war, which he was observed to conduct much more warily than before; for Metellus, which one would not have imagined, was grown excessively luxurious in his habits, having given himself over to self-indulgence and pleasure, and from a moderate and temperate, became suddenly a sumptuous and ostentatious liver, so that this very thing gained Pompey great reputation and goodwill, as he made himself somewhat specially an example of frugality, although that virtue was habitual in him, and required no great industry to exercise it, as he was naturally inclined to temperance, and no ways inordinate in his desires. The fortune of the war was very various; nothing however annoyed Pompey so much as the taking of the town of Lauron by Sertorius. For when Pompey thought he had him safe inclosed, and had boasted somewhat largely of raising the siege, he found himself all of a sudden encompassed; insomuch that he durst not move out of his camp, but was forced to sit still whilst the city was taken and burnt before his face. However, afterwards in a battle near Valentia, he gave a great defeat to Herennius and Perpenna, two commanders among the refugees who had fled to Sertorius, and now lieutenants under him, in which he slew above ten thousand men.

Pompey, being elated and filled with confidence by this victory, made all haste to engage Sertorius himself, and the rather lest Metellus should come in for a share in the honor of the victory. Late in the day, towards sunset, they joined battle near the river Sucro, both being in fear lest Metellus should come; Pompey, that he might engage alone, Sertorius, that he might have one alone to engage with. The issue of the battle proved doubtful, for a wing of each side had the better; but of the generals, Sertorius had the greater honor, for that he maintained his post, having put to flight the entire division that was opposed to him, whereas Pompey was himself almost made a prisoner; for being set upon by a strong man at arms that fought on foot, (he being on horseback,) as they were closely engaged hand to hand, the strokes of their swords chanced to light upon their hands, but with a different success; for Pompey's was a slight wound only, whereas he cut off the other's hand. However, it happened so, that many now falling upon

Pompey together, and his own forces there being put to the rout, he made his escape beyond expectation, by quitting his horse, and turning him out among the enemy. For the horse being richly adorned with golden trappings, and having a caparison of great value, the soldiers quarrelled among themselves for the booty, so that while they were fighting with one another, and dividing the spoil, Pompey made his escape. By break of day the next morning, each drew out his forces into the field to claim the victory; but Metellus coming up, Sertorius vanished, having broken up and dispersed his army. For this was the way in which he used to raise and disband his armies, so that sometimes he would be wandering up and down all alone, and at other times again he would come pouring into the field at the head of no less than one hundred and fifty thousand fighting-men, swelling of a sudden like a winter torrent.

When Pompey was going after the battle to meet and welcome Metellus, and when they were near one another, he commanded his attendants to lower their rods in honor of Metellus, as his senior and superior. But Metellus on the other side forbade it, and behaved himself in general very obligingly to him, not claiming any prerogative either in respect of his consular rank or seniority; excepting only that when they encamped together, the watchword was given to the whole camp by Metellus. But generally they had their camps asunder, being divided and distracted by the enemy, who took all shapes, and being always in motion, would by some skilful artifice appear in a variety of places almost in the same instant, drawing them from one attack to another, and at last keeping them from foraging, wasting the country, and holding the dominion of the sea, Sertorius drove them both out of that part of Spain which was under his control, and forced them for want of necessaries to retreat into provinces that did not belong to them.

Pompey, having made use of and expended the greatest part of his own private revenues upon the war, sent and demanded moneys of the senate, adding, that in case they did not furnish him speedily, he should be forced to return into Italy with his army. Lucullus being consul at that time, though at variance with Pompey, yet in consideration that he himself was a candidate for the command against Mithridates, procured and hastened these supplies, fearing lest there should be any pretence or occasion given to Pompey of returning home, who of himself was no less desirous of leaving Sertorius, and of undertaking the war against Mithridates, as an enterprise which by all appearance would prove much more honorable and not so dangerous. In the mean time Sertorius died, being treacherously murdered by some of his own party; and Perpenna, the chief among them, took the command, and attempted to carry on the same enterprises with Sertorius, having indeed the same forces and the same means, only wanting the same skill and conduct in the use of them. Pompey therefore marched directly against Perpenna, and finding him acting merely at random in his affairs, had a decoy ready for him, and sent out a detachment of ten cohorts into the level country with orders to range up and down and disperse themselves abroad. The bait took accordingly, and no sooner had Perpenna turned upon the prey and had them in chase, but Pompey appeared suddenly with all his army and joining battle, gave him a total overthrow. Most of his officers were slain in the field, and he himself being brought prisoner to Pompey, was by his order put to death. Neither was Pompey guilty in this of ingratitude or unmindfulness of what had occurred in Sicily, which some have laid to his charge, but was guided by a high-minded policy and a deliberate counsel for the security of his country. For Perpenna, having in his custody all Sertorius's papers, offered to produce several letters from the greatest men in Rome, who, desirous of a change and subversion of the government, had invited Sertorius into Italy. And Pompey, fearing that these might be the occasion of worse wars than those which were now ended, thought it advisable to put Perpenna to death, and burnt the letters without reading them.

Pompey continued in Spain after this so long a time as was necessary for the suppression of all the greatest disorders in the province; and after moderating and allaying the more violent heats of affairs there, returned with his army into Italy, where he arrived, as chance would have it, in the height of the servile war. Accordingly, upon his arrival, Crassus, the commander in that war, at some hazard precipitated a battle, in which he had great success, and slew upon the place twelve thousand three hundred of the insurgents. Nor yet was he so quick, but that fortune reserved to Pompey some share of honor in the success of this war, for five thousand of those that had escaped out of the battle fell into his hands; and when he had totally cut them off, he wrote to the senate, that Crassus had overthrown the slaves in battle, but that he had plucked up the whole war by the roots. And it was agreeable to the people in Rome both thus to say, and thus to hear said, because of the general favor of Pompey. But of the Spanish war and the conquest of Sertorius, no one, even in jest, could have ascribed the honor to any one else. Nevertheless, all this high respect for him, and this desire to see him come home, were not unmixed with apprehensions and suspicions that he might perhaps not disband his army, but take his way by the force of arms and a supreme command to the seat of Sylla. And so in the number of all those that ran out to meet him and congratulate his return, as many went out of fear as affection. But after Pompey had removed this alarm, by declaring beforehand that he would discharge the army after his triumph, those that envied him could now only complain that he affected popularity, courting the common people more than the nobility, and that whereas Sylla had abolished the tribuneship of the people, he designed to gratify the people by restoring that office, which was indeed the fact. For there was not any one thing that the people of Rome were more wildly eager for, or more passionately desired, than the restoration of that office, insomuch that Pompey thought himself extremely fortunate in this opportunity, despairing (if he were anticipated by some one else in this) of ever meeting with any other sufficient means of expressing his gratitude for the favors which he had received from the people.

Though a second triumph was decreed him, and he was declared consul, yet all these honors did not seem so great an evidence of his power and glory, as the ascendant which he had over Crassus; for he, the wealthiest among all the statesmen of his time, and the most eloquent and greatest too, who had looked down on Pompey himself, and on all others as beneath him, durst not appear a candidate for the consulship before he had applied to Pompey.

The request was made accordingly, and was eagerly embraced by Pompey, who had long sought an occasion to oblige him in some friendly office; so that he solicited for Crassus, and entreated the people heartily, declaring, that their favor would be no less to him in choosing Crassus his colleague, than in making himself consul. Yet for all this, when they were created consuls, they were always at variance, and opposing one another. Crassus prevailed most in the senate, and Pompey's power was not less with the people, he having restored to them the office of tribune, and having allowed the courts of judicature to be transferred back to the knights by a new law. He himself in person, too, afforded them a most grateful spectacle, when he appeared and craved his discharge from the military service. For it is an ancient custom among the Romans, that the knights, when they had served out their legal time in the wars, should lead their horses into the market-place before the two officers, called censors, and having given an account of the commanders and generals under whom they served, as also of the places and actions of their service, should be discharged, every man with honor or disgrace, according to his deserts. There were then sitting in state upon the bench two censors, Gellius and Lentulus, inspecting the knights, who were passing by in muster before them, when Pompey was seen coming down into the forum, with all the ensigns of a consul, but leading his horse in his hand. When he came up, he bade his lictors make way for him, and so he led his horse to the bench; the people being all this while in a sort of amaze, and all in silence, and the censors themselves regarding the sight with a mixture of respect and gratification. Then the senior censor examined him: " Pompeius

Magnus, I demand of you whether you have served the full time in the wars that is prescribed by the law?" "Yes," replied Pompey with a loud voice, "I have served all, and all under myself as general." The people hearing this gave a great shout, and made such an outcry for delight, that there was no appeasing it; and the censors rising from their judgment-seat, accompanied him home to gratify the multitude, who followed after, clapping their hands and shouting.

Pompey's consulship was now expiring, and yet his difference with Crassus increasing, when one Caius Aurelius, a knight, a man who had declined public business all his lifetime, mounted the hustings, and addressed himself in an oration to the assembly, declaring that Jupiter had appeared to him in a dream, commanding him to tell the consuls, that they should not give up office until they were friends. After this was said, Pompey stood silent, but Crassus took him by the hand, and spoke in this manner: "I do not think, fellow-citizens, that I shall do any thing mean or dishonorable, in yielding first to Pompey, whom you were pleased to ennoble with the title of Great, when as yet he scarce had a hair on his face; and granted the honor of two triumphs, before he had a place in the senate." Hereupon they were reconciled and laid down their office. Crassus resumed the manner of life which he had always pursued before; but Pompey in the great generality of causes for judgment declined appearing on either side and by degrees withdrew himself totally from the forum, showing himself but seldom in public; and whenever he did, it was with a great train after him. Neither was it easy to meet or visit him without a crowd of people about him; he was most pleased to make his appearance before large numbers at once, as though he wished to maintain in this way his state and majesty, and as if he held himself bound to preserve his dignity from contact with the addresses and conversation of common people. And life in the robe of peace is only too apt to lower the reputation of men that have grown great by arms, who naturally find difficulty in adapting themselves to the habits of civil equality. They expect to be treated as the first in the city, even as they were in the camp; and on the other hand, men who in war were nobody, think it intolerable if in the city at any rate they are not to take the lead. And so, when a warrior renowned for victories and triumphs shall turn advocate and appear among them in the forum, they endeavor their utmost to obscure and depress him; whereas, if he gives up any pretensions here and retires, they will maintain his military honor and authority beyond the reach of envy. Events themselves not long after showed the truth of this.

The power of the pirates first commenced in Cilicia, having in truth but a precarious and obscure beginning, but gained life and boldness afterwards in the wars of Mithridates, where they hired themselves out, and took employment in the king's service. Afterwards, whilst the Romans were embroiled in their civil wars, being engaged against one another even before the very gates of Rome, the seas lay waste and unguarded, and by degrees enticed and drew them on not only to seize upon and spoil the merchants and ships upon the seas, but also to lay waste the islands and seaport towns. So that now there embarked with these pirates men of wealth and noble birth and superior abilities, as if it had been a natural occupation to gain distinction in. They had divers arsenals, or piratic harbors, as likewise watch towers and beacons, all along the seacoast; and fleets were here received that were well manned with the finest mariners, and well served with the expertest pilots, and composed of swift-sailing and light-built vessels adapted for their special purpose. Nor was it merely their being thus formidable that excited indignation; they were even more odious for their ostentation than they were feared for their force. Their ships had gilded masts at their stems; the sails woven of purple, and the oars plated with silver, as if their delight were to glory in their iniquity. There was nothing but music and dancing, banqueting and revels, all along the shore. Officers in command were taken prisoners, and cities put under contribution, to the reproach and dishonor of the Roman supremacy. There were of these corsairs above one thousand sail, and they had taken no less than four hundred cities, committing sacrilege upon the temples of the gods, and enriching themselves with the spoils of many never violated before, such as were those of Claros, Didyma, and Samothrace; and the temple of the Earth in Hermione, and that of Æsculapius in Epidaurus, those of Neptune at the Isthmus, at Tænarus, and at Calauria; those of Apollo at Actium and Leucas, and those of Juno, in Samos, at Argos, and at Lacinium. They themselves offered strange sacrifices upon Mount Olympus,[5] and

---

[5] *Olympus* (it is *Olympus* alone in the Greek) is not *Mount Olympus*, say the commentators, at any rate not that of Thessaly, nor that of Prusa, the modern Broussa, but Olympus in Lycia, which, however, appears to have been a mountain as well as a town. "It was the strong-hold," says Strabo (*XII.*, 7), "of the pirate Zenicetus, a mountain and a fortified place of the same

performed certain secret rites or religious mysteries, among which those of Mithras have been preserved to our own time, having received their previous institution from them. But besides these insolencies by sea, they were also injurious to the Romans by land; for they would often go inland up the roads, plundering and destroying their villages and country-houses. And once they seized upon two Roman prætors, Sextilius and Bellinus, in their purple-edged robes, and carried them off together with their officers and lictors. The daughter also of Antonius, a man that had had the honor of a triumph, taking a journey into the country, was seized, and redeemed upon payment of a large ransom. But it was most abusive of all, that when any of the captives declared himself to be a Roman and told his name, they affected to be surprised, and feigning fear, smote their thighs and fell down at his feet, humbly beseeching him to be gracious and forgive them. The captive seeing them so humble and suppliant, believed them to be in earnest; and some of them now would proceed to put Roman shoes on his feet, and to dress him in a Roman gown, to prevent, they said, his being mistaken another time. After all this pageantry, when they had thus deluded and mocked him long enough, at last putting out a ship's ladder, when they were in the midst of the sea, they told him he was free to go, and wished him a pleasant journey; and if he resisted, they themselves threw him overboard, and drowned him.

name, from whence there is a view of all Lycia, Pamphylia, and Pisidia." The strong-hold had been wrested from the pirates before Pompey's time by Servilius Isauricus, when Zenicetus burnt himself and all his household in it; but it had doubtless soon been re-occupied.

POMPEY

This piratic power having got the dominion and control of all the Mediterranean, there was left no place for navigation or commerce. And this it was which most of all made the Romans, finding themselves to be extremely straitened in their markets, and considering that if it should continue, there would be a dearth and famine in the land, determine at last to send out Pompey to recover the seas from the pirates. Gabinius, one of Pompey's friends, preferred a law, whereby there was granted to him, not only the government of the seas as admiral, but in direct words, sole and irresponsible sovereignty over all men. For the decree gave him absolute power and authority in all the seas within the pillars of Hercules, and in the adjacent main-land for the space of four hundred furlongs from the sea. Now there were but few regions in the Roman empire out of that compass; and the greatest of the nations and most powerful of the kings were included in the limit. Moreover by this decree he had a power of selecting fifteen lieutenants out of the senate, and of assigning to each his province in charge; then he might take likewise out of the treasury and out of the hands of the revenue-farmers what moneys he pleased; as also two hundred sail of ships, with a power to press and levy what soldiers and seamen he thought fit. When this law was read, the common people approved of it exceedingly, but the chief men and most important among the senators looked upon it as an exorbitant power, even beyond the reach of envy, but well deserving their fears. Therefore concluding with themselves that such unlimited authority was dangerous, they agreed unanimously to oppose the bill, and all went against it, except Cæsar, who gave his vote for the law, not to gratify Pompey, but the people, whose favor he had

courted underhand from the beginning, and hoped
to compass for himself. The rest inveighed bitterly
against Pompey, insomuch that one of the consuls
told him, that if he was ambitious of the place of
Romulus, he would scarce avoid his end, but he was
in danger of being torn in pieces by the multitude
for his speech. Yet when Catulus stood up to
speak against the law, the people in reverence to
him were silent and attentive. And when, after
saying much in the most honorable terms in favor
of Pompey, he proceeded to advise the people in
kindness to spare him, and not to expose a man of
his value to such a succession of dangers and wars,
"For," said he, "where could you find another
Pompey, or whom would you have in case you
should chance to lose him?" they all cried out with
one voice, "Yourself." And so Catulus, finding all
his rhetoric ineffectual, desisted. Then Roscius attempted to speak, but could obtain no hearing, and
made signs with his fingers, intimating, "Not him
alone," but that there might be a second Pompey or
colleague in authority with him. Upon this, it is
said, the multitude being extremely incensed, made
such a loud outcry, that a crow flying over the
market-place at that instant was struck, and dropt
down among the crowd; whence it would appear
that the cause of birds falling down to the ground,
is not any rupture or division of the air causing a
vacuum, but purely the actual stroke of the voice,
which when carried up in a great mass and with
violence, raises a sort of tempest and billow, as it
were, in the air.

The assembly broke up for that day; and when
the day was come, on which the bill was to pass by
suffrage into a decree, Pompey went privately into
the country; but hearing that it was passed and

confirmed, he returned again into the city by night, to avoid the envy that might be occasioned by the concourse of people that would meet and congratulate him. The next morning he came abroad and sacrificed to the gods, and having audience at an open assembly, so handled the matter that they enlarged his power, giving him many things besides what was already granted, and almost doubling the preparation appointed in the former decree. Five hundred ships were manned for him, and an army raised of one hundred and twenty thousand foot, and five thousand horse. Twenty-four senators that had been generals of armies were appointed to serve as lieutenants under him, and to these were added two quæstors. Now it happened within this time that the prices of provisions were much reduced, which gave an occasion to the joyful people of saying, that the very name of Pompey had ended the war. However, Pompey in pursuance of his charge divided all the seas, and the whole Mediterranean into thirteen parts, allotting a squadron to each, under the command of his officers; and having thus dispersed his power into all quarters, and encompassed the pirates everywhere, they began to fall into his hands by whole shoals, which he seized and brought into his harbors. As for those that withdrew themselves betimes, or otherwise escaped his general chase, they all made to Cilicia, where they hid themselves as in their hive; against whom Pompey now proceeded in person with sixty of his best ships, not however until he had first scoured and cleared all the seas near Rome, the Tyrrhenian, and the African, and all the waters of Sardinia, Corsica, and Sicily; all which he performed in the space of forty days, by his own indefatigable industry, and the zeal of his lieutenants.

Pompey met with some interruption in Rome, through the malice and envy of Piso, the consul, who had given some check to his proceedings, by withholding his stores and discharging his seamen; whereupon he sent his fleet round to Brundusium, himself going the nearest way by land through Tuscany to Rome; which was no sooner known by the people, than they all flocked out to meet him upon the way, as if they had not sent him out but a few days before. What chiefly excited their joy, was the unexpectedly rapid change in the markets, which abounded now with the greatest plenty, so that Piso was in great danger to have been deprived of his consulship, Gabinius having a law ready prepared for that purpose; but Pompey forbade it, behaving himself as in that, so in all things else, with great moderation, and when he had made sure of all that he wanted or desired, he departed for Brundusium, whence he set sail in pursuit of the pirates. And though he was straitened in time, and his hasty voyage forced him to sail by several cities without touching, yet he would not pass by the city of Athens unsaluted; but landing there, after he had sacrificed to the gods, and made an address to the people, as he was returning out of the city, he read at the gates two epigrams, each in a single line, written in his own praise; one within the gate:—

>Thy humbler thoughts make thee a god the more;[6]

the other without:—

>Adieu we bid, who welcome bade before.

[6] *Thy humbler thoughts make thee a god the more.* Literally, In so far as you know yourself man, even so far you are a god; an Attic conceit, expressing the same meaning as Horace's *Dîs te minorem quod geris, imperas.*

Now because Pompey had shown himself merciful to some of these pirates that were yet roving in bodies about the seas, having upon their supplication ordered a seizure of their ships and persons only, without any further process or severity, therefore the rest of their comrades in hopes of mercy too, made their escape from his other commanders, and surrendered themselves with their wives and children into his protection. He continued to pardon all that came in, and the rather because by them he might make discovery of those who fled from his justice, as conscious that their crimes were beyond an act of indemnity. The most numerous and important part of these conveyed their families and treasures, with all their people that were unfit for war, into castles and strong forts about Mount Taurus; but they themselves having well manned their galleys, embarked for Coracesium in Cilicia, where they received Pompey and gave him battle. Here they had a final overthrow, and retired to the land, where they were besieged. At last, having despatched their heralds to him with a submission, they delivered up to his mercy themselves, their towns, islands, and strong-holds, all which they had so fortified that they were almost impregnable, and scarcely even accessible.

Thus was this war ended, and the whole power of the pirates at sea dissolved everywhere in the space of three months, wherein, besides a great number of other vessels, he took ninety men-of-war with brazen beaks; and likewise prisoners of war to the number of no less than twenty thousand.

As regarded the disposal of these prisoners, he never so much as entertained the thought of putting them to death; and yet it might be no less dangerous on the other hand to disperse them, as they might reunite and make head again, being numerous, poor, and warlike. Therefore wisely weighing with himself, that man by nature is not a wild or unsocial creature, neither was he born so, but makes himself what he naturally is not, by vicious habit; and that again on the other side, he is civilized and grows gentle by a change of place, occupation, and manner of life, as beasts themselves that are wild by nature, become tame and tractable by housing and gentler usage, upon this consideration he determined to translate these pirates from sea to land, and give them a taste of an honest and innocent course of life, by living in towns, and tilling the ground. Some therefore were admitted into the small and half-peopled towns of the Cilicians, who for an enlargement of their territories, were willing to receive them. Others he planted in the city of the Solians, which had been lately laid waste by Tigranes, king of Armenia, and which he now restored. But the largest number were settled in Dyme, the town of Achæa, at that time extremely depopulated, and possessing an abundance of good land.

However, these proceedings could not escape the envy and censure of his enemies; and the course he took against Metellus in Crete was disapproved of even by the chiefest of his friends. For Metellus, a relation of Pompey's former colleague in Spain, had been sent prætor into Crete, before this province of the seas was assigned to Pompey. Now Crete was the second source of pirates next to Cilicia, and Metellus having shut up a number of them in their strong-holds there, was engaged in reducing and extirpating them. Those that were yet remaining and besieged sent their supplications to Pompey, and invited him into the island as a part of his province, alleging it to fall, every part of it, within the distance from the sea specified in his commission, and so within the precincts of his charge. Pompey receiving the submission, sent letters to Metellus, commanding him to leave off the war; and others in like manner to the cities, in which he charged them not to yield any obedience to the commands of Metellus. And after these, he sent Lucius Octavius, one of his lieutenants, to act as general, who entering the besieged fortifications and fighting in defence of the pirates, rendered Pompey not odious only, but even ridiculous too; that he should lend his name as a guard to a nest of thieves, that knew neither god nor law, and make his reputation serve as a sanctuary to them, only out of pure envy and emulation to Metellus. For neither was Achilles thought to act the part of a man, but rather of a mere boy, mad after glory, when by signs he forbade the rest of the Greeks to strike at Hector:—

" for fear
Some other hand should give the blow, and he
Lose the first honor of the victory." [7]

Whereas Pompey even sought to preserve the common enemies of the world, only that he might deprive a Roman prætor, after all his labors, of the honor of a triumph. Metellus however was not daunted, but prosecuted the war against the pirates, expelled them from their strong-holds and punished them; and dismissed Octavius with the insults and reproaches of the whole camp.

When the news came to Rome that the war with the pirates was at an end, and that Pompey was unoccupied, diverting himself in visits to the

[7] For the death of Hector see Iliad, XXII., 207.

cities for want of employment, one Manlius,[8] a tribune of the people, preferred a law that Pompey should have all the forces of Lucullus, and the provinces under his government, together with Bithynia, which was under the command of Glabrio; and that he should forthwith conduct the war against the two kings, Mithridates and Tigranes, retaining still the same naval forces and the sovereignty of the seas as before. But this was nothing less than to constitute one absolute monarch of all the Roman empire. For the provinces which seemed to be exempt from his commission by the former decree, such as were Phrygia, Lycaonia, Galatia, Cappadocia, Cilicia, the upper Colchis, and Armenia, were all added in by this latter law, together with all the troops and forces with which Lucullus had defeated Mithridates and Tigranes. And though Lucullus was thus simply robbed of the glory of his achievements in having a successor assigned him, rather to the honor of his triumph, than the danger of the war; yet this was of less moment in the eyes of the aristocratical party, though they could not but admit the injustice and ingratitude to Lucullus. But their great grievance was, that the power of Pompey should be converted into a manifest tyranny; and they therefore exhorted and encouraged one another privately to bend all their forces in opposition to this law, and not tamely to cast away their liberty; yet when the day came on which it was to pass into a decree, their hearts failed them for fear of the people, and all were silent except Catulus, who boldly inveighed against the law and its proposer, and when he found

[8] i. e. Manilius; in support of whose law Cicero made his speech, Pro Lege Manilia.

that he could do nothing with the people, turned
to the senate, crying out and bidding them seek out
some mountain as their forefathers had done, and
fly to the rocks where they might preserve their
liberty. The law passed into a decree, as it is said,
by the suffrages of all the tribes. And Pompey in
his absence was made lord of almost all that power,
which Sylla only obtained by force of arms, after
a conquest of the very city itself. When Pompey
had advice by letters of the decree, it is said that in
the presence of his friends, who came to give him
joy of his honor, he seemed displeased, frowning
and smiting his thigh, and exclaimed as one over-
burdened, and weary of government, "Alas, what
a series of labors upon labors! If I am never to
end my service as a soldier, nor to escape from this
invidious greatness, and live at home in the country
with my wife, I had better have been an unknown
man." But all this was looked upon as mere trifling,
neither indeed could the best of his friends call it
any thing else, well knowing that his enmity with
Lucullus, setting a flame just now to his natural
passion for glory and empire, made him feel more
than usually gratified.

As indeed appeared not long afterwards by his
actions, which clearly unmasked him; for in the first
place, he sent out his proclamations into all quarters,
commanding the soldiers to join him, and summoned
all the tributary kings and princes within his charge;
and in short, as soon as he had entered upon his
province, he left nothing unaltered that had been
done and established by Lucullus. To some he remitted their penalties, and deprived others of their
rewards, and acted in all respects as if with the
express design that the admirers of Lucullus might
know that all his authority was at an end. Lucullus

expostulated by friends, and it was thought fitting that there should be a meeting betwixt them; and accordingly they met in the country of Galatia. As they were both great and successful generals, their officers bore their rods before them all wreathed with branches of laurel; Lucullus came through a country full of green trees and shady woods, but Pompey's march was through a cold and barren district. Therefore the lictors of Lucullus, perceiving Pompey's laurels were withered and dry, helped him to some of their own, and adorned and crowned his rods with fresh laurels. This was thought ominous, and looked as if Pompey came to take away the reward and honor of Lucullus's victories. Lucullus had the priority in the order of consulships, and also in age; but Pompey's two triumphs made him the greater man. Their first addresses in this interview were dignified and friendly, each magnifying the other's actions, and offering congratulations upon his success. But when they came to the matter of their conference or treaty, they could agree on no fair or equitable terms of any kind, but even came to harsh words against each other, Pompey upbraiding Lucullus with avarice, and Lucullus retorting ambition upon Pompey, so that their friends could hardly part them. Lucullus, remaining in Galatia, made a distribution of the lands within his conquests, and gave presents to whom he pleased; and Pompey encamping not far distant from him, sent out his prohibitions, forbidding the execution of any of the orders of Lucullus, and commanded away all his soldiers, except sixteen hundred, whom he thought likely to be unserviceable to himself, being disorderly and mutinous, and whom he knew to be hostile to Lucullus; and to these acts he added satirical speeches, detracting openly from the glory

of his actions, and giving out, that the battles of
Lucullus had been but with the mere stage-shows
and idle pictures of royal pomp, whereas the real
war against a genuine army, disciplined by defeat,
was reserved to him, Mithridates having now begun
to be in earnest, and having betaken himself to his
shields, swords, and horses. Lucullus, on the other
side, to be even with him, replied, that Pompey
came to fight with the mere image and shadow of
war, it being his usual practice, like a lazy bird of
prey, to come upon the carcass, when others had
slain the dead, and to tear in pieces the relics of a
war. Thus he had appropriated to himself the victories over Sertorius, over Lepidus, and over the
insurgents under Spartacus; whereas this last had
been achieved by Crassus, that obtained by Catulus,
and the first won by Metellus. And therefore it
was no great wonder, that the glory of the Pontic
and Armenian war should be usurped by a man
who had condescended to any artifices to work himself into the honor of a triumph over a few runaway
slaves.

After this Lucullus went away, and Pompey
having placed his whole navy in guard upon the
seas betwixt Phœnicia and Bosporus,[9] himself
marched against Mithridates, who had a phalanx of
thirty thousand foot, with two thousand horse, yet
durst not bid him battle. He had encamped upon a
strong mountain where it would have been hard
to attack him, but abandoned it in no long time, as
destitute of water. No sooner was he gone but
Pompey occupied it, and observing the plants that
were thriving there, together with the hollows which

---

[9] The kingdom of Bosporus here, as in the lives of Lucullus
and Sylla, is the southern part of the Crimea.

he found in several places, conjectured that such a plot could not be without springs, and therefore ordered his men to sink wells in every corner. After which there was, in a little time, great plenty of water throughout all the camp, insomuch that he wondered how it was possible for Mithridates to be ignorant of this, during all that time of his encampment there. After this Pompey followed him to his next camp, and there drawing lines round about him, shut him in. But he, after having endured a siege of forty-five days, made his escape secretly, and fled away with all the best part of his army, having first put to death all the sick and unserviceable. Not long after Pompey overtook him again near the banks of the river Euphrates, and encamped close by him; but fearing lest he should pass over the river and give him the slip there too, he drew up his army to attack him at midnight. And at that very time Mithridates, it is said, saw a vision in his dream foreshowing what should come to pass. For he seemed to be under sail in the Euxine Sea with a prosperous gale, and just in view of Bosporus, discoursing pleasantly with the ship's company, as one overjoyed for his past danger and present security, when on a sudden he found himself deserted of all, and floating upon a broken plank of the ship at the mercy of the sea. Whilst he was thus laboring under these passions and phantasms, his friends came and awaked him with the news of Pompey's approach; who was now indeed so near at hand, that the fight must be for the camp itself, and the commanders accordingly drew up the forces in battle array. Pompey perceiving how ready they were and well prepared for defence, began to doubt with himself whether he should put it to the hazard of a fight in the dark,

judging it more prudent to encompass them only
at present, lest they should fly, and to give them
battle with the advantage of numbers the next day.
But his oldest officers were of another opinion, and
by entreaties and encouragements obtained permission that they might charge them immediately.
Neither was the night so very dark, but that, though
the moon was going down, it yet gave light enough
to discern a body. And indeed this was one especial
disadvantage to the king's army. For the Romans
coming upon them with the moon on their backs,
the moon, being very low, and just upon setting,
cast the shadows a long way before their bodies,
reaching almost to the enemy, whose eyes were
thus so much deceived that not exactly discerning
the distance, but imagining them to be near at
hand, they threw their darts at the shadows, without
the least execution. The Romans therefore perceiving this, ran in upon them with a great shout;
but the barbarians, all in a panic, unable to endure
the charge, turned and fled, and were put to great
slaughter, above ten thousand being slain; the camp
also was taken. As for Mithridates himself, he at
the beginning of the onset, with a body of eight
hundred horse charged through the Roman army,
and made his escape. But before long all the rest
dispersed, some one way, some another, and he was
left only with three persons, among whom was his
concubine, Hypsicratia, a girl always of a manly
and daring spirit, and the king called her on that
account Hypsicrates. She being attired and
mounted like a Persian horseman, accompanied the
king in all his flight, never weary even in the longest
journey, nor ever failing to attend the king in person, and look after his horse too, until they came
to Inora, a castle of the king's, well stored with gold

and treasure. From thence Mithridates took his richest apparel, and gave it among those that had resorted to him in their flight; and to every one of his friends he gave a deadly poison, that they might not fall into the power of the enemy against their wills. From thence he designed to have gone to Tigranes in Armenia, but being prohibited by Tigranes, who put out a proclamation with a reward of one hundred talents to any one that should apprehend him, he passed by the head-waters of the river Euphrates, and fled through the country of Colchis.

Pompey in the mean time made an invasion into Armenia, upon the invitation of young Tigranes, who was now in rebellion against his father, and gave Pompey a meeting about the river Araxes, which rises near the head of Euphrates, but turning its course and bending towards the east, falls into the Caspian Sea. They two, therefore, marched together through the country, taking in all the cities by the way, and receiving their submission. But king Tigranes, having lately suffered much in the war with Lucullus, and understanding that Pompey was of a kind and gentle disposition, admitted Roman troops into his royal palaces, and taking along with him his friends and relations, went in person to surrender himself into the hands of Pompey. He came as far as the trenches on horseback, but there he was met by two of Pompey's lictors, who commanded him to alight and walk on foot, for no man ever was seen on horseback within a Roman camp. Tigranes submitted to this immediately, and not only so, but loosing his sword, delivered up that too; and last of all, as soon as he appeared before Pompey, he pulled off his royal turban, and attempted to have laid it at his feet.

Nay, worst of all, even he himself had fallen prostrate as an humble suppliant at his knees, had not Pompey prevented it, taking him by the hand and placing him near him, Tigranes himself on one side of him and his son upon the other. Pompey now told him that the rest of his losses were chargeable upon Lucullus, by whom he had been dispossessed of Syria, Phœnicia, Cilicia, Galatia, and Sophene; but all that he had preserved to himself entire till that time he should peaceably enjoy, paying the sum of six thousand talents as a fine or penalty for injuries done to the Romans, and that his son should have the kingdom of Sophene. Tigranes himself was well pleased with these conditions of peace, and when the Romans saluted him king, seemed to be overjoyed, and promised to every common soldier half a mina of silver, to every centurion ten minas, and to every tribune a talent; but the son was displeased, insomuch that when he was invited to supper, he replied, that he did not stand in need of Pompey for that sort of honor, for he would find out some other Roman to sup with. Upon this he was put into close arrest, and reserved for the triumph.

Not long after this Phraates, king of Parthia, sent to Pompey, and demanded to have young Tigranes, as his son-in-law, given up to him, and that the river Euphrates should be the boundary of the empires. Pompey replied, that for Tigranes, he belonged more to his own natural father than his father-in-law, and for the boundaries, he would take care that they should be according to right and justice.

So Pompey, leaving Armenia in the custody of Afranius, went himself in chase of Mithridates; to do which he was forced of necessity to march through several nations inhabiting about Mount Caucasus. Of these the Albanians and Iberians were the two chiefest. The Iberians stretch out as far as the Moschian mountains and the Pontus; the Albanians lie more eastwardly, and towards the Caspian Sea. These Albanians at first permitted Pompey, upon his request, to pass through the country; but when winter had stolen upon the Romans whilst they were still in the country, and they were busy celebrating the festival of Saturn, they mustered a body of no less than forty thousand fighting men, and set upon them, having passed over the river Cyrnus,[10] which rising from the mountains of Iberia, and receiving the river Araxes in its course from Armenia, discharges itself by twelve mouths into the Caspian. Or, according to others, the Araxes does not fall into it, but they flow near one another, and so discharge themselves as neighbors into the same sea. It was in the power of Pompey to have obstructed the enemy's passage over the river, but he suffered them to pass over quietly; and then leading on his forces and giving battle, he routed them, and slew great numbers of them in the field. The king sent ambassadors with his submission, and Pompey upon his supplication pardoned the offence, and making a treaty with him, he marched directly against the Iberians, a nation no less in number than the other, but much more warlike, and extremely desirous of gratifying Mithridates, and driving out Pompey. These Iberians were never subject to the Medes or Persians, and they happened likewise to escape the dominion of the Macedonians, because Alexander was so quick in his march through

---

[10] Or Cyrus, which is the correct name, and was probably well known to Plutarch, the modern Koor.

Hyrcania. But these also Pompey subdued in a
great battle, where there were slain nine thousand
upon the spot, and more than ten thousand taken
prisoners. From thence he entered into the country
of Colchis, where Servilius met him by the river
Phasis, bringing the fleet with which he was guarding the Pontus.

The pursuit of Mithridates, who had thrown
himself among the tribes inhabiting Bosporus and
the shores of the Mæotian Sea, presented great
difficulties. News was also brought to Pompey
that the Albanians had again revolted. This made
him turn back, out of anger and determination not
to be beaten by them, and with difficulty and great
danger he passed back over the Cyrnus, which the
barbarous people had fortified a great way down the
banks with palisadoes. And after this, having a
tedious march to make through a waterless and
difficult country, he ordered ten thousand skins to
be filled with water, and so advanced towards the
enemy; whom he found drawn up in order of battle
near the river Abas, to the number of sixty thousand horse, and twelve thousand foot, ill armed
generally, and most of them covered only with
the skins of wild beasts. Their general was Cosis,
the king's brother, who as soon as the battle was
begun, singled out Pompey, and rushing in upon
him, darted his javelin into the joints of his breastplate; while Pompey, in return, struck him through
the body with his lance, and slew him. It is related
that in this battle there were Amazons fighting as
auxiliaries with the barbarians, and that they came
down from the mountains by the river Thermodon.
For that after the battle, when the Romans were
taking the spoil and plunder of the field, they met
with several targets and buskins of the Amazons;

but no woman's body was found among the dead. They inhabit the parts of Mount Caucasus that reach down to the Hyrcanian Sea, not immediately bordering upon the Albanians, for the Gelæ and the Leges lie betwixt; and they keep company with these people yearly, for two months only, near the river Thermodon; after which they retire to their own habitations, and live alone all the rest of the year.

After this engagement, Pompey was eager to advance with his forces upon the Hyrcanian and Caspian Sea, but was forced to retreat at a distance of three days' march from it, by the number of venomous serpents, and so he retreated into Armenia the Less. Whilst he was there, the kings of the Elymæans and Medes sent ambassadors to him, to whom he gave friendly answer by letter; and sent against the king of Parthia, who had made incursions upon Gordyene, and despoiled the subjects of Tigranes, an army under the command of Afranius, who put him to the rout, and followed him in chase as far as the district of Arbela.

Of the concubines of king Mithridates that were brought before Pompey, he took none to himself, but sent them all away to their parents and relations; most of them being either the daughters or wives of princes and great commanders. Stratonice, however, who had the greatest power and influence with him, and to whom he had committed the custody of his best and richest fortress, had been, it seems, the daughter of a musician, an old man, and of no great fortune, and happening to sing one night before Mithridates at a banquet, she struck his fancy so, that immediately he took her with him, and sent away the old man much dissatisfied, the king having not so much as said one kind word to himself.

But when he rose in the morning, and saw tables in his house richly covered with gold and silver plate, a great retinue of servants, eunuchs, and pages, bringing him rich garments, and a horse standing before the door richly caparisoned, in all respects as was usual with the king's favorites, he looked upon it all as a piece of mockery, and thinking himself trifled with, attempted to make off and run away. But the servants laying hold upon him, and informing him really that the king had bestowed on him the house and furniture of a rich man lately deceased, and that these were but the first-fruits or earnests of greater riches and possessions that were to come, he was persuaded at last with much difficulty to believe them. And so putting on his purple robes, and mounting his horse, he rode through the city, crying out, "All this is mine;" and to those that laughed at him, he said, there was no such wonder in this, but it was a wonder rather that he did not throw stones at all he met, he was so transported with joy. Such was the parentage and blood of Stratonice. She now delivered up this castle into the hands of Pompey, and offered him many presents of great value, of which he accepted only such as he thought might serve to adorn the temples of the gods, and add to the splendor of his triumph; the rest he left to Stratonice's disposal, bidding her please herself in the enjoyment of them.

And in the same manner he dealt with the presents offered him by the king of Iberia, who sent him a bedstead, table, and a chair of state, all of gold, desiring him to accept of them; but he delivered them all into the custody of the public treasurers, for the use of the commonwealth.

In another castle called Cænum, Pompey found

and read with pleasure several secret writings of Mithridates, containing much that threw light on his character. For there were memoirs by which it appeared that besides others, he had made away with his son Ariarathes by poison, as also with Alcæus the Sardian, for having robbed him of the first honors in a horse-race. There were several judgments upon the interpretation of dreams, which either he himself or some of his mistresses had had; and besides these, there was a series of wanton letters to and from his concubine Monime. Theophanes tells us that there was found also an address by Rutilius, in which he attempted to exasperate him to the slaughter of all the Romans in Asia; though most men justly conjecture this to be a malicious invention of Theophanes, who probably hated Rutilius because he was a man in nothing like himself; or perhaps it might be to gratify Pompey, whose father is described by Rutilius in his history, as the vilest man alive.

From thence Pompey came to the city of Amisus, where his passion for glory put him into a position which might be called a punishment on himself. For whereas he had often sharply reproached Lucullus, in that while the enemy was still living, he had taken upon him to issue decrees, and distribute rewards and honors, as conquerors usually do only when the war is brought to an end, yet now was he himself, while Mithridates was paramount in the kingdom of Bosporus, and at the head of a powerful army, as if all were ended, just doing the same thing, regulating the provinces, and distributing rewards, many great commanders and princes having flocked to him, together with no less than twelve barbarian kings; insomuch that to gratify these other kings, when he wrote to the king of Parthia, he would not condescend, as others used to do, in the superscription of his letter, to give him his title of king of kings.

Moreover, he had a great desire and emulation to occupy Syria, and to march through Arabia to the Red Sea,[11] that he might thus extend his conquests every way to the great ocean that encompasses the habitable earth; as in Africa he was the first Roman that advanced his victories to the ocean; and again in Spain he made the Atlantic Sea the limit of the empire; and then thirdly, in his late pursuit of the Albanians, he had wanted but little of reaching the Hyrcanian Sea. Accordingly he raised his camp, designing to bring the Red Sea within the circuit of his expedition, especially as he saw how difficult it was to hunt after Mithridates with an army, and that he would prove a worse enemy flying than fighting. But yet he declared, that he would leave a sharper enemy behind him than himself, namely, famine; and therefore he appointed a guard of ships to lie in wait for the merchants that sailed to Bosporus, death being the penalty for any who should attempt to carry provisions thither.

Then he set forward with the greatest part of his army, and in his march casually fell in with several dead bodies still uninterred, of those soldiers who were slain with Triarius in his unfortunate engagement with Mithridates; these he buried splendidly and honorably. The neglect of whom, it is thought, caused, as much as any thing, the hatred that was felt against Lucullus, and alienated the

---

[11] The Red or Erythræan Sea of the ancients was rather the Indian Ocean, though within this it may have included our Red Sea.

affections of the soldiers from him. Pompey having now by his forces under the command of Afranius, subdued the Arabians about the mountain Amanus, himself entered Syria, and finding it destitute of any natural and lawful prince, reduced it into the form of a province, as a possession of the people of Rome. He conquered also Judæa, and took its king, Aristobulus, captive. Some cities he built anew, and to others he gave their liberty, chastising their tyrants. Most part of the time that he spent there was employed in the administration of justice, in deciding controversies of kings and States; and where he himself could not be present in person, he gave commissions to his friends, and sent them. Thus when there arose a difference betwixt the Armenians and Parthians about some territory, and the judgment was referred to him, he gave a power by commission to three judges and arbiters to hear and determine the controversy. For the reputation of his power was great; nor was the fame of his justice and clemency inferior to that of his power, and served indeed as a veil for a multitude of faults committed by his friends and familiars. For although it was not in his nature to check or chastise wrongdoers, yet he himself always treated those that had to do with him in such a manner, that they submitted to endure with patience the acts of covetousness and oppression done by others.

Among these friends of his, there was one Demetrius, who had the greatest influence with him of all; he was a freed slave, a youth of good understanding, but somewhat too insolent in his good fortune, of whom there goes this story. Cato, the philosopher, being as yet a very young man, but of great repute and a noble mind, took a journey of pleasure to Antioch, at a time when Pompey was not there, having a great desire to see the city. He, as his custom was, walked on foot, and his friends accompanied him on horseback; and seeing before the gates of the city a multitude dressed in white, the young men on one side of the road, and the boys on the other, he was somewhat offended at it, imagining that it was officiously done in honor of him, which was more than he had any wish for. However, he desired his companions to alight and walk with him; but when they drew near, the master of the ceremonies in this procession came out with a garland and a rod in his hand, and met them, inquiring, where they had left Demetrius, and when he would come? Upon which Cato's companions burst out into laughter, but Cato said only, " Alas, poor city!" and passed by without any other answer. However, Pompey rendered Demetrius less odious to others by enduring his presumption and impertinence to himself. For it is reported how that Pompey, when he had invited his friends to an entertainment, would be very ceremonious in waiting till they all came and were placed, while Demetrius would be already stretched upon the couch as if he cared for no one, with his dress over his ears, hanging down from his head. Before his return into Italy, he had purchased the pleasantest country-seat about Rome, with the finest walks and places for exercise, and there were sumptuous gardens, called by the name of Demetrius, while Pompey his master, up to his third triumph, was contented with an ordinary and simple habitation. Afterwards, it is true, when he had erected his famous and stately theatre [12] for the

---

[12] Of Pompey's *famous and stately theatre* some small remains are still supposed to exist. It was the first building for theatrical shows which was erected in Rome for permanent use.

people of Rome, he built as a sort of appendix to it, a house for himself, much more splendid than his former, and yet no object even this to excite men's envy, since he who came to be master of it after Pompey could not but express wonder and inquire where Pompey the Great used to sup. Such is the story told us.

The king of the Arabs near Petra, who had hitherto despised the power of the Romans, now began to be in great alarm at it, and sent letters to him promising to be at his commands, and to do whatever he should see fit to order. However, Pompey having a desire to confirm and keep him in the same mind, marched forwards for Petra, an expedition not altogether irreprehensible in the opinion of many; who thought it a mere running away from their proper duty, the pursuit of Mithridates, Rome's ancient and inveterate enemy, who was now rekindling the war once more, and making preparations, it was reported, to lead his army

Up to that time, all had been temporary stages, pulled down after the occasion for which they were set up. This stood far out from the walls, with a large portico, and plane trees planted about it, on the very edge of the Campus Martius, beyond the public buildings which had by this time covered the new quarter (the Prata Flaminia), outside and under the Capitoline. Agrippa went a little beyond it with the Pantheon. Whether the house which Pompey *built as a sort of appendix to it for himself* was near the theatre, and different from his house within the walls, in the Carinæ, is made a question. Plutarch's words certainly do not require us to suppose that it was locally an appendix or appendage to the theatre, and there seems no doubt that the house in the Carinæ was his real residence. See the story of the Life of Antony (*Vol. V.*), of the retort made to Antony by Sextus Pompeius.

POMPEY

through Scythia and Pæonia,[18] into Italy. Pompey, on the other side, judging it easier to destroy his forces in battle, than to seize his person in flight, resolved not to tire himself out in a vain pursuit, but rather to spend his leisure upon another enemy, as a sort of digression in the mean while. But fortune resolved the doubt; for when he was now not far from Petra, and had pitched his tents and encamped for that day, as he was taking exercise with his horse outside the camp, couriers came riding up from Pontus, bringing good news, as was known at once by the heads of their javelins, which it is the custom to carry crowned with branches of laurel. The soldiers, as soon as they saw them, flocked immediately to Pompey, who notwithstanding was minded to finish his exercise; but when they began to be clamorous and importunate, he alighted from his horse, and taking the letters went before them into the camp. Now there being no tribunal erected there, not even that military substitute for one which they make by cutting up thick turfs of earth and piling them one upon another, they, through eagerness and impatience, heaped up a pile of packsaddles, and Pompey standing upon that, told them the news of Mithridates's death, how that he had himself put an end to his life upon the revolt of his son Pharnaces, and that Pharnaces had taken all things there into his hands and possession, which he did, his letters said, in right of himself and the Romans. Upon this news, the whole army expressing their joy, as was to be expected, fell to sacrificing to the gods, and feasting, as if in the person of Mithridates alone there had died many thousands of their enemies.

[18] Or Pannonia. The Greeks appear to have confused the two names.

Pompey by this event having brought this war to its completion, with much more ease than was expected, departed forthwith out of Arabia, and passing rapidly through the intermediate provinces, he came at length to the city Amisus. There he received many presents brought from Pharnaces, with several dead bodies of the royal blood, and the corpse of Mithridates himself, which was not easy to be known by the face, for the physicians that embalmed him had not dried up his brain, but those who were curious to see him knew him by the scars there. Pompey himself would not endure to see him, but to deprecate the divine jealousy, sent it away to the city of Sinope. He admired the richness of his robes, no less than the size and splendor of his armor. His sword-belt, however, which had cost four hundred talents, was stolen by Publius, and sold to Ariarathes; his tiara also, a piece of admirable workmanship, Gaius, the foster-brother of Mithridates, gave secretly to Faustus, the son of Sylla, at his request. All which Pompey was ignorant of, but afterwards, when Pharnaces came to understand it, he severely punished those that embezzled them.

Pompey now having ordered all things, and established that province, took his journey homewards in greater pomp and with more festivity. For when he came to Mitylene, he gave the city their freedom upon the intercession of Theophanes,[14] and was present at the contest, there periodically held,

---

[14] This Lesbian Greek, who is mentioned several times in the life of Pompey, and again in that of Cicero, rose early into favor with Pompey, whose confidence in him is mentioned in several places by Cicero, and also by Cæsar. He left a son named Marcus Pompeius, who was employed both by Augustus and

of the poets, who took at that time no other theme
or subject than the actions of Pompey. He was
extremely pleased with the theatre itself, and had
a model of it taken, intending to erect one in Rome
on the same design, but larger and more magnificent.
When he came to Rhodes, he attended the
lectures of all the philosophers there, and gave to
every one of them a talent. Posidonius has published
the disputation which he held before him
against Hermagoras the rhetorician, upon the subject
of Invention [15] in general. At Athens, also,
he showed similar munificence to the philosophers,
and gave fifty talents towards the repairing and
beautifying the city. So that now by all these
acts he well hoped to return into Italy in the greatest
splendor and glory possible to man, and find
his family as desirous to see him, as he felt himself
to come home to them. But that supernatural
agency, whose province and charge it is always to
mix some ingredient of evil with the greatest and
most glorious goods of fortune, had for some time
back been busy in his household, preparing him a
sad welcome. For Mucia during his absence had
dishonored his bed. Whilst he was abroad at a
distance, he had refused all credence to the report;
but when he drew nearer to Italy, where his
thoughts were more at leisure to give consideration
to the charge, he sent her a bill of divorce; but

Tiberius; but at the end of the reign of Tiberius his descendants
were put to death.

[15] As in Cicero's *de Inventione,* the first of the five points of
Rhetoric; the other four being elocutio, dispositio, memoria, actio.
We are first to *find out* what to say, then to express it in proper
diction, to arrange it judiciously, to remember our speech, and,
lastly, to deliver it well.

neither then in writing, nor afterwards by word of mouth, did he ever give a reason why he discharged her; the cause of it is mentioned in Cicero's epistles.

Rumors of every kind were scattered abroad about Pompey, and were carried to Rome before him, so that there was a great tumult and stir, as if he designed forthwith to march with his army into the city, and establish himself securely as sole ruler. Crassus withdrew himself, together with his children and property, out of the city, either that he was really afraid, or that he counterfeited rather, as is most probable, to give credit to the calumny and exasperate the jealousy of the people. Pompey, therefore, as soon as he entered Italy, called a general muster of the army; and having made a suitable address and exchanged a kind farewell with his soldiers, he commanded them to depart every man to his country and place of habitation, only taking care that they should not fail to meet again at his triumph. Thus the army being disbanded, and the news commonly reported, a wonderful result ensued. For when the cities saw Pompey the Great passing through the country unarmed, and with a small train of familiar friends only, as if he was returning from a journey of pleasure, not from his conquests, they came pouring out to display their affection for him, attending and conducting him to Rome with far greater forces than he disbanded; insomuch that if he had designed any movement or innovation in the State, he might have done it without his army.

Now, because the law permitted no commander to enter into the city before his triumph, he sent to the senate entreating them as a favor to him to prorogue the election of consuls, that thus he might be able to attend and give countenance to Piso, one of the candidates. The request was resisted by Cato, and met with a refusal. However, Pompey could not but admire the liberty and boldness of speech which Cato alone had dared to use in the maintenance of law and justice. He therefore had a great desire to win him over, and purchase his friendship at any rate; and to that end, Cato having two nieces, Pompey asked for one in marriage for himself, the other for his son. But Cato looked unfavorably on the proposal, regarding it as a design for undermining his honesty, and in a manner bribing him by a family alliance; much to the displeasure of his wife and sister, who were indignant that he should reject a connection with Pompey the Great. About that time Pompey having a design of setting up Afranius for the consulship, gave a sum of money among the tribes for their votes, and people came and received it in his own gardens, a proceeding which, when it came to be generally known, excited great disapprobation, that he should thus for the sake of men who could not obtain the honor by their own merits, make merchandise of an office which had been given to himself as the highest reward of his services. "Now," said Cato to his wife and sister, "had we contracted an alliance with Pompey, we had been allied to this dishonor too," and this they could not but acknowledge, and allow his judgment of what was right and fitting to have been wiser and better than theirs.

The splendor and magnificence of Pompey's triumph was such that though it took up the space of two days, yet they were extremely straitened in time, so that of what was prepared for that pageantry, there was as much withdrawn as would have set out and adorned another triumph. In the first place, there were tables carried, inscribed with the names and titles of the nations over whom he triumphed, Pontus, Armenia, Cappadocia, Paphlagonia, Media, Colchis, the Iberians, the Albanians, Syria, Cilicia, and Mesopotamia, together with Phœnicia and Palestine, Judæa, Arabia, and all the power of the pirates subdued by sea and land. And in these different countries there appeared the capture of no less than one thousand fortified places, nor much less than nine hundred cities, together with eight hundred ships of the pirates, and the foundation of thirty-nine towns. Besides, there was set forth in these tables an account of all the tributes throughout the empire, and how that before these conquests the revenue amounted but to fifty millions, whereas from his acquisitions they had a revenue of eighty-five millions; and that in present payment he was bringing into the common treasury ready money, and gold and silver plate, and ornaments, to the value of twenty thousand talents, over and above what had been distributed among the soldiers, of whom he that had least had fifteen hundred drachmas for his share. The prisoners of war that were led in triumph, besides the chief pirates, were the son of Tigranes, king of Armenia, with his wife and daughter; as also Zosime, wife of king Tigranes himself, and Aristobulus, king of Judæa, the sister of king Mithridates and her five sons, and some Scythian women. There were likewise the hostages of the Albanians and Iberians, and of the king of Commagene, besides a vast number of trophies, one for every battle in which he was conqueror, either himself in person, or by his lieutenants. But that which seemed to be his greatest glory, being one which no other Roman ever attained to, was this, that he made his third triumph over the third division of the world. For others among the Romans had the honor of triumphing thrice, but his first triumph was over Africa, his second, over Europe, and this last, over Asia; so that he seemed in these three triumphs to have led the whole world captive.

As for his age, those who affect to make the parallel exact in all things betwixt him and Alexander the Great, do not allow him to have been quite thirty-four, whereas in truth at that time he was near forty. And well had it been for him had he terminated his life at this date, while he still enjoyed Alexander's fortune, since all his aftertime served only either to bring him prosperity that made him odious, or calamities too great to be retrieved. For that great authority which he had gained in the city by his merits, he made use of only in patronizing the iniquities of others, so that by advancing their fortunes, he detracted from his own glory, till at last he was overthrown even by the force and greatness of his own power. And as the strongest citadel or fort in a town, when it is taken by an enemy, does then afford the same strength to the foe, as it had done to friends before; so Cæsar, after Pompey's aid had made him strong enough to defy his country, ruined and overthrew at last the power which had availed him against the rest. The course of things was as follows. Lucullus, when he returned out of Asia, where he had been treated with insult by Pompey, was received by the senate with great honor, which was yet increased when Pompey came home; to check whose ambition they encouraged him to assume the administration of the government, whereas he was now grown cold and disinclined to business, having given himself over to the pleasures of ease and the enjoyment of a splendid fortune. However, he began for the time to exert himself against Pompey, attacked him sharply, and succeeded in having his own acts and decrees, which were repealed by Pompey, reëstablished, and with the assistance of Cato, gained the superiority in the senate. Pompey having fallen from his hopes in such an unworthy repulse, was forced to fly to the tribunes of the people for refuge, and to attach himself to the young men, among whom was Clodius, the vilest and most impudent wretch alive, who took him about, and exposed him as a tool to the people, carrying him up and down among the throngs in the market-place, to countenance those laws and speeches which he made to cajole the people and ingratiate himself. And at last for his reward, he demanded of Pompey, as if he had not disgraced, but done him a great kindness, that he should forsake (as in the end he did forsake) Cicero, his friend, who on many public occasions had done him the greatest service. And so when Cicero was in danger, and implored his aid, he would not admit him into his presence, but shutting up his gates against those that came to mediate for him, slipt out at a back door, whereupon Cicero fearing the result of his trial, departed privately from Rome.

About that time Cæsar, returning from military service, started a course of policy which brought him great present favor, and much increased his power for the future, and proved extremely destructive both to Pompey and the commonwealth. For now he stood candidate for his first consulship, and well observing the enmity betwixt Pompey and Crassus, and finding that by joining with one he should make the other his enemy, he endeavored by all means to reconcile them, an object in itself honorable and tending to the public good, but as he undertook it, a mischievous and subtle intrigue. For he well knew that opposite parties or factions in a commonwealth, like passengers in a boat, serve to trim and balance the unsteady motions of power there; whereas if they combine and come all over to one side; they cause a shock which will be sure to overset the vessel and carry down everything. And therefore Cato wisely told those who charged all the calamities of Rome upon the disagreement betwixt Pompey and Cæsar, that they were in error in charging all the crime upon the last cause; for it was not their discord and enmity, but their unanimity and friendship, that gave the first and greatest blow to the commonwealth.

Cæsar being thus elected consul, began at once to make an interest with the poor and meaner sort, by preferring and establishing laws for planting colonies and dividing lands, lowering the dignity of his office, and turning his consulship into a sort of tribuneship rather. And when Bibulus, his colleague, opposed him, and Cato was prepared to second Bibulus, and assist him vigorously, Cæsar brought Pompey upon the hustings, and addressing him in the sight of the people, demanded his opinion upon the laws that were proposed. Pompey gave his approbation. "Then," said Cæsar, "in case any man should offer violence to these laws, will you be ready to give assistance to the people?" "Yes," replied Pompey, "I shall be ready, and against those that threaten the sword, I will appear with sword and buckler." Nothing ever was said or done by Pompey up to that day, that seemed more insolent or overbearing; so that his friends endeavored to apologize for it as a word spoken inadvertently, but by his actions afterwards it appeared plainly that he was totally devoted to Cæsar's service. For on a sudden, contrary to all expectation, he married Julia, the daughter of Cæsar, who had been affianced before and was to be married within a few days to Cæpio. And to appease Cæpio's wrath, he gave him his own daughter in marriage, who had been espoused before to Faustus, the son of Sylla. Cæsar himself married Calpurnia, the daughter of Piso.

Upon this Pompey, filling the city with soldiers, carried all things by force as he pleased. As Bibulus, the consul, was going to the forum, accompanied by Lucullus and Cato, they fell upon him on a sudden and broke his rods; and somebody threw a vessel of ordure upon the head of Bibulus himself; and two tribunes of the people, who escorted him, were desperately wounded in the fray. And thus having cleared the forum of all their adversaries, they got their bill for the division of lands established and passed into an act; and not only so, but the whole populace being taken with this bait, became totally at their devotion, inquiring into nothing and without a word giving their suffrages to whatever they propounded. Thus they confirmed all those acts and decrees of Pompey, which were questioned and contested by Lucullus; and to Cæsar they granted the provinces of Gaul, both within and without the Alps, together with Illyricum, for five years, and likewise an army of four entire legions; then they created consuls for the year ensuing, Piso, the father-in-law of Cæsar, and Gabinius, the most extravagant of Pompey's flatterers.

During all these transactions, Bibulus kept close within doors, nor did he appear publicly in person for the space of eight months together, notwithstanding he was consul, but sent out proclamations full of bitter invectives and accusations against them both. Cato turned prophet, and, as if he had been possessed with a spirit of divination, did nothing else in the senate but foretell what evils should befall the commonwealth and Pompey. Lucullus pleaded old age, and retired to take his ease, as superannuated for affairs of State; which gave occasion to the saying of Pompey, that the fatigues of luxury were not more seasonable for an old man than those of government. Which in truth proved a reflection upon himself; for he not long after let his fondness for his young wife seduce him also into effeminate habits. He gave all his time to her, and passed his days in her company in country-houses and gardens, paying no heed to what was going on in the forum. Insomuch that Clodius, who was then tribune of the people, began to despise him, and engage in the most audacious attempts. For when he had banished Cicero, and sent away Cato into Cyprus under pretence of military duty, and when Cæsar was gone upon his expedition to Gaul, finding the populace now looking to him as the leader who did every thing according to their pleasure, he attempted forthwith to repeal some of Pompey's decrees; he took Tigranes, the captive, out of prison, and kept him about him as his companion; and commenced actions against several of Pompey's friends, thus designing to try the extent of his power. At last, upon a time when Pompey was present at the hearing of a certain cause, Clodius, accompanied with a crowd of profligate and impudent ruffians, standing up in a place above the rest, put questions to the populace as follows: "Who is the dissolute general? who is the man that seeks another man? who scratches his head with one finger?" and the rabble, upon the signal of his shaking his gown, with a great shout to every question, like singers making responses in a chorus, made answer, "Pompey."

This indeed was no small annoyance to Pompey,

who was quite unaccustomed to hear any thing ill of himself, and unexperienced altogether in such encounters; and he was yet more vexed, when he saw that the senate rejoiced at this foul usage, and regarded it as a just punishment upon him for his treachery to Cicero. But when it came even to blows and wounds in the forum, and that one of Clodius's bondslaves was apprehended, creeping through the crowd towards Pompey with a sword in his hand, Pompey laid hold of this pretence, though perhaps otherwise apprehensive of Clodius's insolence and bad language, and never appeared again in the forum during all the time he was tribune, but kept close at home, and passed his time in consulting with his friends, by what means he might best allay the displeasure of the senate and nobles against him. Among other expedients, Culleo advised the divorce of Julia, and to abandon Cæsar's friendship to gain that of the senate; this he would not hearken to. Others again advised him to call home Cicero from banishment, a man who was always the great adversary of Clodius, and as great a favorite of the senate; to this he was easily persuaded. And therefore he brought Cicero's brother into the forum, attended with a strong party, to petition for his return; where, after a warm dispute, in which several were wounded and some slain, he got the victory over Clodius. No sooner was Cicero returned home upon this decree, but immediately he used his efforts to reconcile the senate to Pompey; and by speaking in favor of the law upon the importation of corn, did again, in effect, make Pompey sovereign lord of all the Roman possessions by sea and land. For by that law, there were placed under his control all ports, markets, and storehouses, and in short, all the concerns both of the merchants and the husbandmen; which gave occasion to the charge brought against it by Clodius, that the law was not made because of the scarcity of corn, but the scarcity of corn was made, that they might pass a law, whereby that power of his, which was now grown feeble and consumptive, might be revived again, and Pompey reinstated in a new empire. Others look upon it as a politic device of Spinther, the consul, whose design it was to secure Pompey in a greater authority, that he himself might be sent in assistance to king Ptolemy. However, it is certain that Canidius, the tribune, preferred a law to despatch Pompey in the character of an ambassador, without an army, attended only with two lictors, as a mediator betwixt the king and his subjects of Alexandria. Neither did this proposal seem unacceptable to Pompey, though the senate cast it out upon the specious pretence, that they were unwilling to hazard his person. However, there were found several writings scattered about the forum and near the senate-house, intimating how grateful it would be to Ptolemy to have Pompey appointed for his general instead of Spinther. And Timagenes even asserts that Ptolemy went away and left Egypt, not out of necessity, but purely upon the persuasion of Theophanes, who was anxious to give Pompey the opportunity for holding a new command, and gaining further wealth. But Theophanes's want of honesty does not go so far to make this story credible as does Pompey's own nature, which was averse, with all its ambition, to such base and disingenuous acts, to render it improbable.

Thus Pompey being appointed chief purveyor, and having within his administration and management all the corn trade, sent abroad his factors and agents into all quarters, and he himself sailing into

Sicily, Sardinia, and Africa, collected vast stores of corn. He was just ready to set sail upon his voyage home, when a great storm arose upon the sea, and the ships' commanders doubted whether it were safe. Upon which Pompey himself went first abroad, and bid the mariners weigh anchor, declaring with a loud voice, that there was a necessity to sail, but no necessity to live.[16] So that with this spirit and courage, and having met with favorable fortune, he made a prosperous return, and filled the markets with corn, and the sea with ships. So much so that this great plenty and abundance of provisions yielded a sufficient supply, not only to the city of Rome, but even to other places too, dispersing itself, like waters from a spring, into all quarters.

Meantime Cæsar grew great and famous with his wars in Gaul, and while in appearance he seemed far distant from Rome, entangled in the affairs of the Belgians, Suevians, and Britons, in truth he was working craftily by secret practices in the midst of the people, and countermining Pompey in all political matters of most importance. He himself with his army close about him, as if it had been his own body, not with mere views of conquest over the barbarians, but as though his contests with them were but mere sports and exercises of the chase, did his utmost with this training and discipline to make it invincible and alarming. And in the mean time his gold and silver and other spoils and treasure which he took from the enemy in his conquests, he sent to Rome in presents, tempting people with his gifts, and aiding ædiles, prætors, and consuls, as also their

---

[16] *There was a necessity to sail, but no necessity to live.* "Necesse est ut eam, non ut vivam."

POMPEY

wives, in their expenses, and thus purchasing himself numerous friends. Insomuch, that when he passed back again over the Alps, and took up his winter quarters in the city of Luca, there flocked to him an infinite number of men and women, striving who should get first to him, two hundred senators included, among whom were Pompey and Crassus; so that there were to be seen at once before Cæsar's door no less than six score rods of proconsuls and prætors. The rest of his addressers he sent all away full fraught with hopes and money; but with Crassus and Pompey, he entered into special articles of agreement, that they should stand candidates for the consulship next year; that Cæsar on his part should send a number of his soldiers to give their votes at the election; that as soon as they were elected, they should use their interest to have the command of some provinces and legions assigned to themselves, and that Cæsar should have his present charge confirmed to him for five years more. When these arrangements came to be generally known, great indignation was excited among the chief men in Rome; and Marcellinus, in an open assembly of the people, demanded of them both, whether they designed to sue for the consulship or no. And being urged by the people for their answer, Pompey spoke first, and told them, perhaps he would sue for it, perhaps he would not. Crassus was more temperate, and said, that he would do what should be judged most agreeable with the interest of the commonwealth; and when Marcellinus persisted in his attack on Pompey, and spoke, as it was thought, with some vehemence, Pompey remarked that Marcellinus was certainly the unfairest of men, to show him no gratitude for having thus made him an orator out of a mute, and converted him from a hungry starveling into a man so full-fed that he could not contain himself.

Most of the candidates nevertheless abandoned their canvass for the consulship; Cato alone persuaded and encouraged Lucius Domitius not to desist, "since," said he, "the contest now is not for office, but for liberty against tyrants and usurpers." Therefore those of Pompey's party, fearing this inflexible constancy in Cato, by which he kept with him the whole senate, lest by this he should likewise pervert and draw after him all the well-affected part of the commonalty, resolved to withstand Domitius at once, and to prevent his entrance into the forum. To this end, therefore, they sent in a band of armed men, who slew the torchbearer of Domitius, as he was leading the way before him, and put all the rest to flight; last of all, Cato himself retired, having received a wound in his right arm while defending Domitius. Thus by these means and practices they obtained the consulship; neither did they behave themselves with more decency in their further proceedings; but in the first place, when the people were choosing Cato prætor, and just ready with their votes for the poll, Pompey broke up the assembly, upon a pretext of some inauspicious appearance, and having gained the tribes by money, they publicly proclaimed Vatinius prætor. Then, in pursuance of their covenants with Cæsar, they introduced several laws by Trebonius, the tribune, continuing Cæsar's commission to another five years' charge of his province; to Crassus there were appointed Syria, and the Parthian war; and to Pompey himself, all Africa, together with both Spains, and four legions of soldiers, two of which he lent to Cæsar upon his request, for the wars in Gaul.

Crassus, upon the expiration of his consulship,

departed forthwith into his province; but Pompey spent some time in Rome, upon the opening or dedication of his theatre, where he treated the people with all sorts of games, shows, and exercises, in gymnastics alike and in music. There was likewise the hunting or baiting of wild beasts, and combats with them, in which five hundred lions were slain; but above all, the battle of elephants was a spectacle full of horror and amazement.

These entertainments brought him great honor and popularity; but on the other side he created no less envy to himself, in that he committed the government of his provinces and legions into the hands of friends as his lieutenants, whilst he himself was going about and spending his time with his wife in all the places of amusement in Italy; whether it were he was so fond of her himself, or she so fond of him, and he unable to distress her by going away, for this also is stated. And the love displayed by this young wife for her elderly husband was a matter of general note, to be attributed, it would seem, to his constancy in married life, and to his dignity of manner, which in familiar intercourse was tempered with grace and gentleness, and was particularly attractive to women, as even Flora, the courtesan, may be thought good enough evidence to prove. It once happened in a public assembly, as they were at an election of the ædiles, that the people came to blows, and several about Pompey were slain, so that he, finding himself all bloody, ordered a change of apparel; but the servants who brought home his clothes, making a great bustle and hurry about the house, it chanced that the young lady, who was then with child, saw his gown all stained with blood; upon which she dropped immediately into a swoon, and was hardly brought to life again; however, what with her fright and suffering, she fell into labor and miscarried; even those who chiefly censured Pompey for his friendship to Cæsar, could not reprove him for his affection to so attached a wife. Afterwards she was great again, and brought to bed of a daughter, but died in childbed; neither did the infant outlive her mother many days. Pompey had prepared all things for the interment of her corpse at his house near Alba, but the people seized upon it by force, and performed the solemnities in the field of Mars, rather in compassion for the young lady, than in favor either for Pompey or Cæsar; and yet of these two, the people seemed at that time to pay Cæsar a greater share of honor in his absence, than to Pompey, though he was present.

For the city now at once began to roll and swell, so to say, with the stir of the coming storm. Things everywhere were in a state of agitation, and everybody's discourse tended to division, now that death had put an end to that relation which hitherto had been a disguise rather than restraint to the ambition of these men. Besides, not long after came messengers from Parthia with intelligence of the death of Crassus there, by which another safeguard against civil war was removed, since both Cæsar and Pompey kept their eyes on Crassus, and awe of him held them together more or less within the bounds of fair-dealing all his lifetime. But when fortune had taken away this second, whose province it might have been to revenge the quarrel of the conquered, you might then say with the comic poet,

> The combatants are waiting to begin,
> Smearing their hands with dust and oiling each his skin.[17]

[17] *The combatants are waiting to begin* is an unknown comic fragment.

So inconsiderable a thing is fortune in respect of human nature, and so insufficient to give content to a covetous mind, that an empire of that mighty extent and sway could not satisfy the ambition of two men; and though they knew and had read, that

> The gods, when they divided out 'twixt three,[18]
> This massive universe, heaven, hell, and sea,
> Each one sat down contented on his throne,
> And undisturbed each god enjoys his own,

yet they thought the whole Roman empire not sufficient to contain them, though they were but two.

Pompey once in an oration to the people, told them, that he had always come into office before he expected he should, and that he had always left it sooner than they expected he would; and, indeed, the disbanding of all his armies witnessed as much. Yet when he perceived that Cæsar would not so willingly discharge his forces, he endeavored to strengthen himself against him by offices and com-

---

[18] The four verses are a very liberal translation of one quoted by Plutarch. *All was divided in three, and each had a portion assigned him.* It is from the passage in the fifteenth Iliad (189), the reply of Neptune when Jupiter, waking out of sleep, sees the Trojans flying and Neptune busy aiding the Greeks, and sends Iris to order him to quit the field; *somewhat an arrogant message,* replies Neptune in anger, *to one his equal in honor.* "We are three brothers, all sons of Cronus by Rhea our mother, Zeus, and I, and Hades, the third, in the world underneath us; three shares were made of all things, and each of us had his portion; I had the lot of the white salt sea for my possession; Hades had the thick darkness; Zeus had the open sky and the clouds in the heaven above us; and as common to all remain the earth and the heights of Olympus."

mands in the city; but beyond this he showed no desire for any change, and would not seem to distrust, but rather to disregard and contemn him. And when he saw how they bestowed the places of government quite contrary to his wishes, because the citizens were bribed in their elections, he let things take their course, and allowed the city to be left without any government at all. Hereupon there was mention straightway made of appointing a dictator. Lucilius, a tribune of the people, was the man who first adventured to propose it, urging the people to make Pompey dictator. But the tribune was in danger of being turned out of his office, by the opposition that Cato made against it. And for Pompey, many of his friends appeared and excused him, alleging that he never was desirous of that government, neither would he accept of it. And when Cato therefore made a speech in commendation of Pompey, and exhorted him to support the cause of good order in the commonwealth, he could not for shame but yield to it, and so for the present Domitius and Messala were elected consuls. But shortly afterwards, when there was another anarchy, or vacancy in the government, and the talk of a dictator was much louder and more general than before, those of Cato's party, fearing lest they should be forced to appoint Pompey, thought it policy to keep him from that arbitrary and tyrannical power, by giving him an office of more legal authority. Bibulus himself, who was Pompey's enemy, first gave his vote in the senate, that Pompey should be created consul alone; alleging, that by these means either the commonwealth would be freed from its present confusion, or that its bondage should be lessened by serving the worthiest. This was looked upon as a very strange opinion, considering the man that spoke it; and therefore on Cato's standing up, everybody expected that he would have opposed it; but after silence made, he said that he would never have been the author of that advice himself, but since it was propounded by another, his advice was to follow it, adding, that any form of government was better than none at all; and that in a time so full of distraction, he thought no man fitter to govern than Pompey. This counsel was unanimously approved of, and a decree passed that Pompey should be made sole consul, with this clause, that if he thought it necessary to have a colleague, he might choose whom he pleased, provided it were not till after two months expired.

Thus was Pompey created and declared sole consul by Sulpicius, regent [19] in this vacancy; upon which he made very cordial acknowledgments to Cato, professing himself much his debtor, and requesting his good advice in conducting the government; to this Cato replied, that Pompey had no reason to thank him, for all that he had said was for the service of the commonwealth, not of Pompey; but that he would be always ready to give his advice privately, if he were asked for it; and if not, he should not fail to say what he thought in public. Such was Cato's conduct on all occasions.

On his return into the city Pompey married Cornelia, the daughter of Metellus Scipio, not a maiden, but lately left a widow by Publius, the son of Crassus, her first husband, who had been killed in Parthia. The young lady had other attractions besides those of youth and beauty; for she was highly educated, played well upon the lute, understood geometry, and had been accustomed to listen with profit to lectures on philosophy; all this, too,

[19] Interrex.

without in any degree becoming unamiable or pretentious, as sometimes young women do when they pursue such studies. Nor could any fault be found either with her father's family or reputation. The disparity of their ages was however not liked by everybody; Cornelia being in this respect a fitter match for Pompey's son. And wiser judges thought it rather a slight upon the commonwealth when he, to whom alone they had committed their broken fortunes, and from whom alone, as from their physician, they expected a cure to these distractions, went about crowned with garlands and celebrating his nuptial feasts; never considering, that his very consulship was a public calamity, which would never have been given him, contrary to the rules of law, had his country been in a flourishing state. Afterwards, however, he took cognizance of the cases of those that had obtained offices by gifts and bribery, and enacted laws and ordinances, setting forth the rules of judgment by which they should be arraigned; and regulating all things with gravity and justice, he restored security, order, and silence to their courts of judicature, himself giving his presence there with a band of soldiers. But when his father-in-law Scipio was accused, he sent for the three hundred and sixty judges to his house, and entreated them to be favorable to him; whereupon his accuser, seeing Scipio come into the court, accompanied by the judges themselves, withdrew the prosecution. Upon this Pompey was very ill spoken of, and much worse in the case of Plancus; for whereas he himself had made a law, putting a stop to the practice of making speeches in praise of persons under trial, yet notwithstanding this prohibition, he came into court, and spoke openly in commendation of Plancus, insomuch that Cato, who happened to be one of the judges at that time, stopping his ears with his hands, told him, he could not in conscience listen to commendations contrary to law. Cato upon this was refused, and set aside from being a judge, before sentence was given, but Plancus was condemned by the rest of the judges, to Pompey's dishonor. Shortly after, Hypsæus, a man of consular dignity, who was under accusation, waited for Pompey's return from his bath to his supper, and falling down at his feet, implored his favor; but he disdainfully passed him by, saying, that he did nothing else but spoil his supper. Such partiality was looked upon as a great fault in Pompey, and highly condemned; however, he managed all things else discreetly, and having put the government in very good order, he chose his father-in-law to be his colleague in the consulship for the last five months. His provinces were continued to him for the term of four years longer, with a commission to take one thousand talents yearly out of the treasury for the payment of his army.

This gave occasion to some of Cæsar's friends to think it reasonable, that some consideration should be had of him too, who had done such signal services in war, and fought so many battles for the empire, alleging, that he deserved at least a second consulship, or to have the government of his province continued, that so he might command and enjoy in peace what he had obtained in war, and no successor come in to reap the fruits of his labor, and carry off the glory of his actions. There arising some debate about this matter, Pompey took upon him, as it were out of kindness to Cæsar, to plead his cause, and allay any jealousy that was conceived against him, telling them, that he had letters from Cæsar, expressing his desire for a successor, and his own discharge from the command; but it would be only right that they should give him leave to stand for the consulship though in his absence. But those of Cato's party withstood this, saying, that if he expected any favor from the citizens, he ought to leave his army, and come in a private capacity to canvass for it. And Pompey's making no rejoinder, but letting it pass as a matter in which he was overruled, increased the suspicion of his real feelings towards Cæsar. Presently, also, under pretence of a war with Parthia, he sent for his two legions which he had lent him. However, Cæsar, though he well knew why they were asked for, sent them home very liberally rewarded.

About that time Pompey recovered of a dangerous fit of sickness which seized him at Naples, where the whole city, upon the suggestion of Praxagoras, made sacrifices of thanksgiving to the gods for his recovery. The neighboring towns likewise happening to follow their example, the thing then went its course throughout all Italy, so that there was not a city either great or small, that did not feast and rejoice for many days together. And the company of those that came from all parts to meet him was so numerous, that no place was able to contain them, but the villages, seaport towns, and the very highways, were all full of people, feasting and sacrificing to the gods. Nay, many went to meet him with garlands on their heads, and flambeaux in their hands, casting flowers and nosegays upon him as he went along; so that this progress of his, and reception, was one of the noblest and most glorious sights imaginable. And yet it is thought that this very thing was not one of the least causes and occasions of the civil war. For Pompey, yielding to a feeling of exultation, which in the greatness of the present display of joy lost sight of more solid grounds of consideration, and abandoning that prudent temper which had guided him hitherto to a safe use of all his good fortune and his successes, gave himself up to an extravagant confidence in his own, and contempt of Cæsar's power; insomuch that he thought neither force of arms nor care necessary against him, but that he could pull him down much easier than he had set him up. Besides this, Appius, under whose command those legions which Pompey lent to Cæsar were returned, coming lately out of Gaul, spoke slightingly of Cæsar's actions there, and spread scandalous reports about him, at the same time telling Pompey, that he was unacquainted with his own strength and reputation, if he made use of any other forces against Cæsar than Cæsar's own; for such was the soldiers' hatred to Cæsar, and their love to Pompey so great, that they would all come over to him upon his first appearance. By these flatteries Pompey was so puffed up, and led on into such a careless security, that he could not choose but laugh at those who seemed to fear a war; and when some were saying, that if Cæsar should march against the city, they could not see what forces there were to resist him, he replied with a smile, bidding them be in no concern, "for," said he, "whenever I stamp with my foot in any part of Italy, there will rise up forces enough in an instant, both horse and foot."

Cæsar, on the other side, was more and more vigorous in his proceedings, himself always at hand about the frontiers of Italy, and sending his soldiers continually into the city to attend all elections with their votes. Besides, he corrupted several of the magistrates, and kept them in his pay; among others, Paulus, the consul, who was brought over by a bribe of one thousand and five hundred talents; and Curio, tribune of the people, by a discharge of the debts with which he was overwhelmed; together with Mark Antony, who, out of friendship to Curio, had become bound with him in the same obligations for them all. And it was stated as a fact, that a centurion of Cæsar's waiting at the senate-house, and hearing that the senate refused to give him a longer term of his government, clapped his hand upon his sword, and said, "But this shall give it." And indeed all his practices and preparations seemed to bear this appearance. Curio's demands, however, and requests in favor of Cæsar, were more popular in appearance; for he desired one of these two things, either that Pompey also should be called upon to resign his army, or that Cæsar's should not be taken away from him; for if both of them became private persons, both would be satisfied with simple justice; or if both retained their present power, each being a match for the other, they would be contented with what they already had; but he that weakens one, does at the same time strengthen the other, and so doubles that very strength and power which he stood in fear of before. Marcellus, the consul, replied nothing to all this, but that Cæsar was a robber, and should be proclaimed an enemy to the state, if he did not disband his army. However, Curio, with the assistance of Antony and Piso, prevailed, that the matter in debate should be put to the question, and decided by vote in the senate. So that it being ordered upon the question for those to withdraw, who were of opinion, that Cæsar only should lay down his army, and Pompey command, the majority withdrew. But when it was ordered again for those to withdraw, whose vote was, that both should lay down their arms, and neither command, there were but twenty-two for Pompey, all the rest remained on Curio's side. Whereupon he, as one proud of his conquest, leaped out in triumph among the people, who received him with as great tokens of joy, clapping their hands, and crowning him with garlands and flowers. Pompey was not then present in the senate, because it is not lawful for generals in command of an army to come into the city. But Marcellus rising up, said, that he would not sit there hearing speeches, when he saw ten legions already passing the Alps on their march toward the city, but on his own authority would send some one to oppose them in defence of the country.

Upon this the city went into mourning, as in a public calamity, and Marcellus, accompanied by the senate, went solemnly through the forum to meet Pompey, and made him this address. "I hereby give you orders, O Pompey, to defend your country, to employ the troops you now command, and to levy more." Lentulus, consul elect for the year following, spoke to the same purpose. Antony, however, contrary to the will of the senate, having in a public assembly read a letter of Cæsar's, containing various plausible overtures such as were likely to gain the common people, proposing, namely, that both Pompey and he quitting their governments, and dismissing their armies, should submit to the judgment of the people, and give an account of their actions before them, the consequence was that when Pompey began to make his levies, he found himself disappointed in his expectations. Some few, indeed, came in, but those very unwillingly; others would not answer to their names, and the generality cried out for peace. Lentulus, notwithstanding he was now entered upon his consulship, would not assemble the senate; but Cicero, who was lately returned from Cilicia, labored for a reconciliation, proposing that Cæsar should leave his province of Gaul and army, reserving two legions only, together with the government of Illyricum, and should thus be put in nomination for a second consulship. Pompey disliking this motion, Cæsar's friends were contented that he should surrender one of the two; but Lentulus still opposing, and Cato crying out that Pompey did ill to be deceived again, the reconciliation did not take effect.

In the mean time, news was brought that Cæsar had occupied Ariminum, a great city in Italy, and was marching directly towards Rome with all his forces. But this latter was altogether false, for he had no more with him at that time than three hundred horse and five thousand foot; and he did not mean to tarry for the body of his army, which lay beyond the Alps, choosing rather to fall in on a sudden upon his enemies, while they were in confusion, and did not expect him, than to give them time, and fight them after they had made preparations. For when he came to the banks of the Rubicon, a river that made the bounds of his province, there he made a halt, pausing a little, and considering, we may suppose, with himself the greatness of the enterprise which he had undertaken; then, at last, like men that are throwing themselves headlong from some precipice into a vast abyss, having shut, as it were, his mind's eyes and put away from his sight the idea of danger, he merely uttered to those near him in Greek the words, "Anerriphtho kubos," (let the die be cast,) and led his army through it. No sooner was the news arrived, but there was an uproar throughout all the city, and a consternation in the people even to astonishment, such as never was known in Rome before; all the senate ran immediately to Pompey, and the magistrates followed. And when Tullus[20] made inquiry about his legions and forces, Pompey seemed to pause a little, and answered with some hesitation, that he had those two legions ready that Cæsar sent back, and that out of the men who had been previously enrolled he believed he could shortly make up a body of thirty thousand men. On which Tullus crying out aloud, "O Pompey, you have deceived us," gave his advice to send off a deputation to Cæsar. Favonius, a man of fair character, except that he used to suppose his own petulance and abusive talking a copy of Cato's straight-forwardness, bade Pompey stamp upon the ground, and call forth the forces he had promised. But Pompey bore patiently with this unseasonable raillery; and on Cato putting him in mind of what he had foretold from the very beginning about Cæsar, made this answer only, that Cato indeed had spoken more like a prophet, but he had acted more like a friend. Cato then advised them to choose Pompey general with absolute power and authority, saying that the same men who do great evils, know best how to cure them. He himself went his way forthwith into Sicily, the province that was allotted him, and all the rest of the senators likewise departed every one to his respective government.

Thus all Italy in a manner being up in arms, no one could say what was best to be done. For those that were without, came from all parts flocking into the city; and they who were within, seeing the confusion and disorder so great there, all good things impotent, and disobedience and insubordination grown too strong to be controlled by the magistrates, were quitting it as fast as the others came in. Nay, it was so far from being possible to allay their

[20] Lucius Volcatius Tullus, the "Consule Tullo" of Horace.

fears, that they would not suffer Pompey to follow out his own judgment, but every man pressed and urged him according to his particular fancy, whether it proceeded from doubt, fear, grief, or any meaner passion; so that even in the same day quite contrary counsels were acted upon. Then, again, it was as impossible to have any good intelligence of the enemy; for what each man heard by chance upon a flying rumor, he would report for truth, and exclaim against Pompey if he did not believe it. Pompey, at length, seeing such a confusion in Rome, determined with himself to put an end to their clamors by his departure, and therefore commanding all the senate to follow him, and declaring, that whosoever tarried behind, should be judged a confederate of Cæsar's, about the dusk of the evening he went out and left the city. The consuls also followed after in a hurry, without offering the sacrifices to the gods, usual before a war. But in all this, Pompey himself had the glory, that in the midst of such calamities, he had so much of men's love and good-will. For though many found fault with the conduct of the war, yet no man hated the general; and there were more to be found of those that went out of Rome, because that they could not forsake Pompey, than of those that fled for love of liberty.

Some few days after Pompey was gone out, Cæsar came into the city, and made himself master of it, treating every one with a great deal of courtesy, and appeasing their fears, except only Metellus, one of the tribunes; on whose refusing to let him take any money out of the treasury, Cæsar threatened him with death, adding words yet harsher than the threat, that it was far easier for him to do it than say it. By this means removing Metellus, and taking what moneys were of use for his occasions, he set forwards in pursuit of Pompey, endeavoring with all speed to drive him out of Italy before his army, that was in Spain, could join him.

But Pompey arriving at Brundusium, and having plenty of ships there, bade the two consuls embark immediately, and with them shipped thirty cohorts of foot, bound before him for Dyrrhachium. He sent likewise his father-in-law Scipio, and Cnæus his son, into Syria, to provide and fit out a fleet there; himself in the mean time having blocked up the gates, placed his lightest soldiers as guards upon the walls; and giving express orders that the citizens should keep within doors, he dug up all the ground inside the city, cutting trenches, and fixing stakes and palisades throughout all the streets of the city, except only two that led down to the sea-side. Thus in three days space having with ease put all the rest of his army on shipboard, he suddenly gave the signal to those that guarded the walls, who nimbly repairing to the ships, were received on board and carried off. Cæsar meantime perceiving their departure by seeing the walls unguarded hastened after, and in the heat of pursuit was all but entangled himself among the stakes and trenches. But the Brundusians discovering the danger to him, and showing him the way, he wheeled about, and taking a circuit round the city, made towards the haven, where he found all the ships on their way, excepting only two vessels that had but a few soldiers aboard.

Most are of opinion, that this departure of Pompey's is to be counted among the best of his military performances, but Cæsar himself could not but wonder that he, who was thus ingarrisoned in a city well fortified, who was in expectation of his forces from Spain, and was master of the sea besides, should leave and abandon Italy. Cicero accuses him [21] of imitating the conduct of Themistocles, rather than of Pericles, when the circumstances were more like those of Pericles than they were like those of Themistocles. However, it appeared plainly, and Cæsar showed it by his actions, that he was in great fear of delay, for when he had taken Numerius, a friend of Pompey's, prisoner, he sent him as an ambassador to Brundusium, with offers of peace and reconciliation upon equal terms; but Numerius sailed away with Pompey. And now Cæsar having become master of all Italy in sixty days, without a drop of blood shed, had a great desire forthwith to follow Pompey; but being destitute of shipping, he was forced to divert his course, and march into Spain, designing to bring over Pompey's forces there to his own.

In the mean time Pompey raised a mighty army both by sea and land. As for his navy, it was irresistible. For there were five hundred men of war, besides an infinite company of light vessels, Liburnians, and others; and for his land forces, the cavalry made up a body of seven thousand horse, the very flower of Rome and Italy, men of family, wealth, and high spirit; but the infantry was a mixture of unexperienced soldiers drawn from different quarters, and these he exercised and trained near Berœa, where he quartered his army; himself noways slothful, but performing all his exercises as if he had been in the flower of his youth, conduct which raised the spirits of his soldiers extremely. For it was no

---

[21] *Cicero accuses him* (of deserting the city *like Themistocles* in the Persian, when he ought to have maintained it *like Pericles* in the Peloponnesian war), in the letters to Atticus (*VII.*, 11), "Fecit idem Themistocles. At idem Pericles non fecit." *Would he do so*, he continues, *if the Gauls came?*

small encouragement for them to see Pompey the Great, sixty years of age wanting two, at one time handling his arms among the foot, then again mounted among the horse, drawing out his sword with ease in full career, and sheathing it up as easily; and in darting the javelin, showing not only skill and dexterity in hitting the mark, but also strength and activity in throwing it so far that few of the young men went beyond him.

Several kings and princes of nations came thither to him, and there was a concourse of Roman citizens who had held the magistracies, so numerous that they made up a complete senate. Labienus forsook his old friend Cæsar, whom he had served throughout all his wars in Gaul, and came over to Pompey; and Brutus, son to that Brutus that was put to death in Gaul, a man of a high spirit, and one that to that day had never so much as saluted or spoke to Pompey, looking upon him as the murderer of his father, came then and submitted himself to him as the defender of their liberty. Cicero likewise, though he had written and advised otherwise, yet was ashamed not to be accounted in the number of those that would hazard their lives and fortunes for the safeguard of their country. There came to him also into Macedonia, Tidius [22] Sextius, a man extremely old, and lame of one leg; so that others indeed mocked and laughed at the spectacle, but Pompey, as soon as he saw him, rose and ran to meet him, esteeming it no small testimony in his favor, when men of such age and infirmities should rather choose to be with him in danger, than in safety at home. Afterwards in a meeting of their senate they passed a

[22] Tidius does not appear to be a Roman name. Didius, perhaps, was the original.

decree, on the motion of Cato, that no Roman citizen should be put to death but in battle, and that they should not sack or plunder any city that was subject to the Roman empire, a resolution which gained Pompey's party still greater reputation, insomuch that those who were noways at all concerned in the war, either because they dwelt afar off, or were thought incapable of giving help, were yet, in their good wishes, upon his side, and in all their words, so far as that went, supported the good or just cause, as they called it; esteeming those as enemies to the gods and men that wished not victory to Pompey.

Neither was Pompey's clemency such, but that Cæsar likewise showed himself as merciful a conqueror; for when he had taken and overthrown all Pompey's forces in Spain, he gave them easy terms, leaving the commanders at their liberty, and taking the common soldiers into his own pay. Then repassing the Alps, and making a running march through Italy, he came to Brundusium about the winter solstice, and crossing the sea there landed at the port of Oricum. And having Jubius,[23] an intimate friend of Pompey's, with him as his prisoner, he despatched him to Pompey with an invitation, that they, meeting together in a conference, should disband both their armies within three days, and renewing their former friendship with solemn oaths, should return together into Italy. Pompey looked upon this again as some new stratagem, and therefore marching down in all haste to the sea-coast, possessed himself of all forts and places of strength suitable

[23] Lucius Vibullius Rufus is pretty certainly the real name of the person meant by *Jubius;* but the manuscripts of Cæsar write it corruptly, sometimes Jubellius, or Jubilius, or Jubulus; and one of these bad readings Plutarch may have had in his copy.

to encamp in, and to secure his land forces, as likewise of all ports and harbors commodious to receive any that came by sea, so that what wind soever blew, it must needs in some way or other be favorable to him, bringing in either provision, men, or money; while Cæsar, on the contrary, was so hemmed in both by sea and land, that he was forced to desire battle, daily provoking the enemy, and assailing them in their very forts; and in these light skirmishes for the most part had the better. Once only he was dangerously overthrown, and was within a little of losing his whole army, Pompey having fought nobly, routing the whole force, and killing two thousand on the spot. But either he was not able, or was afraid, to go on and force his way into their camp with them, so that Cæsar made the remark, that " To-day the victory had been the enemy's, had there been any one among them to gain it." Pompey's soldiers were so encouraged by this victory that they were eager now to have all put to the decision of a battle; but Pompey himself, though he wrote to distant kings, generals, and states in confederacy with him, as a conqueror, yet was afraid to hazard the success of a battle, choosing rather by delays, and distress of provisions, to tire out a body of men, who had never yet been conquered by force of arms, and had long been used to fight and conquer together; while their time of life, now an advanced one, which made them quickly weary of those other hardships of war, such as were long marches, and frequent decampings, making trenches, and building fortifications, made them eager to come to close combat and venture a battle with all speed.

Pompey had all along hitherto by his persuasions pretty well quieted his soldiers; but after this last engagement, when Cæsar for want of provisions was forced to raise his camp, and passed through Athamania into Thessaly, it was impossible to curb or allay the heat of their spirits any longer. For all crying out with a general voice, that Cæsar was fled, some were for pursuing and pressing upon him, others for returning into Italy; some there were that sent their friends and servants beforehand to Rome, to hire houses near the forum, that they might be in readiness to sue for offices; several of their own motion sailed off at once to Lesbos to carry to Cornelia, (whom Pompey had conveyed thither to be in safety,) the joyful news, that the war was ended. And a senate being called, and the matter being under debate, Afranius was of opinion, that Italy should first be regained, for that it was the grand prize and crown of all the war; and they who were masters of that, would quickly have at their devotion all the provinces of Sicily, Sardinia, Corsica, Spain, and Gaul; but what was of greatest weight and moment to Pompey, it was his own native country that lay near, reaching out her hand for his help; and certainly it could not be consistent with his honor to leave her thus exposed to all indignities, and in bondage under slaves and the flatterers of a tyrant. But Pompey himself, on the contrary, thought it neither honorable to fly a second time before Cæsar, and be pursued, when fortune had given him the advantage of a pursuit; nor indeed lawful before the gods to forsake Scipio and divers other men of consular dignity dispersed throughout Greece and Thessaly, who must necessarily fall into Cæsar's hands, together with large sums of money and numerous forces; and as to his care for the city of Rome, that would most eminently appear, by removing the scene of war to a greater distance, and

POMPEY

leaving her, without feeling the distress or even hearing the sound of these evils, to await in peace the return of whichever should be the victor.

With this determination, Pompey marched forwards in pursuit of Cæsar, firmly resolved with himself not to give him battle, but rather to besiege and distress him, by keeping close at his heels, and cutting him short. There were other reasons that made him continue this resolution, but especially because a saying that was current among the Romans serving in the cavalry came to his ear, to the effect, that they ought to beat Cæsar as soon as possible, and then humble Pompey too. And some report, it was for this reason that Pompey never employed Cato in any matter of consequence during the whole war, but now when he pursued Cæsar, left him to guard his baggage by sea, fearing lest, if Cæsar should be taken off, he himself also by Cato's means not long after should be forced to give up his power.

Whilst he was thus slowly attending the motions of the enemy, he was exposed on all sides to outcries, and imputations of using his generalship to defeat, not Cæsar, but his country and the senate, that he might always continue in authority, and never cease to keep those for his guards and servants, who themselves claimed to govern the world. Domitius Ænobarbus, continually calling him Agamemnon, and king of kings, excited jealousy against him; and Favonius, by his unseasonable raillery, did him no less injury than those who openly attacked him, as when he cried out, " Good friends, you must not expect to gather any figs in Tusculum this year." But Lucius Afranius, who had lain under an imputation of treachery for the loss of the army in Spain, when he saw Pompey purposely declining an engagement, declared openly, that he could not but admire, why those who were so ready to accuse him, did not go themselves and fight this buyer and seller of their provinces.

With these and many such speeches they wrought upon Pompey, who never could bear reproach, or resist the expectations of his friends; and thus they forced him to break his measures, so that he forsook his own prudent resolution to follow their vain hopes and desires: weakness that would have been blamable in the pilot of a ship, how much more in the sovereign commander of such an army, and so many nations. But he, though he had often commended those physicians who did not comply with the capricious appetites of their patients, yet himself could not but yield to the malady and disease of his companions and advisers in the war, rather than use some severity in their cure. Truly who could have said that health was not disordered and a cure not required in the case of men who went up and down the camp, suing already for the consulship and office of prætor, while Spinther, Domitius, and Scipio made friends, raised factions, and quarrelled among themselves, who should succeed Cæsar in the dignity of his high-priesthood, esteeming all as lightly, as if they were to engage only with Tigranes, king of Armenia, or some petty Nabathæan king, not with that Cæsar and his army that had stormed a thousand towns, and subdued more than three hundred several nations; that had fought innumerable battles with the Germans and Gauls, and always carried the victory; that had taken a million of men prisoners, and slain as many upon the spot in pitched battles?

But they went on soliciting and clamoring, and on reaching the plain of Pharsalia, they forced Pompey by their pressure and importunities to call a council of war, where Labienus, general of the horse, stood up first and swore that he would not return out of the battle if he did not rout the enemies; and all the rest took the same oath. That night Pompey dreamed that as he went into the theatre, the people received him with great applause, and that he himself adorned the temple of Venus the Victorious,[24] with many spoils. This vision partly encouraged, but partly also disheartened him, fearing lest that splendor and ornament to Venus should be made with spoils furnished by himself to Cæsar, who derived his family from that goddess. Besides there were some panic fears and alarms that ran through the camp, with such a noise that it awaked him out of his sleep. And about the time of renewing the watch towards morning, there appeared a great light over Cæsar's camp, whilst they were all at rest, and from thence a ball of flaming fire was carried into Pompey's camp, which Cæsar himself says he saw, as he was walking his rounds.

Now Cæsar having designed to raise his camp with the morning and move to Scotussa, whilst the soldiers were busy in pulling down their tents, and sending on their cattle and servants before them with their baggage, there came in scouts who brought word that they saw arms carried to and fro in the enemy's camp, and heard a noise and running up and down, as of men preparing for battle; not long after there came in other scouts with further intelligence, that the first ranks were already set in battle array. Thereupon Cæsar when he had told them that the wished for day was come at last, when they should fight with men, not with hunger and famine,

---

[24] A temple or chapel dedicated to *Venus Victrix*, or, *the Victorious*, formed the highest part of Pompey's theatre at Rome.

instantly gave orders for the red colors to be set up before his tent, that being the ordinary signal of battle among the Romans. As soon as the soldiers saw that, they left their tents, and with great shouts of joy ran to their arms; the officers, likewise, on their parts drawing up their companies in order of battle, every man fell into his proper rank without any trouble or noise, as quietly and orderly as if they had been in a dance.

Pompey himself led the right wing of his army against Antony, and placed his father-in-law Scipio in the middle against Lucius Calvinus. The left wing was commanded by Lucius Domitius; and supported by the great mass of the horse. For almost the whole cavalry was posted there, in the hope of crushing Cæsar, and cutting off the tenth legion, which was spoken of as the stoutest in all the army, and in which Cæsar himself usually fought in person. Cæsar observing the left wing of the enemy to be lined and fortified with such a mighty guard of horse, and alarmed at the gallantry of their appearance, sent for a detachment of six cohorts out of the reserves, and placed them in the rear of the tenth legion, commanding them not to stir, lest they should be discovered by the enemy; but when the enemy's horse should begin to charge, and press upon them, that they should make up with all speed to the front through the foremost ranks, and not throw their javelins at a distance, as is usual with brave soldiers, that they may come to a close fight with their swords the sooner, but that they should strike them upwards into the eyes and faces of the enemy; telling them that those fine young dancers would never endure the steel shining in their eyes, but would fly to save their handsome faces. This was Cæsar's employment at that time. But while

POMPEY

he was thus instructing his soldiers, Pompey on horseback was viewing the order of both armies, and when he saw how well the enemy kept their ranks, expecting quietly the signal of battle; and, on the contrary, how impatient and unsteady his own men were, waving up and down in disorder for want of experience, he was very much afraid that their ranks would be broken upon the first onset; and therefore he gave out orders that the van should make a stand, and keeping close in their ranks, should receive the enemy's charge. Cæsar much condemns this command;[25] which he says not only took off from the strength of the blows, which would otherwise have been made with a spring; but also lost the men the impetus, which, more than any thing, in the moment of their coming upon the enemy, fills soldiers with impulse and inspiration, the very shouts and rapid pace adding to their fury; of which Pompey deprived his men, arresting them in their course and cooling down their heat.

Cæsar's army consisted of twenty-two thousand, and Pompey's of somewhat above twice as many. When the signal of battle was given on both sides, and the trumpets began to sound a charge, most men of course were fully occupied with their own matters; only some few of the noblest Romans, together with certain Greeks there present, standing as spectators without the battle, seeing the armies now ready to join, could not but consider in themselves to what a pass private ambition and emulation had brought the empire. Common arms, and kindred ranks drawn up under the self-same standards, the whole

---

[25] *Cæsar much condemns this command.* Cæsar de Bello Civili, III., 92.

flower and strength of the same single city here meeting in collision with itself, offered plain proof how blind and how mad a thing human nature is, when once possessed with any passion; for if they had been desirous only to rule, and enjoy in peace what they had conquered in war, the greatest and best part of the world was subject to them both by sea and land. But if there was yet a thirst in their ambition, that must still be fed with new trophies and triumphs, the Parthian and German wars would yield matter enough to satisfy the most covetous of honor. Scythia, moreover, was yet unconquered, and the Indians too, where their ambition might be colored over with the specious pretext of civilizing barbarous nations. And what Scythian horse, Parthian arrows, or Indian riches, could be able to resist seventy thousand Roman soldiers, well appointed in arms, under the command of two such generals as Pompey and Cæsar, whose names they had heard of before that of the Romans, and whose prowess, by their conquests of such wild, remote, savage, and brutish nations, was spread further than the fame of the Romans themselves? To-day they met in conflict, and could no longer be induced to spare their country, even out of regard for their own glory or the fear of losing the name which till this day both had held, of having never yet been defeated. As for their former private ties, and the charms of Julia, and the marriage that had made them near connections, these could now only be looked upon as tricks of state, the mere securities of a treaty made to serve the needs of an occasion, not the pledges of any real friendship.

Now, therefore, as soon as the plains of Pharsalia were covered with men, horse, and armor, and that the signal of battle was raised on either side,

POMPEY

Caius Crassianus,[26] a centurion, who commanded a company of one hundred and twenty men, was the first that advanced out of Cæsar's army, to give the charge, and acquit himself of a solemn engagement that he had made to Cæsar. He had been the first man that Cæsar had seen going out of the camp in the morning, and Cæsar, after saluting him, had asked him what he thought of the coming battle. To which he, stretching out his right hand, replied aloud, "Thine is the victory, O Cæsar, thou shalt conquer gloriously, and I myself this day will be the subject of thy praise either alive or dead." In pursuance of this promise he hastened forward, and being followed by many more, charged into the midst of the enemy. There they came at once to a close fight with their swords, and made a great slaughter; but as he was still pressing forward, and breaking the ranks of the vanguard, one of Pompey's soldiers ran him in at the mouth, so that the point of the sword came out behind at his neck; and Crassianus being thus slain, the fight became doubtful, and continued equal on that part of the battle.

Pompey had not yet brought on the right wing, but stayed and looked about, waiting to see what execution his cavalry would do on the left. They had already drawn out their squadrons in form, designing to turn Cæsar's flank, and force those few horse, which he had placed in the front, to give back upon the battalion of foot. But Cæsar, on the other side, having given the signal, his horse retreated back a little, and gave way to those six subsidiary cohorts, which had been posted in the rear, as a reserve to cover the flank; and which now came out,

---

[26] The name is given as Crassinius in the life of Cæsar; and in Cæsar De Bello Civili is written Crastinus.

three thousand men in number, and met the enemy; and when they came up, standing by the horses, struck their javelins upwards, according to their instructions, and hit the horsemen full in their faces. They, unskilful in any manner of fight, and least of all expecting or understanding such a kind as this, had not courage enough to endure the blows upon their faces, but turning their backs, and covering their eyes with their hands, shamefully took to flight. Cæsar's men, however, did not follow them, but marched upon the foot, and attacked the wing, which the flight of the cavalry had left unprotected, and liable to be turned and taken in the rear, so that this wing now being attacked in the flank by these, and charged in the front by the tenth legion, was not able to abide the charge, or make any longer resistance, especially when they saw themselves surrounded and circumvented in the very way in which they had designed to invest the enemy. Thus these being likewise routed and put to flight, when Pompey, by the dust flying in the air, conjectured the fate of his horse, it were very hard to say what his thoughts or intentions were, but looking like one distracted and beside himself, and without any recollection or reflection that he was Pompey the Great, he retired slowly towards his camp, without speaking a word to any man, exactly according to the description in the verses,

> But Jove from heaven struck Ajax with a fear;
> Ajax the bold then stood astonished there,
> Flung o'er his back the mighty sevenfold shield,
> And trembling gazed and spied about the field.[27]

[27] The translation from the Iliad (*XI.*, 543), should have been made a little less epigrammatic; the following rough correction is truer to Homer's swift plain-speaking:—

> But Jove from heaven struck Ajax with a fear;
> He stopped and stood as in amazement there;
> Put on his back his shield of sevenfold hide,
> And trembling on the advancing numbers spied.

In this state and condition he went into his own tent, and sat down, speechless still, until some of the enemy fell in together with his men that were flying into the camp, and then he let fall only this one word, "What? into the very camp?" and said no more, but rose up, and putting on a dress suitable to his present fortune, made his way secretly out.

By this time the rest of the army was put to flight, and there was a great slaughter in the camp among the servants and those that guarded the tents, but of the soldiers themselves there were not above six thousand slain, as is stated by Asinius Pollio, who himself fought in this battle on Cæsar's side. When Cæsar's soldiers had taken the camp, they saw clearly the folly and vanity of the enemy; for all their tents and pavilions were richly set out with garlands of myrtle, embroidered carpets and hangings, and tables laid and covered with goblets. There were large bowls of wine ready, and every thing prepared and put in array, in the manner rather of people who had offered sacrifice and were going to celebrate a holiday, than of soldiers who had armed themselves to go out to battle, so possessed with the expectation of success and so full of empty confidence had they gone out that morning.

When Pompey had got a little way from the camp, he dismounted and forsook his horse, having but a small retinue with him; and finding that no man pursued him, walked on softly afoot, taken up altogether with thoughts, such as probably might possess a man that for the space of thirty-four years together had been accustomed to conquest and victory, and was then at last, in his old age, learning for the first time what defeat and flight were. And it was no small affliction to consider, that he had lost in one hour all the glory and power, which he had been getting in so many wars, and bloody battles; and that he who but a little before was guarded with such an army of foot, so many squadrons of horse, and such a mighty fleet, was now flying in so mean a condition, and with such a slender retinue, that his very enemies who fought him could not know him. Thus, when he had passed by the city of Larissa, and came into the pass of Tempe, being very thirsty, he kneeled down and drank out of the river; then rising up again, he passed through Tempe, until he came to the seaside, and there he betook himself to a poor fisherman's cottage, where he rested the remainder of the night. The next morning about break of day he went into one of the river boats, and taking none of those that followed him except such as were free, dismissed his servants, advising them to go boldly to Cæsar, and not be afraid. As he was rowing up and down near the shore, he chanced to spy a large merchant-ship, lying off, just ready to set sail; the master of which was a Roman citizen, named Peticius, who, though he was not familiarly acquainted with Pompey, yet knew him well by sight. Now it happened that this Peticius dreamed, the night before, that he saw Pompey, not like the man he had often seen him, but in a humble and dejected condition, and in that posture discoursing with him. He was then telling his dream to the people on board, as men do when at leisure, and especially dreams of that consequence, when of a sudden one of the mariners told him, he saw a river boat with oars putting off from shore, and that some of the men there shook their garments, and held out their hands, with signs to take them in; thereupon Peticius looking attentively, at once recognized Pompey, just as he appeared in his dream, and smiting his hand on his head, ordered the mariners to let down the ship's boat, he himself waving his hand, and calling to him by his name, already assured of his change and the change of his fortune by that of his garb. So that without waiting for any further entreaty or discourse, he took him into his ship, together with as many of his company as he thought fit, and hoisted sail. There were with him the two Lentuli, and Favonius; and a little after they spied king Deiotarus, making up towards them from the shore; so they stayed and took him in along with them. At supper time, the master of the ship having made ready such provisions as he had aboard, Pompey, for want of his servants, began to undo his shoes himself, which Favonius noticing ran to him and undid them, and helped him to anoint himself, and always after continued to wait upon, and attend him in all things, as servants do their masters, even to the washing of his feet, and preparing his supper. Insomuch that any one there present, observing the free and unaffected courtesy of these services, might have well exclaimed,

> O heavens, in those that noble are,
> Whate'er they do is fit and fair.[28]

Pompey, sailing by the city of Amphipolis, crossed over from thence to Mitylene, with a design

---

[28] *O heaven in those that noble are* is an uncertain fragment of Euripides. (*Matthiæ Fragm. Incert.*, 119.)

to take in Cornelia and his son; and as soon as he arrived at the port in that island, he despatched a messenger into the city, with news very different from Cornelia's expectation. For she, by all the former messages and letters sent to please her, had been put in hopes that the war was ended at Dyrrhachium, and that there was nothing more remaining for Pompey, but the pursuit of Cæsar. The messenger finding her in the same hopes still, was not able to salute or speak to her, but declaring the greatness of her misfortune by his tears rather than by his words, desired her to make haste if she would see Pompey, with one ship only, and that not of his own. The young lady hearing this, fell down in a swoon, and continued a long time senseless and speechless. And when with some trouble she was brought to her senses again, being conscious to herself that this was no time for lamentation and tears, she started up and ran through the city towards the seaside, where Pompey meeting and embracing her, as she sank down, supported by his arms, "This, sir," she exclaimed, "is the effect of my fortune, not of yours, that I see you thus reduced to one poor vessel, who before your marriage with Cornelia, were wont to sail in these seas with a fleet of five hundred ships. Why therefore should you come to see me, or why not rather have left to her evil genius one who has brought upon you her own ill-fortune? How happy a woman had I been, if I had breathed out my last, before the news came from Parthia of the death of Publius, the husband of my youth, and how prudent if I had followed his destiny, as I designed! But I was reserved for a greater mischief, even the ruin of Pompey the Great."

Thus, they say, Cornelia spoke to him, and this

was Pompey's reply: "You have had, Cornelia, but one season of a better fortune, which it may be, gave you unfounded hopes, by attending me a longer time than is usual. It behoves us, who are mortals born, to endure these events, and to try fortune yet again; neither is it any less possible to recover our former state, than it was to fall from that into this." Thereupon Cornelia sent for her servants and baggage out of the city. The citizens also of Mitylene came out to salute and invite Pompey into the city, but he refused, advising them to be obedient to the conqueror, and fear not, for that Cæsar was a man of great goodness and clemency. Then turning to Cratippus, the philosopher, who came among the rest out of the city to visit him, he began to find some fault, and briefly argued with him upon Providence, but Cratippus modestly declined the dispute, putting him in better hopes only, lest by opposing, he might seem too austere or unseasonable. For he might have put Pompey a question in his turn, in defence of Providence; and might have demonstrated the necessity there was that the commonwealth should be turned into a monarchy, because of their ill government in the state; and could have asked, "How, O Pompey, and by what token or assurance can we ascertain, that if the victory had been yours, you would have used your fortune better than Cæsar? We must leave the divine power to act as we find it do." [29]

Pompey having taken his wife and friends

---

[29] Or perhaps, simply dismissing the subject, "However, we must let questions about the gods rest as they are." The words, *we must leave the divine power to act as we find it do,* have been wrongly included between the inverted commas.

aboard, set sail, making no port, nor touching anywhere, but when he was necessitated to take in provisions, or fresh water. The first city he entered was Attalia, in Pamphylia, and whilst he was there, there came some galleys thither to him out of Cilicia, together with a small body of soldiers, and he had almost sixty senators with him again; then hearing that his navy was safe too, and that Cato had rallied a considerable body of soldiers after their overthrow, and was crossing with them over into Africa, he began to complain and blame himself to his friends that he had allowed himself to be driven into engaging by land, without making use of his other forces, in which he was irresistibly the stronger, and had not kept near enough to his fleet, that failing by land, he might have reinforced himself from the sea, and would have been again at the head of a power quite sufficient to encounter the enemy on equal terms. And in truth, neither did Pompey during all the war commit a greater oversight, nor Cæsar use a more subtle stratagem, than in drawing the fight so far off from the naval forces.

As it now was, however, since he must come to some decision, and try some plan within his present ability, he despatched his agents to the neighboring cities, and himself sailed about in person to others, requiring their aid in money and men for his ships. But, fearing lest the rapid approach of the enemy might cut off all his preparations, he began to consider what place would yield him the safest refuge and retreat at present. A consultation was held, and it was generally agreed that no province of the Romans was secure enough. As for foreign kingdoms, he himself was of opinion, that Parthia would be the fittest to receive and defend them in their present weakness, and best able to furnish them with new means and send them out again with large forces. Others of the council were for going into Africa, and to king Juba. But Theophanes the Lesbian, thought it madness to leave Egypt, that was but at a distance of three days' sailing, and make no use of Ptolemy, who was still a boy, and was highly indebted to Pompey for the friendship and favor he had shown to his father, only to put himself under the Parthian, and trust the most treacherous nation in the world; and rather than make any trial of the clemency of a Roman, and his own near connection, to whom if he would yield to be second, he might be the first and chief over all the rest, to go and place himself at the mercy of Arsaces, which even Crassus had not submitted to, while alive; and, moreover, to expose his young wife, of the family of the Scipios, among a barbarous people, who govern by their lusts, and measure their greatness by their power to commit affronts and insolencies; from whom, though she suffered no dishonor, yet it might be thought she did, being in the hands of those who had the power to do it. This argument alone, they say, was persuasive enough to divert his course, that was designed towards Euphrates, if it were so indeed that any counsel of Pompey's, and not some superior power, made him take this other way.

As soon, therefore, as it was resolved upon, that he should fly into Egypt, setting sail from Cyprus in a galley of Seleucia, together with Cornelia, while the rest of his company sailed along near him, some in ships of war, and others in merchant vessels, he passed over sea without danger. But on hearing that king Ptolemy was posted with his army at the city of Pelusium, making war against his sister, he steered his course that way, and sent a messenger before to acquaint the king with his arrival, and to crave his protection. Ptolemy himself was quite young, and therefore Pothinus, who had the principal administration of all affairs, called a council of the chief men, those being the greatest whom he pleased to make so, and commanded them every man to deliver his opinion touching the reception of Pompey. It was, indeed, a miserable thing, that the fate of the great Pompey should be left to the determinations of Pothinus the eunuch, Theodotus of Chios, the paid rhetoric master, and Achillas the Egyptian. For these, among the chamberlains and menial domestics, that made up the rest of the council, were the chief and leading men. Pompey, who thought it dishonorable for him to owe his safety to Cæsar, riding at anchor at a distance from shore, was forced to wait the sentence of this tribunal. It seems they were so far different in their opinions that some were for sending the man away, and others again for inviting and receiving him; but Theodotus, to show his cleverness and the cogency of his rhetoric, undertook to demonstrate, that neither the one nor the other was safe in that juncture of affairs. For if they entertained him, they would be sure to make Cæsar their enemy, and Pompey their master; or if they dismissed him, they might render themselves hereafter obnoxious to Pompey, for that inhospitable expulsion, and to Cæsar, for the escape; so that the most expedient course would be to send for him and take away his life, for by that means they would ingratiate themselves with the one, and have no reason to fear the other; adding, it is related, with a smile, that "a dead man cannot bite."

This advice being approved of, they committed the execution of it to Achillas. He, therefore, taking with him as his accomplices one Septimius, a man that had formerly held a command under Pompey, and Salvius, another centurion, with three or four attendants, made up towards Pompey's galley. In the mean time, all the chiefest of those who accompanied Pompey in this voyage, were come into his ship to learn the event of their embassy. But when they saw the manner of their reception, that in appearance it was neither princely nor honorable, nor indeed in any way answerable to the hopes of Theophanes, or their expectation, (for there came but a few men in a fisherman's boat to meet them,) they began to suspect the meanness of their entertainment, and gave warning to Pompey that he should row back his galley, whilst he was out of their reach, and make for the sea. By this time, the Egyptian boat drew near, and Septimius standing up first, saluted Pompey in the Latin tongue, by the title of imperator. Then Achillas, saluting him in the Greek language, desired him to come aboard his vessel, telling him, that the sea was very shallow towards the shore, and that a galley of that burden could not avoid striking upon the sands. At the same time they saw several of the king's galleys getting their men on board, and all the shore covered with soldiers; so that even if they changed their minds, it seemed impossible for them to escape, and besides, their distrust would have given the assassins a pretence for their cruelty. Pompey, therefore, taking his leave of Cornelia, who was already lamenting his death before it came, bade two centurions, with Philip, one of his freedmen, and a slave called Scythes, go on board the boat before him. And as some of the crew with Achillas were reaching out their hands to help him, he turned about towards his wife and son, and repeated those iambics of Sophocles,

> He that once enters at a tyrant's door,
> Becomes a slave, though he were free before.[30]

These were the last words he spoke to his friends, and so he went aboard. Observing presently that notwithstanding there was a considerable distance betwixt his galley and the shore, yet none of the company addressed any words of friendliness or welcome to him all the way, he looked earnestly upon Septimius, and said, "I am not mistaken, surely, in believing you to have been formerly my fellow-soldier." But he only nodded with his head, making no reply at all, nor showing any other courtesy. Since, therefore, they continued silent, Pompey took a little book in his hand, in which was written out an address in Greek, which he intended to make to king Ptolemy, and began to read it. When they drew near to the shore, Cornelia, together with the rest of his friends in the galley, was very impatient to see the event, and began to take courage at last, when she saw several of the royal escort coming to meet him, apparently to give him a more honorable reception; but in the mean time, as Pompey took Philip by the hand to rise up more easily, Septimius first stabbed him from behind with his sword; and after him likewise Salvius and Achillas drew out their swords. He, therefore, taking up his gown with both hands, drew it over his face, and neither saying nor doing any thing unworthy of himself, only groaning a little, endured the wounds they gave him, and so ended his life, in the fifty-ninth year of his age, the very next day after the day of his birth.

Cornelia, with her company from the galley,

[30] The verses are a fragment from a lost and unknown play. Fragm. Incert., 54; in Dindorf, 711.

POMPEY

seeing him murdered, gave such a cry that it was heard to the shore, and weighing anchor with all speed, they hoisted sail, and fled. A strong breeze from the shore assisted their flight into the open sea, so that the Egyptians, though desirous to overtake them, desisted from the pursuit. But they cut off Pompey's head, and threw the rest of his body overboard, leaving it naked upon the shore, to be viewed by any that had the curiosity to see so sad a spectacle. Philip stayed by and watched till they had glutted their eyes in viewing it; and then washing it with sea-water, having nothing else, he wrapped it up in a shirt of his own for a winding-sheet. Then seeking up and down about the sands, at last he found some rotten planks of a little fisher-boat, not much, but yet enough to make up a funeral pile for a naked body, and that not quite entire. As Philip was busy in gathering and putting these old planks together, an old Roman citizen, who in his youth had served in the wars under Pompey, came up to him and demanded, who he was that was preparing the funeral of Pompey the Great. And Philip making answer, that he was his freedman, " Nay, then," said he, " you shall not have this honor alone; let even me, too, I pray you, have my share in such a pious office, that I may not altogether repent me of this pilgrimage in a strange land, but in compensation of many misfortunes, may obtain this happiness at last, even with mine own hands to touch the body of Pompey, and do the last duties to the greatest general among the Romans." And in this manner were the obsequies of Pompey performed. The next day Lucius Lentulus, not knowing what had passed, came sailing from Cyprus along the shore of that coast, and seeing a funeral pile, and Philip standing by, exclaimed, before he was yet seen by any one, "Who is this that has found his end here?" adding, after a short pause, with a sigh, "Possibly even thou, Pompeius Magnus!" and so going ashore, he was presently apprehended and slain. This was the end of Pompey.

Not long after, Cæsar arrived in the country that was polluted with this foul act, and when one of the Egyptians was sent to present him with Pompey's head, he turned away from him with abhorrence as from a murderer; and on receiving his seal, on which was engraved a lion holding a sword in his paw, he burst into tears. Achillas and Pothinus he put to death; and king Ptolemy himself, being overthrown in battle upon the banks of the Nile, fled away and was never heard of afterwards. Theodotus, the rhetorician, flying out of Egypt, escaped the hands of Cæsar's justice, but lived a vagabond in banishment, wandering up and down, despised and hated of all men, till at last Marcus Brutus, after he had killed Cæsar, finding him in his province of Asia, put him to death, with every kind of ignominy. The ashes of Pompey were carried to his wife Cornelia, who deposited them at his country house near Alba.

COMPARISON OF POMPEY AND AGESILAUS

Thus having drawn out the history of the lives of Agesilaus and Pompey, the next thing is to compare them; and in order to this, to take a cursory view, and bring together the points in which they chiefly disagree; which are these. In the first place, Pompey attained to all his greatness and glory by the fairest and justest means, owing his advancement to his own efforts, and to the frequent and important aid which he rendered Sylla, in delivering Italy from its tyrants. But Agesilaus appears to have obtained his kingdom, not without offence both towards gods and towards men, towards these, by procuring judgment of bastardy against Leotychides, whom his brother had declared his lawful son, and towards those, by putting a false gloss upon the oracle, and eluding its sentence against his lameness. Secondly, Pompey never ceased to display his respect for Sylla during his lifetime, and expressed it also after his death, by enforcing the honorable interment of his corpse, in despite of Lepidus, and by giving his daughter in marriage to his son Faustus. But Agesilaus, upon a slight pretence, cast off Lysander with reproach and dishonor. Yet Sylla in fact had owed to Pompey's services, as much as Pompey ever received from him, whereas Lysander made Agesilaus king of Sparta, and general of all Greece. Thirdly, Pompey's transgressions of right and justice in his political life were occasioned chiefly by his relations with other people, and most of his errors had some affinity, as well as himself, to Cæsar and Scipio, his fathers-in-law. But Agesilaus, to gratify the fondness of his son, saved the life of Sphodrias by a sort of violence, when he deserved death for the wrong he had done to the Athenians; and when Phœbidas treacherously broke the peace with Thebes, zealously abetted him for the sake, it was clear, of the unjust act itself. In short, what mischief soever Pompey might be said to have brought on Rome through compliance with the wishes of his friends or through inadvertency, Agesilaus may be said to have brought on Sparta out of obstinacy and malice, by kindling the Bœotian war. And if, moreover, we are to attribute any part of these disasters to some personal ill-fortune attaching to the men themselves, in the case of Pompey, certainly, the Romans had no reason to anticipate it. Whereas Agesilaus would not suffer the Lacedæmonians to avoid what they foresaw and were forewarned must attend the "lame sovereignty." For had Leotychides been chargeable ten thousand times as foreign and spurious, yet the race of the Eurypontidæ was still in being, and could easily have furnished Sparta with a lawful king, that was sound in his limbs, had not Lysander darkened and disguised the true sense of the oracle in favor of Agesilaus.

Such a politic piece of sophistry as was devised by Agesilaus, in that great perplexity of the people as to the treatment to be given to those who had played the coward at the battle of Leuctra, when after that unhappy defeat, he decreed, that the laws should sleep for that day, it would be hard to find any parallel to; neither indeed have we the fellow of it in all Pompey's story. But on the contrary, Pompey for a friend thought it no sin to break those very laws which he himself had made, as if to show at once the force of his friendship, and the greatness of his power; whereas Agesilaus, under the necessity, as it seemed, of either rescinding the laws, or not saving the citizens, contrived an expedient by the help of which the laws should not touch these citizens, and yet should not, to avoid it, be overthrown. Then I must commend it as an incomparable act of civil virtue and obedience in Agesilaus, that immediately upon the receipt of the scytala, he left the wars in Asia, and returned into his country. For he did not like Pompey merely advance his country's interest by acts that contributed at the same time to promote his own greatness, but looking to his country's good, for its sake laid aside as great authority and honor as ever any man had before or since, except Alexander the Great.

But now to take another point of view, if we sum up Pompey's military expeditions and exploits of war, the number of his trophies, and the greatness of the powers which he subdued, and the multitude of battles in which he triumphed, I am persuaded even Xenophon himself would not put the victories of Agesilaus in balance with his, though Xenophon has this privilege allowed him, as a sort of special reward for his other excellences, that he may write and speak, in favor of his hero, whatever he pleases. Methinks, too, there is a great deal of difference betwixt these men, in their clemency and moderation towards their enemies. For Agesilaus, while attempting to enslave Thebes and exterminate Messene, the latter, his country's ancient associate, and Thebes, the mother-city of his own royal house,[1] almost lost Sparta itself, and did really lose the

---

[1] Messene and Sparta were associates in the famous division by lot of Peloponnesus; and from Alcmena, the Theban mother of Hercules, Agesilaus himself claimed descent.

government of Greece; whereas Pompey gave cities to those of the pirates who were willing to change their manner of life; and when it was in his power to lead Tigranes, king of Armenia, in triumph, he chose rather to make him a confederate of the Romans, saying that a single day was worth less than all future time. But if the preëminence in that which relates to the office and virtues of a general, should be determined by the greatest and most important acts and counsels of war, the Lacedæmonian would not a little exceed the Roman. For Agesilaus never deserted his city, though it was besieged by an army of seventy thousand men, when there were very few soldiers within to defend it, and those had been defeated too, but a little before, at the battle of Leuctra. But Pompey, when Cæsar with a body only of fifty-three hundred men, had taken but one town in Italy, departed in a panic out of Rome, either through cowardice, when there were so few, or at least through a false and mistaken belief that there were more; and having conveyed away his wife and children, he left all the rest of the citizens defenceless, and fled; whereas he ought either to have conquered in fight for the defence of his country, or yielded upon terms to the conqueror, who was moreover his fellow-citizen, and allied to him; but now to the same man to whom he refused a prolongation of the term of his government, and thought it intolerable to grant another consulship, to him he gave the power, by letting him take the city, to tell Metellus, together with all the rest, that they were his prisoners.

That which is chiefly the office of a general, to force the enemy into fighting when he finds himself the stronger, and to avoid being driven into it himself when he is the weaker, this excellence Agesilaus

POMPEY AND AGESILAUS

always displayed, and by it kept himself invincible; whereas in contending with Pompey, Cæsar, who was the weaker, successfully declined the danger, and his own strength being in his land forces, drove him into putting the conflict to issue with these, and thus made himself master of the treasure, stores, and the sea too, which were all in his enemy's hands, and by the help of which the victory could have been secured without fighting. And what is alleged as an apology in vindication of Pompey, is to a general of his age and standing the greatest of disgraces. For, granting that a young commander might by clamor and outcry be deprived of his fortitude and strength of mind, and weakly forsake his better judgment, and the thing be neither strange nor altogether unpardonable, yet for Pompey the Great, whose camp the Romans called their country, and his tent the senate, styling the consuls, prætors, and all other magistrates who were conducting the government at Rome, by no better title than that of rebels and traitors, for him, whom they well knew never to have been under the command of any but himself, having served all his campaigns under himself as sole general, for him upon so small a provocation as the scoffs of Favonius and Domitius, and lest he should bear the nickname of Agamemnon, to be wrought upon, and even forced to hazard the whole empire and liberty of Rome upon the cast of a die, was surely indeed intolerable. Who, if he had so much regarded a present infamy, should have guarded the city at first with his arms, and fought the battle in defence of Rome, not have left it as he did; nor while declaring his flight from Italy an artifice in the manner of Themistocles, nevertheless be ashamed in Thessaly of a prudent delay before engaging. Heaven had not appointed the Pharsa-

lian fields to be the stage and theatre upon which
they should contend for the empire of Rome,
neither was he summoned thither by any herald
upon challenge, with intimation that he must either
undergo the combat, or surrender the prize to
another. There were many other fields, thousands
of cities, and even the whole earth, placed at
his command, by the advantage of his fleet, and his
superiority at sea, if he would but have followed
the examples of Maximus, Marius, Lucullus, and
even Agesilaus himself, who endured no less tumults
within the city of Sparta, when the Thebans provoked him to come out and fight in defence of the
land, and sustained in Egypt also numerous calumnies, slanders, and suspicions on the part of the
king, whom he counselled to abstain from a battle.
And thus following always what he had determined
in his own judgment upon mature advice, by that
means he not only preserved the Egyptians, against
their wills, not only kept Sparta, in those desperate
convulsions, by his sole act, safe from overthrow, but
even was able to set up trophies likewise in the
city over the Thebans, having given his countrymen
an occasion of being victorious afterwards by not at
first leading them out, as they tried to force him to
do, to their own destruction. The consequence was
that in the end Agesilaus was commended by the
very men, when they found themselves saved, upon
whom he had put this compulsion, whereas Pompey,
whose error had been occasioned by others, found
those his accusers whose advice had misled him. Some
indeed profess that he was deceived by his father-in-
law Scipio, who, designing to conceal and keep to
himself the greatest part of that treasure which he
had brought out of Asia, pressed Pompey to battle,
upon the pretence that there would be a want of

money. Yet admitting he was deceived, one in his place ought not to have been so, nor should have allowed so slight an artifice to cause the hazard of such mighty interests. And thus we have taken a view of each, by comparing together their conduct, and actions in war.

As to their voyages into Egypt, one steered his course thither out of necessity in flight; the other neither honorably, nor of necessity, but as a mercenary soldier, having enlisted himself into the service of a barbarous nation for pay, that he might be able afterwards to wage war upon the Greeks. And secondly, what we charge upon the Egyptians in the name of Pompey, the Egyptians lay to the charge of Agesilaus. Pompey trusted them and was betrayed and murdered by them; Agesilaus accepted their confidence and deserted them, transferring his aid to the very enemies who were now attacking those whom he had been brought over to assist.

ALEXANDER[1]

TRANSLATED BY MR. EVELYN, (ONE OF THE MINOR COMPOSITIONS OF THE AUTHOR OF SYLVA AND NOT UNWORTHY OF HIM).

It being my purpose to write the lives of Alexander the king, and of Cæsar, by whom Pompey was destroyed, the multitude of their great actions affords so large a field that I were to blame if I should not by way of apology forewarn my reader that I have chosen rather to epitomize the most celebrated parts of their story, than to insist at large on every particular circumstance of it. It must be borne in mind that my design is not to write histories, but lives. And the most glorious exploits do not always furnish us with the clearest discoveries of virtue or vice in men; sometimes a matter of less moment, an expression or a jest, informs us better of their characters and inclinations, than the most famous sieges, the greatest armaments, or the bloodiest battles whatsoever. Therefore as portrait-painters are more exact in the lines and features of the face, in which the character is seen, than in the other parts of the body, so I must

---

[1] Alexander the Great was born at Pella 356 B.C. He must rank as one of the most remarkable men of all ages and countries; especially when we remember that all his achievements were crowded into twelve years and that he died before he reached middle life, younger in fact at the time of his death than Julius Cæsar was when he began his career. As a general, he has no proved superior in history, and he had political capacity also, such as rarely has been surpassed. He died 323 B.C. at the age of 32.—DR. WILLIAM SMITH.

be allowed to give my more particular attention to the marks and indications of the souls of men, and while I endeavor by these to portray their lives, may be free to leave more weighty matters and great battles to be treated of by others.

It is agreed on by all hands, that on the father's side, Alexander descended from Hercules by Caranus, and from Æacus by Neoptolemus on the mother's side. His father Philip, being in Samothrace, when he was quite young, fell in love there with Olympias, in company with whom he was initiated in the religious ceremonies of the country, and her father and mother being both dead, soon after, with the consent of her brother Arymbas, he married her. The night before the consummation of their marriage, she dreamed that a thunderbolt fell upon her body, which kindled a great fire, whose divided flames dispersed themselves all about, and then were extinguished. And Philip some time after he was married, dreamt that he sealed up his wife's body with a seal, whose impression, as he fancied, was the figure of a lion. Some of the diviners interpreted this as a warning to Philip to look narrowly to his wife; but Aristander of Telmessus, considering how unusual it was to seal up any thing that was empty, assured him the meaning of his dream was, that the queen was with child of a boy, who would one day prove as stout and courageous as a lion. Once, moreover, a serpent was found lying by Olympias as she slept, which more than any thing else, it is said, abated Philip's passion for her; and whether he feared her as an enchantress, or thought she had commerce with some god, and so looked on himself as excluded, he was ever after less fond of her conversation. Others say, that the women of this country having always been extremely addicted to the enthusiastic Orphic rites, and the wild worship of Bacchus, (upon which account they were called Clodones, and Mimallones,) imitated in many things the practices of the Edonian and Thracian women about Mount Hæmus, from whom the word *threskeuein*,[2] seems to have been derived, as a special term for superfluous and over-curious forms of adoration; and that Olympias, zealously affecting these fanatical and enthusiastic inspirations, to perform them with more barbaric dread, was wont in the dances proper to these ceremonies to have great tame serpents about her, which sometimes creeping out of the ivy and the mystic fans, sometimes winding themselves about the sacred spears, and the women's chaplets, made a spectacle which the men could not look upon without terror.

Philip, after this vision, sent Chæron of Megalopolis to consult the oracle of Apollo at Delphi, by which he was commanded to perform sacrifice, and henceforth pay particular honor, above all other gods, to Ammon; and was told he should one day lose that eye with which he presumed to peep through the chink of the door, when he saw the god, under the form of a serpent, in the company of his

---

[2] *Threskeuein*, as though from *thressa*, a Thracian woman. It occurs several times in the New Testament,—" voluntary humility and *worshipping* of angels;" " If any man among you seem to be *religious*, and bridleth not his tongue, but deceiveth his own heart, this man's *religion* is vain. Pure *religion* and undefiled before God," etc. By this time it had naturally, from the notion of performances for the propitiation of a deity, been extended to that of habits and practices of religious living, and was selected as the proper word for what we call a religion, " according to the most straitest sect of our *religion*."

wife. Eratosthenes says that Olympias, when she attended Alexander on his way to the army in his first expedition, told him the secret of his birth, and bade him behave himself with courage suitable to his divine extraction. Others again affirm that she wholly disclaimed any pretensions of the kind, and was wont to say, " When will Alexander leave off slandering me to Juno?"

Alexander was born the sixth of Hecatombæon, which month the Macedonians call Lous, the same day that the temple of Diana at Ephesus was burnt; which Hegesias of Magnesia makes the occasion of a conceit, frigid enough to have stopped the conflagration. The temple, he says, took fire and was burnt while its mistress was absent, assisting at the birth of Alexander. And all the Eastern soothsayers [3] who happened to be then at Ephesus, looking upon the ruin of this temple to be the forerunner of some other calamity, ran about the town, beating their faces, and crying, that this day had brought forth something that would prove fatal and destructive to all Asia.

Just after Philip had taken Potidæa, he received these three messages at one time, that Parmenio had overthrown the Illyrians in a great battle, that his race-horse had won the course at the Olympic games, and that his wife had given birth to Alexander; with which being naturally well pleased, as an addition to his satisfaction, he was assured by the diviners that a son, whose birth was accompanied

---

[3] Literally *Magians,* which however Plutarch perhaps does not use in its strict original sense. Diana, it will be remembered, was the goddess who gave assistance in childbirth. The epithet *cold* was the ordinary Greek expression in the case of a poor joke, or a stupid, unsuccessful piece of wit.

with three such successes, could not fail of being invincible.

The statues that gave the best representation of Alexander's person, were those of Lysippus, (by whom alone he would suffer his image to be made,) those peculiarities which many of his successors afterwards and his friends used to affect to imitate, the inclination of his head a little on one side towards his left shoulder, and his melting eye, having been expressed by this artist with great exactness. But Apelles, who drew him with thunderbolts in his hand, made his complexion browner and darker than it was naturally; for he was fair and of a light color, passing into ruddiness in his face and upon his breast. Aristoxenus in his Memoirs tells us that a most agreeable odor exhaled from his skin, and that his breath and body all over was so fragrant as to perfume the clothes which he wore next him; the cause of which might probably be the hot and adust temperament of his body. For sweet smells, Theophrastus conceives, are produced by the concoction of moist humors by heat, which is the reason that those parts of the world which are driest and most burnt up, afford spices of the best kind, and in the greatest quantity; for the heat of the sun exhausts all the superfluous moisture which lies in the surface of bodies, ready to generate putrefaction. And this hot constitution, it may be, rendered Alexander so addicted to drinking, and so choleric. His temperance, as to the pleasures of the body, was apparent in him in his very childhood, as he was with much difficulty incited to them, and always used them with great moderation; though in other things he was extremely eager and vehement, and in his love of glory, and the pursuit of it, he showed a solidity of

ARISTOTLES AND HIS PUPIL ALEXANDER

high spirit and magnanimity far above his age. For he neither sought nor valued it upon every occasion, as his father Philip did, (who affected to show his eloquence almost to a degree of pedantry, and took care to have the victories of his racing chariots at the Olympic games engraven on his coin,) but when he was asked by some about him, whether he would run a race in the Olympic games, as he was very swift-footed, he answered, he would, if he might have kings to run with him. Indeed, he seems in general to have looked with indifference, if not with dislike, upon the professed athletes. He often appointed prizes, for which not only tragedians and musicians, pipers and harpers, but rhapsodists also, strove to outvie one another; and delighted in all manner of hunting and cudgel-playing, but never gave any encouragement to contests either of boxing or of the pancratium.[4]

While he was yet very young, he entertained the ambassadors from the king of Persia, in the absence of his father, and entering much into conversation with them, gained so much upon them by his affability, and the questions he asked them, which were far from being childish or trifling, (for he inquired of them the length of the ways, the nature of the road into inner Asia, the character of their king, how he carried himself to his enemies, and what forces he was able to bring into the field,) that they were struck with admiration of him, and looked upon the ability so much famed of Philip, to be nothing in comparison with the forwardness and high purpose that appeared thus early in his son. Whenever

[4] Rhapsodists were reciters of Epic verses. In the pancratium, wrestling and boxing were combined.

he heard Philip had taken any town of importance, or won any signal victory, instead of rejoicing at it altogether, he would tell his companions that his father would anticipate every thing, and leave him and them no opportunities of performing great and illustrious actions. For being more bent upon action and glory than either upon pleasure or riches, he esteemed all that he should receive from his father as a diminution and prevention of his own future achievements; and would have chosen rather to succeed to a kingdom involved in troubles and wars, which would have afforded him frequent exercise of his courage, and a large field of honor, than to one already flourishing and settled, where his inheritance would be an inactive life, and the mere enjoyment of wealth and luxury.

The care of his education, as it might be presumed, was committed to a great many attendants, preceptors, and teachers, over the whole of whom Leonidas, a near kinsman of Olympias, a man of an austere temper, presided, who did not indeed himself decline the name of what in reality is a noble and honorable office,[5] but in general his dignity, and his near relationship, obtained him from other people the title of Alexander's foster-father and governor. But he who took upon him the actual place and style of his pedagogue, was Lysimachus the Acarnanian, who, though he had nothing specially to recommend him, but his lucky fancy of calling himself Phœnix, Alexander Achilles, and Philip Peleus, was therefore well enough esteemed, and ranked in the next degree after Leonidas.

Philonicus the Thessalian brought the horse

[5] The paidagogus or pædagogus, was usually a slave, who *took the boy about.*

Bucephalas[6] to Philip, offering to sell him for thirteen talents; but when they went into the field to try him, they found him so very vicious and unmanageable, that he reared up when they endeavored to mount him, and would not so much as endure the voice of any of Philip's attendants. Upon which, as they were leading him away as wholly useless and untractable, Alexander, who stood by, said, "What an excellent horse do they lose, for want of address and boldness to manage him!" Philip at first took no notice of what he said; but when he heard him repeat the same thing several times, and saw he was much vexed to see the horse sent away, "Do you reproach," said he to him, "those who are older than yourself, as if you knew more, and were better able to manage him than they?" "I could manage this horse," replied he, "better than others do." "And if you do not," said Philip, "what will you forfeit for your rashness?" "I will pay," answered Alexander, "the whole price of the horse." At this the whole company fell a laughing; and as soon as the wager was settled amongst them, he immediately ran to the horse, and taking hold of the bridle, turned him directly towards the sun, having, it seems, observed that he was disturbed at and afraid of the motion of his own shadow; then letting him go forward a little, still keeping the reins in his hand, and stroking him gently when he found him begin to grow eager and fiery, he let fall his upper garment softly, and with one nimble leap securely mounted him, and when he was seated, by little and little drew in the bridle, and curbed him without either striking or

[6] Bucephalas, not Bucephalus, appears to be the correct form, although authority is not wanting for the latter.

spurring him. Presently, when he found him free from all rebelliousness, and only impatient for the course, he let him go at full speed, inciting him now with a commanding voice, and urging him also with his heel. Philip and his friends looked on at first in silence and anxiety for the result, till seeing him turn at the end of his career, and come back rejoicing and triumphing for what he had performed, they all burst out into acclamations of applause; and his father, shedding tears, it is said, for joy, kissed him as he came down from his horse, and in his transport, said, "O my son, look thee out a kingdom equal to and worthy of thyself, for Macedonia is too little for thee."

After this, considering him to be of a temper easy to be led to his duty by reason, but by no means to be compelled, he always endeavored to persuade rather than to command or force him to any thing; and now looking upon the instruction and tuition of his youth to be of greater difficulty and importance, than to be wholly trusted to the ordinary masters in music and poetry, and the common school subjects, and to require, as Sophocles says, .

<blockquote>The bridle and the rudder too,[7]</blockquote>

he sent for Aristotle, the most learned and most celebrated philosopher of his time, and rewarded him with a munificence proportionable to and becoming the care he took to instruct his son. For he repeopled his native city Stagira, which he had caused to be demolished a little before, and restored all the citizens who were in exile or slavery, to

---

[7] *The bridle and the rudder too.* Sophocles, Fragm. Incert., 55; in Dindorf, 712.

their habitations. As a place for the pursuit of their studies and exercises, he assigned the temple of the Nymphs, near Mieza, where, to this very day, they show you Aristotle's stone seats, and the shady walks which he was wont to frequent. It would appear that Alexander received from him not only his doctrines of Morals and of Politics, but also something of those more abstruse and profound theories which these philosophers, by the very names they gave them,[8] professed to reserve for oral communication to the initiated, and did not allow many to become acquainted with. For when he was in Asia, and heard Aristotle had published some treatises of that kind, he wrote to him, using very plain language to him in behalf of philosophy, the following letter. "Alexander to Aristotle greeting. You have not done well to publish your books of oral doctrine; for what is there now that we excel others in, if those things which we have been particularly instructed in be laid open to all? For my part, I assure you, I had rather excel others in the knowledge of what is excellent, than in the extent of my power and dominion. Farewell." And Aristotle, soothing this passion for preëminence, speaks, in his excuse for himself, of these doctrines, as in fact both published and not published: as indeed, to say the truth, his books on metaphysics are written in a style which makes them useless for ordinary teaching, and instructive only, in the way of memoranda, for those who have been already conversant in that sort of learning.

[8] Acroamatica and Epoptica, Oral, and Secret, were terms applied by the Peripatetics to what we should call Esoteric doctrines. The *Epoptes* was one who had been admitted to the Greater Mysteries.

Doubtless also it was to Aristotle, that he owed the inclination he had, not to the theory only, but likewise to the practice of the art of medicine. For when any of his friends were sick, he would often prescribe them their course of diet, and medicines proper to their disease, as we may find in his epistles. He was naturally a great lover of all kinds of learning and reading; and Onesicritus informs us, that he constantly laid Homer's Iliads, according to the copy corrected by Aristotle, called the casket copy, with his dagger under his pillow, declaring that he esteemed it a perfect portable treasure of all military virtue and knowledge. When he was in the upper Asia, being destitute of other books, he ordered Harpalus to send him some; who furnished him with Philistus's History, a great many of the plays of Euripides, Sophocles, and Æschylus, and some dithyrambic odes, composed by Telestes and Philoxenus. For awhile he loved and cherished Aristotle no less, as he was wont to say himself, than if he had been his father, giving this reason for it, that as he had received life from the one, so the other had taught him to live well. But afterwards, upon some mistrust of him, yet not so great as to make him do him any hurt, his familiarity and friendly kindness to him abated so much of its former force and affectionateness, as to make it evident he was alienated from him. However, his violent thirst after and passion for learning, which were once implanted, still grew up with him, and never decayed; as appears by his veneration of Anaxarchus, by the present of fifty talents which he sent to Xenocrates, and his particular care and esteem of Dandamis and Calanus.

While Philip went on his expedition against the Byzantines, he left Alexander, then sixteen years old, his lieutenant in Macedonia, committing the charge of his seal to him; who, not to sit idle, reduced the rebellious Mædi, and having taken their chief town by storm, drove out the barbarous inhabitants, and planting a colony of several nations in their room, called the place after his own name, Alexandropolis. At the battle of Chæronea, which his father fought against the Grecians, he is said to have been the first man that charged the Thebans' sacred band. And even in my remembrance, there stood an old oak near the river Cephisus, which people called Alexander's oak, because his tent was pitched under it. And not far off are to be seen the graves of the Macedonians who fell in that battle. This early bravery made Philip so fond of him, that nothing pleased him more than to hear his subjects call himself their general and Alexander their king.

But the disorders of his family, chiefly caused by his new marriages and attachments, (the troubles that began in the women's chambers spreading, so to say, to the whole kingdom,) raised various complaints and differences between them, which the violence of Olympias, a woman of a jealous and implacable temper, made wider, by exasperating Alexander against his father. Among the rest, this accident contributed most to their falling out. At the wedding of Cleopatra, whom Philip fell in love with and married, she being much too young for him, her uncle Attalus in his drink desired the Macedonians would implore the gods to give them a lawful successor to the kingdom by his niece. This so irritated Alexander, that throwing one of the cups at his head, "You villain," said he, "what, am I then a bastard?" Then Philip taking Attalus's part, rose up and would have run his son through;

but by good fortune for them both, either his overhasty rage, or the wine he had drunk, made his foot slip, so he fell down on the floor. At which Alexander reproachfully insulted over him: " See there," said he, " the man, who makes preparations to pass out of Europe into Asia, overturned in passing from one seat to another." After this debauch, he and his mother Olympias withdrew from Philip's company, and when he had placed her in Epirus, he himself retired into Illyria.

About this time, Demaratus the Corinthian, an old friend of the family, who had the freedom to say any thing among them without offence, coming to visit Philip, after the first compliments and embraces were over, Philip asked him, whether the Grecians were at amity with one another. " It ill becomes you," replied Demaratus, " to be solicitous about Greece, when you have involved your own house in so many dissensions and calamities." He was so convinced by this seasonable reproach, that he immediately sent for his son home, and by Demaratus's mediation prevailed with him to return. But this reconciliation lasted not long; for when Pixodorus, viceroy of Caria, sent Aristocritus to treat for a match between his eldest daughter and Philip's son Arrhidæus, hoping by this alliance to secure his assistance upon occasion, Alexander's mother, and some who pretended to be his friends, presently filled his head with tales and calumnies, as if Philip, by a splendid marriage and important alliance, were preparing the way for settling the kingdom upon Arrhidæus. In alarm at this, he despatched Thessalus, the tragic actor, into Caria, to dispose Pixodorus to slight Arrhidæus, both as illegitimate and a fool, and rather to accept of himself for his son-in-law. This proposition was much more agreeable to Pixodorus than the former. But Philip, as soon as he was made acquainted with this transaction, went to his son's apartment, taking with him Philotas, the son of Parmenio, one of Alexander's intimate friends and companions, and there reproved him severely, and reproached him bitterly, that he should be so degenerate, and unworthy of the power he was to leave him, as to desire the alliance of a mean Carian, who was at best but the slave of a barbarous prince. Nor did this satisfy his resentment, for he wrote to the Corinthians, to send Thessalus to him in chains, and banished Harpalus, Nearchus, Erigyius, and Ptolemy, his son's friends and favorites, whom Alexander afterwards recalled, and raised to great honor and preferment.

Not long after this, Pausanias, having had an outrage done to him at the instance of Attalus and Cleopatra, when he found he could get no reparation for his disgrace at Philip's hands, watched his opportunity and murdered him. The guilt of which fact was laid for the most part upon Olympias, who was said to have encouraged and exasperated the enraged youth to revenge; and some sort of suspicion attached even to Alexander himself, who, it was said, when Pausanias came and complained to him of the injury he had received, repeated the verse out of Euripides's Medea:—

On husband, and on father, and on bride.[9]

However, he took care to find out and punish the

[9] Upon all of whom, says Jason, Creon, king of Corinth, and Glauce, in the speech from which the line is quoted, Medea was threatening to take vengeance. Euripides, Medea, 283.

accomplices of the conspiracy severely, and was very angry with Olympias for treating Cleopatra inhumanly in his absence.

Alexander was but twenty years old when his father was murdered, and succeeded to a kingdom beset on all sides with great dangers, and rancorous enemies. For not only the barbarous nations that bordered on Macedonia, were impatient of being governed by any but their own native princes; but Philip likewise, though he had been victorious over the Grecians, yet, as the time had not been sufficient for him to complete his conquest and accustom them to his sway, had simply left all things in a general disorder and confusion. It seemed to the Macedonians a very critical time, and some would have persuaded Alexander to give up all thought of retaining the Grecians in subjection by force of arms. and rather to apply himself to win back by gentle means the allegiance of the tribes who were designing revolt, and try the effect of indulgence in arresting the first motions towards revolution. But he rejected this counsel as weak and timorous, and looked upon it to be more prudence to secure himself by resolution and magnanimity, than, by seeming to truckle to any, to encourage all to trample on him. In pursuit of this opinion, he reduced the barbarians to tranquillity, and put an end to all fear of war from them, by a rapid expedition into their country as far as the river Danube, where he gave Syrmus, king of the Triballians, an entire overthrow. And hearing the Thebans were in revolt, and the Athenians in correspondence with them, he immediately marched through the pass of Thermopylæ, saying that to Demosthenes who had called him a child while he was in Illyria and in the country of the Triballians, and a youth when he was in Thessaly, he would appear a man before the walls of Athens.

When he came to Thebes, to show how willing he was to accept of their repentance for what was past, he only demanded of them Phœnix and Prothytes, the authors of the rebellion, and proclaimed a general pardon to those who would come over to him. But when the Thebans merely retorted by demanding Philotas and Antipater to be delivered into their hands, and by a proclamation on their part, invited all who would assert the liberty of Greece to come over to them, he presently applied himself to make them feel the last extremities of war. The Thebans indeed defended themselves with a zeal and courage beyond their strength, being much outnumbered by their enemies. But when the Macedonian garrison sallied out upon them from the citadel, they were so hemmed in on all sides, that the greater part of them fell in the battle; the city itself being taken by storm, was sacked and razed, Alexander's hope being that so severe an example might terrify the rest of Greece into obedience, and also in order to gratify the hostility of his confederates, the Phocians and Platæans. So that, except the priests, and some few who had heretofore been the friends and connections of the Macedonians, the family of the poet Pindar, and those who were known to have opposed the public vote for the war, all the rest, to the number of thirty thousand, were publicly sold for slaves; and it is computed that upwards of six thousand were put to the sword. Among the other calamities that befell the city, it happened that some Thracian soldiers having broken into the house of a matron of high character and repute, named Timoclea, their captain, after he had used violence with her, to satisfy his avarice as well as lust, asked her, if she knew of any money concealed; to which she readily answered she did, and bade him follow her into a garden, where she showed him a well, into which, she told him, upon the taking of the city she had thrown what she had of most value. The greedy Thracian presently stooping down to view the place where he thought the treasure lay, she came behind him, and pushed him into the well, and then flung great stones in upon him, till she had killed him. After which, when the soldiers led her away bound to Alexander, her very mien and gait showed her to be a woman of dignity, and of a mind no less elevated, not betraying the least sign of fear or astonishment. And when the king asked her who she was, "I am," said she, "the sister of Theagenes, who fought the battle of Chæronea with your father Philip, and fell there in command for the liberty of Greece." Alexander was so surprised, both at what she had done, and what she said, that he could not choose but give her and her children their freedom to go whither they pleased.

After this he received the Athenians into favor, although they had shown themselves so much concerned at the calamity of Thebes that out of sorrow they omitted the celebration of the Mysteries, and entertained those who escaped with all possible humanity. Whether it were, like the lion, that his passion was now satisfied, or that after an example of extreme cruelty, he had a mind to appear merciful, it happened well for the Athenians; for he not only forgave them all past offences, but bade them to look to their affairs with vigilance, remembering that if he should miscarry, they were likely to be the arbiters of Greece. Certain it is, too, that in after-time he often repented of his severity to the Thebans, and his remorse had such influence on his temper as to make him ever after less rigorous to all others. He imputed also the murder of Clitus, which he committed in his wine, and the unwillingness of the Macedonians to follow him against the Indians, by which his enterprise and glory was left imperfect, to the wrath and vengeance of Bacchus, the protector of Thebes. And it was observed that whatsoever any Theban, who had the good fortune to survive this victory, asked of him, he was sure to grant without the least difficulty.

Soon after, the Grecians, being assembled at the Isthmus, declared their resolution of joining with Alexander in the war against the Persians, and proclaimed him their general. While he stayed here, many public ministers and philosophers came from all parts to visit him, and congratulated him on his election, but contrary to his expectation, Diogenes of Sinope, who then was living at Corinth, thought so little of him, that instead of coming to compliment him, he never so much as stirred out of the suburb called the Cranium, where Alexander found him lying along in the sun. When he saw so much company near him, he raised himself a little, and vouchsafed to look upon Alexander; and when he kindly asked him whether he wanted any thing, "Yes," said he, "I would have you stand from between me and the sun." Alexander was so struck at this answer, and surprised at the greatness of the man, who had taken so little notice of him, that as he went away, he told his followers who were laughing at the moroseness of the philosopher, that if he were not Alexander, he would choose to be Diogenes.

Then he went to Delphi, to consult Apollo concerning the success of the war he had undertaken, and happening to come on one of the forbidden days, when it was esteemed improper to give any answers from the oracle, he sent messengers to desire the priestess to do her office; and when she refused, on the plea of a law to the contrary, he went up himself, and began to draw her by force into the temple, until tired and overcome with his importunity, "My son," said she, "thou art invincible." Alexander taking hold of what she spoke, declared he had received such an answer as he wished for, and that it was needless to consult the god any further. Among other prodigies that attended the departure of his army, the image of Orpheus at Libethra, made of cypress-wood, was seen to sweat in great abundance, to the discouragement of many. But Aristander told him, that far from presaging any ill to him, it signified he should perform acts so important and glorious as would make the poets and musicians of future ages labor and sweat to describe and celebrate them.

His army, by their computation who make the smallest amount, consisted of thirty thousand foot, and four thousand horse; and those who make the most of it, speak but of forty-three thousand foot, and three thousand horse.[10] Aristobulus says, he had not a fund of above seventy talents for their pay, nor had he more than thirty days' provision, if we may believe Duris; Onesicritus tells us, he was two hundred talents in debt. However narrow

---

[10] *Forty-three thousand foot and three thousand horse* should be *forty-three thousand foot and five thousand horse*. The numbers in this passage are, as numbers very generally are in manuscripts, given with variations. This, however, is the reading established by comparison with the corresponding passage in

ALEXANDER

and disproportionable the beginnings of so vast an undertaking might seem to be, yet he would not embark his army until he had informed himself particularly what means his friends had to enable them to follow him, and supplied what they wanted, by giving good farms to some, a village to one, and the revenue of some hamlet or harbor town to another. So that at last he had portioned out or engaged almost all the royal property; which giving Perdiccas an occasion to ask him what he would leave himself, he replied, his hopes. "Your soldiers," replied Peridiccas, "will be your partners in those," and refused to accept of the estate he had assigned him. Some others of his friends did the like, but to those who willingly received, or desired assistance of him, he liberally granted it, as far as his patrimony in Macedonia would reach, the most part of which was spent in these donations.

With such vigorous resolutions, and his mind thus disposed, he passed the Hellespont, and at Troy sacrificed to Minerva, and honored the memory of the heroes who were buried there, with solemn libations; especially Achilles, whose gravestone he anointed, and with his friends, as the ancient custom is, ran naked about his sepulchre, and crowned it with garlands, declaring how happy he esteemed him, in having while he lived so faithful a friend, and when he was dead, so famous a poet to proclaim his actions. While he was viewing the rest of the antiquities and curiosities of the place, being

Plutarch's own treatise on the Merit or Fortune of Alexander. He says there, that Aristobulus made it 30,000 foot and 4,000 horse; Ptolemy, the king, 30,000 foot and 5,000 horse; and Anaximenes, 43,000 foot and 5,000 horse (*De Alexandri s. Virtute s. Fortuna, I., 3*).

told he might see Paris's harp, if he pleased, he said, he thought it not worth looking on, but he should be glad to see that of Achilles,[11] to which he used to sing the glories and great actions of brave men.

In the mean time Darius's captains having collected large forces, were encamped on the further bank of the river Granicus, and it was necessary to fight, as it were, in the gate of Asia for an entrance into it. The depth of the river, with the unevenness and difficult ascent of the opposite bank, which was to be gained by main force, was apprehended by most, and some pronounced it an improper time to engage, because it was unusual for the kings of Macedonia to march with their forces in the month called Dæsius. But Alexander broke through these scruples, telling them they should call it a second Artemisius. And when Parmenio advised him not to attempt any thing that day, because it was late, he told him that he should disgrace the Hellespont, should he fear the Granicus. And so without more saying, he immediately took the river with thirteen troops of horse, and advanced against whole showers of darts thrown from the steep opposite side, which was covered with armed multitudes of the enemy's horse and foot, notwithstanding the disadvantage of the ground and the rapidity of the stream; so that the action seemed to have more of frenzy and desperation in it, than of prudent conduct. However, he persisted obstinately to gain the passage, and at last with much ado making his way up the

---

[11] Iliad, IX. 189. When Ajax, Ulysses, and Phœnix came with the offers of reconciliation from Agamemnon, they found Achilles seated with Patroclus in the tent singing to his harp " the glories of men."

banks, which were extremely muddy and slippery, he had instantly to join in a mere confused hand-to-hand combat with the enemy, before he could draw up his men, who were still passing over, into any order. For the enemy pressed upon him with loud and warlike outcries; and charging horse against horse, with their lances, after they had broken and spent these, they fell to it with their swords. And Alexander, being easily known by his buckler, and a large plume of white feathers on each side of his helmet, was attacked on all sides, yet escaped wounding, though his cuirass was pierced by a javelin in one of the joinings. And Rhœsaces and Spithridates, two Persian commanders, falling upon him at once, he avoided one of them, and struck at Rhœsaces, who had a good cuirass on, with such force, that his spear breaking in his hand, he was glad to betake himself to his dagger. While they were thus engaged, Spithridates came up on one side of him, and raising himself upon his horse, gave him such a blow with his battle-axe on the helmet, that he cut off the crest of it, with one of his plumes, and the helmet was only just so far strong enough to save him, that the edge of the weapon touched the hair of his head. But as he was about to repeat his stroke, Clitus, called the black Clitus, prevented him, by running him through the body with his spear. At the same time Alexander despatched Rhœsaces with his sword. While the horse were thus dangerously engaged, the Macedonian phalanx passed the river, and the foot on each side advanced to fight. But the enemy hardly sustaining the first onset, soon gave ground and fled, all but the mercenary Greeks, who, making a stand upon a rising ground, desired quarter, which Alexander, guided rather by passion than judgment, refused to grant, and charging them himself first, had his horse, (not Bucephalas, but another) killed under him. And this obstinacy of his to cut off these experienced desperate men, cost him the lives of more of his own soldiers than all the battle before, besides those who were wounded. The Persians lost in this battle twenty thousand foot, and two thousand five hundred horse. On Alexander's side, Aristobulus says there were not wanting above four and thirty, of whom nine were foot-soldiers; and in memory of them he caused so many statues of brass, of Lysippus's making, to be erected. And that the Grecians might participate the honor of his victory, he sent a portion of the spoils home to them, particularly to the Athenians three hundred bucklers, and upon all the rest he ordered this inscription to be set: " Alexander the son of Philip, and the Grecians, except the Lacedæmonians, won these from the barbarians who inhabit Asia." All the plate and purple garments, and other things of the same kind that he took from the Persians, except a very small quantity which he reserved for himself, he sent as a present to his mother.

This battle presently made a great change of affairs to Alexander's advantage. For Sardis itself, the chief seat of the barbarian's power in the maritime provinces, and many other considerable places were surrendered to him; only Halicarnassus and Miletus stood out, which he took by force, together with the territory about them. After which he was a little unsettled in his opinion how to proceed. Sometimes he thought it best to find out Darius as soon as he could, and put all to the hazard of a battle; another while he looked upon it as a more prudent course to make an entire reduction of the sea-coast, and not to seek the enemy till he had first exercised his power here and made himself secure of the resources of these provinces. While he was thus deliberating what to do, it happened that a spring of water near the city of Xanthus in Lycia, of its own accord swelled over its banks, and threw up a copper plate upon the margin, in which was engraven in ancient characters, that the time would come, when the Persian empire should be destroyed by the Grecians. Encouraged by this accident, he proceeded to reduce the maritime parts of Cilicia and Phœnicia, and passed his army along the sea-coasts of Pamphylia with such expedition that many historians have described and extolled it with that height of admiration, as if it were no less than a miracle, and an extraordinary effect of divine favor, that the waves which usually come rolling in violently from the main, and hardly ever leave so much as a narrow beach under the steep, broken cliffs at any time uncovered, should on a sudden retire to afford him passage. Menander, in one of his comedies, alludes to this marvel when he says,

> Was Alexander ever favored more?
> Each man I wish for meets me at my door,
> And should I ask for passage through the sea,
> The sea I doubt not would retire for me.[12]

[12] The passage from Menander is only known by this quotation. It may perhaps belong to the character of some Boastful Soldier, like a fragment in Athenæus from his play called the Flatterer, in which it is made a compliment to say, "You have drunk more than king Alexander." The twelve years of the campaigns of Alexander were those of the boyhood of Menander, who was not quite twenty-one when his first play was acted two years after Alexander's death (321 B.C.).

But Alexander himself in his epistles mentions nothing unusual in this at all, but says he went from Phaselis, and passed through what they call the ladders.[13] At Phaselis he stayed some time, and finding the statue of Theodectes, who was a native of this town and was now dead, erected in the market-place, after he had supped, having drunk pretty plentifully, he went and danced about it, and crowned it with garlands, honoring not ungracefully in his sport, the memory of a philosopher whose conversation he had formerly enjoyed, when he was Aristotle's scholar.

Then he subdued the Pisidians who made head against him, and conquered the Phrygians, at whose chief city Gordium, which is said to be the seat of the ancient Midas, he saw the famous chariot fastened with cords made of the rind of the cornel-tree, which whosoever should untie, the inhabitants had a tradition, that for him was reserved the empire of the world. Most authors tell the story that Alexander, finding himself unable to untie the knot, the ends of which were secretly twisted round and folded up within it, cut it asunder with his sword. But Aristobulus tells us it was easy for him to undo it, by only pulling the pin out of the pole to which the yoke was tied, and afterwards drawing off the yoke itself from below. From hence he advanced into Paphlagonia and Cappadocia, both which countries he soon reduced to obedience, and then hearing of the death of Memnon, the best commander Darius had upon the sea-coasts, who,

---

[13] Mount Climax was the name of the headland, round the foot of which the narrow strip of beach offered a passage. Strabo describes it, and says, Alexander found the waters nearly breast-high.

if he had lived, might, it was supposed, have put
many impediments and difficulties in the way of the
progress of his arms, he was the rather encouraged
to carry the war into the upper provinces of Asia.

Darius [14] was by this time upon his march from
Susa, very confident, not only in the number of
his men, which amounted to six hundred thousand,
but likewise in a dream, which the Persian soothsayers interpreted rather in flattery to him, than
according to the natural probability. He dreamed
that he saw the Macedonian phalanx all on fire,
and Alexander waiting on him, clad in the same
dress which he himself had been used to wear when
he was courier to the late king; after which, going
into the temple of Belus, he vanished out of his
sight. The dream would appear to have super-
naturally signified to him the illustrious actions the
Macedonians were to perform, and that as he from
a courier's place had risen to the throne, so Alexander should come to be master of Asia, and not
long surviving his conquests, conclude his life with
glory. Darius's confidence increased the more, because Alexander spent so much time in Cilicia, which
he imputed to his cowardice. But it was sickness
that detained him there, which some say he contracted from his fatigues, others from bathing in
the river Cydnus, whose waters were exceedingly

---

[14] Darius had been one of the royal *Couriers* (*Courtier*, in the twenty-second line, is a misprint), or king's messengers. *Astandes,* the Greek word of the original, is of Persian derivation. The system of regular relays of horses and couriers for conveying the government despatches seems to have been one of the good points in the Persian imperial system. It was adopted in the Macedonian kingdoms, and passed from them to the Romans.

cold. However it happened, none of his physicians would venture to give him any remedies, they thought his case so desperate, and were so afraid of the suspicions and ill-will of the Macedonians if they should fail in the cure; till Philip, the Acarnanian, seeing how critical his case was, but relying on his own well-known friendship for him, resolved to try the last efforts of his art, and rather hazard his own credit and life, than suffer him to perish for want of physic, which he confidently administered to him, encouraging him to take it boldly, if he desired a speedy recovery, in order to prosecute the war. At this very time, Parmenio wrote to Alexander from the camp, bidding him have a care of Philip, as one who was bribed by Darius to kill him, with great sums of money, and a promise of his daughter in marriage. When he had perused the letter, he put it under his pillow, without showing it so much as to any of his most intimate friends, and when Philip came in with the potion, he took it with great cheerfulness and assurance, giving him meantime the letter to read. This was a spectacle well worth being present at, to see Alexander take the draught, and Philip read the letter at the same time, and then turn and look upon one another, but with different sentiments; for Alexander's looks were cheerful and open, to show his kindness to and confidence in his physician, while the other was full of surprise and alarm at the accusation, appealing to the gods to witness his innocence, sometimes lifting up his hands to heaven, and then throwing himself down by the bedside, and beseeching Alexander to lay aside all fear, and follow his directions without apprehension. For the medicine at first worked so strongly as to drive, so to say, the vital forces into the interior; he lost his speech, and falling into a swoon, had scarce any sense or pulse left. However, in no long time, by Philip's means, his health and strength returned, and he showed himself in public to the Macedonians, who were in continual fear and dejection until they saw him abroad again.

There was at this time in Darius's army a Macedonian refugee, named Amyntas, one who was pretty well acquainted with Alexander's character. This man, when he saw Darius intended to fall upon the enemy in the passes and defiles, advised him earnestly to keep where he was, in the open and extensive plains, it being the advantage of a numerous army to have field-room enough when it engages with a lesser force. Darius, instead of taking his counsel, told him he was afraid the enemy would endeavor to run away, and so Alexander would escape out of his hands. "That fear," replied Amyntas, "is needless, for assure yourself that far from avoiding you, he will make all the speed he can to meet you, and is now most likely on his march towards you." But Amyntas's counsel was to no purpose, for Darius immediately decamping, marched into Cilicia, at the same time that Alexander advanced into Syria to meet him; and missing one another in the night, they both turned back again. Alexander, greatly pleased with the event, made all the haste he could to fight in the defiles, and Darius to recover his former ground, and draw his army out of so disadvantageous a place. For now he began to perceive his error in engaging himself too far in a country in which the sea, the mountains, and the river Pinarus running through the midst of it, would necessitate him to divide his forces, render his horse almost unserviceable, and only cover and support the weakness of the enemy. Fortune was not kinder to Alexander in the choice of the ground, than he was careful to improve it to his advantage. For being much inferior in numbers, so far from allowing himself to be outflanked, he stretched his right wing much further out than the left wing of his enemies, and fighting there himself in the very foremost ranks, put the barbarians to flight. In this battle he was wounded in the thigh, Chares says by Darius, with whom he fought hand to hand. But in the account which he gave Antipater of the battle, though indeed he owns he was wounded in the thigh with a sword, though not dangerously, yet he takes no notice who it was that wounded him.

Nothing was wanting to complete this victory, in which he overthrew above an hundred and ten thousand of his enemies, but the taking the person of Darius, who escaped very narrowly by flight. However, having taken his chariot and his bow, he returned from pursuing him, and found his own men busy in pillaging the barbarians' camp, which (though to disburden themselves they had left most of their baggage at Damascus) was exceedingly rich. But Darius's tent, which was full of splendid furniture, and quantities of gold and silver, they reserved for Alexander himself, who after he had put off his arms, went to bathe himself, saying, "Let us now cleanse ourselves from the toils of war in the bath of Darius." "Not so," replied one of his followers, "but in Alexander's rather; for the property of the conquered is, and should be called the conqueror's." Here, when he beheld the bathing vessels, the water-pots, the pans, and the ointment boxes, all of gold, curiously wrought, and smelt the fragrant odors with which the whole place was exquisitely perfumed, and from thence passed into a pavilion of great size and height, where the couches and tables and preparations for an entertainment were perfectly magnificent, he turned to those about him and said, "This, it seems, is royalty."

But as he was going to supper, word was brought him that Darius's mother and wife and two unmarried daughters, being taken among the rest of the prisoners, upon the sight of his chariot and bow were all in mourning and sorrow, imagining him to be dead. After a little pause, more livelily affected with their affliction than with his own success, he sent Leonnatus to them to let them know Darius was not dead, and that they need not fear any harm from Alexander, who made war upon him only for dominion; they should themselves be provided with every thing they had been used to receive from Darius. This kind message could not but be very welcome to the captive ladies, especially being made good by actions no less humane and generous. For he gave them leave to bury whom they pleased of the Persians, and to make use for this purpose of what garments and furniture they thought fit out of the booty. He diminished nothing of their equipage, or of the attentions and respect formerly paid them, and allowed larger pensions for their maintenance than they had before. But the noblest and most royal part of their usage was, that he treated these illustrious prisoners according to their virtue and character, not suffering them to hear, or receive, or so much as to apprehend any thing that was unbecoming. So that they seemed rather lodged in some temple, or some holy virgin chambers, where they enjoyed their privacy sacred and uninterrupted, than in the camp of an enemy. Nevertheless Darius's wife was accounted the most beautiful princess then living, as her husband the tallest and handsomest man of his time, and the

daughters were not unworthy of their parents. But
Alexander, esteeming it more kingly to govern
himself than to conquer his enemies, sought no
intimacy with any one of them, nor indeed with
any other woman before marriage, except Barsine,
Memnon's widow, who was taken prisoner at Damascus. She had been instructed in the Grecian learning, was of a gentle temper, and, by her father
Artabazus, royally descended, which good qualities,
added to the solicitations and encouragement of
Parmenio, as Aristobulus tells us, made him the
more willing to attach himself to so agreeable and
illustrious a woman. Of the rest of the female
captives, though remarkably handsome and well
proportioned, he took no further notice than to say
jestingly, that Persian women were terrible eyesores. And he himself, retaliating, as it were, by the
display of the beauty of his own temperance and
self-control, bade them be removed, as he would
have done so many lifeless images. When Philoxenus,
his lieutenant on the sea-coast, wrote to him to know
if he would buy two young boys, of great beauty,
whom one Theodorus, a Tarentine, had to sell, he
was so offended, that he often expostulated with
his friends, what baseness Philoxenus had ever
observed in him, that he should presume to make
him such a reproachful offer. And he immediately
wrote him a very sharp letter, telling him Theodorus
and his merchandise might go with his good-will
to destruction. Nor was he less severe to Hagnon,
who sent him word he would buy a Corinthian youth
named Crobylus, as a present for him. And hearing
that Damon and Timotheus, two of Parmenio's
Macedonian soldiers, had abused the wives of some
strangers who were in his pay, he wrote to Parmenio, charging him strictly, if he found them guilty,

to put them to death, as wild beasts that were only made for the mischief of mankind. In the same letter he added, that he had not so much as seen or desired to see the wife of Darius, no, nor suffered anybody to speak of her beauty before him. He was wont to say, that sleep and the act of generation chiefly made him sensible that he was mortal; as much as to say, that weariness and pleasure proceed both from the same frailty and imbecility of human nature.

In his diet, also, he was most temperate, as appears, omitting many other circumstances, by what he said to Ada, whom he adopted, with the title of mother, and afterwards created queen of Caria. For when she out of kindness sent him every day many curious dishes, and sweetmeats, and would have furnished him with some cooks and pastry-men, who were thought to have great skill, he told her he wanted none of them, his preceptor, Leonidas, having already given him the best, which were a night march to prepare for breakfast, and a moderate breakfast to create an appetite for supper. Leonidas also, he added, used to open and search the furniture of his chamber, and his wardrobe, to see if his mother had left him any thing that was delicate or superfluous. He was much less addicted to wine than was generally believed; that which gave people occasion to think so of him was, that when he had nothing else to do, he loved to sit long and talk, rather than drink, and over every cup hold a long conversation. For when his affairs called upon him, he would not be detained, as other generals often were, either by wine, or sleep, nuptial solemnities, spectacles, or any other diversion whatsoever; a convincing argument of which is, that in the short time he lived, he accomplished so many and so great actions. When he was free from employment, after he was up, and had sacrificed to the gods, he used to sit down to breakfast, and then spend the rest of the day in hunting, or writing memoirs, giving decisions on some military questions, or reading. In marches that required no great haste, he would practise shooting as he went along, or to mount a chariot, and alight from it in full speed. Sometimes, for sport's sake, as his journals tell us, he would hunt foxes and go fowling. When he came in for the evening, after he had bathed and was anointed, he would call for his bakers and chief cooks, to know if they had his dinner ready. He never cared to dine till it was pretty late and beginning to be dark, and was wonderfully circumspect at meals that every one who sat with him should be served alike and with proper attention; and his love of talking, as was said before, made him delight to sit long at his wine. And then, though otherwise no prince's conversation was ever so agreeable, he would fall into a temper of ostentation and soldierly boasting, which gave his flatterers a great advantage to ride him, and made his better friends very uneasy. For though they thought it too base to strive who should flatter him most, yet they found it hazardous not to do it; so that between the shame and the danger, they were in a great strait how to behave themselves. After such an entertainment, he was wont to bathe, and then perhaps he would sleep till noon, and sometimes all day long. He was so very temperate in his eating, that when any rare fish or fruits were sent him, he would distribute them among his friends, and often reserve nothing for himself. His table, however, was always magnificent, the expense of it still increasing with his good fortune, till it amounted to ten thousand drachmas

ALEXANDER 211

a day, to which sum he limited it, and beyond this he would suffer none to lay out in any entertainment where he himself was the guest.

After the battle of Issus, he sent to Damascus to seize upon the money and baggage, the wives and children of the Persians, of which spoil the Thessalian horsemen had the greatest share; for he had taken particular notice of their gallantry in the fight, and sent them thither on purpose to make their reward suitable to their courage. Not but that the rest of the army had so considerable a part of the booty as was sufficient to enrich them all. This first gave the Macedonians such a taste of the Persian wealth and women and barbaric splendor of living, that they were ready to pursue and follow upon it with all the eagerness of hounds upon a scent. But Alexander, before he proceeded any further, thought it necessary to assure himself of the sea-coast.[15] Those who governed in Cyprus, put that island into his possession, and Phœnicia, Tyre only excepted, was surrendered to him. During the siege of this city, which with mounds of earth cast up, and battering engines, and two hundred galleys by sea, was carried on for seven months together, he dreamt that he saw Hercules upon the walls, reaching out his hands, and calling to him. And many of the Tyrians in their sleep, fancied that Apollo told them he was displeased with their actions, and was about to leave them and go over to Alexander. Upon which, as if the god had been a deserting soldier, they seized him, so to say, in the

---

[15] Until the Phœnician cities were reduced, the Persian fleet would continue to be superior at sea and to interrupt his communications with Greece and Macedonia, and make every thing unsafe in his rear.

act, tied down the statue with ropes, and nailed it to the pedestal, reproaching him, that he was a favorer of Alexander. Another time, Alexander dreamed he saw a Satyr mocking him at a distance, and when he endeavored to catch him, he still escaped from him, till at last with much perseverance and running about after him, he got him into his power. The soothsayers making two words of *Satyrus*,[16] assured him, that Tyre should be his own. The inhabitants at this time show a spring of water, near which they say Alexander slept, when he fancied the Satyr appeared to him.

While the body of the army lay before Tyre, he made an excursion against the Arabians who inhabit the Mount Antilibanus, in which he hazarded his life extremely to bring off his master Lysimachus, who would needs go along with him, declaring he was neither older nor inferior in courage to Phœnix, Achilles's guardian. For when, quitting their horses, they began to march up the hills on foot, the rest of the soldiers outwent them a great deal, so that night drawing on, and the enemy near, Alexander was fain to stay behind so long, to encourage and help up the lagging and tired old man, that before he was aware, he was left behind, a great way from his soldiers, with a slender attendance, and forced to pass an extremely cold night, in the dark, and in a very inconvenient place; till seeing a great many scattered fires of the enemy at some distance, and trusting to his agility of body, and as he was always wont by undergoing toils and labors himself to cheer and support the Macedonians in any distress, he ran straight to one of the nearest fires, and with his dagger despatching two of the bar-

---

[16] Satyrus or Saturos, a Satyr; Sa Turos, *Thine* shall be *Tyre*.

barians that sat by it, snatched up a lighted brand, and returned with it to his own men. They immediately made a great fire, which so alarmed the enemy that most of them fled, and those that assaulted them were soon routed, and thus they rested securely the remainder of the night. Thus Chares writes.

But to return to the siege, it had this issue. Alexander, that he might refresh his army, harassed with many former encounters, had led only a small party towards the walls, rather to keep the enemy busy, than with any prospect of much advantage. It happened at this time that Aristander, the soothsayer, after he had sacrificed, upon view of the entrails, affirmed confidently to those who stood by, that the city should be certainly taken that very month, upon which there was a laugh and some mockery among the soldiers, as this was the last day of it. The king seeing him in perplexity, and always anxious to support the credit of the predictions, gave order that they should not count it as the thirtieth, but as the twenty-third of the month, and ordering the trumpets to sound, attacked the walls more seriously than he at first intended. The sharpness of the assault so inflamed the rest of his forces who were left in the camp, that they could not hold from advancing to second it, which they performed with so much vigor, that the Tyrians retired, and the town was carried that very day. The next place he sat down before was Gaza, one of the largest cities of Syria, where this accident befell him. A large bird flying over him, let a clod of earth fall upon his shoulder, and then settling upon one of the battering engines, was suddenly entangled and caught in the nets composed of sinews, which protected the ropes with which the machine was managed. This fell out exactly according to Aristander's prediction, which was, that Alexander should be wounded, and the city reduced.

From hence he sent great part of the spoils to Olympias, Cleopatra, and the rest of his friends, not omitting his preceptor Leonidas, on whom he bestowed five hundred talents weight of frankincense, and an hundred of myrrh, in remembrance of the hopes he had once expressed of him when he was but a child. For Leonidas, it seems, standing by him one day while he was sacrificing, and seeing him take both his hands full of incense to throw into the fire, told him it became him to be more sparing in his offerings, and not be so profuse till he was master of the countries which those sweet gums and spices came from. So Alexander now wrote to him, saying, "We have sent you abundance of myrrh and frankincense, that for the future you may not be stingy to the gods." Among the treasures and other booty that was taken from Darius, there was a very precious casket, which being brought to Alexander for a great rarity, he asked those about him what they thought fittest to be laid up in it; and when they had delivered their various opinions, he told them he should keep Homer's Iliad in it. This is attested by many credible authors, and if what those of Alexandria tell us, relying upon the authority of Heraclides, be true, Homer was neither an idle, nor an unprofitable companion to him in his expedition. For when he was master of Egypt, designing to settle a colony of Grecians there, he resolved to build a large and populous city, and give it his own name. In order to which, after he had measured and staked out the ground with the advice of the best architects, he chanced one night in his sleep to see a wonderful vision; a grey-headed old man, of a venerable aspect, appeared to stand by him, and pronounce these verses:—

> An island lies, where loud the billows roar,
> Pharos they call it, on the Egyptian shore.[17]

Alexander upon this immediately rose up and went to Pharos, which, at that time, was an island lying a little above the Canobic mouth of the river Nile, though it has now been joined to the main land by a mole. As soon as he saw the commodious situation of the place, it being a long neck of land, stretching like an isthmus between large lagoons and shallow waters on one side, and the sea on the other, the latter at the end of it making a spacious harbor, he said, Homer, besides his other excellences, was a very good architect, and ordered the plan of a city to be drawn out answerable to the place. To do which, for want of chalk, the soil being black, they laid out their lines with flour, taking in a pretty large compass of ground in a semicircular figure, and drawing into the inside of the circumference equal straight lines from each end, thus giving it something of the form of a cloak or cape. While he was pleasing himself with his design, on a sudden an infinite number of great birds of several kinds, rising like a black cloud out of the river and the lake, devoured every morsel of the flour that had been used in setting out the lines; at which omen even Alexander himself was troubled, till the augurs restored his confidence again by telling him, it was

---

[17] *An island lies where loud the billows roar* is from Menelaus's story of his return from Troy, told by him to Telemachus at Sparta in the fourth Odyssey (354). *A neck of land* would be better, *a strip* (it is literally *a ribbon*) *of land*.

a sign the city he was about to build would not only abound in all things within itself, but also be the nurse and feeder of many nations. He commanded the workmen to proceed, while he went to visit the temple of Ammon.

This was a long and painful, and in two respects, a dangerous journey; first, if they should lose their provision of water, as for several days none could be obtained; and, secondly, if a violent south wind should rise upon them, while they were travelling through the wide extent of deep sands, as it is said to have done when Cambyses led his army that way, blowing the sand together in heaps, and raising, as it were, the whole desert like a sea upon them, till fifty thousand were swallowed up and destroyed by it. All these difficulties were weighed and represented to him; but Alexander was not easily to be diverted from any thing he was bent upon. For fortune having hitherto seconded him in his designs, made him resolute and firm in his opinions, and the boldness of his temper raised a sort of passion in him for surmounting difficulties; as if it were not enough to be always victorious in the field, unless places and seasons and nature herself submitted to him. In this journey, the relief and assistance the gods afforded him in his distresses, were more remarkable, and obtained greater belief than the oracles he received afterwards, which, however, were valued and credited the more on account of those occurrences. For first, plentiful rains that fell, preserved them from any fear of perishing by drought, and, allaying the extreme dryness of the sand, which now became moist and firm to travel on, cleared and purified the air. Besides this, when they were out of their way, and were wandering

up and down, because the marks which were wont to
direct the guides were disordered and lost, they
were set right again by some ravens, which flew
before them when on their march, and waited for
them when they lingered and fell behind; and the
greatest miracle, as Callisthenes tells us, was that if
any of the company went astray in the night they
never ceased croaking and making a noise, till by
that means they had brought them into the right
way again. Having passed through the wilderness,
they came to the place where the high-priest [18] at
the first salutation bade Alexander welcome from
his father Ammon. And being asked by him
whether any of his father's murderers had escaped
punishment, he charged him to speak with more
respect, since his was not a mortal father. Then
Alexander, changing his expression, desired to know
of him if any of those who murdered Philip were
yet unpunished, and further concerning dominion,
whether the empire of the world was reserved for
him? This, the god answered, he should obtain,
and that Philip's death was fully revenged, which
gave him so much satisfaction, that he made splendid offerings to Jupiter, and gave the priests very
rich presents. This is what most authors write concerning the oracles. But Alexander, in a letter to
his mother, tells her there were some secret answers,
which at his return he would communicate to her
only. Others say that the priest, desirous as a
piece of courtesy to address him in Greek, "O Pai-

---

[18] Literally the *Prophet,* but the word in English naturally
implies a power of prediction possessed by the individual himself; whereas the Greek *prophetes,* which would not be used in
our sense, means merely an utterer of words placed, as it were,
in his mouth by the direct act of a divinity.

dion," [19] by a slip in pronunciation ended with the *s* instead of the *n*, and said, " O Paidios," which mistake Alexander was well enough pleased with, and it went for current that the oracle had called him so.

Among the sayings of one Psammon, a philosopher, whom he heard in Egypt, he most approved of this, that all men are governed by God, because in every thing, that which is chief and commands, is divine. But what he pronounced himself upon this subject, was even more like a philosopher, for he said, God was the common father of us all, but more particularly of the best of us. To the barbarians he carried himself very haughtily, as if he were fully persuaded of his divine birth and parentage; but to the Grecians more moderately, and with less affectation of divinity, except it were once in writing to the Athenians about Samos, when he tells them that he should not himself have bestowed upon them that free and glorious city; " You received it," he says, " from the bounty of him who at that time was called my lord and father," meaning Philip. However, afterwards being wounded with an arrow, and feeling much pain, he turned to those about him, and told them, " This, my friends, is real flowing blood, not Ichor,[20]

' Such as immortal gods are wont to shed.' "

And another time, when it thundered so much that everybody was afraid, and Anaxarchus, the sophist, asked him if he who was Jupiter's son could do any

---

[19] O Paidion, O my son, O Pai Dios, O Son of Jupiter.

[20] *Ichor, such as immortal gods are wont to shed,* flows from the wounded hand of Venus (*Iliad V.,* 340).

thing like this, "Nay," said Alexander, laughing, "I have no desire to be formidable to my friends, as you would have me, who despised my table for being furnished with fish, and not with the heads of governors of provinces." For in fact it is related as true, that Anaxarchus seeing a present of small fishes, which the king sent to Hephæstion, had used this expression, in a sort of irony, and disparagement of those who undergo vast labors and encounter great hazards in pursuit of magnificent objects, which after all bring them little more pleasure or enjoyment than what others have. From what I have said upon this subject, it is apparent that Alexander in himself was not foolishly affected, or had the vanity to think himself really a god, but merely used his claims to divinity as a means of maintaining among other people the sense of his superiority.

At his return out of Egypt into Phœnicia, he sacrificed and made solemn processions, to which were added shows of lyric dances and tragedies, remarkable not merely for the splendor of the equipage and decorations, but for the competition among those who exhibited them. For the kings of Cyprus were here the exhibitors,[21] just in the same manner as at Athens those who are chosen by lot out of the tribes. And, indeed, they showed the greatest emulation to outvie each other; especially Nicocreon, king of Salamis, and Pasicrates

---

[21] In Greek, *choragi* or chorus-masters; the chorus or musical part being always regarded as the basis of the play. To pay the expenses of a dramatic exhibition at the festivals, was one of the public duties expected of every wealthier citizen. It was regarded as an opportunity for displaying munificence, and there was accordingly much competition.

of Soli, who furnished the chorus, and defrayed the expenses of the two most celebrated actors, Athenodorus and Thessalus, the former performing for Pasicrates, and the latter for Nicocreon. Thessalus was most favored by Alexander, though it did not appear till Athenodorus was declared victor by the plurality of votes. For then at his going away, he said the judges deserved to be commended for what they had done, but that he would willingly have lost part of his kingdom, rather than to have seen Thessalus overcome. However, when he understood Athenodorus was fined by the Athenians for being absent at the festivals of Bacchus, though he refused his request that he would write a letter in his behalf, he gave him a sufficient sum to satisfy the penalty. Another time, when Lycon of Scarphia happened to act with great applause in the theatre, and in a verse which he introduced into the comic part which he was acting, begged for a present of ten talents, he laughed and gave him the money.

Darius wrote him a letter, and sent friends to intercede with him, requesting him to accept as a ransom of his captives the sum of a thousand talents, and offering him in exchange for his amity and alliance, all the countries on this side the river Euphrates, together with one of his daughters in marriage. These propositions he communicated to his friends, and when Parmenio told him, that for his part, if he were Alexander, he should readily embrace them, "So would I," said Alexander, "if I were Parmenio." Accordingly, his answer to Darius was, that if he would come and yield himself up into his power, he would treat him with all possible kindness; if not, he was resolved immediately to go himself and seek him. But the death of Darius's wife in childbirth made him soon after regret one part of this answer, and he showed evident marks of grief, at being thus deprived of a further opportunity of exercising his clemency and good nature, which he manifested, however, as far as he could, by giving her a most sumptuous funeral.

Among the eunuchs who waited in the queen's chamber, and were taken prisoners with the women, there was one Tireus, who getting out of the camp, fled away on horseback to Darius, to inform him of his wife's death. He, when he heard it, beating his head, and bursting into tears and lamentations, said, "Alas! how great is the calamity of the Persians! Was it not enough that their king's consort and sister was a prisoner in her lifetime, but she must, now she is dead also, be but meanly and obscurely buried?" "Oh king," replied the eunuch, "as to her funeral rites, or any respect or honor that should have been shown in them, you have not the least reason to accuse the ill-fortune of your country; for to my knowledge neither your queen Statira when alive, nor your mother, nor children, wanted any thing of their former happy condition, unless it were the light of your countenance, which I doubt not but the lord Oromasdes will yet restore to its former glory. And after her decease, I assure you, she had not only all due funeral ornaments, but was honored also with the tears of your very enemies; for Alexander is as gentle after victory, as he is terrible in the field." At the hearing of these words, such was the grief and emotion of Darius's mind, that they carried him into extravagant suspicions; and taking Tireus aside into a more private part of his tent, "Unless thou likewise," said he to him, "hast deserted me, together with the good fortune of Persia, and art become a Macedonian in thy heart; if thou yet ownest me for thy master Darius, tell me, I charge thee, by the veneration thou payest the light of Mithras, and this right hand of thy king, do I not lament the least of Statira's misfortunes in her captivity and death? Have I not suffered something more injurious and deplorable in her lifetime? And had I not been miserable with less dishonor, if I had met with a more severe and inhuman enemy? For how is it possible a young man as he is, should treat the wife of his opponent with so much distinction, were it not from some motive that does me disgrace?" Whilst he was yet speaking, Tierus threw himself at his feet, and besought him neither to wrong Alexander so much, nor his dead wife and sister, as to give utterance to any such thoughts, which deprived him of the greatest consolation left him in his adversity, the belief that he was overcome by a man whose virtues raised him above human nature; that he ought to look upon Alexander with love and admiration, who had given no less proofs of his continence towards the Persian women, than of his valor among the men. The eunuch confirmed all he said with solemn and dreadful oaths, and was further enlarging upon Alexander's moderation and magnanimity on other occasions, when Darius, breaking away from him into the other division of the tent, where his friends and courtiers were, lifted up his hands to heaven, and uttered this prayer, "Ye gods," said he, " of my family, and of my kingdom, if it be possible, I beseech you to restore the declining affairs of Persia, that I may leave them in as flourishing a condition as I found them, and have it in my power to make a grateful return to Alexander for the kindness which in my adversity he has shown to those who are dearest to me. But if, indeed, the fatal time be come, which is to give a period to the Persian monarchy, if our ruin be a debt that must be paid to the divine jealousy and the vicissitude of things, then I beseech you grant that no other man but Alexander may sit upon the throne of Cyrus." Such is the narrative given by the greater number of the historians.

But to return to Alexander. After he had reduced all Asia on this side the Euphrates, he advanced towards Darius, who was coming down against him with a million of men. In his march, a very ridiculous passage happened. The servants who followed the camp, for sport's sake divided themselves into two parties, and named the commander of one of them Alexander, and of the other Darius. At first they only pelted one another with clods of earth, but presently took to their fists, and at last, heated with the contention, they fought in good earnest with stones and clubs, so that they had much ado to part them; till Alexander, upon hearing of it, ordered the two captains to decide the quarrel by single combat, and armed him who bore his name himself, while Philotas did the same to him who represented Darius. The whole army were spectators of this encounter, willing from the event of it to derive an omen of their own future success. After they had fought stoutly a pretty long while, at last he who was called Alexander had the better, and for a reward of his prowess, had twelve villages given him, with leave to wear the Persian dress. So we are told by Eratosthenes.

But the great battle of all that was fought with Darius, was not, as most writers tell us, at Arbela, but at Gaugamela, which, in their language, signifies the camel's house, forasmuch as one of their ancient kings having escaped the pursuit of his enemies on a swift camel, in gratitude to his beast, settled him at this place, with an allowance of certain villages and rents for his maintenance. It came to pass that in the month Boëdromion, about the beginning of the feast of Mysteries at Athens, there was an eclipse of the moon, the eleventh night after which, the two armies being now in view of one another, Darius kept his men in arms, and by torchlight took a general review of them. But Alexander, while his soldiers slept, spent the night before his tent with his diviner Aristander, performing certain mysterious ceremonies, and sacrificing to the god Fear. In the mean while the oldest of his commanders, and chiefly Parmenio, when they beheld all the plain between Niphates and the Gordæan mountains shining with the lights and fires which were made by the barbarians, and heard the uncertain and confused sound of voices out of their camp, like the distant roaring of a vast ocean, were so amazed at the thoughts of such a multitude, that after some conference among themselves, they concluded it an enterprise too difficult and hazardous for them to engage so numerous an enemy in the day, and therefore meeting the king as he came from sacrificing, besought him to attack Darius by night, that the darkness might conceal the danger of the ensuing battle. To this he gave them the celebrated answer, "I will not steal a victory," which though some at the time thought a boyish and inconsiderate speech, as if he played with danger, others, however, regarded as an evidence that he confided in his present condition, and acted on a true judgment of the future, not wishing to leave

Darius, in case he were worsted, the pretext of trying his fortune again, which he might suppose himself to have, if he could impute his overthrow to the disadvantage of the night, as he did before to the mountains, the narrow passages, and the sea. For while he had such numerous forces and large dominions still remaining, it was not any want of men or arms that could induce him to give up the war, but only the loss of all courage and hope upon the conviction of an undeniable and manifest defeat.

After they were gone from him with this answer, he laid himself down in his tent and slept the rest of the night more soundly than was usual with him, to the astonishment of the commanders, who came to him early in the morning, and were fain themselves to give order that the soldiers should breakfast. But at last, time not giving them leave to wait any longer, Parmenio went to his bedside, and called him twice or thrice by his name, till he waked him, and then asked him how it was possible, when he was to fight the most important battle of all, he could sleep as soundly as if he were already victorious. "And are we not so, indeed," replied Alexander, smiling, "since we are at last relieved from the trouble of wandering in pursuit of Darius through a wide and wasted country, hoping in vain that he would fight us?" And not only before the battle, but in the height of the danger, he showed himself great, and manifested the self-possession of a just foresight and confidence. For the battle for some time fluctuated and was dubious. The left wing, where Parmenio commanded, was so impetuously charged by the Bactrian horse that it was disordered and forced to give ground, at the same time that Mazæus had sent a detachment round about to fall upon those who guarded the baggage, which so disturbed Parmenio, that he sent messengers to acquaint Alexander that the camp and baggage would be all lost unless he immediately relieved the rear by a considerable reinforcement drawn out of the front. This message being brought him just as he was giving the signal to those about him for the onset, he bade them tell Parmenio that he must have surely lost the use of his reason, and had forgotten, in his alarm, that soldiers, if victorious, become masters of their enemies' baggage; and if defeated, instead of taking care of their wealth or their slaves, have nothing more to do but to fight gallantly and die with honor. When he had said this, he put on his helmet, having the rest of his arms on before he came out of his tent, which were a coat of the Sicilian make, girt close about him, and over that a breastpiece of thickly quilted linen, which was taken among other booty at the battle of Issus. The helmet, which was made by Theophilus, though of iron, was so well wrought and polished, that it was as bright as the most refined silver. To this was fitted a gorget of the same metal, set with precious stones. His sword, which was the weapon he most used in fight, was given him by the king of the Citieans, and was of an admirable temper and lightness. The belt which he also wore in all engagements, was of much richer workmanship than the rest of his armor. It was a work of the ancient Helicon, and had been presented to him by the Rhodians, as a mark of their respect to him. So long as he was engaged in drawing up his men, or riding about to give orders or directions, or to view them, he spared Bucephalas, who was now growing old, and made use of another horse; but when he was actually to fight, he sent for him again, and as soon as he was mounted, commenced the attack.

He made the longest address that day to the Thessalians and other Greeks, who answered him with loud shouts, desiring him to lead them on against the barbarians, upon which he shifted his javelin into his left hand, and with his right lifted up towards heaven, besought the gods, as Callisthenes tells us, that if he was of a truth the son of Jupiter, they would be pleased to assist and strengthen the Grecians. At the same time the augur Aristander, who had a white mantle about him, and a crown of gold on his head, rode by and showed them an eagle that soared just over Alexander, and directed his flight towards the enemy; which so animated the beholders, that after mutual encouragements and exhortations, the horse charged at full speed, and were followed in a mass by the whole phalanx of the foot. But before they could well come to blows with the first ranks, the barbarians shrunk back, and were hotly pursued by Alexander, who drove those that fled before him into the middle of the battle, where Darius himself was in person, whom he saw from a distance over the foremost ranks, conspicuous in the midst of his life-guard, a tall and fine-looking man, drawn in a lofty chariot, defended by an abundance of the best horse, who stood close in order about it, ready to receive the enemy. But Alexander's approach was so terrible, forcing those who gave back upon those who yet maintained their ground, that he beat down and dispersed them almost all. Only a few of the bravest and valiantest opposed the pursuit, who were slain in their king's presence, falling in heaps upon one another, and in the very pangs of death striving to catch hold of the horses. Darius now seeing all was lost, that those who were placed in front to defend him were broken and beat back upon him, that he could not turn or disengage his chariot without great difficulty, the wheels being clogged and entangled among the dead bodies, which lay in such heaps as not only stopped, but almost covered the horses, and made them rear and grow so unruly, that the frighted charioteer could govern them no longer, in this extremity was glad to quit his chariot and his arms, and mounting, it is said, upon a mare that had been taken from her foal, betook himself to flight. But he had not escaped so either, if Parmenio had not sent fresh messengers to Alexander, to desire him to return and assist him against a considerable body of the enemy which yet stood together, and would not give ground. For, indeed, Parmenio is on all hands accused of having been sluggish and unserviceable in this battle, whether age had impaired his courage, or that, as Callisthenes says, he secretly disliked and envied Alexander's growing greatness. Alexander, though he was not a little vexed to be so recalled and hindered from pursuing his victory, yet concealed the true reason from his men, and causing a retreat to be sounded, as if it were too late to continue the execution any longer, marched back towards the place of danger, and by the way met with the news of the enemy's total overthrow and flight.

This battle being thus over, seemed to put a period to the Persian empire; and Alexander, who was now proclaimed king of Asia, returned thanks to the gods in magnificent sacrifices, and rewarded his friends and followers with great sums of money, and places, and governments of provinces. And eager to gain honor with the Grecians, he wrote to them that he would have all tyrannies abolished, that they might live free according to their own laws, and specially to the Plataeans, that their city should be rebuilt, because their ancestors had permitted their countrymen of old to make their territory the seat of the war, when they fought with the barbarians for their common liberty. He sent also part of the spoils into Italy, to the Crotoniats, to honor the zeal and courage of their citizen Phayllus, the wrestler, who, in the Median war, when the other Grecian colonies in Italy disowned Greece, that he might have a share in the danger, joined the fleet at Salamis, with a vessel set forth at his own charge. So affectionate was Alexander to all kind of virtue, and so desirous to preserve the memory of laudable actions.

From hence he marched through the province of Babylon, which immediately submitted to him, and in Ecbatana [22] was much surprised at the sight of the place where fire issues in a continuous stream, like a spring of water, out of a cleft in the earth, and the stream of naphtha, which, not far from this spot, flows out so abundantly as to form a sort of lake. This naphtha, in other respects resembling bitumen, is so subject to take fire, that before it touches the flame, it will kindle at the very light that surrounds it, and often inflame the intermediate air also. The barbarians, to show the power and nature of it, sprinkled the street that led to the king's lodgings with little drops of it, and when it was almost night, stood at the further end with torches, which being applied to the moistened places, the

---

[22] "In Ecbatana," should probably be omitted. Nothing is known of any Ecbatana in the province of Babylon, and Ecbatana, the capital of Media, was not reached by Alexander till long after this. Darius had retreated to it. A spot corresponding to the description is mentioned in the neighborhood of Arbela.

first at once taking fire, instantly, as quick as a man could think of it, it caught from one end to another, in such a manner that the whole street was one continued flame. Among those who used to wait on the king and find occasion to amuse him when he anointed and washed himself, there was one Athenophanes, an Athenian, who desired him to make an experiment of the naphtha upon Stephanus, who stood by in the bathing place, a youth with a ridiculously ugly face, whose talent was singing well, "For," said he, "if it take hold of him and is not put out, it must undeniably be allowed to be of the most invincible strength." The youth, as it happened, readily consented to undergo the trial, and as soon as he was anointed and rubbed with it, his whole body broke out into such a flame, and was so seized by the fire, that Alexander was in the greatest perplexity and alarm for him, and not without reason; for nothing could have prevented his being consumed by it, if by good chance there had not been people at hand with a great many vessels of water for the service of the bath, with all which they had much ado to extinguish the fire; and his body was so burned all over, that he was not cured of it a good while after. And thus it is not without some plausibility that they endeavor to reconcile the fable to truth, who say this was the drug in the tragedies with which Medea anointed the crown and veil which she gave to Creon's daughter. For neither the things themselves, nor the fire could kindle of its own accord, but being prepared for it by the naphtha, they imperceptibly attracted and caught a flame which happened to be brought near them. For the rays and emanations of fire at a distance have no other effect upon some bodies than bare light and heat, but in others, where they meet with airy dryness, and also sufficient rich moisture, they collect themselves and soon kindle and create a transformation. The manner, however, of the production of naphtha admits of a diversity of opinion [23] . . . . . . or whether this liquid substance that feeds the flame does not rather proceed from a soil that is unctuous and productive of fire, as that of the province of Babylon is, where the ground is so very hot, that oftentimes the grains of barley leap up, and are thrown out, as if the violent inflammation had made the earth throb; and in the extreme heats the inhabitants are wont to sleep upon skins filled with water. Harpalus, who was left governor of this country, and was desirous to adorn the palace gardens and walks with Grecian plants, succeeded in raising all but ivy, which the earth would not bear, but constantly killed. For being a plant that loves a cold soil, the temper of this hot and fiery earth was improper for it. But such digressions as these the impatient reader will be more willing to pardon, if they are kept within a moderate compass.

At the taking of Susa, Alexander found in the palace forty thousand talents in money ready coined, besides an unspeakable quantity of other furniture and treasure; amongst which was five thousand talents' worth of Hermionian purple, that had been laid up there an hundred and ninety years, and yet kept its color as fresh and lively as at first. The reason of which, they say, is that in dyeing the purple they made use of honey, and of white oil in the white tincture, both which after the like space of time preserve the clearness and brightness of their lustre. Dinon also relates that the Persian kings had water fetched from the Nile and the Danube, which they

[23] Some words have here been lost out of the text.

laid up in their treasuries as a sort of testimony of the greatness of their power and universal empire.

The entrance into Persia [24] was through a most difficult country, and was guarded by the noblest of the Persians, Darius himself having escaped further. Alexander, however, chanced to find a guide in exact correspondence with what the Pythia had foretold when he was a child, that a lycus [25] should conduct him into Persia. For by such an one, whose father was a Lycian, and his mother a Persian, and who spoke both languages, he was now led into the country, by a way something about, yet without fetching any considerable compass. Here a great many of the prisoners were put to the sword, of which himself gives this account, that he commanded them to be killed in the belief that it would be for his advantage. Nor was the money found here less, he says, than at Susa, besides other movables and treasure, as much as ten thousand pair of mules and five thousand camels could well carry away. Amongst other things he happened to observe a large statue of Xerxes thrown carelessly down to the ground in the confusion made by the multitude of soldiers pressing into the palace. He stood still, and accosting it as if it had been alive, "Shall we," said he, "neglectfully pass thee by, now thou art prostrate on the ground, because thou once invadedst Greece, or shall we erect thee again in consideration of the greatness of thy mind and thy other virtues?" But at last, after he had paused some time, and silently considered with himself, he went on without taking any further notice of it. In this place he took up his winter quarters,

---

[24] The district of Persia proper, or Persis; Farsistan.
[25] *Lycus* being indifferently a *wolf* or a man of *Lycia*.

and stayed four months to refresh his soldiers. It is related that the first time he sat on the royal throne of Persia, under the canopy of gold, Demaratus, the Corinthian, who was much attached to him and had been one of his father's friends, wept, in an old man's manner, and deplored the misfortune of those Greeks whom death had deprived of the satisfaction of seeing Alexander seated on the throne of Darius.

From hence designing to march against Darius, before he set out, he diverted himself with his officers at an entertainment of drinking and other pastimes, and indulged so far as to let every one's mistress sit by and drink with them. The most celebrated of them was Thais, an Athenian, mistress of Ptolemy, who was afterwards king of Egypt. She, partly as a sort of well-turned compliment to Alexander, partly out of sport, as the drinking went on, at last was carried so far as to utter a saying, not misbecoming her native country's character, though somewhat too lofty for her own condition. She said it was indeed some recompense for the toils she had undergone in following the camp all over Asia, that she was that day treated in, and could insult over, the stately palace of the Persian monarchs. But, she added, it would please her much better, if while the king looked on, she might in sport, with her own hands, set fire to the court of that Xerxes who reduced the city of Athens to ashes, that it might be recorded to posterity, that the women who followed Alexander had taken a severer revenge on the Persians for the sufferings and affronts of Greece, than all the famed commanders had been able to do by sea or land. What she said was received with such universal liking and murmurs of applause, and so seconded by the encouragement and eagerness of the company, that the king himself, persuaded to be of the party, started from his seat, and with a chaplet of flowers on his head, and a lighted torch in his hand, led them the way, while they went after him in a riotous manner dancing and making loud cries about the place; which when the rest of the Macedonians perceived, they also in great delight ran thither with torches; for they hoped the burning and destruction of the royal palace was an argument that he looked homeward, and had no design to reside among the barbarians. Thus some writers give their account of this action, while others say it was done deliberately; however, all agree that he soon repented of it, and gave order to put out the fire.

Alexander was naturally most munificent, and grew more so as his fortune increased, accompanying what he gave with that courtesy and freedom, which, to speak truth, is necessary to make a benefit really obliging. I will give a few instances of this kind. Ariston, the captain of the Pæonians, having killed an enemy, brought his head to show him, and told him that in his country, such a present was recompensed with a cup of gold. "With an empty one," said Alexander, smiling, "but I drink to you in this, which I give you full of wine." Another time, as one of the common soldiers was driving a mule laden with some of the king's treasure, the beast grew tired, and the soldier took it upon his own back, and began to march with it, till Alexander seeing the man so overcharged, asked what was the matter; and when he was informed, just as he was ready to lay down his burden for weariness, "Do not faint now," said he to him, "but finish the journey, and carry what you have there to your own tent for yourself." He was always more displeased with those who would not accept of what he gave than with those who begged of him. And therefore he wrote to Phocion, that he would not own him for his friend any longer, if he refused his presents. He had never given any thing to Serapion, one of the youths that played at ball with him, because he did not ask of him, till one day, it coming to Serapion's turn to play, he still threw the ball to others, and when the king asked him why he did not direct it to him, "Because you do not ask for it," said he; which answer pleased him so, that he was very liberal to him afterwards. One Proteas, a pleasant, jesting, drinking fellow, having incurred his displeasure, got his friends to intercede for him, and begged his pardon himself with tears, which at last prevailed, and Alexander declared he was friends with him. "I cannot believe it," said Proteas, "unless you first give me some pledge of it." The king understood his meaning, and presently ordered five talents to be given him. How magnificent he was in enriching his friends, and those who attended on his person, appears by a letter which Olympias wrote to him, where she tells him he should reward and honor those about him in a more moderate way, "For now," said she, "you make them all equal to kings, you give them power and opportunity of making many friends of their own, and in the mean time you leave yourself destitute." She often wrote to him to this purpose, and he never communicated her letters to anybody, unless it were one which he opened when Hephæstion was by, whom he permitted, as his custom was, to read it along with him; but then as soon as he had done, he took off his ring, and set the seal upon Hephæstion's lips. Mazæus, who was the most considerable man in Darius's court, had a son who was already governor of a province. Alexander bestowed another upon him that was better; he, however, modestly refused, and told him, instead of one Darius, he went the way to make many Alexanders. To Parmenio he gave Bagoas's house,[26] in which he found a wardrobe of apparel worth more than a thousand talents. He wrote to Antipater, commanding him to keep a life-guard about him for the security of his person against conspiracies. To his mother he sent many presents, but would never suffer her to meddle with matters of state or war, not indulging her busy temper, and when she fell out with him upon this account, he bore her ill-humor very patiently. Nay more, when he read a long letter from Antipater, full of accusations against her, "Antipater," he said, "does not know that one tear of a mother effaces a thousand such letters as these."

But when he perceived his favorites grow so luxurious and extravagant in their way of living and expenses, that Hagnon, the Teian, wore silver nails in his shoes, that Leonnatus employed several camels, only to bring him powder out of Egypt to use when he wrestled, and that Philotas had hunting nets a hundred furlongs in length, that more used precious ointment than plain oil when they went to bathe, and that they carried about servants everywhere with them to rub them and wait upon them in their chambers, he reproved them in gentle and reasonable terms, telling them he wondered that they who had been engaged in so many signal battles did not know by experience, that those who

---

[26] *Bagoas's house,* at Susa, is probably the sense, but the words *at Susa,* omitted in the translation, are doubtful.

labor sleep more sweetly and soundly than those who are labored for, and could fail to see by comparing the Persians' manner of living with their own, that it was the most abject and slavish condition to be voluptuous, but the most noble and royal to undergo pain and labor. He argued with them further, how it was possible for any one who pretended to be a soldier, either to look well after his horse, or to keep his armor bright and in good order, who thought it much to let his hands be serviceable to what was nearest to him, his own body. "Are you still to learn," said he, "that the end and perfection of our victories is to avoid the vices and infirmities of those whom we subdue?" And to strengthen his precepts by example, he applied himself now more vigorously than ever to hunting and warlike expeditions, embracing all opportunities of hardship and danger, insomuch that a Lacedæmonian, who was there on an embassy to him, and chanced to be by when he encountered with and mastered a huge lion, told him he had fought gallantly with the beast, which of the two should be king. Craterus caused a representation to be made of this adventure, consisting of the lion and the dogs, of the king engaged with the lion, and himself coming in to his assistance, all expressed in figures of brass, some of which were by Lysippus, and the rest by Leochares; and had it dedicated in the temple of Apollo at Delphi. Alexander exposed his person to danger in this manner, with the object both of inuring himself, and inciting others to the performance of brave and virtuous actions.

But his followers, who were grown rich, and consequently proud, longed to indulge themselves in pleasure and idleness, and were weary of marches and expeditions, and at last went on so far as to censure and speak ill of him. All which at first he bore very patiently, saying, it became a king well to do good to others, and be evil spoken of. Meantime, on the smallest occasions that called for a show of kindness to his friends, there was every indication on his part of tenderness and respect. Hearing Peucestes was bitten by a bear, he wrote to him, that he took it unkindly he should send others notice of it, and not make him acquainted with it; " But now," said he, " since it is so, let me know how you do, and whether any of your companions forsook you when you were in danger, that I may punish them." He sent Hephæstion, who was absent about some business, word how while they were fighting for their diversion with an ichneumon, Craterus was by chance run through both thighs with Perdiccas's javelin. And upon Peucestes's recovery from a fit of sickness, he sent a letter of thanks to his physician Alexippus. When Craterus was ill, he saw a vision in his sleep, after which he offered sacrifices for his health, and bade him to do so likewise. He wrote also to Pausanias, the physician, who was about to purge Craterus with hellebore, partly out of an anxious concern for him, and partly to give him a caution how he used that medicine. He was so tender of his friends' reputation that he imprisoned Ephialtes and Cissus, who brought him the first news of Harpalus's flight and withdrawal from his service, as if they had falsely accused him. When he sent the old and infirm soldiers home, Eurylochus, a citizen of Ægæ, got his name enrolled among the sick, though he ailed nothing, which being discovered, he confessed he was in love with a young woman named Telesippa, and wanted to go along with her to the seaside. Alexander inquired to whom the woman belonged, and being told she was a free courtesan, "I will assist you," said he to Eurylochus, "in your armour, if your mistress be to be gained either by presents or persuasions; but we must use no other means, because she is free-born."

It is surprising to consider upon what slight occasions he would write letters to serve his friends. As when he wrote one in which he gave order to search for a youth that belonged to Seleucus, who was run away into Cilicia; and in another, thanked and commended Peucestes for apprehending Nicon, a servant of Craterus; and in one to Megabyzus, concerning a slave that had taken sanctuary in a temple, gave direction that he should not meddle with him while he was there, but if he could entice him out by fair means, then he gave leave to seize him. It is reported of him that when he first sat in judgment upon capital causes, he would lay his hand upon one of his ears while the accuser spoke, to keep it free and unprejudiced in behalf of the party accused. But afterwards such a multitude of accusations were brought before him, and so many proved true, that he lost his tenderness of heart, and gave credit to those also that were false; and especially when anybody spoke ill of him, he would be transported out of his reason, and show himself cruel and inexorable, valuing his glory and reputation beyond his life or kingdom.

He now, as we said,[27] set forth to seek Darius, expecting he should be put to the hazard of another battle, but heard he was taken and secured by Bessus, upon which news he sent home the Thessalians, and gave them a largess of two thousand talents over and above the pay that was due to them. This long and painful pursuit of Darius, for in

[27] Above, page 233.

eleven days he marched thirty-three hundred furlongs, harassed his soldiers so that most of them were ready to give it up, chiefly for want of water. While they were in this distress, it happened that some Macedonians who had fetched water in skins upon their mules from a river they had found out, came about noon to the place where Alexander was, and seeing him almost choked with thirst, presently filled an helmet and offered it him. He asked them to whom they were carrying the water; they told him to their children, adding, that if his life were but saved, it was no matter for them, they should be able well enough to repair that loss, though they all perished. Then he took the helmet into his hands, and looking round about, when he saw all those who were near him stretching their heads out and looking earnestly after the drink, he returned it again with thanks without tasting a drop of it. "For," said he, "if I alone should drink, the rest will be out of heart." The soldiers no sooner took notice of his temperance and magnanimity upon this occasion, but they one and all cried out to him to lead them forward boldly, and began whipping on their horses. For whilst they had such a king, they said, they defied both weariness and thirst, and looked upon themselves to be little less than immortal. But though they were all equally cheerful and willing, yet not above threescore horse were able, it is said, to keep up, and to fall in with Alexander upon the enemy's camp, where they rode over abundance of gold and silver that lay scattered about, and passing by a great many chariots full of women that wandered here and there for want of drivers, they endeavored to overtake the first of those that fled, in hopes to meet with Darius among them. And at last, after much trouble, they found

ALEXANDER AT THE DEAD BODY OF DARIUS CODOMANUS

him lying in a chariot, wounded all over with darts, just at the point of death. However, he desired they would give him some drink, and when he had drunk a little cold water, he told Polystratus, who gave it him, that it had become the last extremity of his ill fortune, to receive benefits and not be able to return them. "But Alexander," said he, "whose kindness to my mother, my wife, and my children I hope the gods will recompense, will doubtless thank you for your humanity to me. Tell him, therefore, in token of my acknowledgment, I give him this right hand," with which words he took hold of Polystratus's hand and died. When Alexander came up to them, he showed manifest tokens of sorrow, and taking off his own cloak, threw it upon the body to cover it. And sometime afterwards, when Bessus was taken, he ordered him to be torn in pieces in this manner. They fastened him to a couple of trees which were bound down so as to meet, and then being let loose, with a great force returned to their places, each of them carrying that part of the body along with it that was tied to it. Darius's body was laid in state, and sent to his mother with pomp suitable to his quality. His brother Exathres, Alexander received into the number of his intimate friends.

And now with the flower of his army he marched into Hyrcania, where he saw a large bay of an open sea, apparently not much less than the Euxine, with water, however, sweeter than that of other seas, but could learn nothing of certainty concerning it, further than that in all probability it seemed to him to be an arm issuing from the lake of Mæotis. However, the naturalists were better informed of the truth, and had given an account of it many years before Alexander's expedition; that of four gulfs which out of the main sea enter into the continent, this, known indifferently as the Caspian and as the Hyrcanian sea, is the most northern. Here the barbarians, unexpectedly meeting with those who led Bucephalas, took them prisoners, and carried the horse away with them, at which Alexander was so much vexed, that he sent an herald to let them know he would put them all to the sword, men, women, and children, without mercy, if they did not restore him. But on their doing so, and at the same time surrendering their cities into his hands, he not only treated them kindly, but also paid a ransom for his horse to those who took him.

From hence he marched into Parthia, where not having much to do, he first put on the barbaric dress, perhaps with the view of making the work of civilizing them the easier, as nothing gains more upon men than a conformity to their fashions and customs. Or it may have been as a first trial, whether the Macedonians might be brought to *adore* him, as the Persians did their kings, by accustoming them by little and little to bear with the alteration of his rule and course of life in other things. However, he followed not the Median fashion, which was altogether foreign and uncouth, and adopted neither the trousers nor the sleeved vest, nor the tiara for the head, but taking a middle way between the Persian mode and the Macedonian,[28] so contrived his habit that it was not so flaunting as the one, and yet more pompous and magnificent than the other. At first he wore this habit only when he conversed with the barbarians, or within doors, among his

---

[28] Another reading is *Median;* the Median dress being the more sumptuous, and the Persian the plainer.

intimate friends and companions, but afterwards he appeared in it abroad, when he rode out, and at public audiences, a sight which the Macedonians beheld with grief; but they so respected his other virtues and good qualities that they felt it reasonable in some things to gratify his fancies and his passion of glory, in pursuit of which he hazarded himself so far, that besides his other adventures, he had but lately been wounded in the leg by an arrow, which had so shattered the shank-bone that splinters were taken out. And on another occasion he received a violent blow with a stone upon the nape of the neck, which dimmed his sight for a good while afterwards. And yet all this could not hinder him from exposing himself freely to any dangers, insomuch that he passed the river Orexartes, which he took to be the Tanais, and putting the Scythians to flight, followed them above a hundred furlongs, though suffering all the time from a diarrhœa.

Here many affirm that the Amazon came to give him a visit. So Clitarchus, Polyclitus, Onesicritus, Antigenes, and Ister, tell us. But Aristobulus and Chares, who held the office of reporter of requests, Ptolemy and Anticlides, Philon the Theban, Philip of Theangela, Hecatæus the Eretrian, Philip the Chalcidian, and Duris the Samian, say it is wholly a fiction. And truly Alexander himself seems to confirm the latter statement, for in a letter in which he gives Antipater an account of all that happened, he tells him that the king of Scythia offered him his daughter in marriage, but makes no mention at all of the Amazon. And many years after, when Onesicritus read this story in his fourth book to Lysimachus, who then reigned, the king laughed quietly and asked, " Where could I have been at that time?"

But it signifies little to Alexander whether this be credited or no. Certain it is, that apprehending the Macedonians would be weary of pursuing the war, he left the greater part of them in their quarters; and having with him in Hyrcania the choice of his men only, amounting to twenty thousand foot, and three thousand horse, he spoke to them to this effect: That hitherto the barbarians had seen them no otherwise than as it were in a dream, and if they should think of returning when they had only alarmed Asia, and not conquered it, their enemies would set upon them as upon so many women. However, he told them he would keep none of them with him against their will, they might go if they pleased; he should merely enter his protest, that when on his way to make the Macedonians the masters of the world, he was left alone with a few friends and volunteers. This is almost word for word as he wrote in a letter to Antipater, where he adds, that when he had thus spoken to them, they all cried out, they would go along with him whithersoever it was his pleasure to lead them. After succeeding with these, it was no hard matter for him to bring over the multitude, which easily followed the example of their betters. Now, also, he more and more accommodated himself in his way of living to that of the natives, and tried to bring them, also, as near as he could to the Macedonian customs, wisely considering that whilst he was engaged in an expedition which would carry him far from thence, it would be wiser to depend upon the good-will which might arise from intermixture and association as a means of maintaining tranquillity, than upon force and compulsion. In order to this, he chose out thirty thousand boys, whom he put under masters to teach them the Greek tongue, and to train them up to arms in the Macedonian discipline. As for his marriage with Roxana, whose youthfulness and beauty had charmed him at a drinking entertainment, where he first happened to see her, taking part in a dance, it was, indeed, a love affair, yet it seemed at the same time to be conducive to the object he had in hand. For it gratified the conquered people to see him choose a wife from among themselves, and it made them feel the most lively affection for him, to find that in the only passion which he, the most temperate of men, was overcome by, he yet forbore till he could obtain her in a lawful and honorable way.

Noticing, also, that among his chief friends and favorites, Hephæstion most approved all that he did, and complied with and imitated him in his change of habits, while Craterus continued strict in the observation of the customs and fashions of his own country, he made it his practice to employ the first in all transactions with the Persians, and the latter when he had to do with the Greeks or Macedonians. And in general he showed more affection for Hephæstion, and more respect for Craterus; Hephæstion, as he used to say, being Alexander's, and Craterus the king's friend. And so these two friends always bore in secret a grudge to each other, and at times quarrelled openly, so much so, that once in India they drew upon one another, and were proceeding in good earnest, with their friends on each side to second them, when Alexander rode up and publicly reproved Hephæstion, calling him fool and madman, not to be sensible that without his favor he was nothing. He rebuked Craterus, also, in private, severely, and then causing them both to come into his presence, he reconciled them, at the same time swearing by Ammon and the rest of the gods, that he loved them two above all other men, but if ever he perceived them fall out again he would be sure to put both of them to death, or at least the aggressor. After which they neither ever did or said any thing, so much as in jest, to offend one another.

There was scarcely any one who had greater repute among the Macedonians than Philotas, the son of Parmenio. For besides that he was valiant and able to endure any fatigue of war, he was also next to Alexander himself the most munificent, and the greatest lover of his friends, one of whom asking him for some money, he commanded his steward to give it him; and when he told him he had not wherewith, "Have you not any plate then," said he, "or any clothes of mine to sell?" But he carried his arrogance and his pride of wealth and his habits of display and luxury to a degree of assumption unbecoming a private man, and affecting all the loftiness without succeeding in showing any of the grace or gentleness of true greatness, by this mistaken and spurious majesty he gained so much envy and ill-will, that Parmenio would sometimes tell him, "My son, to be not quite so great would be better." For he had long before been complained of, and accused to Alexander. Particularly when Darius was defeated in Cilicia, and an immense booty was taken at Damascus, among the rest of the prisoners who were brought into the camp, there was one Antigone of Pydna, a very handsome woman, who fell to Philotas's share. The young man one day in his cups, in the vaunting, outspoken, soldier's manner, declared to his mistress, that all the great actions were performed by him and his father, the glory and benefit of which, he said, together

with the title of king, the boy Alexander reaped
and enjoyed by their means. She could not hold,
but discovered what he had said to one of her
acquaintance, and he, as is usual in such cases, to
another, till at last the story came to the ears of
Craterus, who brought the woman secretly to the
king. When Alexander had heard what she had to
say, he commanded her to continue her intrigue with
Philotas, and give him an account from time to
time of all that should fall from him to this purpose.
He thus unwittingly caught in a snare, to gratify
sometimes a fit of anger, sometimes a mere love
of vainglory, let himself utter numerous foolish,
indiscreet speeches against the king in Antigone's
hearing, of which though Alexander was informed
and convinced by strong evidence, yet he would
take no notice of it at present, whether it was that
he confided in Parmenio's affection and loyalty, or
that he apprehended their authority and interest in
the army. But about this time one Limnus,[29] a
Macedonian of Chalastra, conspired against Alexander's life, and communicated his design to a youth
whom he was fond of, named Nicomachus, inviting
him to be of the party. But he not relishing the
thing, revealed it to his brother Balinus, who immediately addressed himself to Philotas, requiring
him to introduce them both to Alexander, to whom
they had something of great moment to impart
which very nearly concerned him. But he, for what
reason is uncertain, went not with them, professing
that the king was engaged with affairs of more importance. And when they had urged him a second
time, and were still slighted by him, they applied
themselves to another, by whose means being admitted into Alexander's presence, they first told

[29] Limnus is in other authors Dimnus, and Balinus, Cebalinus.

about Limnus's conspiracy, and by the way let Philotas's negligence appear, who had twice disregarded their application to him. Alexander was greatly incensed, and on finding that Limnus had defended himself, and had been killed by the soldier who was sent to seize him, he was still more discomposed, thinking he had thus lost the means of detecting the plot. As soon as his displeasure against Philotas began to appear, presently all his old enemies showed themselves, and said openly, the king was too easily imposed on, to imagine that one so inconsiderable as Limnus, a Chalastrian, should of his own head undertake such an enterprise; that in all likelihood he was but subservient to the design, an instrument that was moved by some greater spring; that those ought to be more strictly examined about the matter whose interest it was so much to conceal it. When they had once gained the king's ear for insinuations of this sort, they went on to show a thousand grounds of suspicion against Philotas, till at last they prevailed to have him seized and put to the torture, which was done in the presence of the principal officers, Alexander himself being placed behind some tapestry to understand what passed. Where, when he heard in what a miserable tone, and with what abject submissions Philotas applied himself to Hephæstion, he broke out, it is said, in this manner: "Are you so mean-spirited and effeminate, Philotas, and yet can engage in so desperate a design?" After his death, he presently sent into Media, and put also Parmenio, his father, to death, who had done brave service under Philip, and was the only man, of his older friends and counsellors, who had encouraged Alexander to invade Asia. Of three sons whom he had had in the army, he had already lost two, and now was himself put to death with the third. These actions rendered Alexander an object of terror to many of his friends, and chiefly to Antipater, who, to strengthen himself, sent messengers privately to treat for an alliance with the Ætolians, who stood in fear of Alexander, because they had destroyed the town of the Œniadæ; on being informed of which Alexander had said the children of the Œniadæ need not revenge their fathers' quarrel, for he would himself take care to punish the Ætolians.

Not long after this happened the deplorable end of Clitus, which to those who barely hear the matter-of-fact, may seem more inhuman than that of Philotas; but if we consider the story with its circumstance of time, and weigh the cause, we shall find it to have occurred rather through a sort of mischance of the king's, whose anger and overdrinking offered an occasion to the evil genius of Clitus. The king had a present of Grecian fruit brought him from the sea-coast, which was so fresh and beautiful, that he was surprised at it, and called Clitus to him to see it, and to give him a share of it. Clitus was then sacrificing, but he immediately left off and came, followed by three sheep, on whom the drink-offering had been already poured preparatory to sacrificing them. Alexander, being informed of this, told his diviners, Aristander and Cleomantis the Lacedæmonian, and asked them what it meant; on whose assuring him, it was an ill omen, he commanded them in all haste to offer sacrifices for Clitus's safety, forasmuch as three days before he himself had seen a strange vision in his sleep, of Clitus all in mourning, sitting by Parmenio's sons who were dead. Clitus, however, stayed not to finish his devotions, but came straight to supper with the king, who had sacrificed to Castor and Pollux. And when they had drunk pretty hard, some of the company fell a singing the verses of one Pranichus, or as others say of Pierion, which were made upon those captains who had been lately worsted by the barbarians, on purpose to disgrace and turn them to ridicule. This gave offence to the older men who were there, and they upbraided both the author and the singer of the verses, though Alexander and the younger men about him were much amused to hear them, and encouraged them to go on, till at last Clitus, who had drunk too much, and was besides of a froward and wilful temper, was so nettled that he could hold no longer, saying, it was not well done to expose the Macedonians so before the barbarians and their enemies, since though it was their unhappiness to be overcome, yet they were much better men than those who laughed at them. And when Alexander remarked, that Clitus was pleading his own cause, giving cowardice the name of misfortune, Clitus started up; "This cowardice, as you are pleased to term it," said he to him, "saved the life of a son of the gods, when in flight from Spithridates's sword; and it is by the expense of Macedonian blood, and by these wounds, that you are now raised to such a height, as to be able to disown your father Philip, and call yourself the son of Ammon." "Thou base fellow," said Alexander, who was now thoroughly exasperated, "dost thou think to utter these things everywhere of me, and stir up the Macedonians to sedition, and not be punished for it?" "We are sufficiently punished already," answered Clitus, "if this be the recompense of our toils, and we must esteem theirs a happy lot, who have not lived to see their countrymen scourged with Median rods, and forced to sue to the Persians to have access to their king." While he talked thus at random, and those near Alexander got up from their seats and began to revile him in turn, the elder men did what they could to compose the disorder. Alexander, in the mean time turning about to Xenodochus, the Cardian, and Artemius, the Colophonian, asked them if they were not of opinion that the Greeks, in comparison with the Macedonians, behaved themselves like so many demi-gods among wild beasts. But Clitus for all this would not give over, desiring Alexander to speak out if he had any thing more to say, or else why did he invite men who were free-born and accustomed to speak their minds openly without restraint, to sup with him. He had better live and converse with barbarians and slaves who would not scruple to bow the knee to his Persian girdle and his white tunic. Which words so provoked Alexander, that not able to suppress his anger any longer, he threw one of the apples that lay upon the table at him, and hit him, and then looked about for his sword. But Aristophanes, one of his life-guard, had hid that out of the way, and others came about him and besought him, but in vain. For breaking from them, he called out aloud to his guards in the Macedonian language, which was a certain sign of some great disturbance in him, and commanded a trumpeter to sound, giving him a blow with his clenched fist for not instantly obeying him; though afterwards the same man was commended for disobeying an order which would have put the whole army into tumult and confusion. Clitus still refusing to yield, was with much trouble forced by his friends out of the room. But he came in again immediately at another door, very irreverently and confidently singing the verses out of Euripides's Andromache,—

In Greece, alas! how ill things ordered are! [30]

Upon this, at last, Alexander, snatching a spear from one of the soldiers, met Clitus as he was coming forward and was putting by the curtain that hung before the door, and ran him through the body. He fell at once with a cry and a groan. Upon which the king's anger immediately vanishing, he came perfectly to himself, and when he saw his friends about him all in a profound silence, he pulled the spear out of the dead body, and would have thrust it into his own throat, if the guards had not held his hands, and by main force carried him away into his chamber, where all that night and the next day he wept bitterly, till being quite spent with lamenting and exclaiming, he lay as it were speechless, only fetching deep sighs. His friends ap-

---

[30] The offensiveness is in what follows:—

> When trophies rise for victories in war,
> Men count the praise not theirs who did the deed,
> But to the one commander give the meed;
> Who, sharing with ten thousand more the fight,
> For one man's service takes the general right.
> So in the city set with lofty air,
> Worthless themselves, they scorn their fellows there
> Who, better far than these they serve below,
> Want but the will and boldness for the blow.

The passage from the Andromache is a speech of Peleus to Menelaus (693-702). The fragment (two pages further on), in disparagement of the wise man who is *not wise to his own interest* (*miso sophisten hostis oukh hautoi sophos*), is quoted also, once in Greek, and twice in a Latin form given it by Ennius (qui ipse sibi sapiens prodesse non quit, nequidquam sapit), by Cicero (*Ad Diversos, XIII.*, 15, a letter to Cæsar, & *VII.*, 6, & *de Officiis, III.*, 15). It is No. CXI. in Matthiæ's Uncertain Fragments.

prehending some harm from his silence, broke into the room, but he took no notice of what any of them said, till Aristander putting him in mind of the vision he had seen concerning Clitus, and the prodigy that followed, as if all had come to pass by an unavoidable fatality, he then seemed to moderate his grief. They now brought Callisthenes, the philosopher, who was the near friend of Aristotle, and Anaxarchus of Abdera, to him. Callisthenes used moral language, and gentle and soothing means, hoping to find access for words of reason, and get a hold upon the passion. But Anaxarchus, who had always taken a course of his own in philosophy, and had a name for despising and slighting his contemporaries, as soon as he came in, cried out aloud, "Is this the Alexander whom the whole world looks to, lying here

'Tis easy on good subjects to excel is from the mouth of Tiresias in the Bacchæ (266-267). *In civil strife e'en villains rise to fame* (three pages later) is a verse which Plutarch has already used twice in the Lives, once in that of Nicias, and again in the comparison between Lysander and Sylla, and it occurs a third time in the Essay on Brotherly Love; but where it comes from is, I believe, unknown. *Death seized at last on great Patroclus too* is from the *uncompassionate answer* returned by Achilles to the prayers of Lycaon, one of Priam's sons, in the battle of the rivers (*Iliad XXI.*, 107). *While yet Patroclus lived, he might haply have thought upon pity, now death was the doom of every Trojan man, and above all, of the children of Priam; wherefore,*

> Be content, good friend, and die, and do not lament it;
> Patroclus died also, who was much better than you are.
> Look at me and observe my size and beauty of person,
> Yet for me too death is at hand, and the fated appointment.
> Either in the morning, or the evening, or at the noonday,
> Some one in the battle shall take the life from my body
> With the stroke of a spear or arrow shot from the bowstring.

weeping like a slave, for fear of the censure and reproach of men, to whom he himself ought to be a law and measure of equity, if he would use the right his conquests have given him as supreme lord and governor of all, and not be the victim of a vain and idle opinion? Do not you know," said he, "that Jupiter is represented to have Justice and Law on each hand of him, to signify that all the actions of a conqueror are lawful and just?" With these and the like speeches, Anaxarchus indeed allayed the king's grief, but withal corrupted his character, rendering him more audacious and lawless than he had been. Nor did he fail by these means to insinuate himself into his favor, and to make Callisthenes's company, which at all times, because of his austerity, was not very acceptable, more uneasy and disagreeable to him.

It happened that these two philosophers meeting at an entertainment, where conversation turned on the subject of climate and the temperature of the air, Callisthenes joined with their opinion, who held that those countries were colder, and the winter sharper there than in Greece. Anaxarchus would by no means allow this, but argued against it with some heat. "Surely," said Callisthenes, "you cannot but admit this country to be colder than Greece, for there you used to have but one threadbare cloak to keep out the coldest winter, and here you have three good warm mantles one over another." This piece of raillery irritated Anaxarchus and the other pretenders to learning, and the crowd of flatterers in general could not endure to see Callisthenes so much admired and followed by the youth, and no less esteemed by the older men for his orderly life, and his gravity, and for being contented with his condition; all con-

ALEXANDER

firming what he had professed about the object he had in his journey to Alexander, that it was only to get his countrymen recalled from banishment, and to rebuild and repeople his native town.[31] Besides the envy which his great reputation raised, he also, by his own deportment, gave those who wished him ill, opportunity to do him mischief. For when he was invited to public entertainments, he would most times refuse to come, or if he were present at any, he put a constraint upon the company by his austerity and silence, which seemed to intimate his disapproval of what he saw. So that Alexander himself said in application to him,

> That vain pretence to wisdom I detest,
> Where a man's blind to his own interest.[32]

Being with many more invited to sup with the king, he was called upon when the cup came to him,

---

[31] Olynthus, which Philip had destroyed, and for which Callisthenes hoped to obtain from Alexander the same favor which Philip showed for Aristotle's sake to Stagira.

[32] A fragment from a lost play of Euripides. In the original it is, "I hate the *sophist* who is not *sophos* for himself." The word sophist, however, is far from expressing to us the original Greek meaning. Knowledge that does not know its own good, or cleverness that is not clever for itself, would be phrases more nearly equivalent. *Sophistes*, which at first meant one who professed superior knowledge and cleverness, had passed by this time into the common name for lecturers and teachers in logic and (less properly) in rhetoric. It was used, much as our word *doctor* is for physician, as the familiar and half-disparaging term for the higher class of *reasoners* rather than arguers, the philosophers, the moralists, who at this time exercised among the Greeks, as may be seen just above in the story of Clitus, a sort of clerical function.

to make an oration extempore in praise of the Macedonians; and he did it with such a flow of eloquence, that all who heard it rose from their seats to clap and applaud him, and threw their garland upon him; only Alexander told him out of Euripides,

> I wonder not that you have spoke so well,
> 'Tis easy on good subjects to excel.

"Therefore," said he, "if you will show the force of your eloquence, tell my Macedonians their faults, and dispraise them, that by hearing their errors they may learn to be better for the future." Callisthenes presently obeyed him, retracting all he had said before, and, inveighing against the Macedonians with great freedom, added, that Philip thrived and grew powerful, chiefly by the discord of the Grecians, applying this verse to him:—

> In civil strife e'en villains rise to fame;

which so offended the Macedonians, that he was odious to them ever after. And Alexander said, that instead of his eloquence, he had only made his ill-will appear in what he had spoken. Hermippus assures us, that one Strœbus, a servant whom Callisthenes kept to read to him, gave this account of these passages afterwards to Aristotle; and that when he perceived the king grow more and more averse to him, two or three times, as he was going away, he repeated the verses,—

> Death seiz'd at last on great Patroclus too,
> Though he in virtue far exceeded you.

Not without reason, therefore, did Aristotle give this character of Callisthenes, that he was, indeed, a

powerful speaker, but had no judgment. He acted
certainly a true philosopher's part in positively refusing, as he did, to pay adoration; and by speaking out openly against that which the best and
gravest of the Macedonians only repined at in
secret, he delivered the Grecians and Alexander
himself from a great disgrace, when the practice
was given up. But he ruined himself by it, because
he went too roughly to work, as if he would have
forced the king to that which he should have effected
by reason and persuasion. Chares of Mitylene
writes, that at a banquet, Alexander, after he had
drunk, reached the cup to one of his friends, who,
on receiving it, rose up towards the domestic altar,
and when he had drunk, first adored, and then
kissed Alexander, and afterwards laid himself down
at the table with the rest. Which they all did one
after another, till it came to Callisthenes's turn, who
took the cup and drank, while the king who was
engaged in conversation with Hephæstion was not
observing, and then came and offered to kiss him.
But Demetrius, surnamed Phidon, interposed, saying, " Sir, by no means let him kiss you, for he
only of us all has refused to adore you;" upon
which the king declined it, and all the concern
Callisthenes showed was, that he said aloud, " Then
I go away with a kiss less than the rest." The
displeasure he incurred by this action procured
credit for Hephæstion's declaration that he had
broken his word to him in not paying the king the
same veneration that others did, as he had faithfully
promised to do. And to finish his disgrace, a number of such men as Lysimachus and Hagnon now
came in with their asseverations that the sophist
went about everywhere boasting of his resistance
to arbitrary power, and that the young men all

ran after him, and honored him as the only man among so many thousands who had the courage to preserve his liberty. Therefore when Hermolaus's conspiracy came to be discovered, the charges which his enemies brought against him were the more easily believed, particularly that when the young man asked him what he should do to be the most illustrious person on earth, he told him the readiest way was to kill him who was already so; and that to incite him to commit the deed, he bade him not be awed by the golden couch, but remember Alexander was a man equally infirm and vulnerable as another. However, none of Hermolaus's accomplices, in the utmost extremity, made any mention of Callisthenes's being engaged in the design. Nay, Alexander himself, in the letters which he wrote soon after to Craterus, Attalus, and Alcetas, tells them that the young men who were put to the torture, declared they had entered into the conspiracy of themselves, without any others being privy to, or guilty of it. But yet afterwards, in a letter to Antipater, he accuses Callisthenes. "The young men," he says, "were stoned to death by the Macedonians, but for the sophist," (meaning Callisthenes,) "I will take care to punish him with them too who sent him to me, and who harbor those in their cities who conspire against my life," an unequivocal declaration against Aristotle, in whose house Callisthenes, for his relationship's sake, being his niece Hero's son, had been educated. His death is variously related. Some say he was hanged by Alexander's orders; others, that he died of sickness in prison; but Chares writes he was kept in chains seven months after he was apprehended, on purpose that he might be proceeded against in full council, when Aristotle should be present; and that growing very fat, and contracting a disease of vermin, he there died, about the time that Alexander was wounded in India, in the country of the Malli Oxydracæ,[33] all which came to pass afterwards.

For to go on in order, Demaratus of Corinth, now quite an old man, had made a great effort, about this time, to pay Alexander a visit; and when he had seen him, said he pitied the misfortune of those Grecians, who were so unhappy as to die before they had beheld Alexander seated on the throne of Darius. But he did not long enjoy the benefit of the king's kindness for him, any otherwise than that soon after falling sick and dying, he had a magnificent funeral, and the army raised him a monument of earth, fourscore cubits high, and of a vast circumference. His ashes were conveyed in a very rich chariot, drawn by four horses, to the seaside.

Alexander now intent upon his expedition into India, took notice that his soldiers were so charged with booty that it hindered their marching. Therefore, at break of day, as soon as the baggage waggons were laden, first he set fire to his own, and to those of his friends, and then commanded those to be burnt which belonged to the rest of the army. An act which in the deliberation of it had seemed more dangerous and difficult than it proved in the execution, with which few were dissatisfied; for most of the soldiers, as if they had been inspired,

---

[33] One of these names must be omitted, as the Malli and Oxydracæ are distinct tribes. Probably the whole clause has been interpolated from the margin, where one annotator may have named the Malli, and another the Oxydracæ. Plutarch having merely said, in India.

uttering loud outcries and warlike shoutings, supplied one another with what was absolutely necessary, and burnt and destroyed all that was superfluous, the sight of which redoubled Alexander's zeal and eagerness for his design. And, indeed, he was now grown very severe and inexorable in punishing those who committed any fault. For he put Menander, one of his friends, to death, for deserting a fortress where he had placed him in garrison, and shot Orsodates, one of the barbarians who revolted from him, with his own hand.

At this time a sheep happened to yean a lamb, with the perfect shape and color of a tiara upon the head, and testicles on each side; which portent Alexander regarded with such dislike, that he immediately caused his Babylonian priests, whom he usually carried about with him for such purposes, to purify him, and told his friends he was not so much concerned for his own sake as for theirs, out of an apprehension that after his death the divine power might suffer his empire to fall into the hands of some degenerate, impotent person. But this fear was soon removed by a wonderful thing that happened not long after, and was thought to presage better. For Proxenus, a Macedonian, who was the chief of those who looked to the king's furniture, as he was breaking up the ground near the river Oxus, to set up the royal pavilion, discovered a spring of a fat, oily liquor, which after the top was taken off, ran pure, clear oil, without any difference either of taste or smell, having exactly the same smoothness and brightness, and that, too, in a country where no olives grew. The water, indeed, of the river Oxus, is said to be the smoothest to the feeling of all waters, and to leave a gloss on the skins of those who bathe themselves in it.

Whatever might be the cause, certain it is that Alexander was wonderfully pleased with it, as appears by his letters to Antipater, where he speaks of it as one of the most remarkable presages that God had ever favored him with. The diviners told him it signified his expedition would be glorious in the event, but very painful, and attended with many difficulties; for oil, they said, was bestowed on mankind by God as a refreshment of their labors.

Nor did they judge amiss, for he exposed himself to many hazards in the battles which he fought, and received very severe wounds, but the greatest loss in his army was occasioned through the unwholesomeness of the air, and the want of necessary provisions. But he still applied himself to overcome fortune and whatever opposed him, by resolution and virtue, and thought nothing impossible to true intrepidity, and on the other hand nothing secure or strong for cowardice. It is told of him that when he besieged Sisimithres, who held an inaccessible, impregnable rock against him, and his soldiers began to despair of taking it, he asked Oxyartes whether Sisimithres was a man of courage, who assuring him he was the greatest coward alive, "Then you tell me," said he, "that the place may easily be taken, since what is in command of it is weak." And in a little time he so terrified Sisimithres that he took it without any difficulty. At an attack which he made upon such another precipitous place with some of his Macedonian soldiers, he called to one whose name was Alexander, and told him, he at any rate must fight bravely, if it were but for his name's sake. The youth fought gallantly and was killed in the action, at which he was sensibly afflicted. Another time, seeing his men march slowly and unwillingly to the siege of the place called Nysa, because of a deep river between them and the town, he advanced before them, and standing upon the bank, "What a miserable man," said he, "am I, that I have not learned to swim!" and then was hardly dissuaded from endeavoring to pass it upon his shield. Here, after the assault was over, the ambassadors who from several towns which he had blocked up, came to submit to him and make their peace, were surprised to find him still in his armor, without any one in waiting or attendance upon him, and when at last some one brought him a cushion, he made the eldest of them, named Acuphis, take it and sit down upon it. The old man, marvelling at his magnanimity and courtesy, asked him what his countrymen should do to merit his friendship. "I would have them," said Alexander, "choose you to govern them, and send one hundred of the most worthy men among them to remain with me as hostages." Acuphis laughed and answered, "I shall govern them with more ease, Sir, if I send you so many of the worst, rather than the best of my subjects."

The extent of king Taxiles's dominions in India was thought to be as large as Egypt, abounding in good pastures, and producing beautiful fruits. The king himself had the reputation of a wise man, and at his first interview with Alexander, he spoke to him in these terms: "To what purpose," said he, "should we make war upon one another, if the design of your coming into these parts be not to rob us of our water or our necessary food, which are the only things that wise men are indispensably obliged to fight for? As for other riches and possessions, as they are accounted in the eye of the world, if I am better provided of them than you, I am ready to let you share with me; but if fortune has been more liberal to you than me, I have no objection to be obliged to you." This discourse pleased Alexander so much, that embracing him, " Do you think," said he to him, " your kind words and courteous behavior will bring you off in this interview without a contest? No, you shall not escape so. I shall contend and do battle with you so far, that how obliging soever you are, you shall not have the better of me." Then receiving some presents from him, he returned him others of greater value, and to complete his bounty, gave him in money ready coined one thousand talents; at which his old friends were much displeased, but it gained him the hearts of many of the barbarians. But the best soldiers of the Indians now entering into the pay of several of the cities, undertook to defend them, and did it so bravely, that they put Alexander to a great deal of trouble, till at last, after a capitulation, upon the surrender of the place, he fell upon them as they were marching away, and put them all to the sword. This one breach of his word remains as a blemish upon his achievements in war, which he otherwise had performed throughout with that justice and honor that became a king. Nor was he less incommoded by the Indian philosophers, who inveighed against those princes who joined his party, and solicited the free nations to oppose him. He took several of these also, and caused them to be hanged.

Alexander, in his own letters, has given us an account of his war with Porus. He says the two armies were separated by the river Hydaspes, on whose opposite bank Porus continually kept his elephants in order of battle, with their heads towards their enemies, to guard the passage; that he, on the other hand, made every day a great noise and clamor in his camp, to dissipate the apprehensions of the barbarians; that one stormy dark night he passed the river, at a distance from the place where the enemy lay, into a little island, with part of his foot, and the best of his horse. Here there fell a most violent storm of rain, accompanied with lightning and whirlwinds, and seeing some of his men burnt and dying with the lightning, he nevertheless quitted the island and made over to the other side. The Hydaspes, he says, now after the storm, was so swollen and grown so rapid, as to have made a breach in the bank, and a part of the river was now pouring in here, so that when he came across, it was with difficulty he got a footing on the land, which was slippery and unsteady, and exposed to the force of the currents on both sides. This is the occasion when he is related to have said, "O ye Athenians, will ye believe what dangers I incur to merit your praise?" This, however, is Onesicritus's story. Alexander says, here the men left their boats, and passed the breach in their armor, up to the breast in water, and that then he advanced with his horse about twenty furlongs before his foot, concluding that if the enemy charged him with their cavalry, he should be too strong for them; if with their foot, his own would come up time enough to his assistance. Nor did he judge amiss; for being charged by a thousand horse, and sixty armed chariots, which advanced before their main body, he took all the chariots, and killed four hundred horse upon the place. Porus, by this time guessing that Alexander himself had crossed over, came on with his whole army, except a party which he left behind, to hold the rest of the Macedonians in play, if they should attempt to pass the river. But he, apprehending the multitude of the enemy, and to avoid the shock of their elephants, dividing his forces, attacked their left wing himself, and commanded Cœnus to fall upon the right, which was performed with good success. For by this means both wings being broken, the enemies fell back in their retreat upon the center, and crowded in upon their elephants. There rallying, they fought a hand to hand battle, and it was the eighth hour of the day before they were entirely defeated. This description the conqueror himself has left us in his own epistles.

Almost all the historians agree in relating that Porus was four cubits and a span high, and that when he was upon his elephant, which was of the largest size, his stature and bulk were so answerable, that he appeared to be proportionably mounted, as a horseman on his horse. This elephant, during the whole battle, gave many singular proofs of sagacity and of particular care of the king, whom as long as he was strong and in a condition to fight, he defended with great courage, repelling those who set upon him; and as soon as he perceived him overpowered with his numerous wounds and the multitude of darts that were thrown at him, to prevent his falling off, he softly knelt down and began to draw out the darts with his proboscis. When Porus was taken prisoner, and Alexander asked him how he expected to be used, he answered, "As a king." For that expression, he said, when the same question was put to him a second time, comprehended every thing. And Alexander, accordingly not only suffered him to govern his own kingdom as satrap under himself, but gave him also the additional territory of various independent tribes whom he subdued, a district which, it is said, contained fifteen several nations, and five thousand considerable towns, besides abundance of villages. To another government, three times as large as this, he appointed Philip, one of his friends.

Some little time after the battle with Porus, Bucephalas died, as most of the authorities state, under cure of his wounds, or as Onesicritus says, of fatigue and age, being thirty years old. Alexander was no less concerned at his death, than if he had lost an old companion or an intimate friend, and built a city, which he named Bucephalia, in memory of him, on the bank of the river Hydaspes. He also, we are told, built another city, and called it after the name of a favorite dog, Peritas, which he had brought up himself. So Sotion assures us he was informed by Potamon of Lesbos.

But this last combat with Porus took off the edge of the Macedonians' courage, and stayed their further progress into India. For having found it hard enough to defeat an enemy who brought but twenty thousand foot and two thousand horse into the field, they thought they had reason to oppose Alexander's design of leading them on to pass the Ganges too, which they were told was thirty-two furlongs broad and a hundred fathoms deep, and the banks on the further side covered with multitudes of enemies. For they were told that the kings of the Gandaritans and Præsians expected them there with eighty thousand horse, two hundred thousand foot, eight thousand armed chariots, and six thousand fighting elephants. Nor was this a mere vain report, spread to discourage them. For Androcottus,[34]

---

[34] Or Sandrocottus, as the name is given in Arrian and other writers, identical, it is generally presumed, with the Sandragupta

who not long after reigned in those parts, made a present of five hundred elephants at once to Seleucus, and with an army of six hundred thousand men subdued all India. Alexander at first was so grieved and enraged at his men's reluctancy, that he shut himself up in his tent, and threw himself upon the ground, declaring, if they would not pass the Ganges, he owed them no thanks for any thing they had hitherto done, and that to retreat now, was plainly to confess himself vanquished. But at last the reasonable persuasions of his friends and the cries and lamentations of his soldiers, who in a suppliant manner crowded about the entrance of his tent, prevailed with him to think of returning. Yet he could not refrain from leaving behind him various deceptive memorials of his expedition, to impose upon after-times, and to exaggerate his glory with posterity, such as arms larger than were really worn, and mangers for horses, with bits of bridles above the usual size, which he set up and distributed in several places. He erected altars, also, to the gods, which the kings of the Præsians even in our time do honor to when they pass the river, and offer sacrifice upon them after the Grecian manner. Androcottus, then a boy, saw Alexander there, and is said often afterwards to have been heard to say, that he missed but little of making himself master of those countries; their king, who then reigned, was so hated and despised for the viciousness of his life, and the meanness of his extraction.

of Indian history and literature. At his court Megasthenes, the envoy of Seleucus, met apparently some of the Buddhist ascetics and philosophers. Calanus and the gymnosophists, whom we read of here, were pretty certainly of the old Brahminical religion.

Alexander was now eager to see the ocean. To which purpose he caused a great many row-boats and rafts to be built, in which he fell gently down the rivers at his leisure, yet so that his navigation was neither unprofitable nor inactive. For by several descents upon the banks, he made himself master of the fortified towns, and consequently of the country on both sides. But at a siege of a town of the Mallians, who have the repute of being the bravest people of India, he ran in great danger of his life. For having beaten off the defendants with showers of arrows, he was the first man that mounted the wall by a scaling ladder, which, as soon as he was up, broke and left him almost alone, exposed to the darts which the barbarians threw at him in great numbers from below. In this distress, turning himself as well as he could, he leaped down in the midst of his enemies, and had the good fortune to light upon his feet. The brightness and clattering of his armor when he came to the ground, made the barbarians think they saw rays of light, or some bright phantom playing before his body, which frightened them so at first, that they ran away and dispersed. Till seeing him seconded but by two of his guards, they fell upon him hand to hand, and some, while he bravely defended himself, tried to wound him through his armor with their swords and spears. And one who stood further off, drew a bow with such just strength, that the arrow finding its way through his cuirass, stuck in his ribs under the breast. This stroke was so violent, that it made him give back, and set one knee to the ground, upon which the man ran up with his drawn scimitar, thinking to despatch him, and had done it, if Peucestes and Limnæus had not interposed, who were both wounded, Limnæus mortally, but Peucestes stood his ground, while Alexander killed the barbarian. But this did not free him from danger; for besides many other wounds, at last he received so weighty a stroke of a club upon his neck, that he was forced to lean his body against the wall, still, however, facing the enemy. At this extremity, the Macedonians made their way in and gathered round him. They took him up, just as he was fainting away, having lost all sense of what was done near him, and conveyed him to his tent, upon which it was presently reported all over the camp that he was dead. But when they had with great difficulty and pains sawed off the shaft of the arrow, which was of wood, and so with much trouble got off his cuirass, they came to cut out the head of it, which was three fingers broad and four long, and stuck fast in the bone. During the operation, he was taken with almost mortal swoonings, but when it was out he came to himself again. Yet though all danger was past, he continued very weak, and confined himself a great while to a regular diet and the method of his cure, till one day hearing the Macedonians clamoring outside in their eagerness to see him, he took his cloak and went out. And having sacrificed to the gods, without more delay he went on board again, and as he coasted along, subdued a great deal of the country on both sides, and several considerable cities.

In this voyage, he took ten of the Indian philosophers prisoners, who had been most active in persuading Sabbas to revolt, and had caused the Macedonians a great deal of trouble. These men, called Gymnosophists, were reputed to be extremely ready and succinct in their answers, which he made trial of, by putting difficult questions to them, letting them know that those whose answers were not pertinent, should be put to death, of which he made the eldest of them judge. The first being asked which he thought most numerous, the dead or the living, answered, "The living, because those who are dead are not at all." Of the second, he desired to know whether the earth or the sea produced the largest beast; who told him, "The earth, for the sea is but a part of it." His question to the third was, Which is the cunningest of beasts? "That," said he, "which men have not yet found out." He bade the fourth tell him what argument he used to Sabbas to persuade him to revolt. "No other," said he, "than that he should either live or die nobly." Of the fifth he asked, Which was eldest, night or day? The philosopher replied, "Day was eldest, by one day at least." But perceiving Alexander not well satisfied with that account, he added, that he ought not to wonder if strange questions had as strange answers made to them. Then he went on and inquired of the next, what a man should do to be exceedingly beloved. "He must be very powerful," said he, "without making himself too much feared." The answer of the seventh to his question, how a man might become a god, was, "By doing that which was impossible for men to do." The eighth told him, "Life is stronger than death, because it supports so many miseries." And the last being asked, how long he thought it decent for a man to live, said, "Till death appeared more desirable than life." Then Alexander turned to him whom he had made judge, and commanded him to give sentence. "All that I can determine," said he, "is, that they have every one answered worse than another." "Nay," said the king, "then you shall die first, for giving such a sentence." "Not so, O king," replied the gymnosophist, "unless you said falsely that he should die first who made the worst answer." In conclusion he gave them presents and dismissed them.

But to those who were in greatest reputation among them, and lived a private quiet life, he sent Onesicritus, one of Diogenes the Cynic's disciples, desiring them to come to him. Calanus, it is said, very arrogantly and roughly commanded him to strip himself, and hear what he said, naked, otherwise he would not speak a word to him, though he came from Jupiter himself. But Dandamis received him with more civility, and hearing him discourse of Socrates, Pythagoras, and Diogenes, told him he thought them men of great parts, and to have erred in nothing so much, as in having too great respect for the laws and customs of their country. Others say, Dandamis only asked him the reason why Alexander undertook so long a journey to come into those parts. Taxiles, however, persuaded Calanus to wait upon Alexander. His proper name was Sphines, but because he was wont to say *Cale,* which in the Indian tongue is a form of salutation, to those he met with anywhere, the Greeks called him Calanus. He is said to have shown Alexander an instructive emblem of government, which was this. He threw a dry shrivelled hide upon the ground, and trod upon the edges of it. The skin when it was pressed in one place, still rose up in another, wheresoever he trod round about it, till he set his foot in the middle, which made all the parts lie even and quiet. The meaning of this similitude being that he ought to reside most in the middle of his empire, and not spend too much time on the borders of it.

His voyage down the rivers took up seven months' time, and when he came to the sea, he sailed to an island which he himself called Scillustis, others Psiltucis, where going ashore, he sacrificed, and made what observations he could as to the nature of the sea and the sea-coast. Then having besought the gods that no other man might ever go beyond the bounds of this expedition, he ordered his fleet, of which he made Nearchus admiral, and Onesicritus pilot, to sail round about, keeping the Indian shore on the right hand, and returned himself by land through the country of the Orites, where he was reduced to great straits for want of provisions, and lost a vast number of men, so that of an army of one hundred and twenty thousand foot and fifteen thousand horse, he scarcely brought back above a fourth part out of India, they were so diminished by diseases, ill diet, and the scorching heats, but most by famine. For their march was through an uncultivated country whose inhabitants fared hardly, possessing only a few sheep, and those of a wretched kind, whose flesh was rank and unsavory, by their continual feeding upon sea-fish.

After sixty days march he came into Gedrosia, where he found great plenty of all things, which the neighboring kings and governors of provinces, hearing of his approach, had taken care to provide. When he had here refreshed his army, he continued his march through Carmania, feasting all the way for seven days together. He with his most intimate friends banqueted and revelled night and day upon a platform erected on a lofty, conspicuous scaffold, which was slowly drawn by eight horses. This was followed by a great many chariots, some covered with purple and embroidered canopies, and some with green boughs, which were continually supplied afresh, and in them the rest of his friends and commanders drinking, and crowned with garlands of flowers. Here was now no target or helmet or spear to be seen; instead of armor, the soldiers handled nothing but cups and goblets and Thericlean drinking vessels, which, along the whole way, they dipped into large bowls and jars, and drank healths to one another, some seating themselves to it, others as they went along. All places resounded with music of pipes and flutes, with harping and singing, and women dancing as in the rites of Bacchus. For this disorderly, wandering march, besides the drinking part of it, was accompanied with all the sportiveness and insolence of bacchanals, as much as if the god himself had been there to countenance and lead the procession. As soon as he came to the royal palace of Gedrosia, he again refreshed and feasted his army; and one day after he had drunk pretty hard, it is said, he went to see a prize of dancing contended for, in which his favorite Bagoas, having gained the victory, crossed the theatre in his dancing habit, and sat down close by him, which so pleased the Macedonians, that they made loud acclamations for him to kiss Bagoas, and never stopped clapping their hands and shouting till Alexander put his arms round him and kissed him.

Here his admiral, Nearchus, came to him, and delighted him so with the narrative of his voyage, that he resolved himself to sail out of the mouth of Euphrates with a great fleet, with which he designed to go round by Arabia and Africa, and so by Hercules's Pillars into the Mediterranean; in order for which, he directed all sorts of vessels to be built at Thapsacus, and made great provision everywhere of seamen and pilots. But the tidings of the difficulties he had gone through in his Indian expedition, the danger of his person among the Mallians, the reported loss of a considerable part of his forces, and a general doubt as to his own safety, had begun to give occasion for revolt among many of the conquered nations, and for acts of great injustice, avarice, and insolence on the part of the satraps and commanders in the provinces, so that there seemed to be an universal fluctuation and disposition to change. Even at home, Olympias and Cleopatra had raised a faction against Antipater, and divided his government between them, Olympias seizing upon Epirus, and Cleopatra upon Macedonia. When Alexander was told of it, he said his mother had made the best choice, for the Macedonians would never endure to be ruled by a woman. Upon this he despatched Nearchus again to his fleet, to carry the war into the maritime provinces, and as he marched that way himself, he punished those commanders who had behaved ill, particularly Oxyartes,[35] one of the sons of Abuletes, whom he killed with his own hand, thrusting him through the body with his spear. And when Abuletes, instead of the necessary provisions which he ought to have furnished, brought him three thousand talents in coined money, he ordered it to be thrown to his horses, and when they would not touch it, "What good," he said, "will this provision do us?" and sent him away to prison.

When he came into Persia, he distributed money among the women, as their own kings had been wont to do, who as often as they came thither, gave every one of them a piece of gold; on account of which custom, some of them, it is said, had come but seldom, and Ochus was so sordidly covetous, that to avoid this expense, he never visited his

---

[35] Or Oxathres.

native country once in all his reign. Then finding
Cyrus's sepulchre opened [36] and rifled, he put Polymachus, who did it, to death, though he was a man
of some distinction, a born Macedonian of Pella.
And after he had read the inscription, he caused
it to be cut again below the old one in Greek
characters; the words being these: "O man, whosoever thou art, and from whencesoever thou comest
(for I know thou wilt come), I am Cyrus, the
founder of the Persian empire; do not grudge me
this little earth which covers my body." The reading of this sensibly touched Alexander, filling him
with the thought of the uncertainty and mutability
of human affairs. At the same time, Calanus having
been a little while troubled with a disease in the bowels,
requested that he might have a funeral pile erected,
to which he came on horseback, and after he had
said some prayers and sprinkled himself and cut
off some of his hair to throw into the fire, before he
ascended it, he embraced and took leave of the
Macedonians who stood by, desiring them to pass
that day in mirth and good-fellowship with their
king, whom in a little time, he said, he doubted
not but to see again at Babylon. Having thus said,
he lay down, and covering up his face, he stirred not
when the fire came near him, but continued still in
the same posture as at first, and so sacrificed himself, as it was the ancient custom of the philosophers
in those countries to do. The same thing was done
long after by another Indian, who came with Cæsar
to Athens, where they still show you "the Indian's
monument." At his return from the funeral pile,
Alexander invited a great many of his friends and

---

[36] At Pasargadæ, not far from Persepolis. Persia is, as before, Persis, or Persia proper.

principal officers to supper, and proposed a drinking match, in which the victor should receive a crown. Promachus drank twelve quarts of wine, and won the prize, which was a talent,[37] from them all; but he survived his victory but three days, and was followed, as Chares says, by forty-one more, who died of the same debauch, some extremely cold weather having set in shortly after.

At Susa, he married Darius's daughter Statira, and celebrated also the nuptials of his friends, bestowing the noblest of the Persian ladies upon the worthiest of them, at the same time making it an entertainment in honor of the other Macedonians whose marriages had already taken place. At this magnificent festival, it is reported, there were no less than nine thousand guests, to each of whom he gave a golden cup for the libations. Not to mention other instances of his wonderful magnificence, he paid the debts of his army, which amounted to nine thousand eight hundred and seventy talents. But Antigenes, who had lost one of his eyes, though he owed nothing, got his name set down in the list of those who were in debt, and bringing one who pretended to be his creditor, and to have supplied him from the bank, received the money. But when the cheat was found out, the king was so incensed at it, that he banished him from court, and took away his command, though he was an excellent soldier, and a man of great courage. For when he was but a youth, and served under Philip at the siege of Perinthus, where he was wounded in the

---

[37] *Promachus won the prize* (or *crown*), *which was a talent.* This appears to be the correct reading; the crown is simply taken as equivalent to the prize, and might, like a *cup* in English races, be something else, a sum of money.

eye by an arrow shot out of an engine, he would neither let the arrow be taken out, nor be persuaded to quit the field, till he had bravely repulsed the enemy and forced them to retire into the town. Accordingly he was not able to support such a disgrace with any patience, and it was plain that grief and despair would have made him kill himself, but that the king fearing it, not only pardoned him, but let him also enjoy the benefit of his deceit.

The thirty thousand boys whom he left behind him to be taught and disciplined, were so improved at his return, both in strength and beauty, and performed their exercises with such dexterity and wonderful agility, that he was extremely pleased with them, which grieved the Macedonians, and made them fear he would have the less value for them. And when he proceeded to send down the infirm and maimed soldiers to the sea, they said they were unjustly and infamously dealt with, after they were worn out in his service upon all occasions, now to be turned away with disgrace and sent home into their country among their friends and relations, in a worse condition than when they came out; therefore they desired him to dismiss them one and all, and to account his Macedonians useless, now he was so well furnished with a set of dancing boys, with whom, if he pleased, he might go on and conquer the world. These speeches so incensed Alexander, that after he had given them a great deal of reproachful language in his passion, he drove them away, and committed the watch to Persians, out of whom he chose his guards and attendants. When the Macedonians saw him escorted by these men, and themselves excluded and shamefully disgraced, their high spirits fell, and conferring with one another, they found that jealousy and rage had almost distracted them. But at last coming to themselves again, they went without their arms, with only their under garments on, crying and weeping, to offer themselves at his tent, and desired him to deal with them as their baseness and ingratitude deserved. However, this would not prevail; for though his anger was already something mollified, yet he would not admit them into his presence, nor would they stir from thence, but continued two days and nights before his tent, bewailing themselves, and imploring him as their lord to have compassion on them. But the third day he came out to them, and seeing them very humble and penitent, he wept himself a great while, and after a gentle reproof spoke kindly to them, and dismissed those who were unserviceable with magnificent rewards, and with this recommendation to Antipater, that when they came home, at all public shows and in the theatres, they should sit on the best and foremost seats, crowned with chaplets of flowers. He ordered, also, that the children of those who had lost their lives in his service, should have their fathers' pay continued to them.

When he came to Ecbatana in Media, and had despatched his most urgent affairs, he began to divert himself again with spectacles and public entertainments, to carry on which he had a supply of three thousand actors and artists, newly arrived out of Greece. But they were soon interrupted by Hephæstion's falling sick of a fever, in which, being a young man and a soldier too, he could not confine himself to so exact a diet as was necessary; for whilst his physician Glaucus was gone to the theatre, he ate a fowl for his dinner, and drank a large draught of wine, upon which he became very ill, and shortly after died. At this misfortune, Alexander was so beyond all reason transported, that to express his sorrow, he immediately ordered the manes and tails of all his horses and mules to be cut, and threw down the battlements of the neighboring cities. The poor physician he crucified, and forbade playing on the flute, or any other musical instrument in the camp a great while, till directions came from the oracle of Ammon, and enjoined him to honor Hephæstion, and sacrifice to him as to a hero. Then seeking to alleviate his grief in war, he set out, as it were, to a hunt and chase of men, for he fell upon the Cossæans, and put the whole nation to the sword. This was called a sacrifice to Hephæstion's ghost. In his sepulchre and monument and the adorning of them, he intended to bestow ten thousand talents; and designing that the excellence of the workmanship and the singularity of the design might outdo the expense, his wishes turned, above all other artists, to Stasicrates, because he always promised something very bold, unusual, and magnificent in his projects. Once when they had met before, he had told him, that of all the mountains he knew, that of Athos in Thrace was the most capable of being adapted to represent the shape and lineaments of a man; that if he pleased to command him, he would make it the noblest and most durable statue in the world, which in its left hand should hold a city of ten thousand inhabitants, and out of its right should pour a copious river into the sea. Though Alexander declined this proposal, yet now he spent a great deal of time with workmen to invent and contrive others even more extravagant and sumptuous.

As he was upon his way to Babylon, Nearchus,

who had sailed back out of the ocean up the mouth of the river Euphrates, came to tell him he had met with some Chaldæan diviners, who had warned him against Alexander's going thither. Alexander, however, took no thought of it, and went on, and when he came near the walls of the place, he saw a great many crows fighting with one another, some of whom fell down just by him. After this, being privately informed that Apollodorus, the governor of Babylon, had sacrificed, to know what would become of him, he sent for Pythagoras, the soothsayer, and on his admitting the thing, asked him, in what condition he found the victim; and when he told him the liver was defective in its lobe, " A great presage indeed!" said Alexander. However, he offered Pythagoras no injury, but was sorry that he had neglected Nearchus's advice, and stayed for the most part outside the town, removing his tent from place to place, and sailing up and down the Euphrates. Besides this, he was disturbed by many other prodigies. A tame ass fell upon the biggest and handsomest lion that he kept, and killed him by a kick. And one day after he had undressed himself to be anointed, and was playing at ball, just as they were going to bring his clothes again, the young men who played with him perceived a man clad in the king's robes, with a diadem upon his head, sitting silently upon his throne. They asked him who he was, to which he gave no answer a good while, till at last coming to himself, he told them his name was Dionysius, that he was of Messenia, that for some crime of which he was accused, he was brought thither from the sea-side, and had been kept long in prison, that Serapis appeared to him, had freed him from his chains, conducted him to that place, and commanded him to put on the king's robe and diadem, and to sit where they found him, and to say nothing. Alexander, when he heard this, by the direction of his soothsayers, put the fellow to death, but he lost his spirits, and grew diffident of the protection and assistance of the gods, and suspicious of his friends. His greatest apprehension was of Antipater and his sons, one of whom, Iolaus, was his chief cupbearer; and Cassander, who had lately arrived, and had been bred up in Greek manners, the first time he saw some of the barbarians adore the king, could not forbear laughing at it aloud, which so incensed Alexander, that he took him by the hair with both hands, and dashed his head against the wall. Another time, Cassander would have said something in defence of Antipater to those who accused him, but Alexander interrupting him, said, "What is it you say? Do you think people, if they had received no injury, would come such a journey only to calumniate your father?" To which when Cassander replied, that their coming so far from the evidence was a great proof of the falseness of their charges, Alexander smiled, and said those were some of Aristotle's sophisms, which would serve equally on both sides; and added, that both he and his father should be severely punished, if they were found guilty of the least injustice towards those who complained. All which made such a deep impression of terror in Cassander's mind, that long after, when he was king of Macedonia, and master of Greece, as he was walking up and down at Delphi, and looking at the statues, at the sight of that of Alexander he was suddenly struck with alarm, and shook all over, his eyes rolled, his head grew dizzy, and it was long before he recovered himself.

When once Alexander had given way to fears

of supernatural influence, his mind grew so disturbed and so easily alarmed, that if the least unusual or extraordinary thing happened, he thought it a prodigy or a presage, and his court was thronged with diviners and priests whose business was to sacrifice and purify and foretell the future. So miserable a thing is incredulity and contempt of divine power on the one hand, and so miserable also, superstition on the other, which like water, where the level has been lowered, flowing in and never stopping, fills the mind with slavish fears and follies, as now in Alexander's case. But upon some answers which were brought him from the oracle concerning Hephæstion, he laid aside his sorrow, and fell again to sacrificing and drinking; and having given Nearchus a splendid entertainment, after he had bathed, as was his custom, just as he was going to bed, at Medius's request he went to supper with him. Here he drank all the next day, and was attacked with a fever, which seized him, not as some write, after he had drunk of the bowl of Hercules; nor was he taken with any sudden pain in his back, as if he had been struck with a lance, for these are the inventions of some authors who thought it their duty to make the last scene of so great an action as tragical and moving as they could. Aristobulus tells us, that in the rage of his fever and a violent thirst, he took a draught of wine, upon which he fell into delirium, and died on the thirtieth day of the month Dæsius.

But the journals give the following record. On the eighteenth of the month, he slept in the bathing-room on account of his fever. The next day he bathed and removed into his chamber, and spent his time in playing at dice with Medius. In the evening he bathed and sacrificed, and ate freely,

and had the fever on him through the night. On
the twentieth, after the usual sacrifices and bathing,
he lay in the bathing-room and heard Nearchus's
narrative of his voyage, and the observations he had
made in the great sea. The twenty-first he passed
in the same manner, his fever still increasing, and
suffered much during the night. The next day
the fever was very violent, and he had himself removed and his bed set by the great bath, and dis-
coursed with his principal officers about finding fit
men to fill up the vacant places in the army. On
the twenty-fourth he was much worse, and was
carried out of his bed to assist at the sacrifices, and
gave order that the general officers should wait
within the court, whilst the inferior officers kept
watch without doors. On the twenty-fifth he was
removed to his palace on the other side the river,
where he slept a little, but his fever did not abate,
and when the generals came into his chamber, he
was speechless, and continued so the following day.
The Macedonians, therefore, supposing he was
dead, came with great clamors to the gates, and
menaced his friends so they were forced to admit
them, and let them all pass through unarmed along
by his bedside. The same day Python and Seleucus
were despatched to the temple of Serapis to inquire
if they should bring Alexander thither, and were
answered by the god, that they should not remove
him. On the twenty-eighth, in the evening, he died.
This account is most of it word for word as it is
written in the diary.

At the time, nobody had any suspicion of his
being poisoned, but upon some information given
six years after, they say Olympias put many to
death, and scattered the ashes of Iolaus, then dead,
as if he had given it him. But those who affirm that

Aristotle counselled Antipater to do it, and that by his means the poison was brought, adduce one Hagnothemis as their authority, who, they say, heard king Antigonus speak of it, and tell us that the poison was water, deadly cold as ice, distilling from a rock in the district of Nonacris, which they gathered like a thin dew, and kept in an ass's hoof; for it was so very cold and penetrating that no other vessel would hold it. However, most are of opinion that all this is a mere made-up story, no slight evidence of which is, that during the dissensions among the commanders, which lasted several days, the body continued clear and fresh, without any sign of such taint or corruption, though it lay neglected in a close, sultry place.

Roxana, who was now with child, and upon that account much honored by the Macedonians, being jealous of Statira, sent for her by a counterfeit letter, as if Alexander had been still alive; and when she had her in her power, killed her and her sister, and threw their bodies into a well, which they filled up with earth, not without the privity and assistance of Perdiccas, who in the time immediately following the king's death, under cover of the name of Arrhidæus, whom he carried about him as a sort of guard to his person,[38] exercised the chief authority. Arrhidæus, who was Philip's son by an obscure woman of the name of Philinna, was himself of weak intellect, not that he had been originally deficient either in body or mind; on

---

[38] *As a sort of guard to his person* should be rather, perhaps, *as a sort of badge of the royal power* which he himself exercised. The term seems to have been one in use for the mute person who appeared on the stage to attend the actor who represented a king.

the contrary, in his childhood, he had showed a happy and promising character enough. But a diseased habit of body, caused by drugs which Olympias gave him, had ruined not only his health, but his understanding.

CÆSAR [1]

TRANSLATED BY THE REV. DR. JAMES SMALRIDGE

AFTER Sylla became master of Rome, he wished to make Cæsar put away his wife Cornelia, daughter of Cinna, the late sole ruler of the commonwealth, but was unable to effect it either by promises or intimidation, and so contented himself with confiscating her dowry. The ground of Sylla's hostility to Cæsar, was the relationship between him and Marius; for Marius, the elder, married Julia, the sister of Cæsar's father, and had by her the younger Marius, who consequently was Cæsar's first cousin. And though at the beginning, while so many were to be put to death and there was so much to do, Cæsar was overlooked by Sylla, yet he would not keep quiet, but presented himself to the people as a candidate for the priesthood, though he was yet a mere boy. Sylla, without any open opposition, took measures to have him rejected, and in consultation whether he should be put to death,

---

[1] Julius Cæsar is usually considered to have been born in July, 100 B.C. But Mommsen gives strong reasons for fixing his birth in 102 B.C. He was perhaps the greatest man of antiquity, gifted with the most varied talents, a consummate statesman and general, the author of many literary works celebrated for purity of Latin and clearness of style. His main work as a statesman was to reorganize the government of the state, to fit the rule of an empire. The mask ought to be stripped off the false patriots whose object in murdering Cæsar was to gain power for themselves and their party. He was assassinated March 15, 44 B.C.
—DR. WILLIAM SMITH.

when it was urged by some that it was not worth
his while to contrive the death of a boy, he answered,
that they knew little who did not see more than
one Marius in that boy. Cæsar, on being informed
of this saying, concealed himself, and for a considerable time kept out of the way in the country
of the Sabines, often changing his quarters, till one
night, as he was removing from one house to another on account of his health, he fell into the
hands of Sylla's soldiers, who were searching those
parts in order to apprehend any who had absconded.
Cæsar, by a bribe of two talents, prevailed with
Cornelius their captain, to let him go, and was no
sooner dismissed but he put to sea, and made for
Bithynia. After a short stay there with Nicomedes,
the king, in his passage back he was taken near the
island Pharmacusa by some of the pirates, who,
at that time, with large fleets of ships and innumerable smaller vessels infested the seas everywhere.

When these men at first demanded of him twenty
talents for his ransom, he laughed at them for not
understanding the value of their prisoner, and
voluntarily engaged to give them fifty. He presently despatched those about him to several places
to raise the money, till at last he was left among
a set of the most bloodthirsty people in the world,
the Cilicians, only with one friend and two attendants. Yet he made so little of them, that when he
had a mind to sleep, he would send to them, and
order them to make no noise. For thirty-eight days,
with all the freedom in the world, he amused himself with joining in their exercises and games, as
if they had not been his keepers, but his guards.
He wrote verses and speeches, and made them his
auditors, and those who did not admire them, he

called to their faces illiterate and barbarous, and would often, in raillery, threaten to hang them. They were greatly taken with this, and attributed his free talking to a kind of simplicity and boyish playfulness. As soon as his ransom was come from Miletus, he paid it, and was discharged, and proceeded at once to man some ships at the port of Miletus, and went in pursuit of the pirates, whom he surprised with their ships still stationed at the island, and took most of them. Their money he made his prize, and the men he secured in prison at Pergamus, and made application to Junius, who was then governor of Asia, to whose office it belonged, as prætor, to determine their punishment. Junius, having his eye upon the money, for the sum was considerable, said he would think at his leisure what to do with the prisoners, upon which Cæsar took his leave of him, and went off to Pergamus, where he ordered the pirates to be brought forth and crucified; the punishment he had often threatened them with whilst he was in their hands, and they little dreamed he was in earnest.

In the mean time Sylla's power being now on the decline, Cæsar's friends advised him to return to Rome, but he went to Rhodes, and entered himself in the school of Apollonius,[2] Molon's son, a famous rhetorician, one who had the reputation of a worthy man, and had Cicero for one of his scholars. Cæsar is said to have been admirably fitted by nature to make a great statesman and orator, and to have taken such pains to improve his genius this way, that without dispute he might

---

[2] *Apollonius* should not be called, as he is both here and in the Life of Cicero, *Molon's son*, but Molon, or Molo, which was his additional name. It is Plutarch's mistake.

challenge the second place. More he did not aim at, as choosing to be first rather amongst men of arms and power, and, therefore, never rose to that height of eloquence to which nature would have carried him, his attention being diverted to those expeditions and designs, which at length gained him the empire. And he himself, in his answer to Cicero's panegyric on Cato, desires his reader not to compare the plain discourse of a soldier with the harangues of an orator who had not only fine parts, but had employed his life in this study.

When he was returned to Rome, he accused Dolabella of maladministration, and many cities of Greece came in to attest it. Dolabella was acquitted, and Cæsar, in return for the support he had received from the Greeks, assisted them in their prosecution of Publius Antonius for corrupt practices, before Marcus Lucullus, prætor of Macedonia. In this cause he so far succeeded, that Antonius was forced to appeal to the tribunes at Rome, alleging that in Greece he could not have fair play against Grecians. In his pleadings at Rome, his eloquence soon obtained him great credit and favor, and he won no less upon the affections of the people by the affability of his manners and address, in which he showed a tact and consideration beyond what could have been expected at his age; and the open house he kept, the entertainments he gave, and the general splendor of his manner of life contributed little by little to create and increase his political influence. His enemies slighted the growth of it at first, presuming it would soon fail when his money was gone; whilst in the mean time it was growing up and flourishing among the common people. When his power at last was established and not to be overthrown, and now openly tended to the altering of the whole constitution, they were aware too late, that there is no beginning so mean, which continued application will not make considerable, and that despising a danger at first, will make it at last irresistible. Cicero was the first who had any suspicions of his designs upon the government, and, as a good pilot is apprehensive of a storm when the sea is most smiling, saw the designing temper of the man through this disguise of good-humor and affability, and said, that in general, in all he did and undertook, he detected the ambition for absolute power, "but when I see his hair so carefully arranged, and observe him adjusting it with one finger, I cannot imagine it should enter into such a man's thoughts to subvert the Roman state." But of this more hereafter.

The first proof he had of the people's good-will to him, was when he received by their suffrages a tribuneship in the army, and came out on the list with a higher place than Caius Popilius. A second and clearer instance of their favor appeared upon his making a magnificent oration in praise of his aunt Julia, wife to Marius, publicly in the forum, at whose funeral he was so bold as to bring forth the images of Marius, which nobody had dared to produce since the government came into Sylla's hands, Marius's party having from that time been declared enemies of the state. When some who were present had begun to raise a cry against Cæsar, the people answered with loud shouts and clapping in his favor, expressing their joyful surprise and satisfaction at his having, as it were, brought up again from the grave those honors of Marius, which for so long a time had been lost to the city. It had always been the custom at Rome to make funeral orations in praise of elderly matrons, but there was no precedent of any upon young women till Cæsar first made one upon the death of his own wife. This also procured him favor, and by this show of affection he won upon the feelings of the people, who looked upon him as a man of great tenderness and kindness of heart. After he had buried his wife, he went as quæstor into Spain under one of the prætors, named Vetus, whom he honored ever after, and made his son his own quæstor, when he himself came to be prætor. After this employment was ended, he married Pompeia, his third wife, having then a daughter by Cornelia, his first wife, whom he afterwards married to Pompey the Great. He was so profuse in his expenses, that before he had any public employment, he was in debt thirteen hundred talents, and many thought that by incurring such expense to be popular, he changed a solid good for what would prove but a short and uncertain return; but in truth he was purchasing what was of the greatest value at an inconsiderable rate. When he was made surveyor of the Appian Way, he disbursed, besides the public money, a great sum out of his private purse; and when he was ædile, he provided such a number of gladiators, that he entertained the people with three hundred and twenty single combats, and by his great liberality and magnificence in theatrical shows, in processions, and public feastings, he threw into the shade all the attempts that had been made before him, and gained so much upon the people, that every one was eager to find out new offices and new honors for him in return for his munificence.

There being two factions in the city, one that of Sylla, which was very powerful, the other that of

Marius, which was then broken and in a very low condition, he undertook to revive this and to make it his own. And to this end, whilst he was in the height of his repute with the people for the magnificent shows he gave as ædile, he ordered images of Marius, and figures of Victory, with trophies in their hands, to be carried privately in the night and placed in the capitol. Next morning, when some saw them bright with gold and beautifully made, with inscriptions upon them, referring them to Marius's exploits over the Cimbrians, they were surprised at the boldness of him who had set them up, nor was it difficult to guess who it was. The fame of this soon spread and brought together a great concourse of people. Some cried out that it was an open attempt against the established government thus to revive those honors which had been buried by the laws and decrees of the senate; that Cæsar had done it to sound the temper of the people whom he had prepared before, and to try whether they were tame enough to bear his humor, and would quietly give way to his innovations. On the other hand, Marius's party took courage, and it was incredible how numerous they were suddenly seen to be, and what a multitude of them appeared and came shouting into the capitol. Many, when they saw Marius's likeness, cried for joy, and Cæsar was highly extolled as the one man, in the place of all others, who was a relation worthy of Marius. Upon this the senate met, and Catulus Lutatius, one of the most eminent Romans of that time, stood up and inveighed against Cæsar, closing his speech with the remarkable saying, that Cæsar was now not working mines, but planting batteries to overthrow the state. But when Cæsar had made an apology for himself, and satisfied the senate, his admirers were very much animated, and advised him not to depart from his own thoughts for any one, since with the people's good favor he would erelong get the better of them all, and be the first man in the commonwealth.

At this time, Metellus, the High-Priest,[3] died, and Catulus and Isauricus, persons of the highest reputation, and who had great influence in the senate, were competitors for the office; yet Cæsar would not give way to them, but presented himself to the people as a candidate against them. The several parties seeming very equal, Catulus, who, because he had the most honor to lose, was the most apprehensive of the event, sent to Cæsar to buy him off, with offers of a great sum of money. But his answer was, that he was ready to borrow a larger sum than that, to carry on the contest. Upon the day of election, as his mother conducted him out of doors with tears, after embracing her, "My mother," he said, "to-day you will see me either High-Priest, or an exile." When the votes were taken, after a great struggle, he carried it, and excited among the senate and nobility great alarm lest he might now urge on the people to every kind of insolence. And Piso and Catulus found fault with Cicero for having let Cæsar escape, when in the conspiracy of Catiline he had given the government such advantage against him. For Catiline, who had designed not only to change the present state of affairs, but to subvert the whole empire and confound all, had himself taken to flight, while

---

[3] *High Priest* is the Latin Pontifex Maximus. The highest religious dignities were held, at Rome, by laymen. Cæsar, as High Priest, had an official residence, the Regia, in which he lived to the day of his death.

the evidence was yet incomplete against him, before his ultimate purposes had been properly discovered. But he had left Lentulus and Cethegus in the city to supply his place in the conspiracy, and whether they received any secret encouragement and assistance from Cæsar is uncertain; all that is certain, is, that they were fully convicted in the senate, and when Cicero, the consul, asked the several opinions of the senators, how they would have them punished, all who spoke before Cæsar sentenced them to death; but Cæsar stood up and made a set speech, in which he told them, that he thought it without precedent and not just to take away the lives of persons of their birth and distinction before they were fairly tried, unless there was an absolute necessity for it; but that if they were kept confined in any towns of Italy Cicero himself should choose, till Catiline was defeated, then the senate might in peace and at their leisure determine what was best to be done.

This sentence of his carried so much appearance of humanity, and he gave it such advantage by the eloquence with which he urged it, that not only those who spoke after him closed with it, but even they who had before given a contrary opinion, now came over to his, till it came about to Catulus's and Cato's turn to speak. They warmly opposed it, and Cato intimated in his speech the suspicion of Cæsar himself, and pressed the matter so strongly, that the criminals were given up to suffer execution. As Cæsar was going out of the senate, many of the young men who at that time acted as guards to Cicero, ran in with their naked swords to assault him. But Curio, it is said, threw his gown over him, and conveyed him away, and Cicero himself, when the young men looked up to see his wishes, gave a sign not to kill him, either for fear of the people, or because he thought the murder unjust and illegal. If this be true, I wonder how Cicero came to omit all mention of it in his book about his consulship. He was blamed, however, afterwards, for not having made use of so fortunate an opportunity against Cæsar, as if he had let it escape him out of fear of the populace, who, indeed, showed remarkable solicitude about Cæsar, and some time after, when he went into the senate to clear himself of the suspicions he lay under, and found great clamors raised against him, upon the senate in consequence sitting longer than ordinary, they went up to the house in a tumult, and beset it, demanding Cæsar, and requiring them to dismiss him. Upon this, Cato, much fearing some movement among the poor citizens, who were always the first to kindle the flame among the people, and placed all their hopes in Cæsar, persuaded the senate to give them a monthly allowance of corn, an expedient which put the commonwealth to the extraordinary charge of seven million five hundred thousand drachmas[4] in the year, but quite succeeded in removing the great cause of terror for the present, and very much weakened Cæsar's power, who at that time was just going to be made prætor, and consequently would have been more formidable by his office.

But there was no disturbance during his prætorship, only what misfortune he met with in his own domestic affairs. Publius Clodius was a patrician by descent, eminent both for his riches and eloquence, but in licentiousness of life and audacity exceeded the most noted profligates of the day. He was in love with Pompeia, Cæsar's wife, and she

[4] About $1,500,000.

had no aversion to him. But there was strict watch kept on her apartment, and Cæsar's mother, Aurelia, who was a discreet woman, being continually about her, made any interview very dangerous and difficult. The Romans have a goddess whom they call Bona, the same whom the Greeks call Gynæcea. The Phrygians, who claim a peculiar title to her, say she was mother to Midas. The Romans profess she was one of the Dryads, and married to Faunus. The Grecians affirm that she is the mother of Bacchus whose name is not to be uttered, and, for this reason, the women who celebrate her festival, cover the tents with vine-branches, and, in accordance with the fable, a consecrated serpent is placed by the goddess. It is not lawful for a man to be by, nor so much as in the house, whilst the rites are celebrated, but the women by themselves perform the sacred offices, which are said to be much the same with those used in the solemnities of Orpheus. When the festival comes, the husband, who is either consul or prætor, and with him every male creature, quits the house. The wife then taking it under her care, sets it in order, and the principal ceremonies are performed during the night, the women playing together amongst themselves as they keep watch, and music of various kinds going on.

As Pompeia was at that time celebrating this feast, Clodius, who as yet had no beard, and so thought to pass undiscovered, took upon him the dress and ornaments of a singing woman, and so came thither, having the air of a young girl. Finding the doors open, he was without any stop introduced by the maid, who was in the intrigue. She presently ran to tell Pompeia, but as she was away a long time, he grew uneasy in waiting for her, and left his post and traversed the house from one room to another, still taking care to avoid the lights, till at last Aurelia's woman met him, and invited him to play with her, as the women did among themselves. He refused to comply, and she presently pulled him forward, and asked him who he was, and whence he came. Clodius told her he was waiting for Pompeia's own maid, Abra,[5] being in fact her own name also, and as he said so, betrayed himself by his voice. Upon which the woman shrieking, ran into the company where there were lights, and cried out, she had discovered a man. The women were all in a fright. Aurelia covered up the sacred things and stopped the proceedings, and having ordered the doors to be shut, went about with lights to find Clodius, who was got into the maid's room that he had come in with, and was seized there. The women knew him, and drove him out of doors, and at once, that same night, went home and told their husbands the story. In the morning, it was all about the town, what an impious attempt Clodius had made, and how he ought to be punished as an offender, not only against those whom he had affronted, but also against the public and the gods. Upon which one of the tribunes impeached him for profaning the holy rites, and some of the principal senators combined together and gave evidence against him, that besides many other horrible crimes, he had been guilty of incest with his own sister, who was married to Lucullus. But the people set themselves against this combination of the nobility,

[5] Abra was the Greek word for the favorite waiting-maid; and was, also, this girl's own proper name. Clodius said he was waiting for Pompeia's *Abra,* that being, also, as it happened, her name.

and defended Clodius, which was of great service to him with the judges, who took alarm and were afraid to provoke the multitude. Cæsar at once dismissed Pompeia, but being summoned as a witness against Clodius, said he had nothing to charge him with. This looking like a paradox, the accuser asked him why he parted with his wife. Cæsar replied, "I wished my wife to be not so much as suspected." Some say that Cæsar spoke this as his real thought; others, that he did it to gratify the people, who were very earnest to save Clodius. Clodius, at any rate, escaped; most of the judges giving their opinions so written as to be illegible, that they might not be in danger from the people by condemning him, nor in disgrace with the nobility by acquitting him.

Cæsar, in the mean time, being out of his prætorship, had got the province of Spain, but was in great embarrassment with his creditors, who, as he was going off, came upon him, and were very pressing and importunate. This led him to apply himself to Crassus, who was the richest man in Rome, but wanted Cæsar's youthful vigor and heat to sustain the opposition against Pompey. Crassus took upon him to satisfy those creditors who were most uneasy to him, and would not be put off any longer, and engaged himself to the amount of eight hundred and thirty talents, upon which Cæsar was now at liberty to go to his province. In his journey, as he was crossing the Alps, and passing by a small village of the barbarians with but few inhabitants and those wretchedly poor, his companions asked the question among themselves by way of mockery, if there were any canvassing for offices there; any contention which should be uppermost, or feuds of great men one against another. To which Cæsar made answer seriously, "For my part, I had rather be the first man among these fellows, than the second man in Rome." It is said that another time, when free from business in Spain, after reading some part of the history of Alexander, he sat a great while very thoughtful, and at last burst out into tears. His friends were surprised, and asked him the reason of it. "Do you think," said he, "I have not just cause to weep, when I consider that Alexander at my age had conquered so many nations, and I have all this time done nothing that is memorable?" As soon as he came into Spain he was very active, and in a few days had got together ten new cohorts of foot in addition to the twenty which were there before. With these he marched against the Calaici and Lusitani and conquered them, and advancing as far as the ocean, subdued the tribes which never before had been subject to the Romans. Having managed his military affairs with good success, he was equally happy in the course of his civil government. He took pains to establish a good understanding amongst the several states, and no less care to heal the differences between debtors and creditors. He ordered that the creditor should receive two parts of the debtor's yearly income, and that the other part should be managed by the debtor himself, till by this method the whole debt was at last discharged. This conduct made him leave his province with a fair reputation; being rich himself, and having enriched his soldiers, and having received from them the honorable name of Imperator.

There is a law among the Romans, that whoever desires the honor of a triumph must stay without the city and expect his answer. And another, that those who stand for the consulship shall appear personally upon the place. Cæsar was come home at the very time of choosing consuls, and being in a difficulty between these two opposite laws, sent to the senate to desire that since he was obliged to be absent, he might sue for the consulship by his friends. Cato, being backed by the law, at first opposed his request; afterwards perceiving that Cæsar had prevailed with a great part of the senate to comply with it, he made it his business to gain time, and went on wasting the whole day in speaking. Upon which Cæsar thought fit to let the triumph fall, and pursued the consulship. Entering the town and coming forward immediately, he had recourse to a piece of state-policy by which everybody was deceived but Cato. This was the reconciling of Crassus and Pompey, the two men who then were most powerful in Rome. There had been a quarrel between them, which he now succeeded in making up, and by this means strengthened himself by the united power of both, and so under the cover of an action which carried all the appearance of a piece of kindness and good-nature, caused what was in effect a revolution in the government. For it was not the quarrel between Pompey and Cæsar, as most men imagine, which was the origin of the civil wars, but their union, their conspiring together at first to subvert the aristocracy, and so quarrelling afterwards between themselves. Cato, who often foretold what the consequence of this alliance would be, had then the character of a sullen, interfering man, but in the end the reputation of a wise but unsuccessful counsellor.

Thus Cæsar being doubly supported by the interests of Crassus and Pompey, was promoted to the consulship, and triumphantly proclaimed with

Calpurnius Bibulus. When he entered on his
office, he brought in bills which would have been
preferred with better grace by the most audacious
of the tribunes than by a consul, in which he proposed
the plantation of colonies and division of lands,
simply to please the commonalty. The best and
most honorable of the senators opposed it, upon
which, as he had long wished for nothing more
than for such a colorable pretext, he loudly protested how much against his will it was to be driven
to seek support from the people, and how the
senate's insulting and harsh conduct left no other
course possible for him, than to devote himself
henceforth to the popular cause and interest. And
so he hurried out of the senate, and presenting himself to the people, and there placing Crassus and
Pompey, one on each side of him, he asked them
whether they consented to the bills he had proposed.
They owned their assent, upon which he desired
them to assist him against those who had threatened
to oppose him with their swords. They engaged
they would, and Pompey added further, that he
would meet their swords with a sword and buckler
too. These words the nobles much resented, as
neither suitable to his own dignity, nor becoming
the reverence due to the senate, but resembling rather
the vehemence of a boy, or the fury of a madman.
But the people were pleased with it. In order to
get a yet firmer hold upon Pompey, Cæsar having
a daughter, Julia, who had been before contracted to
Servilius Cæpio, now betrothed her to Pompey, and
told Servilius he should have Pompey's daughter,
who was not unengaged either, but promised to Sylla's
son, Faustus. A little time after, Cæsar married
Calpurnia, the daughter of Piso, and got Piso
made consul for the year following. Cato exclaimed

loudly against this, and protested with a great deal of warmth, that it was intolerable the government should be prostituted by marriages, and that they should advance one another to the commands of armies, provinces, and other great posts, by means of women. Bibulus, Cæsar's colleague, finding it was to no purpose to oppose his bills, but that he was in danger of being murdered in the forum, as also was Cato, confined himself to his house, and there let the remaining part of his consulship expire. Pompey, when he was married, at once filled the forum with soldiers, and gave the people his help in passing the new laws, and secured Cæsar the government of all Gaul, both on this and the other side of the Alps, together with Illyricum, and the command of four legions for five years. Cato made some attempts against these proceedings, but was seized and led off on the way to prison by Cæsar, who expected he would appeal to the tribunes. But when he saw that Cato went along without speaking a word, and not only the nobility were indignant, but that the people, also, out of respect for Cato's virtue, were following in silence, and with dejected looks, he himself privately desired one of the tribunes to rescue Cato. As for the other senators, some few of them attended the house, the rest being disgusted, absented themselves. Hence Considius, a very old man, took occasion one day to tell Cæsar, that the senators did not meet because they were afraid of his soldiers. Cæsar asked, "Why don't you then, out of the same fear, keep at home?" To which Considius replied, that age was his guard against fear, and that the small remains of his life were not worth much caution. But the most disgraceful thing that was done in Cæsar's consulship, was his assisting to gain the tribuneship for the same Clodius who had made the attempt upon his wife's chastity, and intruded upon the secret vigils. He was elected on purpose to effect Cicero's downfall; nor did Cæsar leave the city to join his army, till they two had overpowered Cicero, and driven him out of Italy.

Thus far have we followed Cæsar's actions before the wars of Gaul. After this, he seems to begin his course afresh, and to enter upon a new life and scene of action. And the period of those wars which he now fought, and those many expeditions in which he subdued Gaul, showed him to be a soldier and general not in the least inferior to any of the greatest and most admired commanders who had ever appeared at the head of armies. For if we compare him with the Fabii, the Metelli, the Scipios, and with those who were his contemporaries, or not long before him, Sylla, Marius, the two Luculli, or even Pompey himself, whose glory, it may be said, went up at that time to heaven [6] for every excellence in war, we shall find Cæsar's actions to have surpassed them all. One he may be held to have outdone in consideration of the difficulty of the country in which he fought, another in the extent of territory which he conquered; some, in the number and strength of the enemies whom he defeated; one man, because of

---

[6] The words *whose glory went up at that time to heaven* should have perhaps been placed between inverted commas. The form, if not the exact words of the phrase, is from the Odyssey; the nearest passage to it is in the answer made by Ulysses to the inquiry of the Cyclops: "We are Achaians on our way from Troy, driven by the winds, the people of Atrides Agamemnon, whose glory is at this time the greatest under heaven, so great a city he has taken, and so many people has destroyed."

the wildness and perfidiousness of the tribes whose good-will be conciliated, another in his humanity and clemency to those he overpowered; others, again in his gifts and kindnesses to his soldiers; all alike in the number of the battles which he fought and the enemies whom he killed. For he had not pursued the wars in Gaul full ten years, when he had taken by storm above eight hundred towns, subdued three hundred states, and of the three millions of men, who made up the gross sum of those with whom at several times he engaged, he had killed one million, and taken captive a second.

He was so much master of the good-will and hearty service of his soldiers, that those who in other expeditions were but ordinary men, displayed a courage past defeating or withstanding when they went upon any danger where Cæsar's glory was concerned. Such a one was Acilius, who, in the sea-fight before Marseilles, had his right hand struck off with a sword, yet did not quit his buckler out of his left, but struck the enemies in the face with it, till he drove them off, and made himself master of the vessel. Such another was Cassius Scæva, who, in a battle near Dyrrhachium, had one of his eyes shot out with an arrow, his shoulder pierced with one javelin, and his thigh with another; and having received one hundred and thirty darts upon his target, called to the enemy, as though he would surrender himself. But when two of them came up to him, he cut off the shoulder of one with a sword, and by a blow over the face forced the other to retire, and so with the assistance of his friends, who now came up, made his escape. Again, in Britain, when some of the foremost officers had accidentally got into a morass full of water, and there were assaulted by the enemy, a common soldier, whilst Cæsar stood and looked on, threw himself into the midst of them, and after many signal demonstrations of his valor, rescued the officers, and beat off the barbarians. He himself, in the end, took to the water, and with much difficulty, partly by swimming, partly by wading, passed it, but in the passage lost his shield. Cæsar and his officers saw it and admired, and went to meet him with joy and acclamation. But the soldier, much dejected and in tears, threw himself down at Cæsar's feet, and begged his pardon for having let go his buckler. Another time in Africa, Scipio having taken a ship of Cæsar's in which Granius Petro, lately appointed quæstor, was sailing, gave the other passengers as free prize to his soldiers, but thought fit to offer the quæstor his life. But he said it was not usual for Cæsar's soldiers to take, but give mercy, and having said so, fell upon his sword and killed himself.

This love of honor and passion for distinction were inspired into them and cherished in them by Cæsar himself, who, by his unsparing distribution of money and honors, showed them that he did not heap up wealth from the wars for his own luxury, or the gratifying his private pleasures, but that all he received was but a public fund laid by for the reward and encouragement of valor, and that he looked upon all he gave to deserving soldiers as so much increase to his own riches. Added to this, also, there was no danger to which he did not willingly expose himself, no labor from which he pleaded an exemption. His contempt of danger was not so much wondered at by his soldiers, because they knew how much he coveted honor. But his enduring so much hardship, which he did to all appearance beyond his natural strength, very much astonished them. For he was a spare man, had a soft and white skin, was distempered in the head, and subject to an epilepsy, which, it is said, first seized him at Corduba. But he did not make the weakness of his constitution a pretext for his ease, but rather used war as the best physic against his indispositions; whilst by indefatigable journeys, coarse diet, frequent lodging in the field, and continual laborious exercise, he struggled with his diseases, and fortified his body against all attacks. He slept generally in his chariots or litters, employing even his rest in pursuit of action. In the day he was thus carried to the forts, garrisons, and camps, one servant sitting with him, who used to write down what he dictated as he went, and a soldier attending behind with his sword drawn. He drove so rapidly, that when he first left Rome, he arrived at the river Rhone within eight days. He had been an expert rider from his childhood; for it was usual with him to sit with his hands joined together behind his back, and so to put his horse to its full speed. And in this war he disciplined himself so far as to be able to dictate letters from on horseback, and to give directions to two who took notes at the same time, or, as Oppius says, to more. And it is thought that he was the first who contrived means for communicating with friends by cipher, when either press of business, or the large extent of the city, left him no time for a personal conference about matters that required despatch. How little nice he was in his diet, may be seen in the following instance. When at the table of Valerius Leo, who entertained him at supper at Milan, a dish of asparagus was put before him, on which his host instead of oil had poured sweet ointment. Cæsar partook of it without any disgust, and reprimanded his friends for finding fault with it.

"For it was enough," said he, "not to eat what you did not like; but he who reflects on another man's want of breeding, shows he wants it as much himself." Another time upon the road he was driven by a storm into a poor man's cottage, where he found but one room, and that such as would afford but a mean reception to a single person, and therefore told his companions, places of honor should be given up to the greater men, and necessary accommodations to the weaker, and accordingly ordered that Oppius, who was in bad health, should lodge within, whilst he and the rest slept under a shed at the door.

His first war in Gaul was against the Helvetians and Tigurini, who having burnt their own towns, twelve in number, and four hundred villages, would have marched forward through that part of Gaul which was included in the Roman province, as the Cimbrians and Teutons formerly had done. Nor were they inferior to these in courage; and in numbers they were equal, being in all three hundred thousand, of which one hundred and ninety thousand were fighting men. Cæsar did not engage the Tigurini in person, but Labienus, under his directions, routed them near the river Arar. The Helvetians surprised Cæsar, and unexpectedly set upon him as he was conducting his army to a confederate town. He succeeded, however, in making his retreat into a strong position, where, when he had mustered and marshalled his men, his horse was brought to him; upon which he said, "When I have won the battle, I will use my horse for the chase, but at present let us go against the enemy," and accordingly charged them on foot. After a long and severe combat, he drove the main army out of the field, but found the hardest work at their carriages and ramparts, where not only the men stood and fought, but the women also and children defended themselves, till they were cut to pieces; insomuch that the fight was scarcely ended till midnight. This action, glorious in itself, Cæsar crowned with another yet more noble, by gathering in a body all the barbarians that had escaped out of the battle, above one hundred thousand in number, and obliging them to reoccupy the country which they had deserted, and the cities which they had burnt. This he did for fear the Germans should pass in and possess themselves of the land whilst it lay uninhabited.

His second war was in defence of the Gauls against the Germans, though some time before he had made Ariovistus, their king, recognized at Rome as an ally. But they were very insufferable neighbors to those under his government; and it was probable, when occasion offered, they would renounce the present arrangements, and march on to occupy Gaul. But finding his officers timorous, and especially those of the young nobility who came along with him in hopes of turning their campaigns with him into a means for their own pleasure or profit, he called them together, and advised them to march off, and not run the hazard of a battle against their inclinations, since they had such weak and unmanly feelings; telling them that he would take only the tenth legion, and march against the barbarians, whom he did not expect to find an enemy more formidable than the Cimbri, nor, he added, should they find him a general inferior to Marius. Upon this, the tenth legion deputed some of their body to pay him their acknowledgments and thanks, and the other legions blamed their officers, and all, with great vigor and zeal, followed him many days' journey, till they encamped within two hundred furlongs of the enemy. Ariovistus's courage to some extent was cooled upon their very approach; for never expecting the Romans would attack the Germans, whom he had thought it more likely they would not venture to withstand even in defence of their own subjects, he was the more surprised at Cæsar's conduct, and saw his army to be in consternation. They were still more discouraged by the prophecies of their holy women, who foretell the future by observing the eddies of rivers, and taking signs from the windings and noise of streams, and who now warned them not to engage before the next new moon appeared. Cæsar having had intimation of this, and seeing the Germans lie still, thought it expedient to attack them whilst they were under these apprehensions, rather than sit still and wait their time. Accordingly he made his approaches to the strong-holds and hills on which they lay encamped, and so galled and fretted them, that at last they came down with great fury to engage. But he gained a signal victory, and pursued them for four hundred furlongs, as far as the Rhine; all which space was covered with spoils and bodies of the slain. Ariovistus made shift to pass the Rhine with the small remains of an army, for it is said the number of the slain amounted to eighty thousand.

After this action, Cæsar left his army at their winter-quarters in the country of the Sequani, and in order to attend to affairs at Rome, went into that part of Gaul which lies on the Po, and was part of his province; for the river Rubicon divides Gaul, which is on this side the Alps, from the rest of Italy. There he sat down and employed himself in courting people's favor; great numbers coming to him continually, and always finding their requests answered; for he never failed to dismiss all with present pledges of his kindness in hand, and further hopes for the future. And during all this time of the war in Gaul, Pompey never observed how Cæsar was on the one hand using the arms of Rome to effect his conquests, and on the other was gaining over and securing to himself the favor of the Romans, with the wealth which those conquests obtained him. But when he heard that the Belgæ, who were the most powerful of all the Gauls, and inhabited a third part of the country, were revolted, and had got together a great many thousand men in arms, he immediately set out and took his way thither with great expedition, and falling upon the enemy as they were ravaging the Gauls, his allies, he soon defeated and put to flight the largest and least scattered division of them. For though their numbers were great, yet they made but a slender defence, and the marshes and deep rivers were made passable to the Roman foot by the vast quantity of dead bodies. Of those who revolted, all the tribes that lived near the ocean came over without fighting, and he, therefore, led his army against the Nervii, the fiercest and most warlike people of all in those parts. These live in a country covered with continuous woods, and having lodged their children and property out of the way in the depth of the forest, fell upon Cæsar with a body of sixty thousand men, before he was prepared for them, while he was making his encampment. They soon routed his cavalry, and having surrounded the twelfth and seventh legions, killed all the officers, and had not Cæsar himself snatched up a buckler, and forced his way through his own men to come up to the barbarians, or had not the tenth legion, when they saw him in danger, run in from the tops of the hills, where they lay, and broken through the enemy's ranks to rescue him, in all probability not a Roman would have been saved. But now, under the influence of Cæsar's bold example, they fought a battle, as the phrase is, of more than human courage, and yet with their utmost efforts they were not able to drive the enemy out of the field, but cut them down fighting in their defence. For out of sixty thousand men, it is stated that not above five hundred survived the battle, and of four hundred of their senators not above three.

When the Roman senate had received news of this, they voted sacrifices and festivals to the gods, to be strictly observed for the space of fifteen days, a longer space than ever was observed for any victory before. The danger to which they had been exposed by the joint outbreak of such a number of nations was felt to have been great; and the people's fondness for Cæsar gave additional lustre to successes achieved by him. He now, after settling every thing in Gaul, came back again, and spent the winter by the Po, in order to carry on the designs he had in hand at Rome. All who were candidates for offices used his assistance, and were supplied with money from him to corrupt the people and buy their votes, in return of which, when they were chosen, they did all things to advance his power. But what was more considerable, the most eminent and powerful men in Rome in great numbers came to visit him at Lucca, Pompey, and Crassus, and Appius, the governor of Sardinia, and Nepos, the proconsul of Spain, so that there were in the place at one time one hundred and twenty lictors, and more than two hundred senators. In deliberation here held, it was determined that

Pompey and Crassus should be consuls again for the following year; that Cæsar should have a fresh supply of money, and that his command should be renewed to him for five years more. It seemed very extravagant to all thinking men, that those very persons who had received so much money from Cæsar should persuade the senate to grant him more, as if he were in want. Though in truth it was not so much upon persuasion as compulsion, that, with sorrow and groans for their own acts, they passed the measure. Cato was not present, for they had sent him seasonably out of the way into Cyprus; but Favonius, who was a zealous imitator of Cato, when he found he could do no good by opposing it, broke out of the house, and loudly declaimed against these proceedings to the people, but none gave him any hearing; some slighting him out of respect to Crassus and Pompey, and the greater part to gratify Cæsar, on whom depended their hopes.

After this, Cæsar returned again to his forces in Gaul, where he found that country involved in a dangerous war, two strong nations of the Germans having lately passed the Rhine, to conquer it; one of them called the Usipes, the other the Tenteritæ.[7] Of the war with this people, Cæsar himself has given this account in his commentaries, that the barbarians, having sent ambassadors to treat with him, did, during the treaty, set upon him in his march, by which means with eight hundred men

---

[7] The Usipetes and Tencteri of Cæsar's own narrative. The Sugambri below are the same as the Sigambri or Sicambri in the neighborhood of the river Sieg. Tanusius was an historical writer, and is quoted by Suetonius. The bridge was probably a little below Coblenz.

they routed five thousand of his horse, who did not suspect their coming; that afterwards they sent other ambassadors to renew the same fraudulent practices, whom he kept in custody, and led on his army against the barbarians, as judging it mere simplicity to keep faith with those who had so faithlessly broken the terms they had agreed to. But Tanusius states, that when the senate decreed festivals and sacrifices for this victory, Cato declared it to be his opinion that Cæsar ought to be given into the hands of the barbarians, that so the guilt which this breach of faith might otherwise bring upon the state, might be expiated by transferring the curse on him, who was the occasion of it. Of those who passed the Rhine, there were four hundred thousand cut off; those few who escaped were sheltered by the Sugambri, a people of Germany. Cæsar took hold of this pretence to invade the Germans, being at the same time ambitious of the honor of being the first man that should pass the Rhine with an army. He carried a bridge across it, though it was very wide, and the current at that particular point very full, strong, and violent, bringing down with its waters trunks of trees, and other lumber, which much shook and weakened the foundations of his bridge. But he drove great piles of wood into the bottom of the river above the passage, to catch and stop these as they floated down, and thus fixing his bridle upon the stream, successfully finished his bridge, which no one who saw could believe to be the work but of ten days.

In the passage of his army over it, he met with no opposition; the Suevi themselves, who are the most warlike people of all Germany, flying with their effects into the deepest and most densely wooded valleys. When he had burnt all the enemy's country, and encouraged those who embraced the Roman interest, he went back into Gaul, after eighteen days' stay in Germany. But his expedition into Britain was the most famous testimony of his courage. For he was the first who brought a navy into the western ocean, or who sailed into the Atlantic with an army to make war; and by invading an island, the reported extent of which had made its existence a matter of controversy among historians, many of whom questioned whether it were not a mere name and fiction, not a real place, he might be said to have carried the Roman empire beyond the limits of the known world. He passed thither twice from that part of Gaul which lies over against it, and in several battles which he fought, did more hurt to the enemy than service to himself, for the islanders were so miserably poor, that they had nothing worth being plundered of. When he found himself unable to put such an end to the war as he wished, he was content to take hostages from the king, and to impose a tribute, and then quitted the island. At his arrival in Gaul, he found letters which lay ready to be conveyed over the water to him from his friends at Rome, announcing his daughter's death, who died in labor of a child by Pompey. Cæsar and Pompey both were much afflicted with her death, nor were their friends less disturbed, believing that the alliance was now broken, which had hitherto kept the sickly commonwealth in peace, for the child also died within a few days after the mother. The people took the body of Julia, in spite of the opposition of the tribunes, and carried it into the field of Mars, and there her funeral rites were performed, and her remains are laid.

Cæsar's army was now grown very numerous, so that he was forced to disperse them into various camps for their winter-quarters, and he having gone himself to Italy, as he used to do, in his absence a general outbreak throughout the whole of Gaul commenced, and large armies marched about the country, and attacked the Roman quarters, and attempted to make themselves masters of the forts where they lay. The greatest and strongest party of the rebels, under the command of Abriorix, cut off Cotta and Titurius with all their men, while a force sixty thousand strong besieged the legion under the command of Cicero,[8] and had almost taken it by storm, the Roman soldiers being all wounded, and having quite spent themselves by a defence beyond their natural strength. But Cæsar, who was at a great distance, having received the news, quickly got together seven thousand men, and hastened to relieve Cicero. The besiegers were aware of it, and went to meet him, with great confidence that they should easily overpower such an handful of men. Cæsar, to increase their presumption, seemed to avoid fighting, and still marched off, till he found a place conveniently situated for a few to engage against many, where he encamped. He kept his soldiers from making any attack upon the enemy, and commanded them to raise the ramparts higher, and barricade the gates, that by show of fear, they might heighten the enemy's contempt of them. Till at last they came without any order in great security to make an assault, when he issued forth, and put them to flight with the loss of many men.

[8] Quintus Cicero, the orator's brother.   Abriorix is Ambiorix of the Commentares.

This quieted the greater part of the commotions in these parts of Gaul, and Cæsar, in the course of the winter, visited every part of the country, and with great vigilance took precautions against all innovations. For there were three legions now come to him to supply the place of the men he had lost, of which Pompey furnished him with two, out of those under his command; the other was newly raised in the part of Gaul by the Po. But in a while the seeds of war, which had long since been secretly sown and scattered by the most powerful men in those warlike nations, broke forth into the greatest and most dangerous war that ever was in those parts, both as regards the number of men in the vigor of their youth who were gathered and armed from all quarters, the vast funds of money collected to maintain it, the strength of the towns, and the difficulty of the country where it was carried on. It being winter, the rivers were frozen, the woods covered with snow, and the level country flooded, so that in some places the ways were lost through the depth of the snow; in others, the overflowing of marshes and streams made every kind of passage uncertain. All which difficulties made it seem impracticable for Cæsar to make any attempt upon the insurgents. Many tribes had revolted together, the chief of them being the Arverni and Carnutini;[9] the general who had the supreme command in war was Vergentorix, whose

---

[9] The Arverni, the same people whom he presently calls the Aruveni, of the mountains of Auvergne, and the Carnutes of the country around Orleans. Vergentorix appears to be a Greek abbreviation of Vercingetorix, the full name given by Cæsar, which is itself conceived to have been not a proper name, but a title.

father the Gauls had put to death on suspicion of his aiming at absolute government.

He having disposed his army in several bodies, and set officers over them, drew over to him all the country round about as far as those that lie upon the Arar, and having intelligence of the opposition which Cæsar now experienced at Rome, thought to engage all Gaul in the war. Which if he had done a little later, when Cæsar was taken up with the civil wars, Italy had been put into as great a terror as before it was by the Cimbri. But Cæsar, who above all men was gifted with the faculty of making the right use of every thing in war, and most especially of seizing the right moment, as soon as he heard of the revolt, returned immediately the same way he went,[10] and showed the barbarians, by the quickness of his march in such a severe season, that an army was advancing against them which was invincible. For in the time that one would have thought it scarce credible that a courier or express should have come with a message from him, he himself appeared with all his army, ravaging the country, reducing their posts, subduing their towns, receiving into his protection those who declared for him. Till at last the Edui, who hitherto had styled themselves brethren to the Romans, and had been much honored by them, declared against him, and joined the rebels, to the great discouragement of his army. Accordingly he removed thence, and passed the country of the Lingones, desiring to reach the territories of the Sequani, who were his friends, and who lay like a bulwark in front of

---

[10] *Returned the same way he went, and showed the barbarians* —A better reading gives the following sense, *returned, and showed the barbarians by the very roads he took.*

Italy against the other tribes of Gaul. There the enemy came upon him, and surrounded him with many myriads, whom he also was eager to engage; and at last, after some time and with much slaughter, gained on the whole a complete victory; though at first he appears to have met with some reverse, and the Aruveni show you a small sword hanging up in a temple, which they say was taken from Cæsar. Cæsar saw this afterwards himself, and smiled, and when his friends advised it should be taken down, would not permit it, because he looked upon it as consecrated.

After the defeat, a great part of those who had escaped, fled with their king into a town called Alesia, which Cæsar besieged, though the height of the walls, and number of those who defended them, made it appear impregnable; and meantime, from without the walls, he was assailed by a greater danger than can be expressed. For the choice men of Gaul, picked out of each nation, and well armed, came to relieve Alesia, to the number of three hundred thousand; nor were there in the town less than one hundred and seventy thousand. So that Cæsar being shut up betwixt two such forces, was compelled to protect himself by two walls, one towards the town, the other against the relieving army, as knowing if these forces should join, his affairs would be entirely ruined. The danger that he underwent before Alesia,[11] justly gained him great honor on many accounts, and gave him an opportunity of showing greater instances of his valor

---

[11] Alesia is identified with Alise, or with the summit of Mount Auxois, near Flavigny, not far from Dijon. The course of Roman occupation, interposing between Central Gaul and the German competitors for its possession, seems to follow the line of

and conduct than any other contest had done. One wonders much how he should be able to engage and defeat so many thousands of men without the town, and not be perceived by those within, but yet more, that the Romans themselves, who guarded their wall which was next the town, should be strangers to it. For even they knew nothing of the victory, till they heard the cries of the men and lamentations of the women who were in the town, and had from thence seen the Romans at a distance carrying into their camp a great quantity of bucklers, adorned with gold and silver, many breastplates stained with blood, besides cups and tents made in the Gallic fashion. So soon did so vast an army dissolve and vanish like a ghost or dream, the greatest part of them being killed upon the spot. Those who were in Alesia, having given themselves and Cæsar much trouble, surrendered at last; and Vergentorix, who was the chief spring of all the war, putting his best armor on, and adorning his horse, rode out of the gates, and made a turn about Cæsar as he was sitting, then quitted his horse, threw off his armor, and remained seated quietly at Cæsar's feet until he was led away to be reserved for the triumph.

Cæsar had long ago resolved upon the overthrow of Pompey, as had Pompey, for that matter, upon his. For Crassus, the fear of whom had hitherto kept them in peace, having now been killed in Parthia, if the one of them wished to make himself the greatest man in Rome, he had only to overthrow the other; and if he again wished to prevent

---

the Rhone and Saone upwards, and the Meuse and Moselle downwards, from Marseilles and Lyons to Treves and the Rhine. Alesia is near the head waters of the Saone.

his own fall, he had nothing for it but to be beforehand with him whom he feared. Pompey had not been long under any such apprehensions, having till lately despised Cæsar, as thinking it no difficult matter to put down him whom he himself had advanced. But Cæsar had entertained this design from the beginning against his rivals, and had retired, like an expert wrestler, to prepare himself apart for the combat. Making the Gallic wars his exercise-ground, he had at once improved the strength of his soldiery, and had heightened his own glory by his great actions, so that he was looked on as one who might challenge comparison with Pompey. Nor did he let go any of those advantages which were now given him both by Pompey himself and the times, and the ill government of Rome, where all who were candidates for offices publicly gave money, and without any shame bribed the people, who having received their pay, did not contend for their benefactors with their bare suffrages, but with bows, swords, and slings. So that after having many times stained the place of election with the blood of men killed upon the spot, they left the city at last without a government at all, to be carried about like a ship without a pilot to steer her; while all who had any wisdom could only be thankful if a course of such wild and stormy disorder and madness might end no worse than in a monarchy. Some were so bold as to declare openly, that the government was incurable but by a monarchy, and that they ought to take that remedy from the hands of the gentlest physician, meaning Pompey, who, though in words he pretended to decline it, yet in reality made his utmost efforts to be declared dictator. Cato perceiving his design, prevailed with the senate to make him sole consul, that with the

offer of a more legal sort of monarchy he might
be withheld from demanding the dictatorship. They
over and above voted him the continuance of his
provinces, for he had two, Spain and all Africa,
which he governed by his lieutenants, and maintained
armies under him, at the yearly charge of a
thousand talents out of the public treasury.

Upon this Cæsar also sent and petitioned for
the consulship, and the continuance of his provinces.
Pompey at first did not stir in it, but Marcellus and
Lentulus opposed it, who had always hated Cæsar,
and now did every thing, whether fit or unfit, which
might disgrace and affront him. For they took
away the privilege of Roman citizens from the people
of New Comum, who were a colony that Cæsar
had lately planted in Gaul; and Marcellus, who was
then consul, ordered one of the senators of that town,
then at Rome, to be whipped, and told him he laid
that mark upon him to signify he was no citizen of
Rome, bidding him, when he went back again, to
show it to Cæsar. After Marcellus's consulship,
Cæsar began to lavish gifts upon all the public men
out of the riches he had taken from the Gauls; discharged
Curio, the tribune, from his great debts;
gave Paulus, then consul, fifteen hundred talents,
with which he built the noble court of justice [12] adjoining
the forum, to supply the place of that called
the Fulvian. Pompey, alarmed at these preparations,
now openly took steps, both by himself and

---

[12] Or basilica. The first basilica built in Rome was the
Porcian, built by Cato the Elder; see his life, Vol. II., and the
life of the younger Cato, in this volume. The Fulvian was the
next, built by the joint censors Æmilius and Fulvius, adorned by
subsequent members of the Æmilian family, and now restored
with the help of Cæsar's money. This was the Basilica Paulli.

his friends, to have a successor appointed in Cæsar's room, and sent to demand back the soldiers whom he had lent him to carry on the wars in Gaul. Cæsar returned them, and made each soldier a present of two hundred and fifty drachmas. The officers who brought them home to Pompey, spread amongst the people no very fair or favorable report of Cæsar, and flattered Pompey himself with false suggestions that he was wished for by Cæsar's army; and though his affairs here were in some embarrassment through the envy of some, and the ill state of the government, yet there the army was at his command, and if they once crossed into Italy, would presently declare for him; so weary were they of Cæsar's endless expeditions, and so suspicious of his designs for a monarchy. Upon this Pompey grew presumptuous, and neglected all warlike preparations, as fearing no danger, and used no other means against him than mere speeches and votes, for which Cæsar cared nothing. And one of his captains, it is said, who was sent by him to Rome, standing before the senate-house one day, and being told that the senate would not give Cæsar a longer time in his government, clapped his hand on the hilt of his sword, and said, "But this shall."

Yet the demands which Cæsar made had the fairest colors of equity imaginable. For he proposed to lay down his arms, and that Pompey should do the same, and both together should become private men, and each expect a reward of his services from the public. For that those who proposed to disarm him, and at the same time to confirm Pompey in all the power he held, were simply establishing the one in the tyranny which they accused the other of aiming at. When Curio made these proposals to the people in Cæsar's name, he was loudly applauded, and some threw garlands towards him, and dismissed him as they do successful wrestlers, crowned with flowers. Antony, being tribune, produced a letter sent from Cæsar on this occasion, and read it, though the consuls did what they could to oppose it. But Scipio, Pompey's father-in-law, proposed in the senate, that if Cæsar did not lay down his arms within such a time, he should be voted an enemy; and the consuls putting it to the question, whether Pompey should dismiss his soldiers, and again, whether Cæsar should disband his, very few assented to the first, but almost all to the latter. But Antony proposing again, that both should lay down their commissions, all but a very few agreed to it. Scipio was upon this very violent, and Lentulus the consul cried aloud, that they had need of arms, and not of suffrages, against a robber; so that the senators for the present adjourned, and appeared in mourning as a mark of their grief for the dissension.

Afterwards there came other letters from Cæsar, which seemed yet more moderate, for he proposed to quit every thing else, and only to retain Gaul within the Alps, Illyricum, and two legions, till he should stand a second time for consul. Cicero, the orator, who was lately returned from Cilicia, endeavored to reconcile differences, and softened Pompey, who was willing to comply in other things, but not to allow him the soldiers. At last Cicero used his persuasions with Cæsar's friends to accept of the provinces, and six thousand soldiers only, and so to make up the quarrel. And Pompey was inclined to give way to this, but Lentulus, the consul, would not hearken to it, but drove Antony and Curio out of the senate-house with insults, by which he afforded Cæsar the most plausible pretence that could be, and one which he could readily use to inflame the soldiers, by showing them two persons of such repute and authority, who were forced to escape in a hired carriage in the dress of slaves. For so they were glad to disguise themselves, when they fled out of Rome.

There were not about him at that time above three hundred horse, and five thousand foot; for the rest of his army, which was left behind the Alps, was to be brought after him by officers who had received orders for that purpose. But he thought the first motion towards the design which he had on foot did not require large forces at present, and that what was wanted was to make this first step suddenly, and so as to astound his enemies with the boldness of it; as it would be easier, he thought, to throw them into consternation by doing what they never anticipated, than fairly to conquer them, if he had alarmed them by his preparations. And therefore, he commanded his captains and other officers to go only with their swords in their hands, without any other arms, and make themselves masters of Ariminum, a large city of Gaul, with as little disturbance and bloodshed as possible. He committed the care of these forces to Hortensius, and himself spent the day in public as a stander-by and spectator of the gladiators, who exercised before him. A little before night he attended to his person, and then went into the hall, and conversed for some time with those he had invited to supper, till it began to grow dusk, when he rose from table, and made his excuses to the company, begging them to stay till he came back, having already given private directions to a few immediate friends, that they should follow him, not all the same way, but some one way, some another. He himself got into one of the hired carriages, and drove at first another way, but presently turned towards Ariminum. When he came to the river Rubicon, which parts Gaul within the Alps from the rest of Italy, his thoughts began to work, now he was just entering upon the danger, and he wavered much in his mind, when he considered the greatness of the enterprise into which he was throwing himself. He checked his course, and ordered a halt, while he revolved with himself, and often changed his opinion one way and the other, without speaking a word. This was when his purposes fluctuated most; presently he also discussed the matter with his friends who were about him, (of which number Asinius Pollio was one,) computing how many calamities his passing that river would bring upon mankind, and what a relation of it would be transmitted to posterity. At last, in a sort of passion, casting aside calculation, and abandoning himself to what might come, and using the proverb frequently in their mouths who enter upon dangerous and bold attempts, "The die is cast," with these words he took the river. Once over, he used all expedition possible, and before it was day reached Ariminum, and took it. It is said that the night before he passed the river, he had an impious dream, that he was unnaturally familiar with his own mother.

As soon as Ariminum was taken, wide gates, so to say, were thrown open, to let in war upon every land alike and sea, and with the limits of the province, the boundaries of the laws were transgressed. Nor would one have thought that, as at other times, the mere men and women fled from one town of Italy to another in their consternation, but that the very towns themselves left their sites, and fled for succor to each other. The city of Rome was overrun as it were with a deluge, by the conflux of people flying in from all the neighboring places. Magistrates could no longer govern, nor the eloquence of any orator quiet it; it was all but suffering shipwreck by the violence of its own tempestuous agitation. The most vehement contrary passions and impulses were at work everywhere. Nor did those who rejoiced at the prospect of the change altogether conceal their feelings, but when they met, as in so great a city they frequently must, with the alarmed and dejected of the other party, they provoked quarrels by their bold expressions of confidence in the event. Pompey, sufficiently disturbed of himself, was yet more perplexed by the clamors of others; some telling him that he justly suffered for having armed Cæsar against himself and the government; others blaming him for permitting Cæsar to be insolently used by Lentulus, when he made such ample concessions, and offered such reasonable proposals towards an accommodation. Favonius bade him now stamp upon the ground; for once talking big in the senate, he desired them not to trouble themselves about making any preparations for the war, for that he himself, with one stamp of his foot, would fill all Italy with soldiers. Yet still Pompey at that time had more forces than Cæsar; but he was not permitted to pursue his own thoughts, but being continually disturbed with false reports and alarms as if the enemy was close upon him and carrying all before him, he gave way, and let himself be borne down by the general cry. He put forth an edict declaring the city to be in a state of anarchy, and left it with orders that the senate should follow him, and that no one should stay behind who did not prefer tyranny to their country and liberty.

The consuls at once fled, without making even the usual sacrifices; so did most of the senators,

CAESAR CROSSING THE RUBICON

carrying off their own goods in as much haste as if they had been robbing their neighbors. Some, who had formerly much favored Cæsar's cause, in the prevailing alarm, quitted their own sentiments, and without any prospect of good to themselves, were carried along by the common stream. It was a melancholy thing to see the city tossed in these tumults, like a ship given up by her pilots, and left to run, as chance guides her, upon any rock in her way. Yet, in spite of their sad condition, people still esteemed the place of their exile to be their country for Pompey's sake, and fled from Rome, as if it had been Cæsar's camp. Labienus even, who had been one of Cæsar's nearest friends, and his lieutenant, and who had fought by him zealously in the Gallic wars, now deserted him, and went over to Pompey. Cæsar sent all his money and equipage after him, and then sat down before Corfinium, which was garrisoned with thirty cohorts under the command of Domitius. He, in despair of maintaining the defence, requested a physician, whom he had among his attendants, to give him poison; and taking the dose, drank it, in hopes of being despatched by it. But soon after, when he was told that Cæsar showed the utmost clemency towards those he took prisoners, he lamented his misfortune, and blamed the hastiness of his resolution. His physician consoled him, by informing him that he had taken a sleeping draught, not a poison; upon which, much rejoiced, and rising from his bed, he went presently to Cæsar, and gave him the pledge of his hand, yet afterwards again went over to Pompey. The report of these actions at Rome, quieted those who were there, and some who had fled thence returned.

Cæsar took into his army Domitius's soldiers,

as he did all those whom he found in any town enlisted for Pompey's service. Being now strong and formidable enough, he advanced against Pompey himself, who did not stay to receive him, but fled to Brundisium, having sent the consuls before with a body of troops to Dyrrhachium. Soon after, upon Cæsar's approach, he set to sea, as shall be more particularly related in his Life. Cæsar would have immediately pursued him, but wanted shipping, and therefore went back to Rome, having made himself master of all Italy without bloodshed in the space of sixty days. When he came thither, he found the city more quiet than he expected, and many senators present, to whom he addressed himself with courtesy and deference, desiring them to send to Pompey about any reasonable accommodations towards a peace. But nobody complied with this proposal; whether out of fear of Pompey, whom they had deserted, or that they thought Cæsar did not mean what he said, but thought it his interest to talk plausibly. Afterwards, when Metellus, the tribune, would have hindered him from taking money out of the public treasure, and adduced some laws against it, Cæsar replied, that arms and laws had each their own time; "If what I do displeases you, leave the place; war allows no free talking. When I have laid down my arms, and made peace, come back and make what speeches you please. And this," he added, "I tell you in diminution of my own just right, as indeed you and all others who have appeared against me and are now in my power, may be treated as I please." Having said this to Metellus, he went to the doors of the treasury, and the keys being not to be found, sent for smiths to force them open. Metellus again making resistance, and some encouraging him in it,

Cæsar, in a louder tone, told him he would put him to death, if he gave him any further disturbance. "And this," said he, "you know, young man, is more disagreeable for me to say, than to do." These words made Metellus withdraw for fear, and obtained speedy execution henceforth for all orders that Cæsar gave for procuring necessaries for the war.

He was now proceeding to Spain, with the determination of first crushing Afranius and Varro, Pompey's lieutenants, and making himself master of the armies and provinces under them, that he might then more securely advance against Pompey, when he had no enemy left behind him. In this expedition his person was often in danger from ambuscades, and his army by want of provisions, yet he did not desist from pursuing the enemy, provoking them to fight, and hemming them with his fortifications, till by main force he made himself master of their camps and their forces. Only the generals got off, and fled to Pompey.

When Cæsar came back to Rome, Piso, his father-in-law, advised him to send men to Pompey, to treat of a peace; but Isauricus, to ingratiate himself with Cæsar, spoke against it. After this, being created dictator by the senate, he called home the exiles, and gave back their rights as citizens to the children of those who had suffered under Sylla; he relieved the debtors by an act remitting some part of the interest on their debts, and passed some other measures of the same sort, but not many. For within eleven days he resigned his dictatorship, and having declared himself consul, with Servilius Isauricus, hastened again to the war. He marched so fast, that he left all his army behind him, except six hundred chosen horse, and five legions, with which he put to sea in the very middle of winter, about the beginning of the month January, (which corresponds pretty nearly with the Athenian month Posideon,) and having past the Ionian Sea, took Oricum and Apollonia, and then sent back the ships to Brundisium, to bring over the soldiers who were left behind in the march. They, while yet on the march, their bodies now no longer in the full vigor of youth, and they themselves weary with such a multitude of wars, could not but exclaim against Cæsar, "When at last, and where, will this Cæsar let us be quiet? He carries us from place to place, and uses as if we were not to be worn out, and had no sense of labor. Even our iron itself is spent by blows, and we ought to have some pity on our bucklers and breastplates, which have been used so long. Our wounds, if nothing else, should make him see that we are mortal men, whom he commands, subject to the same pains and sufferings as other human beings. The very gods themselves cannot force the winter season, or hinder the storms in their time; yet he pushes forward, as if he were not pursuing, but flying from an enemy." So they talked as they marched leisurely towards Brundisium. But when they came thither, and found Cæsar gone off before them, their feelings changed, and they blamed themselves as traitors to their general. They now railed at their officers for marching so slowly, and placing themselves on the heights overlooking the sea towards Epirus, they kept watch to see if they could espy the vessels which were to transport them to Cæsar.

He in the mean time was posted in Apollonia, but had not an army with him able to fight the enemy, the forces from Brundisium being so long in coming, which put him to great suspense and embarrassment what to do. At last he resolved upon a most hazardous experiment, and embarked, without any one's knowledge, in a boat of twelve oars, to cross over to Brundisium, though the sea was at that time covered with a vast fleet of the enemies. He got on board in the night time, in the dress of a slave, and throwing himself down like a person of no consequence, lay along at the bottom of the vessel. The river Anius [13] was to carry them down to sea, and there used to blow a gentle gale every morning from the land, which made it calm at the mouth of the river, by driving the waves forward; but this night there had blown a strong wind from the sea, which overpowered that from the land, so that where the river met the influx of the seawater and the opposition of the waves, it was extremely rough and angry; and the current was beaten back with such a violent swell, that the master of the boat could not make good his passage, but ordered his sailors to tack about and return. Cæsar, upon this, discovers himself, and taking the man by the hand, who was surprised to see him there, said, " Go on, my friend, and fear nothing; you carry Cæsar and his fortune in your boat." The mariners, when they heard that, forgot the storm, and laying all their strength to their oars, did what they could to force their way down the river. But when it was to no purpose, and the vessel now took in much water, Cæsar finding himself in such danger in the very mouth of the river, much against his will permitted the master to turn back. When he was come to land, his soldiers ran to him in a multitude, reproaching him for what he had done, and indignant that he should think himself not strong enough to get a victory by their sole assistance, but must disturb himself, and expose his life

[13] The Aöus or Æas.

for those who were absent, as if he could not trust those who were with him.

After this, Antony came over with the forces from Brundisium, which encouraged Cæsar to give Pompey battle, though he was encamped very advantageously, and furnished with plenty of provisions both by sea and land, whilst he himself was at the beginning but ill-supplied, and before the end was extremely pinched for want of necessaries, so that his soldiers were forced to dig up a kind of root which grew there, and tempering it with milk, to feed on it. Sometimes they made a kind of bread of it, and advancing up to the enemy's outposts, would throw in these loaves, telling them, that as long as the earth produced such roots they would not give up blockading Pompey. But Pompey took what care he could, that neither the loaves nor the words should reach his men, who were out of heart and despondent, through terror at the fierceness and hardiness of their enemies, whom they looked upon as a sort of wild beasts. There were continual skirmishes about Pompey's outworks, in all which Cæsar had the better, except one, when his men were forced to fly in such a manner that he had like to have lost his camp. For Pompey made such a vigorous sally on them that not a man stood his ground; the trenches were filled with the slaughter, many fell upon their own ramparts and bulwarks, whither they were driven in flight by the enemy. Cæsar met them, and would have turned them back, but could not. When he went to lay hold of the ensigns, those who carried them threw them down, so that the enemies took thirty-two of them. He himself narrowly escaped; for taking hold of one of his soldiers, a big and strong man, that was flying by him, he bade him stand and face about;

but the fellow, full of apprehensions from the danger he was in, laid hold of his sword, as if he would strike Cæsar, but Cæsar's armor-bearer cut off his arm. Cæsar's affairs were so desperate at that time, that when Pompey, either through overcautiousness, or his ill fortune, did not give the finishing stroke to that great success, but retreated after he had driven the routed enemy within their camp, Cæsar, upon seeing his withdrawal, said to his friends, "The victory to-day had been on the enemies' side, if they had had a general who knew how to gain it." When he was retired into his tent, he laid himself down to sleep, but spent that night as miserably as ever he did any, in perplexity and consideration with himself, coming to the conclusion that he had conducted the war amiss. For when he had a fertile country before him, and all the wealthy cities of Macedonia and Thessaly, he had neglected to carry the war thither, and had sat down by the seaside, where his enemies had such a powerful fleet, so that he was in fact rather besieged by the want of necessaries, than besieging others with his arms. Being thus distracted in his thoughts with the view of the difficulty and distress he was in, he raised his camp, with the intention of advancing towards Scipio, who lay in Macedonia; hoping either to entice Pompey into a country where he should fight without the advantage he now had of supplies from the sea, or to overpower Scipio, if not assisted.

This set all Pompey's army and officers on fire to hasten and pursue Cæsar, whom they concluded to be beaten and flying. But Pompey was afraid to hazard a battle on which so much depended, and being himself provided with all necessaries for any length of time, thought to tire out and waste the vigor of Cæsar's army, which could not last long.

For the best part of his men, though they had great experience, and showed an irresistible courage in all engagements, yet by their frequent marches, changing their camps,[14] attacking fortifications, and keeping long night-watches, were getting worn-out and broken; they being now old, their bodies less fit for labor, and their courage, also, beginning to give way with the failure of their strength. Besides, it was said that an infectious disease, occasioned by their irregular diet, was prevailing in Cæsar's army, and what was of greatest moment, he was neither furnished with money nor provisions, so that in a little time he must needs fall of himself.

For these reasons Pompey had no mind to fight him, but was thanked for it by none but Cato, who rejoiced at the prospect of sparing his fellow-citizens. For he when he saw the dead bodies of those who had fallen in the last battle on Cæsar's side, to the number of a thousand, turned away, covered his face, and shed tears. But every one else upbraided Pompey for being reluctant to fight, and tried to goad him on by such nicknames as Agamemnon, and king of kings, as if he were in no hurry to lay down his sovereign authority, but was pleased to see so many commanders attending on him, and paying their attendance at his tent. Favonius, who affected Cato's free way of speaking his mind, complained bitterly that they should eat no figs even this year at Tusculum, because of Pompey's love of command. Afranius, who was lately returned out of Spain, and on account of his ill success there, labored under the suspicion of having

---

[14] Or, perhaps more probably, "raising fortifications," which had been very much their occupation latterly. Up to this point the campaign had been a war of intrenchments.

been bribed to betray the army, asked why they did not fight this purchaser of provinces. Pompey was driven, against his own will, by this kind of language, into offering battle, and proceeded to follow Cæsar. Cæsar had found great difficulties in his march, for no country would supply him with provisions, his reputation being very much fallen since his late defeat. But after he took Gomphi, a town of Thessaly, he not only found provisions for his army, but physic too. For there they met with plenty of wine, which they took very freely, and heated with this, sporting and revelling on their march in bacchanalian fashion, they shook off the disease, and their whole constitution was relieved and changed into another habit.

When the two armies were come into Pharsalia,[15] and both encamped there, Pompey's thoughts ran the same way as they had done before, against fighting, and the more because of some unlucky presages, and a vision he had in a dream.[16] But those who were about him were so confident of success, that Domitius, and Spinther, and Scipio, as if they had already conquered, quarrelled which should succeed Cæsar in the pontificate. And many sent to Rome to take houses fit to accommodate consuls and prætors, as being sure of entering upon those offices,

---

[15] "Into Pharsalia," is properly "into the territory of the town of Pharsalus," and in other passages where the battle is mentioned in the translation by the name, as the Romans used it, of *Pharsalia*, the Greek is *Pharsalus*.

[16] Here follow the words, "He fancied he saw himself in the theatre, receiving the plaudits of the people." Either the text is incomplete, and the remainder of the description has been lost, or else it is the imperfect explanation added in the margin by an annotator. The full account is given in the Life of Pompey.

as soon as the battle was over. The cavalry especially were obstinate for fighting, being splendidly armed and bravely mounted, and valuing themselves upon the fine horses they kept, and upon their own handsome persons; as also upon the advantage of their numbers, for they were five thousand against one thousand of Cæsar's. Nor were the numbers of the infantry less disproportionate, there being forty-five thousand of Pompey's against twenty-two thousand of the enemy.

Cæsar, collecting his soldiers together, told them that Corfinius [17] was coming up to them with two legions, and that fifteen cohorts more under Calenus were posted at Megara and Athens; he then asked them whether they would stay till these joined them, or would hazard the battle by themselves. They all cried out to him not to wait, but on the contrary to do whatever he could to bring about an engagement as soon as possible. When he sacrificed to the gods for the lustration of his army, upon the death of the first victim, the augur told him, within three days he should come to a decisive action. Cæsar asked him whether he saw any thing in the entrails, which promised an happy event. "That," said the priest, "you can best answer yourself; for the gods signify a great alteration from the present posture of affairs. If, therefore, you think yourself well off now, expect worse fortune; if unhappy, hope for better." The night before the battle, as he walked the rounds about midnight, there was a light seen in the heaven, very bright and flaming, which seemed to pass over Cæsar's camp, and fall into Pompey's. And when Cæsar's soldiers came to relieve the watch in the morning, they perceived a panic disorder among the enemies. However, he

[17] Cornificius.

did not expect to fight that day, but set about raising his camp with the intention of marching towards Scotussa.

But when the tents were now taken down, his scouts rode up to him, and told him the enemy would give him battle. With this news he was extremely pleased, and having performed his devotions to the gods, set his army in battle array, dividing them into three bodies. Over the middlemost he placed Domitius Calvinus; Antony commanded the left wing, and he himself the right, being resolved to fight at the head of the tenth legion. But when he saw the enemies' cavalry taking position against him, being struck with their fine appearance and their number, he gave orders that six cohorts from the rear of the army should come round and join him, whom he posted behind the right wing, and instructed them what they should do, when the enemy's horse came to charge. On the other side, Pompey commanded the right wing, Domitius the left, and Scipio, Pompey's father-in-law, the centre. The whole weight of the cavalry was collected on the left wing, with the intent that they should outflank the right wing of the enemy, and rout that part where the general himself commanded. For they thought no phalanx of infantry could be solid enough to sustain such a shock, but that they must necessarily be broken and shattered all to pieces upon the onset of so immense a force of cavalry. When they were ready on both sides to give the signal for battle, Pompey commanded his foot who were in the front, to stand their ground, and without breaking their order, receive quietly the enemy's first attack, till they came within javelin's cast. Cæsar, in this respect, also, blames Pompey's generalship, as if he had not been aware how

the first encounter, when made with an impetus
and upon the run, gives weight and force to the
strokes, and fires the men's spirits into a flame,
which the general concurrence fans to full heat.
He himself was just putting the troops into motion
and advancing to the action, when he found one of
his captains, a trusty and experienced soldier, encouraging his men to exert their utmost. Cæsar
called him by his name, and said, "What hopes,
Caius Crassinius, and what grounds for encouragement?" Crassinius stretched out his hand, and
cried in a loud voice, "We shall conquer nobly,
Cæsar; and I this day will deserve your praises,
either alive or dead." So he said, and was the first
man to run in upon the enemy, followed by the
hundred and twenty soldiers about him, and breaking through the first rank, still pressed on forwards
with much slaughter of the enemy, till at last he
was struck back by the wound of a sword, which
went in at his mouth with such force that it came
out at his neck behind.

Whilst the foot was thus sharply engaged in the
main battle, on the flank Pompey's horse rode up
confidently, and opened their ranks very wide, that
they might surround the right wing of Cæsar. But
before they engaged, Cæsar's cohorts rushed out and
attacked them, and did not dart their javelins at a
distance, nor strike at the thighs and legs, as they
usually did in close battle, but aimed at their faces.
For thus Cæsar had instructed them, in hopes that
young gentlemen, who had not known much of
battles and wounds, but came wearing their hair
long, in the flower of their age and height of their
beauty, would be more apprehensive of such blows,
and not care for hazarding both a danger at present
and a blemish for the future. And so it proved,

for they were so far from bearing the stroke of the javelins, that they could not stand the sight of them, but turned about, and covered their faces to secure them. Once in disorder, presently they turned about to fly; and so most shamefully ruined all. For those who had beat them back, at once outflanked the infantry, and falling on their rear, cut them to pieces. Pompey, who commanded the other wing of the army, when he saw his cavalry thus broken and flying, was no longer himself, nor did he now remember that he was Pompey the Great, but like one whom some god had deprived of his senses, retired to his tent without speaking a word, and there sat to expect the event, till the whole army was routed, and the enemy appeared upon the works which were thrown up before the camp, where they closely engaged with his men, who were posted there to defend it. Then first he seemed to have recovered his senses, and uttering, it is said, only these words, "What, into the camp too?" he laid aside his general's habit, and putting on such clothes as might best favor his flight, stole off. What fortune he met with afterwards, how he took shelter in Egypt, and was murdered there, we tell you in his Life.

Cæsar, when he came to view Pompey's camp, and saw some of his opponents dead upon the ground, others dying, said, with a groan, "This they would have; they brought me to this necessity. I, Caius Cæsar, after succeeding in so many wars, had been condemned, had I dismissed my army." [18] These words, Pollio says, Cæsar spoke in Latin at

---

[18] "Hoc voluerunt; tantis rebus gestis C. Cæsar condemnatus essem, nisi ab exercitu auxilium petissem," quoted from Asinius Pollio by Suetonius.

that time, and that he himself wrote them in Greek; adding, that those who were killed at the taking of the camp, were most of them servants; and that not above six thousand soldiers fell. Cæsar incorporated most of the foot whom he took prisoners, with his own legions, and gave a free pardon to many of the distinguished persons, and amongst the rest, to Brutus, who afterwards killed him. He did not immediately appear after the battle was over, which put Cæsar, it is said, into great anxiety for him; nor was his pleasure less when he saw him present himself alive.

There were many prodigies that foreshowed this victory, but the most remarkable that we are told of, was that at Tralles. In the temple of Victory stood Cæsar's statue. The ground on which it stood was naturally hard and solid, and the stone with which it was paved still harder; yet it is said that a palm-tree shot itself up near the pedestal of this statue. In the city of Padua, one Caius Cornelius, who had the character of a good augur, the fellow-citizen and acquaintance of Livy, the historian, happened to be making some augural observations that very day when the battle was fought. And first, as Livy tells us, he pointed out the time of the fight, and said to those who were by him, that just then the battle was begun, and the men engaged. When he looked a second time, and observed the omens, he leaped up as if he had been inspired, and cried out, "Cæsar, you are victorious." This much surprised the standers by, but he took the garland which he had on from his head, and swore he would never wear it again till the event should give authority to his art. This Livy positively states for a truth.

Cæsar, as a memorial of his victory, gave the

Thessalians their freedom, and then went in pursuit
of Pompey. When he was come into Asia, to gratify
Theopompus, the author of the collection of fables,
he enfranchised the Cnidians, and remitted one third
of their tribute to all the people of the province of
Asia. When he came to Alexandria, where Pompey
was already murdered, he would not look upon
Theodotus, who presented him with his head, but
taking only his signet, shed tears. Those of Pompey's friends who had been arrested by the king
of Egypt, as they were wandering in those parts,
he relieved, and offered them his own friendship. In
his letter to his friends at Rome, he told them that
the greatest and most signal pleasure his victory
had given him, was to be able continually to save
the lives of fellow-citizens who had fought against
him. As to the war in Egypt, some say it was at
once dangerous and dishonorable, and noways necessary, but occasioned only by his passion for Cleopatra. Others blame the ministers of the king, and
especially the eunuch Pothinus, who was the chief
favorite, and had lately killed Pompey, who had
banished Cleopatra, and was now secretly plotting
Cæsar's destruction, (to prevent which, Cæsar from
that time began to sit up whole nights, under pretence of drinking, for the security of his person,)
while openly he was intolerable in his affronts to
Cæsar, both by his words and actions. For when
Cæsar's soldiers had musty and unwholesome corn
measured out to them, Pothinus told them they
must be content with it, since they were fed at
another's cost. He ordered that his table should be
served with wooden and earthen dishes, and said
Cæsar had carried off all the gold and silver plate,
under pretence of arrears of debt. For the present
king's father owed Cæsar one thousand seven hun-

dred and fifty myriads of money; Cæsar had formerly remitted to his children the rest, but thought fit to demand the thousand myriads at that time, to maintain his army. Pothinus told him that he had better go now and attend to his other affairs of greater consequence, and that he should receive his money at another time with thanks. Cæsar replied that he did not want Egyptians to be his counsellors, and soon after privately sent for Cleopatra from her retirement.

She took a small boat, and one only of her confidents, Apollodorus, the Sicilian, along with her, and in the dusk of the evening landed near the palace. She was at a loss how to get in undiscovered, till she thought of putting herself into the coverlet of a bed and lying at length, whilst Apollodorus tied up the bedding and carried it on his back through the gates to Cæsar's apartment. Cæsar was first captivated by this proof of Cleopatra's bold wit, and was afterwards so overcome by the charm of her society, that he made a reconciliation between her and her brother, on condition that she should rule as his colleague in the kingdom. A festival was kept to celebrate this reconciliation, where Cæsar's barber, a busy, listening fellow, whose excessive timidity made him inquisitive into every thing, discovered that there was a plot carrying on against Cæsar by Achillas, general of the king's forces, and Pothinus, the eunuch. Cæsar, upon the first intelligence of it, set a guard upon the hall where the feast was kept, and killed Pothinus. Achillas escaped to the army, and raised a troublesome and embarrassing war against Cæsar, which it was not easy for him to manage with his few soldiers against so powerful a city and so large an army. The first difficulty he met with was want of water, for the enemies had turned the canals.[19] Another was, when the enemy endeavored to cut off his communication by sea, he was forced to divert that danger by setting fire to his own ships, which, after burning the docks, thence spread on and destroyed the great library. A third was, when in an engagement near Pharos, he leaped from the mole into a small boat, to assist his soldiers who were in danger, and when the Egyptians pressed him on every side, he threw himself into the sea, and with much difficulty swam off. This was the time when, according to the story, he had a number of manuscripts in his hand, which, though he was continually darted at, and forced to keep his head often under water, yet he did not let go, but held them up safe from wetting in one hand, whilst he swam with the other. His boat, in the meantime, was quickly sunk. At last, the king having gone off to Achillas and his party, Cæsar engaged and conquered them. Many fell in that battle, and the king himself was never seen after. Upon this, he left Cleopatra queen of Egypt, who soon after had a son by him, whom the Alexandrians called Cæsarion, and then departed for Syria.

Thence he passed to Asia, where he heard that Domitius was beaten by Pharnaces, son of Mithridates, and had fled out of Pontus with a handful of men; and that Pharnaces pursued the victory so eagerly, that though he was already master of Bithynia and Cappadocia, he had a further design of attempting the Lesser Armenia, and was inviting all the kings and tetrarchs there to rise. Cæsar immediately marched against him with three legions,

---

[19] By which Alexandria, there being no springs, was wholly supplied.

fought him near Zela, drove him out of Pontus, and totally defeated his army. When he gave Amantius, a friend of his at Rome, an account of this action, to express the promptness and rapidity of it, he used three words, I came, saw, and conquered, which in Latin [20] having all the same cadence, carry with them a very suitable air of brevity.

Hence he crossed into Italy, and came to Rome at the end of that year, for which he had been a second time chosen dictator, though that office had never before lasted a whole year, and was elected consul for the next. He was ill spoken of, because upon a mutiny of some soldiers, who killed Cosconius and Galba, who had been prætors, he gave them only the slight reprimand of calling them *Citizens,* instead of *Fellow-Soldiers,* and afterwards assigned to each man a thousand drachmas, besides a share of lands in Italy. He was also reflected on for Dolabella's extravagance, Amantius's covetousness, Antony's debauchery, and Corfinius's profuseness,[21] who pulled down Pompey's house, and rebuilt it, as not magnificent enough; for the Romans were much displeased with all these. But Cæsar, for the prosecution of his own scheme of government, though he

---

[20] Veni, Vidi, Vici. A tablet with this inscription was displayed in the triumph which was afterwards celebrated for this war. Amantius does not seem to be a true Roman name. It has been corrected into Caius Matius, a well-known friend of Cæsar's.

[21] *Antony's debauchery and Corfinius's profuseness* ought perhaps to change places, and to stand as Corfinius's debauchery (or drunkenness) and Antony's profuseness: it was certainly Antony who bought Pompey's house; see his Life, Vol. V., and the statement there made is confirmed by Cicero in the second Philippic (c. 26).

knew their characters and disapproved them, was forced to make use of those who would serve him.

After the battle of Pharsalia, Cato and Scipio fled into Africa, and there, with the assistance of king Juba, got together a considerable force, which Cæsar resolved to engage. He, accordingly, passed into Sicily about the winter-solstice, and to remove from his officers' minds all hopes of delay there, encamped by the sea-shore, and as soon as ever he had a fair wind, put to sea with three thousand foot and a few horse. When he had landed them, he went back secretly, under some apprehensions for the larger part of his army, but met them upon the sea, and brought them all to the same camp. There he was informed that the enemies relied much upon an ancient oracle, that the family of the Scipios should be always victorious in Africa. There was in his army a man, otherwise mean and contemptible, but of the house of the Africani, and his name Scipio Sallutio. This man Cæsar, (whether in raillery, to ridicule Scipio, who commanded the enemy, or seriously to bring over the omen to his side, it were hard to say,) put at the head of his troops, as if he were general, in all the frequent battles which he was compelled to fight. For he was in such want both of victualling for his men, and forage for his horses, that he was forced to feed the horses with sea-weed, which he washed thoroughly to take off its saltness, and mixed with a little grass, to give it a more agreeable taste. The Numidians, in great numbers, and well horsed, whenever he went, came up and commanded the country. Cæsar's cavalry being one day unemployed, diverted themselves with seeing an African, who entertained them with dancing and at the same time playing upon the pipe to admiration. They were so taken with this, that they alighted, and gave their horses to some boys, when on a sudden the enemy surrounded them, killed some, pursued the rest, and fell in with them into their camp; and had not Cæsar himself and Asinius Pollio come to their assistance, and put a stop to their flight, the war had been then at an end. In another engagement, also, the enemy had again the better, when Cæsar, it is said, seized a standard-bearer, who was running away, by the neck, and forcing him to face about, said, "Look, that is the way to the enemy."

Scipio, flushed with this success at first, had a mind to come to one decisive action. He therefore left Afranius and Juba in two distinct bodies not far distant, and marched himself towards Thapsus, where he proceeded to build a fortified camp above a lake, to serve as a centre-point for their operations, and also as a place of refuge. Whilst Scipio was thus employed Cæsar with incredible despatch made his way through thick woods, and a country supposed to be impassable, cut off one party of the enemy, and attacked another in the front. Having routed these, he followed up his opportunity and the current of his good fortune, and on the first onset carried Afranius's camp, and ravaged that of the Numidians, Juba, their king, being glad to save himself by flight; so that in a small part of a single day he made himself master of three camps, and killed fifty thousand of the enemy, with the loss only of fifty of his own men. This is the account some give of that fight. Others say, he was not in the action, but that he was taken with his usual distemper just as he was setting his army in order. He perceived the approaches of it, and before it had too far disordered his senses, when he was already beginning to shake under its influence, withdrew into a neighboring fort, where he reposed himself. Of the men of consular and prætorian dignity that were taken after the fight, several Cæsar put to death, others anticipated him by killing themselves.

Cato had undertaken to defend Utica, and for that reason was not in the battle. The desire which Cæsar had to take him alive, made him hasten thither; and upon the intelligence that he had despatched himself, he was much discomposed, for what reason is not so well agreed. He certainly said, "Cato, I must grudge you your death, as you grudged me the honor of saving your life." Yet the discourse he wrote against Cato after his death, is no great sign of his kindness, or that he was inclined to be reconciled to him. For how is it probable that he would have been tender of his life, when he was so bitter against his memory? But from his clemency to Cicero, Brutus, and many others who fought against him, it may be divined that Cæsar's book was not written so much out of animosity to Cato, as in his own vindication. Cicero had written an encomium upon Cato, and called it by his name. A composition by so great a master upon so excellent a subject, was sure to be in every one's hands. This touched Cæsar, who looked upon a panegyric on his enemy, as no better than an invective against himself; and therefore he made in his Anti-Cato, a collection of whatever could be said in his derogation. The two compositions, like Cato and Cæsar themselves, have each of them their several admirers.

Cæsar, upon his return to Rome, did not omit to pronounce before the people a magnificent account of his victory, telling them that he had subdued a country which would supply the public every year with two hundred thousand attic bushels of corn, and

three million pounds weight of oil. He then led
three triumphs for Egypt, Pontus, and Africa, the
last for the victory over, not Scipio, but king Juba,
as it was professed, whose little son was then carried
in the triumph, the happiest captive that ever was,
who of a barbarian Numidian, came by this means
to obtain a place among the most learned historians
of Greece. After the triumph, he distributed rewards to his soldiers, and treated the people with
feasting and shows. He entertained the whole people
together at one feast, where twenty-two thousand
dining couches were laid out; and he made a display
of gladiators, and of battles by sea, in honor, as he
said, of his daughter Julia, though she had been
long since dead. When these shows were over, an
account was taken of the people, who from three
hundred and twenty thousand, were now reduced to
one hundred and fifty thousand. So great a waste
had the civil war made in Rome alone, not to mention what the other parts of Italy and the provinces
suffered.

He was now chosen a fourth time consul, and went
into Spain against Pompey's sons. They were but
young, yet had gathered together a very numerous
army, and showed they had courage and conduct to
command it, so that Cæsar was in extreme danger.
The great battle was near the town of Munda, in
which Cæsar seeing his men hard pressed, and making
but a weak resistance, ran through the ranks among
the soldiers, and crying out, asked them whether
they were not ashamed to deliver him into the hands
of boys? At last, with great difficulty, and the best
efforts he could make, he forced back the enemy,
killing thirty thousand of them, though with the
loss of one thousand of his best men. When he
came back from the fight, he told his friends that

he had often fought for victory, but this was the first time that he had ever fought for life. This battle was won on the feast of Bacchus, the very day in which Pompey, four years before, had set out for the war. The younger of Pompey's sons escaped; but Didius, some days after the fight, brought the head of the elder to Cæsar. This was the last war he was engaged in. The triumph which he celebrated for this victory, displeased the Romans beyond any thing. For he had not defeated foreign generals, or barbarian kings, but had destroyed the children and family of one of the greatest men of Rome, though unfortunate; and it did not look well to lead a procession in celebration of the calamities of his country, and to rejoice in those things for which no other apology could be made either to gods or men, than their being absolutely necessary. Besides that, hitherto he had never sent letters or messengers to announce any victory over his fellow-citizens, but had seemed rather to be ashamed of the action, than to expect honor from it.

Nevertheless his countrymen, conceding all to his fortune, and accepting the bit, in the hope that the government of a single person would give them time to breathe after so many civil wars and calamities, made him dictator for life. This was indeed a tyranny avowed, since his power now was not only absolute, but perpetual too. Cicero made the first proposals to the senate for conferring honors upon him, which might in some sort be said not to exceed the limits of ordinary human moderation. But others, striving which should deserve most, carried them so excessively high, that they made Cæsar odious to the most indifferent and moderate sort of men, by the pretension and the extravagance of the titles which they decreed him. His enemies, too, are thought to have had some share in this, as well as his flatterers. It gave them advantage against him, and would be their justification for any attempt they should make upon him; for since the civil wars were ended, he had nothing else that he could be charged with. And they had good reason to decree a temple to Clemency, in token of their thanks for the mild use he made of his victory. For he not only pardoned many of those who fought against him, but, further, to some gave honors and offices; as particularly to Brutus and Cassius, who both of them were prætors. Pompey's images that were thrown down, he set up again, upon which Cicero also said that by raising Pompey's statues he had fixed his own. When his friends advised him to have a guard, and several offered their service, he would not hear of it; but said it was better to suffer death once, than always to live in fear of it. He looked upon the affections of the people to be the best and surest guard, and entertained them again with public feasting, and general distributions of corn; and to gratify his army, he sent out colonies to several places, of which the most remarkable were Carthage and Corinth; which as before they had been ruined at the same time, so now were restored and repeopled together.

As for the men of high rank, he promised to some of them future consulships ánd prætorships, some he consoled with other offices and honors, and to all held out hopes of favor by the solicitude he showed to rule with the general good-will; insomuch that upon the death of Maximus one day before his consulship was ended, he made Caninius Revilius consul for that day. And when many went to pay the usual compliments and attentions to the new consul, "Let us make haste," said Cicero, "lest the man be gone out of his office before we come."

Cæsar was born to do great things, and had a passion after honor, and the many noble exploits he had done did not now serve as an inducement to him to sit still and reap the fruit of his past labors, but were incentives and encouragements to go on, and raised in him ideas of still greater actions, and a desire of new glory, as if the present were all spent. It was in fact a sort of emulous struggle with himself, as it had been with another, how he might outdo his past actions by his future. In pursuit of these thoughts, he resolved to make war upon the Parthians, and when he had subdued them, to pass through Hyrcania; thence to march along by the Caspian Sea to Mount Caucasus, and so on about Pontus, till he came into Scythia; then to overrun all the countries bordering upon Germany, and Germany itself; and so to return through Gaul into Italy, after completing the whole circle of his intended empire, and bounding it on every side by the ocean. While preparations were making for this expedition, he proposed to dig through the isthmus on which Corinth stands; and appointed Anienus to superintend the work. He had also a design of diverting the Tiber, and carrying it by a deep channel directly from Rome to Ciceii, and so into the sea near Tarracina, that there might be a safe and easy passage for all merchants who traded to Rome. Besides this, he intended to drain all the marshes by Pomentium [22] and Setia, and gain ground enough from the water

---

[22] *Pomentium* is Pometia, or Suessa Pometia, a town that had ceased to exist long before Cæsar's time, which, however, gave its name to the Pomptine marshes.

to employ many thousands of men in tillage. He proposed further to make great mounds on the shore nearest Rome, to hinder the sea from breaking in upon the land, to clear the coast at Ostia of all the hidden rocks and shoals that made it unsafe for shipping, and to form ports and harbors fit to receive the large number of vessels that would frequent them.

These things were designed without being carried into effect; but his reformation of the calendar, in order to rectify the irregularity of time, was not only projected with great scientific ingenuity, but was brought to its completion, and proved of very great use. For it was not only in ancient times that the Romans had wanted a certain rule to make the revolutions of their months fall in with the course of the year, so that their festivals and solemn days for sacrifice were removed by little and little, till at last they came to be kept at seasons quite the contrary to what was at first intended, but even at this time the people had no way of computing the solar year; only the priests could say the time, and they, at their pleasure, without giving any notice, slipped in the intercalary month, which they called Mercedonius. Numa was the first who put in this month, but his expedient was but a poor one and quite inadequate to correct all the errors that arose in the returns of the annual cycles, as we have shown in his Life. Cæsar called in the best philosophers and mathematicians of his time to settle the point, and out of the systems he had before him, formed a new and more exact method of correcting the calendar, which the Romans use to this day, and seem to succeed better than any nation in avoiding the errors occasioned by the inequality of the cycles. Yet even this gave offence to those who looked with an evil eye on his position, and felt oppressed by his power. Cicero, the orator, when some one in his company chanced to say, the next morning Lyra would rise, replied, " Yes, in accordance with the edict," as if even this were a matter of compulsion.

But that which brought upon him the most apparent and mortal hatred, was his desire of being king; which gave the common people the first occasion to quarrel with him, and proved the most specious pretence to those who had been his secret enemies all along. Those, who would have procured him that title, gave it out, that it was foretold in the Sibyls' books that the Romans should conquer the Parthians when they fought against them under the conduct of a king, but not before. And one day, as Cæsar was coming down from Alba to Rome, some were so bold as to salute him by the name of king; but he finding the people disrelish it, seemed to resent it himself, and said his name was Cæsar, not king. Upon this, there was a general silence, and he passed on looking not very well pleased or contented. Another time, when the senate had conferred on him some extravagant honors, he chanced to receive the message as he was sitting on the rostra, where, though the consuls and prætors themselves waited on him, attended by the whole body of the senate, he did not rise, but behaved himself to them as if they had been private men, and told them his honors wanted rather to be retrenched than increased. This treatment offended not only the senate, but the commonalty too, as if they thought the affront upon the senate equally reflected upon the whole republic; so that all who could decently leave him went off, looking much discomposed. Cæsar, perceiving the false step he had made, immediately retired home; and laying his throat bare, told his friends that he was ready to offer this to any one who would give the stroke. But afterwards he made the malady from which he suffered, the excuse for his sitting, saying that those who are attacked by it, lose their presence of mind, if they talk much standing; that they presently grow giddy, fall into convulsions, and quite lose their reason. But this was not the reality, for he would willingly have stood up to the senate, had not Cornelius Balbus, one of his friends, or rather flatterers, hindered him. " Will you not remember," said he, " you are Cæsar, and claim the honor which is due to your merit?"

He gave a fresh occasion of resentment by his affront to the tribunes. The Lupercalia were then celebrated, a feast at the first institution belonging, as some writers say, to the shepherds, and having some connection with the Arcadian Lycæa. Many young noblemen and magistrates run up and down the city with their upper garments off, striking all they meet with thongs of hide, by way of sport; and many women, even of the highest rank, place themselves in the way, and hold out their hands to the lash, as boys in a school do to the master, out of a belief that it procures an easy labor to those who are with child, and makes those conceive who are barren. Cæsar, dressed in a triumphal robe, seated himself in a golden chair at the rostra, to view this ceremony. Antony, as consul, was one of those who ran this course, and when he came into the forum, and the people made way for him, he went up and reached to Cæsar a diadem wreathed with laurel. Upon this, there was a shout, but only a slight one, made by the few who were planted there for that purpose; but when Cæsar refused it, there was universal applause. Upon the second offer, very few, and upon the second refusal, all again applauded. Cæsar finding it would not take, rose up, and ordered the crown to be carried into the capitol. Cæsar's statues were afterwards found with royal diadems on their heads. Flavius and Marullus, two tribunes of the people, went presently and pulled them off, and having apprehended those who first saluted Cæsar as king, committed them to prison. The people followed them with acclamations, and called them by the name of Brutus, because Brutus was the first who ended the succession of kings, and transferred the power which before was lodged in one man into the hands of the senate and people. Cæsar so far resented this, that he displaced Marullus and Flavius; and in urging his charges against them, at the same time ridiculed the people, by himself giving the men more than once the names of Bruti, and Cumæi.[23]

This made the multitude turn their thoughts to Marcus Brutus, who, by his father's side, was thought to be descended from that first Brutus, and by his mother's side from the Servilii, another noble family, being besides nephew and son-in-law to Cato. But the honors and favors he had received from Cæsar, took off the edge from the desires he might himself have felt for overthrowing the new monarchy. For he had not only been pardoned himself after Pompey's defeat at Pharsalia, and had procured the same grace for many of his friends, but was one in whom Cæsar had a particular confidence. He had at that time the most honorable prætorship of the year, and was named

[23] Brutus, in Latin, means heavy and stupid; and the Cumæans were for one reason or other proverbial for dulness.

for the consulship four years after, being preferred before Cassius, his competitor. Upon the question as to the choice, Cæsar, it is related, said that Cassius had the fairer pretensions, but that he could not pass by Brutus. Nor would he afterwards listen to some who spoke against Brutus, when the conspiracy against him was already afoot, but laying his hand on his body, said to the informers, "Brutus will wait for this skin of mine," intimating that he was worthy to bear rule on account of his virtue, but would not be base and ungrateful to gain it. Those who desired a change, and looked on him as the only, or at least the most proper, person to effect it, did not venture to speak with him; but in the night-time laid papers about his chair of state, where he used to sit and determine causes, with such sentences in them as, "You are asleep, Brutus," "You are no longer Brutus." Cassius, when he perceived his ambition a little raised upon this, was more instant than before to work him yet further, having himself a private grudge against Cæsar, for some reasons that we have mentioned in the Life of Brutus. Nor was Cæsar without suspicions of him, and said once to his friends, "What do you think Cassius is aiming at? I don't like him, he looks so pale." And when it was told him that Antony and Dolabella were in a plot against him, he said, he did not fear such fat, luxurious men, but rather the pale, lean fellows, meaning Cassius and Brutus.

Fate, however, is to all appearance more unavoidable than unexpected. For many strange prodigies and apparitions are said to have been observed shortly before the event. As to the lights in the heavens, the noises heard in the night, and the wild birds which perched in the forum, these are not perhaps worth taking notice of in so great a case as this. Strabo, the philosopher, tells us that a number of men were seen, looking as if they were heated through with fire, contending with each other; that a quantity of flame issued from the hand of a soldier's servant, so that they who saw it thought he must be burnt, but that after all he had no hurt. As Cæsar was sacrificing, the victim's heart was missing, a very bad omen, because no living creature can subsist without a heart. One finds it also related by many, that a soothsayer bade him prepare for some great danger on the ides of March. When the day was come, Cæsar, as he went to the senate, met this soothsayer, and said to him by way of raillery, "The ides of March are come;" who answered him calmly, "Yes, they are come, but they are not past." The day before this assassination, he supped with Marcus Lepidus; and as he was signing some letters, according to his custom, as he reclined at table, there arose a question what sort of death was the best. At which he immediately, before any one could speak, said, "A sudden one."

After this, as he was in bed with his wife, all the doors and windows of the house flew open together; he was startled at the noise, and the light which broke into the room, and sat up in his bed, where by the moonshine he perceived Calpurnia fast asleep, but heard her utter in her dream some indistinct words and inarticulate groans. She fancied at that time she was weeping over Cæsar, and holding him butchered in her arms. Others say this was not her dream, but that she dreamed that a pinnacle which the senate, as Livy relates, had ordered to be raised on Cæsar's house by way of ornament and grandeur, was tumbling down, which was the occasion of her tears and ejaculations. When it was day, she begged of Cæsar, if it were possible, not to stir out, but to adjourn the senate to another time; and if he slighted her dreams, that he would be pleased to consult his fate by sacrifices, and other kinds of divination. Nor was he himself without some suspicion and fears; for he never before discovered any womanish superstition in Calpurnia, whom he now saw in such great alarm. Upon the report which the priests made to him, that they had killed several sacrifices, and still found them inauspicious, he resolved to send Antony to dismiss the senate.

In this juncture, Decimus Brutus, surnamed Albinus, one whom Cæsar had such confidence in that he made him his second heir, who nevertheless was engaged in the conspiracy with the other Brutus and Cassius, fearing lest if Cæsar should put off the senate to another day, the business might get wind, spoke scoffingly and in mockery of the diviners, and blamed Cæsar for giving the senate so fair an occasion of saying he had put a slight upon them, for that they were met upon his summons, and were ready to vote unanimously, that he should be declared king of all the provinces out of Italy, and might wear a diadem in any other place but Italy, by sea or land. If any one should be sent to tell them they might break up for the present, and meet again when Calpurnia should chance to have better dreams, what would his enemies say? Or who would with any patience hear his friends, if they should presume to defend his government as not arbitrary and tyrannical? But if he was possessed so far as to think this day unfortunate, yet it were more decent to go himself to the senate, and to adjourn it in his own person.

Brutus, as he spoke these words, took Cæsar by the hand, and conducted him forth. He was not gone far from the door, when a servant of some other person's made towards him, but not being able to come up to him, on account of the crowd of those who pressed about him, he made his way into the house, and committed himself to Calpurnia, begging of her to secure him till Cæsar returned, because he had matters of great importance to communicate to him.

Artemidorus, a Cnidian, a teacher of Greek logic, and by that means so far acquainted with Brutus and his friends as to have got into the secret, brought Cæsar in a small written memorial, the heads of what he had to depose. He had observed that Cæsar, as he received any papers, presently gave them to the servants who attended on him; and therefore came as near to him as he could, and said, " Read this, Cæsar, alone, and quickly, for it contains matter of great importance which nearly concerns you." Cæsar received it, and tried several times to read it, but was still hindered by the crowd of those who came to speak to him. However, he kept it in his hand by itself till he came into the senate. Some say it was another who gave Cæsar this note, and that Artemidorus could not get to him, being all along kept off by the crowd.

All these things might happen by chance. But the place which was destined for the scene of this murder, in which the senate met that day, was the same in which Pompey's statue stood, and was one of the edifices which Pompey had raised and dedicated with his theatre to the use of the public, plainly showing that there was something of a supernatural influence which guided the action, and ordered it to that particular place. Cassius, just before the act, is said to have looked towards Pompey's statue, and silently implored his assistance, though he had been inclined to the doctrines of Epicurus. But this occasion and the instant danger, carried him away out of all his reasonings, and filled him for the time with a sort of inspiration. As for Antony, who was firm to Cæsar, and a strong man, Brutus Albinus kept him outside the house, and delayed him with a long conversation contrived on purpose. When Cæsar entered, the senate stood up to show their respect to him, and of Brutus's confederates, some came about his chair and stood behind it, others met him, pretending to add their petitions to those of Tillius Cimber, in behalf of his brother, who was in exile; and they followed him with their joint supplications till he came to his seat. When he was sat down, he refused to comply with their requests, and upon their urging him further, began to reproach them severally for their importunities, when Tillius, laying hold of his robe with both his hands, pulled it down from his neck, which was the signal for the assault. Casca gave him the first cut, in the neck, which was not mortal nor dangerous, as coming from one who at the beginning of such a bold action was probably very much disturbed. Cæsar immediately turned about, and laid his hand upon the dagger and kept hold of it. And both of them at the same time cried out, he that received the blow, in Latin, " Vile Casca, what does this mean? " and he that gave it, in Greek, to his brother, " Brother, help! " Upon this first onset, those who were not privy to the design were astonished, and their horror and amazement at what they saw were so great, that they durst not fly nor assist Cæsar, nor so much as speak a word. But those who came prepared for the business inclosed him on every side, with their naked daggers in their hands. Which way soever he turned, he met with blows, and saw their swords levelled at his face and eyes, and was encompassed, like a wild beast in the toils, on every side. For it had been agreed they should each of them make a thrust at him, and flesh themselves with his blood; for which reason Brutus also gave him one stab in the groin. Some say that he fought and resisted all the rest, shifting his body to avoid the blows, and calling out for help, but that when he saw Brutus's sword drawn, he covered his face with his robe and submitted, letting himself fall, whether it were by chance, or that he was pushed in that direction by his murderers, at the foot of the pedestal on which Pompey's statue stood, and which was thus wetted with his blood. So that Pompey himself seemed to have presided, as it were, over the revenge done upon his adversary, who lay here at his feet, and breathed out his soul through his multitude of wounds, for they say he received three and twenty. And the conspirators themselves were many of them wounded by each other, whilst they all levelled their blows at the same person.

When Cæsar was despatched, Brutus stood forth to give a reason for what they had done, but the senate would not hear him, but flew out of doors in all haste, and filled the people with so much alarm and distraction, that some shut up their houses, others left their counters and shops. All ran one way or the other, some to the place to see the sad spectacle, others back again after they had seen it. Antony and Lepidus, Cæsar's most faithful friends, got off privately, and hid themselves in some friends' houses. Brutus and his followers, being yet hot from the deed, marched in a body from the senate-house to the capitol with their drawn swords, not like persons who thought of escaping, but with an air of confidence and assurance, and as they went along, called to the people to resume their liberty, and invited the company of any more distinguished people whom they met. And some of these joined the procession and went up along with them, as if they also had been of the conspiracy, and could claim a share in the honor of what had been done. As, for example, Caius Octavius and Lentulus Spinther, who suffered afterwards for their vanity, being taken off by Antony and the young Cæsar, and lost the honor they desired, as well as their lives, which it cost them, since no one believed they had any share in the action. For neither did those who punished them profess to revenge the fact, but the ill-will. The day after, Brutus with the rest came down from the capitol, and made a speech to the people, who listened without expressing either any pleasure or resentment, but showed by their silence that they pitied Cæsar, and respected Brutus. The senate passed acts of oblivion for what was past, and took measures to reconcile all parties. They ordered that Cæsar should be worshipped as a divinity, and nothing, even of the slightest consequence, should be revoked, which he had enacted during his government. At the same time they gave Brutus and his followers the command of provinces, and other considerable posts. So that all people now thought things were well settled, and brought to the happiest adjustment.

But when Cæsar's will was opened, and it was found that he had left a considerable legacy to each one of the Roman citizens, and when his body was seen carried through the market-place all mangled with wounds, the multitude could no longer contain themselves within the bounds of tranquillity and order, but heaped together a pile of benches, bars, and tables, which they placed the corpse on, and setting fire to it, burnt it on them. Then they took brands from the pile, and ran some to fire the houses of the conspirators, others up and down the city, to find out the men and tear them to pieces, but met, however, with none of them, they having taken effectual care to secure themselves.

One Cinna, a friend of Cæsar's, chanced the night before to have an odd dream. He fancied that Cæsar invited him to supper, and that upon his refusal to go with him, Cæsar took him by the hand and forced him, though he hung back. Upon hearing the report that Cæsar's body was burning in the market-place, he got up and went thither, out of respect to his memory, though his dream gave him some ill apprehensions, and though he was suffering from a fever. One of the crowd who saw him there, asked another who that was, and having learned his name, told it to his next neighbor. It presently passed for a certainty that he was one of Cæsar's murderers, as, indeed, there was another Cinna, a conspirator, and they, taking this to be the man, immediately seized him, and tore him limb from limb upon the spot.

Brutus and Cassius, frightened at this, within a few days retired out of the city. What they afterwards did and suffered, and how they died, is written in the Life of Brutus. Cæsar died in his fifty-sixth year, not having survived Pompey above four years. That empire and power which he had pursued through the whole course of his life with so much hazard, he did at last with much difficulty compass, but reaped no other fruits from it than the empty name and invidious glory. But the great genius which attended him through his lifetime, even after his death remained as the avenger of his murder, pursuing through every sea and land all those who were concerned in it, and suffering none to escape, but reaching all who in any sort or kind were either actually engaged in the fact, or by their counsels any way promoted it.

The most remarkable of mere human coincidences was that which befell Cassius, who, when he was defeated at Philippi, killed himself with the same dagger which he had made use of against Cæsar. The most signal preternatural appearances were the great comet, which shone very bright for seven nights after Cæsar's death, and then disappeared, and the dimness of the sun,[24] whose orb continued pale and dull for the whole of that year, never showing its ordinary radiance at its rising, and giving but a weak and feeble heat. The air consequently was damp and gross, for want of stronger rays to open and rarify it. The fruits, for that reason, never properly ripened, and began to wither and fall off for want of heat, before they were fully formed. But above all, the phantom which appeared to Brutus showed the murder was not pleasing to the gods. The story of it is this.

Brutus being to pass his army from Abydos to

---

[24] ———Solem quis dicere falsum
Audeat? ille etiam cæcos instare tumultus
Sæpe monet, fraudemque et operta tumescere bella.
Ille etiam exstincto miseratus Cæsare Romam;
Cum caput obscura nitidum ferrugine texit,
Impiaque æternam timuerunt sæcula noctem.
                    Virg. Georg., I. 463.

the continent on the other side, laid himself down one night, as he used to do, in his tent, and was not asleep, but thinking of his affairs, and what events he might expect. For he is related to have been the least inclined to sleep of all men who have commanded armies, and to have had the greatest natural capacity for continuing awake, and employing himself without need of rest. He thought he heard a noise at the door of his tent, and looking that way, by the light of his lamp, which was almost out, saw a terrible figure, like that of a man, but of unusual stature and severe countenance. He was somewhat frightened at first, but seeing it neither did nor spoke any thing to him, only stood silently by his bed-side, he asked who it was. The spectre answered him, "Thy evil genius, Brutus, thou shalt see me at Philippi." Brutus answered courageously, "Well, I shall see you," and immediately the appearance vanished. When the time was come, he drew up his army near Philippi against Antony and Cæsar, and in the first battle won the day, routed the enemy, and plundered Cæsar's camp. The night before the second battle, the same phantom appeared to him again but spoke not a word. He presently understood his destiny was at hand, and exposed himself to all the danger of the battle. Yet he did not die in the fight, but seeing his men defeated, got up to the top of a rock,[25] and there presenting his sword to his naked breast, and assisted, as they say, by a friend, who helped him to give the thrust, met his death.

[25] *To the top of a rock* is a mistranslation; the Greek is merely *to a rocky place;* and the place which Brutus made his refuge seems, by the account in his Life, to have been at the bottom rather than at the top.

PHOCION [1]

Translated by Ph. Fowke, M.D.

Demades, the orator, when in the height of the power which he obtained at Athens by advising the state in the interest of Antipater and the Macedonians, being necessitated to write and speak many things below the dignity, and contrary to the character, of the city, was wont to excuse himself by saying he steered only the shipwrecks of the commonwealth. This hardy saying of his might have some appearance of truth, if applied to Phocion's government. For Demades indeed was himself the mere wreck of his country, living and ruling so dissolutely, that Antipater took occasion to say of him, when he was now grown old, that he was like a sacrificed beast, all consumed except the tongue and the belly. But Phocion's was a real virtue, only overmatched in the unequal contest with an adverse time, and rendered by the ill fortunes of Greece inglorious and obscure. We must not, indeed, allow ourselves to concur with Sophocles in so far diminishing the force of virtue as to say that

> When fortune fails, the sense we had before
> Deserts us also, and is ours no more.[2]

---

[1] Born probably 402 B.C. and died 317 B.C. His virtue is above suspicion and his public conduct was always influenced by upright motives. His opposition to Demosthenes, however, was a mistaken policy.—Dr. William Smith.

[2] *When fortune fails, the sense we had before, Deserts us also, and is ours no more,* is said by Antigone to Creon, in the play of Sophocles (*Antigone*, 563).

Yet thus much, indeed, must be allowed to happen in the conflicts between good men and ill fortune, that instead of due returns of honor and gratitude, obloquy and unjust surmises may often prevail, to weaken, in a considerable degree, the credit of their virtue.

It is commonly said that public bodies are most insulting and contumelious to a good man, when they are puffed up with prosperity and success. But the contrary often happens; afflictions and public calamities naturally imbittering and souring the minds and tempers of men, and disposing them to such peevishness and irritability, that hardly any word or sentiment of common vigor can be addressed to them, but they will be apt to take offence. He that remonstrates with them on their errors, is presumed to be insulting over their misfortunes, and any free spoken expostulation is construed into contempt. Honey itself is searching in sore and ulcerated parts; and the wisest and most judicious counsels prove provoking to distempered minds, unless offered with those soothing and compliant approaches which made the poet, for instance, characterize agreeable things in general, by a word expressive of a grateful and easy touch,[3] exciting nothing of offence or resistance. Inflamed eyes require a retreat into dusky places, amongst colors of the deepest shades, and are unable to endure the brilliancy of light. So fares it in the body politic, in times of distress and humiliation; a certain sensitiveness and soreness of humor prevail, with a weak incapacity of en-

---

[3] The feast, the banquet, meat and drink, bread and wine, receive in Homer the epithet of *měnoeikes,* " that meets and complies with the wishes and desires."

during any free and open advice, even when the necessity of affairs most requires such plaindealing, and when the consequences of any single error may be beyond retrieving. At such times the conduct of public affairs is on all hands most hazardous. Those who humor the people are swallowed up in the common ruin; those who endeavor to lead them aright, perish the first in their attempt.

Astronomers tell us, the sun's motion is neither exactly parallel with that of the heavens in general, nor yet directly and diametrically opposite, but describing an oblique line, with insensible declination he steers his course in such a gentle, easy curve, as to dispense his light and influence, in his annual revolution, at several seasons, in just proportions to the whole creation. So it happens in political affairs; if the motions of rulers be constantly opposite and cross to the tempers and inclination of the people, they will be resented as arbitrary and harsh; as, on the other side, too much deference, or encouragement, as too often it has been, to popular faults and errors, is full of danger and ruinous consequences. But where concession is the response to willing obedience, and a statesman gratifies his people, that he may the more imperatively recall them to a sense of the common interest, then, indeed, human beings, who are ready enough to serve well and submit to much, if they are not always ordered about and roughly handled, like slaves, may be said to be guided and governed upon the method that leads to safety. Though it must be confessed, it is a nice point and extremely difficult, so to temper this lenity as to preserve the authority of the government. But if such a blessed mixture and temperament may be obtained, it seems to be of all concords and harmonies the most concordant and most harmonious. For thus we are taught even God governs the world, not by irresistible force, but persuasive argument and reason, controlling it into compliance with his eternal purposes.

Cato the younger is a similar instance. His manners were little agreeable or acceptable to the people, and he received very slender marks of their favor; witness his repulse when he sued for the consulship, which he lost, as Cicero says,[4] for acting rather like a citizen in Plato's commonwealth, than among the dregs of Romulus's posterity, the same thing happening to him, in my opinion, as we observe in fruits ripe before their season, which we rather take pleasure in looking at and admiring, than actually use; so much was his old-fashioned virtue out of the present mode, among the depraved customs which time and luxury had introduced, that it appeared indeed remarkable and wonderful, but was too great and too good to suit the present exigencies, being so out of all proportion to the times. Yet his circumstances were not altogether like Phocion's, who came to the helm when the ship of the state was just upon sinking. Cato's time was, indeed, stormy and tempestuous, yet so as he was able to assist in managing the sails, and lend his helping hand to those who, which he was not allowed to do, commanded at the helm. Others were to blame for the result; yet his courage and virtue made it in spite of all a hard task for fortune to ruin the commonwealth, and it was

---

[4] The passage in Cicero is in the letters to Atticus (II., 1): "Dicit enim tanquam in Platonis politeiai, non tanquam in Romuli fæce, sententiam." It does not, however, refer to his repulse as a candidate for the consulship.

only with long time and effort and by slow degrees, when he himself had all but succeeded in averting it, that the catastrophe was at last effected.

Phocion and he may be well compared together, not for any mere general resemblances, as though we should say, both were good men and great statesmen. For assuredly there is difference enough among virtues of the same denomination, as between the bravery of Alcibiades and that of Epaminondas, the prudence of Themistocles and that of Aristides, the justice of Numa and that of Agesilaus. But these men's virtues, even looking to the most minute points of difference, bear the same color, stamp, and character impressed upon them, so as not to be distinguishable. The mixture is still made in the same exact proportions, whether we look at the combination to be found in them both of lenity on the one hand, with austerity on the other; their boldness upon some occasions, and caution on others; their extreme solicitude for the public, and perfect neglect of themselves; their fixed and immovable bent to all virtuous and honest actions, accompanied with an extreme tenderness and scrupulosity as to doing any thing which might appear mean or unworthy; so that we should need a very nice and subtle logic of discrimination to detect and establish the distinctions between them.

As to Cato's extraction, it is confessed by all to have been illustrious, as will be said hereafter, nor was Phocion's, I feel assured, obscure or ignoble. For had he been the son of a turner, as Idomeneus reports, it had certainly not been forgotten to his disparagement by Glaucippus, the son of Hyperides, when heaping up a thousand spiteful things to say against him. Nor, indeed, had it been possible for him, in such circumstances, to have had such a liberal breeding and education in his youth, as to be first Plato's, and afterwards Xenocrates's scholar in the Academy, and to have devoted himself from the first to the pursuit of the noblest studies and practices. His countenance was so composed, that scarcely was he ever seen by any Athenian either laughing, or in tears. He was rarely known, so Duris has recorded, to appear in the public baths, or was observed with his hand exposed outside his cloak, when he wore one. Abroad, and in the camp, he was so hardy in going always thin clad and barefoot, except in a time of excessive and intolerable cold, that the soldiers used to say in merriment, that it was like to be a hard winter when Phocion wore his coat.

Although he was most gentle and humane in his disposition, his aspect was stern and forbidding, so that he was seldom accosted alone by any who were not intimate with him. When Chares once made some remark on his frowning looks, and the Athenians laughed at the jest, "My sullenness," said Phocion, "never yet made any of you sad, but these men's jollities have given you sorrow enough." In like manner Phocion's language, also, was full of instruction, abounding in happy maxims and wise thoughts, but admitted no embellishment to its austere and commanding brevity. Zeno said a philosopher should never speak till his words had been steeped in meaning; and such, it may be said, were Phocion's, crowding the greatest amount of significance into the smallest allowance of space. And to this, probably, Polyeuctus, the Sphettian, referred, when he said that Demosthenes was, indeed, the best orator of his time, but Phocion the most powerful speaker. His oratory, like small coin of great value, was to be estimated, not by its bulk, but its intrinsic worth. He was once observed, it is said, when the theatre was filling with the audience, to walk musing alone behind the scenes, which one of his friends taking notice of, said, "Phocion, you seem to be thoughtful; "Yes," replied he, "I am considering how I may shorten what I am going to say to the Athenians." Even Demosthenes himself, who used to despise the rest of the haranguers, when Phocion stood up, was wont to say quietly to those about him, "Here is the pruning-knife of my periods." This, however, might refer, perhaps, not so much to his eloquence, as to the influence of his character, since not only a word, but even a nod from a person who is esteemed, is of more force than a thousand arguments or studied sentences from others.

In his youth he followed Chabrias, the general, from whom he gained many lessons in military knowledge, and in return did something to correct his unequal and capricious humor. For whereas at other times Chabrias was heavy and phlegmatic, in the heat of battle he used to be so fired and transported, that he threw himself headlong into danger beyond the forwardest, which, indeed, in the end, cost him his life in the island of Chios, he having pressed his own ship foremost to force a landing. But Phocion, being a man of temper as well as courage, had the dexterity at some times to rouse the general, when in his procrastinating mood, to action, and at others to moderate and cool the impetuousness of his unseasonable fury. Upon which account Chabrias, who was a good-natured, kindly-tempered man, loved him much, and procured him commands and opportunities for action, giving him means to make himself known in Greece, and using his assistance in all his affairs of moment.

Particularly the sea-fight at Naxos added not a little to Phocion's reputation, when he had the left squadron committed to him by Chabrias, as in this quarter the battle was sharply contested, and was decided by a speedy victory. And this being the first prosperous sea-battle the city had engaged in with its own force since its captivity, Chabrias won great popularity by it, and Phocion, also, got the reputation of a good commander. The victory was gained at the time of the Great Mysteries, and Chabrias used to keep the commemoration of it, by distributing wine among the Athenians, yearly, on the sixteenth day of Boëdromion.

After this, Chabrias sent Phocion to demand their quota of the charges of the war from the islanders, and offered him a guard of twenty ships. Phocion told him, if he intended him to go against them as enemies, that force was insignificant; if as to friends and allies, one vessel was sufficient. So he took his own single galley, and having visited the cities, and treated with the magistrates in an equitable and open manner, he brought back a number of ships, sent by the confederates to Athens, to convey the supplies. Neither did his friendship and attention close with Chabrias's life, but after his decease he carefully maintained it to all that were related to him, and chiefly to his son Ctesippus, whom he labored to bring to some good, and although he was a stupid and intractable young fellow, always endeavored, so far as in him lay, to correct and cover his faults and follies. Once, however, when the youngster was very impertinent and troublesome to him in the camp, interrupting him with idle questions, and putting forward his opinions and suggestions of how the war should be conducted, he could not forbear exclaiming, "O Chabrias, Chabrias, how grateful I show myself for your friendship, in submitting to endure your son."

Upon looking into public matters, and the way in which they were now conducted, he observed that the administration of affairs was cut and parcelled out, like so much land by allotment, between the military men and the public speakers, so that neither these nor those should interfere with the claims of the others. As the one were to address the assemblies, to draw up votes and prepare motions, men, for example, like Eubulus, Aristophon, Demosthenes, Lycurgus, and Hyperides, and were to push their interests here; so, in the mean time, Diopithes, Menestheus, Leosthenes, and Chares, were to make their profit by war and in military commands. Phocion, on the other hand, was desirous to restore and carry out the old system, more complete in itself, and more harmonious and uniform, which prevailed in the times of Pericles, Aristides, and Solon; when statesmen showed themselves, to use Archilochus's words,—

> Mars' and the Muses' friends alike designed,
> To arts and arms indifferently inclined,[5]

and the presiding goddess of his country was, he did not fail to see, the patroness and protectress of both civil and military wisdom. With these views, while his advice at home was always for peace and quietness, he nevertheless held the office of general more frequently than any of the statesmen, not

[5] The two elegiac verses from Archilochus are quoted also by Athenæus, as said by Archilochus of himself. They are the first fragment in Bergk.

only of his own times, but of those preceding, never, indeed, promoting or encouraging military expeditions, yet never, on the other hand, shunning or declining, when he was called upon by the public voice. Thus much is well known, that he was no less than forty-five several times chosen general, he being never on any one of those occasions present at the election, but having the command, in his absence, by common suffrage, conferred on him, and he sent for on purpose to undertake it. Insomuch that it amazed those who did not well consider, to see the people always prefer Phocion, who was so far from humoring them or courting their favor, that he always thwarted and opposed them. But so it was, as great men and princes are said to call in their flatterers when dinner has been served,[6] so the Athenians, upon slight occasions, entertained and diverted themselves with their spruce speakers and trim orators, but when it came to action, they were sober and considerate enough to single out the austerest and wisest for public employment, however much he might be opposed to their wishes and sentiments. This, indeed, he made no scruple to admit, when the oracle from Delphi was read, which informed them that the Athenians were all of one mind, a single dissentient only excepted, frankly coming forward and declaring that they need look no further; he was the man, there was

---

[6] Literally, "after *water on the hands*," the first of the several points enumerated in the two lines of Aristophanes describing dinner:—

Hudōr kata cheiros, tas trapezas eispherein,
Deipnoumen, aponenimmeth', eita spendŏmen.

Water on the hands; the tables then come in,
We dine, we wash, we offer the libations.

no one but he who was dissatisfied with every thing they did. And when once he gave his opinion to the people, and was met with the general approbation and applause of the assembly, turning to some of his friends, he asked them, " Have I inadvertently said something foolish? "

[7] Upon occasion of a public festivity, being solicited for his contribution by the example of others, and the people pressing him much, he bade them apply themselves to the wealthy; for his part he should blush to make a present here, rather than a repayment *there,* turning and pointing to Callicles, the money-lender. Being still clamored upon and importuned, he told them this tale. A certain cowardly fellow setting out for the wars, hearing the ravens croak in his passage, threw down his arms, resolving to wait. Presently he took them and ventured out again, but hearing the same music, once more made a stop. " For," said he, " you may croak till you are tired, but you shall make no dinner upon me."

The Athenians urging him at an unseasonable time to lead them out against the enemy, he peremptorily refused, and being upbraided by them with cowardice and pusillanimity, he told them, " Just now, do what you will, I shall not be brave;

---

[7] Plutarch tells the story also in his essay on False Modesty (*de Vitioso Pudore,* c. 10), and again in his Political Precepts (*Reipublicæ Gerendæ Præcepta,* c. 31). These calls for subscriptions for public amusements and displays were snares to the unwise in his time also. From the turn he gives to Phocion's answer in the latter passage, it seems to be that he declines to make a gift by incurring a debt, to offer the state a present by borrowing money which he will not be able to repay, not as if he was already in debt to his banker or money-lender.

and do what I will, you will not be cowards. Nevertheless, we know well enough what we are." And when again, in a time of great danger, the people were very harsh upon him, demanding a strict account how the public money had been employed, and the like, he bade them, "First, good friends, make sure you are safe." After a war, during which they had been very tractable and timorous, when, upon peace being made, they began again to be confident and overbearing, and to cry out upon Phocion, as having lost them the honor of victory, to all their clamor he made only this answer, "My friends, you are fortunate in having a leader who knows you; otherwise, you had long since been undone."

Having a controversy with the Bœotians about boundaries, which he counselled them to decide by negotiation, they inclined to blows. "You had better," said he, "carry on the contest with the weapons in which you excel, (your tongues,) and not by war, in which you are inferior." Once, when he was addressing them, and they would not hear him or let him go on, said he, "You may compel me to act against my wishes, but you shall never force me to speak against my judgment." Among the many public speakers who opposed him, Demosthenes, for example, once told him, "The Athenians, Phocion, will kill you some day when they once are in a rage." "And you," said he, "if they once are in their senses." Polyeuctus, the Sphettian, once on a hot day was urging war with Philip, and being a corpulent man, and out of breath and in a great heat with speaking, took numerous draughts of water as he went on. "Here, indeed," said Phocion, "is a fit man to lead us into a war! What think you he will do when he is carrying his corslet and his shield to meet the enemy, if even here, delivering a prepared speech to you has almost killed him with exhaustion?" When Lycurgus in the assembly made many reflections on his past conduct, upbraiding him above all for having advised them to deliver up the ten citizens whom Alexander had demanded, he replied that he had been the author of much safe and wholesome counsel, which had not been followed.

There was a man called Archibiades, nicknamed the Lacedæmonian, who used to go about with a huge overgrown beard, wearing an old threadbare cloak, and affecting a very stern countenance. Phocion once, when attacked in council by the rest, appealed to this man for his support and testimony. And when he got up and began to speak on the popular side, putting his hand to his beard, "O Archibiades," said he, "it is time you should shave." Aristogiton, a common accuser, was a terrible man of war within the assembly, always inflaming the people to battle, but when the muster-roll came to be produced, he appeared limping on a crutch, with a bandage on his leg; Phocion descried him afar off, coming in, and cried out to the clerk, "Put down Aristogiton, too, as lame and worthless."

So that it is a little wonderful, how a man so severe and harsh upon all occasions should, notwithstanding, obtain the name of the Good. Yet, though difficult, it is not, I suppose, impossible for men's tempers, any more than for wines, to be at the same time harsh and agreeable to the taste; just as on the other hand many that are sweet at the first taste, are found, on further use, extremely disagreeable and very unwholesome. Hyperides, we are told, once said 'to the people, "Do not ask yourselves, men of Athens, whether or not

I am bitter, but whether or not I am paid for being so," as though a covetous purpose were the only thing that should make a harsh temper insupportable, and as if men might not even more justly render themselves obnoxious to popular dislike and censure, by using their power and influence in the indulgence of their own private passions of pride and jealousy, anger and animosity. Phocion never allowed himself from any feeling of personal hostility to do hurt to any fellow-citizen, nor, indeed, reputed any man his enemy, except so far as he could not but contend sharply with such as opposed the measures he urged for the public good; in which argument he was, indeed, a rude, obstinate, and uncompromising adversary. For his general conversation, it was easy, courteous, and obliging to all, to that point that he would befriend his very opponents in their distress, and espouse the cause of those who differed most from him, when they needed his patronage. His friends reproaching him for pleading in behalf of a man of indifferent character, he told them the innocent had no need of an advocate. Aristogiton, the sycophant, whom we mentioned before, having after sentence passed upon him, sent earnestly to Phocion to speak with him in the prison, his friends dissuaded him from going; "Nay, by your favor," said he, "where should I rather choose to pay Aristogiton a visit?"

As for the allies of the Athenians, and the islanders, whenever any admiral besides Phocion was sent, they treated him as an enemy suspect, barricaded their gates, blocked up their havens, brought in from the country their cattle, slaves, wives, and children, and put them in garrison; but upon Phocion's arrival, they went out to welcome him in their private boats and barges, with streamers and garlands, and received him at landing with every demonstration of joy and pleasure.

When king Philip was effecting his entry into Eubœa, and was bringing over troops from Macedonia, and making himself master of the cities, by means of the tyrants who ruled in them, Plutarch of Eretria sent to request aid of the Athenians for the relief of the island, which was in imminent danger of falling wholly into the hands of the Macedonians. Phocion was sent thither with a handful of men in comparison, in expectation that the Eubœans themselves would flock in and join him. But when he came, he found all things in confusion, the country all betrayed, the whole ground, as it were, undermined under his feet, by the secret pensioners of king Philip, so that he was in the greatest risk imaginable. To secure himself as far as he could, he seized a small rising ground, which was divided from the level plains about Tamynæ by a deep watercourse, and here he inclosed and fortified the choicest of his army. As for the idle talkers and disorderly bad citizens who ran off from his camp and made their way back, he bade his officers not regard them, since here they would have been not only useless and ungovernable themselves, but an actual hinderance to the rest; and further, being conscious to themselves of the neglect of their duty, they would be less ready to misrepresent the action, or raise a cry against them at their return home. When the enemy drew nigh, he bade his men stand to their arms, until he had finished the sacrifice, in which he spent a considerable time, either by some difficulty of the thing itself, or on purpose to invite the enemy nearer. Plutarch, interpreting this tardiness as a failure in his courage, fell on alone with the mercenaries, which the cavalry perceiving, could not be contained, but issuing also out of the camp, confusedly and in disorder, spurred up to the enemy. The first who came up were defeated, the rest were put to the rout, Plutarch himself took to flight, and a body of the enemy, advanced in the hope of carrying the camp, supposing themselves to have secured the victory. But by this time, the sacrifice being over, the Athenians within the camp came forward, and falling upon them put them to flight, and killed the greater number as they fled among the intrenchments, while Phocion ordering his infantry to keep on the watch and rally those who came in from the previous flight, himself, with a body of his best men, engaged the enemy in a sharp and bloody fight, in which all of them behaved with signal courage and gallantry. Thallus, the son of Cineas, and Glaucus, of Polymedes, who fought near the general, gained the honors of the day. Cleophanes, also, did good service in the battle. Recovering the cavalry from its defeat, and with his shouts and encouragement bringing them up to succor the general, who was in danger, he confirmed the victory obtained by the infantry. Phocion now expelled Plutarch from Eretria, and possessed himself of the very important fort of Zaretra, situated where the island is pinched in, as it were, by the seas on each side, and its breadth most reduced to a narrow girth. He released all the Greeks whom he took out of fear of the public speakers at Athens, thinking they might very likely persuade the people in their anger into committing some act of cruelty.

This affair thus despatched and settled, Phocion set sail homewards, and the allies had soon as good reason to regret the loss of his just and humane dealing, as the Athenians that of his experience and courage. Molossus, the commander who took his place, had no better success than to fall alive into the enemy's hands.

Philip, full of great thoughts and designs, now advanced with all his forces into the Hellespont, to seize the Chersonesus and Perinthus, and after them, Byzantium. The Athenians raised a force to relieve them, but the popular leaders made it their business to prefer Chares to be general, who, sailing thither, effected nothing worthy of the means placed in his hands. The cities were afraid, and would not receive his ships into their harbors, so that he did nothing but wander about, raising money from their friends, and despised by their enemies. And when the people, chafed by the orators, were extremely indignant, and repented having ever sent any help to the Byzantines, Phocion rose and told them they ought not to be angry with the allies for disturbing, but with their generals for being distrusted. "They make you suspected," he said, "even by those who cannot possibly subsist without your succor." The assembly being moved with this speech of his, changed their minds on the sudden, and commanded him immediately to raise another force, and go himself to assist their confederates in the Hellespont; an appointment which, in effect, contributed more than any thing to the relief of Byzantium.

For Phocion's name was already honorably known; and an old acquaintance of his, who had been his fellow-student in the Academy, Leon, a man of high renown for virtue among the Byzantines, having vouched for Phocion to the city, they opened their gates to receive him, not permitting him, though he desired it, to encamp without the walls, but entertained him and all the Athenians with perfect reliance, while they, to requite their confidence, behaved among their new hosts soberly and inoffensively, and exerted themselves on all occasions with the greatest zeal and resolution for their defence. Thus king Philip was driven out of the Hellespont, and was despised to boot, whom till now, it had been thought impossible to match, or even to oppose. Phocion also took some of his ships, and recaptured some of the places he had garrisoned, making besides several inroads into the country, which he plundered and overran, until he received a wound from some of the enemy who came to the defence, and, thereupon, sailed away home.

The Megarians at this time privately praying aid of the Athenians, Phocion, fearing lest the Bœotians should hear of it, and anticipate them, called an assembly at sunrise, and brought forward the petition of the Megarians, and immediately after the vote had been put, and carried in their favor, he sounded the trumpet, and led the Athenians straight from the assembly, to arm and put themselves in posture. The Megarians received them joyfully, and he proceeded to fortify Nisæa, and built two new long walls from the city to the arsenal, and so joined it to the sea, so that having now little reason to regard the enemies on the land side, it placed its dependence entirely on the Athenians.

When final hostilities with Philip were now certain, and in Phocion's absence other generals had been nominated, he on his arrival from the islands, dealt earnestly with the Athenians, that since Philip showed peaceable inclinations towards them, and greatly apprehended the danger, they would consent to a treaty. Being contradicted in this by one of the ordinary frequenters of the courts of justice, a common accuser, who asked him if he durst presume to persuade the Athenians to peace, now their arms were in their hands, "Yes," said he, "though I know that if there be war, I shall be in office over you, and if peace, you over me." But when he could not prevail, and Demosthenes's opinion carried it, advising them to make war as far from home as possible, and fight the battle out of Attica, "Good friend," said Phocion, "let us not ask where we shall fight, but how we may conquer in the war. That will be the way to keep it at a distance. If we are beaten, it will be quickly at our doors." After the defeat,[8] when the clamorers and incendiaries in the town would have brought up Charidemus to the hustings, to be nominated to the command, the best of the citizens were in a panic, and supporting themselves with the aid of the council of the Areopagus, with entreaties and tears hardly prevailed upon the people to have Phocion intrusted with the care of the city. He was of opinion, in general, that the fair terms to be expected from Philip should be accepted, yet after Demades had made a motion that the city should receive the common conditions of peace in concurrence with the rest of the states of Greece, he opposed it, till it were known what the particulars were which Philip demanded. He was overborne in this advice, under the pressure of the time, but almost immediately after, the Athenians repented it, when they understood that by these articles, they were obliged to furnish Philip both with horse and shipping. "It was the fear of this," said Phocion, "that occasioned my opposition. But

[8] The defeat is the battle of Chæronea.

since the thing is done, let us make the best of it, and not be discouraged. Our forefathers were sometimes in command, and sometimes under it; and by doing their duty, whether as rulers or as subjects, saved their own country and the rest of Greece."

Upon the news of Philip's death, he opposed himself to any public demonstrations of joy and jubilee, saying it would be ignoble to show malice upon such an occasion, and that the army that had fought them at Chæronea, was only diminished by a single man.

When Demosthenes made his invectives against Alexander, now on his way to attack Thebes, he repeated those verses of Homer,—

> "Unwise one, wherefore to a second stroke
> His anger be foolhardy to provoke?"[9]

and asked, "Why stimulate his already eager passion for glory? Why take pains to expose the city to the terrible conflagration now so near? We, who accepted office to save our fellow-citizens, will not, however they desire it, be consenting to their destruction."

After Thebes was lost, and Alexander had demanded Demosthenes, Lycurgus, Hyperides, and Charidemus to be delivered up, the whole assembly turning their eyes to him, and calling on him by

[9] *Unwise one, wherefore* is what the sailors say to Ulysses in the story of the Cyclops, when they are rowing their boat from the shore, and Ulysses, though he has already by one bold speech provoked the Cyclops to hurl a rock which had nearly intercepted them, is, nevertheless, eager to accost him once again with a taunt.

name to deliver his opinion, at last he rose up, and showing them one of his most intimate friends, whom he loved and confided in above all others, told them, "You have brought things amongst you to that pass, that for my part, should he demand this my friend Nicocles, I would not refuse to give him up. For as for myself, to have it in my power to sacrifice my own life and fortune for the common safety, I should think the greatest of good fortune. Truly," he added, "it pierces my heart to see those who are fled hither for succor from the desolation of Thebes. Yet it is enough for Greece to have Thebes to deplore. It will be more for the interest of all that we should deprecate the conqueror's anger, and intercede for both, than run the hazard of another battle."

When this was decreed by the people, Alexander is said to have rejected their first address when it was presented, throwing it from him scornfully, and turning his back upon the deputation, who left him in affright. But the second, which was presented by Phocion, he received, understanding from the older Macedonians how much Philip had admired and esteemed him. And he not only gave him audience and listened to his memorial and petition, but also permitted him to advise him, which he did to this effect, that if his designs were for quietness, he should make peace at once; if glory were his aim, he should make war, not upon Greece, but on the barbarians. And with various counsels and suggestions, happily designed to meet the genius and feelings of Alexander, he so won upon him, and softened his temper, that he bade the Athenians not forget their position, as if any thing went wrong with him, the supremacy belonged to them. And to Phocion himself, whom he adopted as his friend and guest, he showed a respect, and admitted him to distinctions, which few of those who were continually near his person ever received. Duris, at any rate, tells us, that when he became great, and had conquered Darius, in the heading of all his letters he left off the word *Greeting*,[10] except in those he wrote to Phocion. To him, and to Antipater alone, he condescended to use it. This, also, is stated by Chares.

As for his munificence to him, it is well known he sent him a present at one time of one hundred talents; and this being brought to Athens, Phocion asked of the bearers, how it came to pass, that among all the Athenians, he alone should be the object of this bounty. And being told that Alexander esteemed him alone a person of honor and worth, "Let him, then," said he, "permit me to continue so, and be still so reputed." Following him to his house, and observing his simple and plain way of living, his wife employed in kneading bread with her own hands, himself drawing water to wash his feet, they pressed him to accept it, with some indignation, being ashamed, as they said, that Alexander's friend should live so poorly and pitifully. So Phocion pointing out to them a poor old fellow, in a dirty worn-out coat, passing by, asked them if they thought him in worse condition than this man. They bade him not mention such a comparison. "Yet," said Phocion, "he with less to live upon than I, finds it sufficient, and in brief," he continued, "if I do not use this

---

[10] *Chairein*, to rejoice; the usual Greek term, used in the superscription of letters, like *Salutem*, in Latin. He wrote, not "Alexander to Phocion," but "Alexander to Phocion, greeting."

money, what good is there in my having it; and if I do use it, I shall procure an ill name, both for myself and for Alexander, among my countrymen." So the treasure went back again from Athens, to prove to Greece by a signal example, that he who could afford to give so magnificent a present, was yet not so rich as he who could afford to refuse it. And when Alexander was displeased, and wrote back to him to say that he could not esteem those his friends, who would not be obliged by him, not even would this induce Phocion to accept the money, but he begged leave to intercede with him in behalf of Echecratides, the sophist, and Athenodorus, the Imbrian, as also for Demaratus and Sparton, two Rhodians, who had been arrested upon some charges, and were in custody at Sardis. This was instantly granted by Alexander, and they were set at liberty. Afterwards, when sending Craterus into Macedonia, he commanded him to make him an offer of four cities in Asia, Cius, Gergithus, Mylasa, and Elæa, any one of which, at his choice, should be delivered to him; insisting yet more positively with him, and declaring he should resent it, should he continue obstinate in his refusal. But Phocion was not to be prevailed with at all, and, shortly after, Alexander died.

Phocion's house is shown to this day in Melita,[11] ornamented with small plates of copper, but otherwise plain and homely. Concerning his wives, of the first of them there is little said, except that she was sister of Cephisodotus, the statuary. The other was a matron of no less reputation for her virtues and simple living among the Athenians, than Phocion was for his probity. It happened

[11] The south-west quarter of the city.

once when the people were entertained with a new tragedy, that the actor, just as he was to enter the stage to perform the part of a queen, demanded to have a number of attendants sumptuously dressed, to follow in his train, and on their not being provided, was sullen and refused to act, keeping the audience waiting, till at last Melanthius, who had to furnish the chorus,[12] pushed him on the stage, crying out, "What, don't you know that Phocion's wife is never attended by more than a single waiting woman, but you must needs be grand, and fill our women's heads with vanity?" This speech of his, spoken loud enough to be heard, was received with great applause, and clapped all round the theatre. She herself, when once entertaining a visitor out of Ionia, who showed her all her rich ornaments, made of gold and set with jewels, her wreaths, necklaces, and the like, "For my part," said she, "all my ornament is my husband Phocion, now for the twentieth year in office as general at Athens."

He had a son named Phocus, who wished to take part in the games at the great feast of Minerva. He permitted him so to do, in the contest of leaping, not with any view to the victory, but in the hope that the training and discipline for it would make him a better man, the youth being in a general way a lover of drinking, and ill-regulated in his habits. On his having succeeded in the sports, many were eager for the honor of his company at banquets in celebration of the victory. Phocion declined all these invitations but one, and when he came to this entertainment and saw the costly preparations, even the water brought to wash the guests' feet being mingled with wine and

[12] The Choragus; see the note in the Life of Alexander, p. 219.

spices, he reprimanded his son, asking him why he would so far permit his friend to sully the honor of his victory. And in the hope of wholly weaning the young man from such habits and company, he sent him to Lacedæmon, and placed him among the youths then under the course of the Spartan discipline. This the Athenians took offence at, as though he slighted and contemned the education at home; and Demades twitted him with it publicly, "Suppose, Phocion, you and I advise the Athenians to adopt the Spartan constitution. If you like, I am ready to introduce a bill to that effect, and to speak in its favor." "Indeed," said Phocion, "you with that strong scent of perfumes about you, and with that mantle on your shoulders, are just the very man to speak in honor of Lycurgus, and recommend the Spartan table."

When Alexander wrote to demand a supply of galleys, and the public speakers objected to sending them, Phocion, on the council requesting his opinion, told them freely, "Sirs, I would either have you victorious yourselves, or friends of those who are so." He took up Pytheas, who about this time first began to address the assembly, and already showed himself a confident, talking fellow, by saying that a young slave whom the people had but bought yesterday,[13] ought to have the manners to hold his tongue. And when Harpalus, who had fled from Alexander out of Asia, carrying off a large sum of money, came to Attica, and there was a perfect

[13] Since the time of Aristophanes, it had been the standing jest to speak of the orators as the domestic servants or slaves, who flattered, plagued, and cheated Demus, the people, their master.

race among the ordinary public men of the assembly who should be the first to take his pay, he distributed amongst these some trifling sums by way of a bait and provocative, but to Phocion he made an offer of no less than seven hundred talents and all manner of other advantages he pleased to demand; with the compliment that he would entirely commit himself and all his affairs to his disposal. Phocion answered sharply, Harpalus should repent of it, if he did not quickly leave off corrupting and debauching the city, which for the time silenced him, and checked his proceedings. But afterwards, when the Athenians were deliberating in council about him, he found those that had received money from him to be his greatest enemies, urging and aggravating matters against him, to prevent themselves being discovered, whereas Phocion, who had never touched his pay, now, so far as the public interest would admit of it, showed some regard to his particular security. This encouraged him once more to try his inclinations, and upon further survey, finding that he himself was a fortress, inaccessible on every quarter to the approaches of corruption, he professed a particular friendship to Phocion's son-in-law, Charicles. And admitting him into his confidence in all his affairs, and continually requesting his assistance, he brought him into some suspicion. Upon the occasion, for example, of the death of Pythonice, who was Harpalus's mistress, for whom he had a great fondness, and had a child by her, he resolved to build her a sumptuous monument, and committed the care of it to his friend Charicles. This commission, disreputable enough in itself, was yet further disparaged by the figure the piece of workmanship made after it was finished. It is yet to be seen in the Hermeum,[14] as you go from Athens to Eleusis, with nothing in its appearance answerable to the sum of thirty talents, with which Charicles is said to have charged Harpalus for its erection. After Harpalus's own decease, his daughter was educated by Phocion and Charicles with great care. But when Charicles was called to account for his dealings with Harpalus, and entreated his father-in-law's protection, begging that he would appear for him in the court, Phocion refused, telling him, "I did not choose you for my son-in-law for any but honorable purposes."

Asclepiades, the son of Hipparchus, brought the first tidings of Alexander's death to Athens, which Demades told them was not to be credited; for, were it true, the whole world would ere this have stunk with the dead body. But Phocion seeing the people eager for an instant revolution, did his best to quiet and repress them. And when numbers of them rushed up to the hustings to speak, and cried out that the news was true, and Alexander was dead, "If he is dead to-day," said he, "he will be so to-morrow and the day after to-morrow equally. So that there is no need to take counsel hastily or before it is safe."

When Leosthenes now had embarked the city in the Lamian war, greatly against Phocion's wishes, to raise a laugh against Phocion, he asked him scoffingly, what the State had been benefited by his having now so many years been general. "It is not a little," said Phocion, "that the citizens have been buried in their own sepulchres." And

[14] Soon after crossing the Cephisus, says Pausanias, who does not mention the temple or sacred ground of Hermes, but calls the monument the most remarkable of all the antiquities of Greece.

when Leosthenes continued to speak boldly and boastfully in the assembly, "Young man," he said, "your speeches are like cypress-trees, stately and tall, and no fruit to come of them." And when he was then attacked by Hyperides, who asked him when the time would come, that he would advise the Athenians to make war, "As soon," said he, "as I find the young men keep their ranks, the rich men contribute their money, and the orators leave off robbing the treasury." Afterwards, when many admired the forces raised, and the preparations for war that were made by Leosthenes, they asked Phocion how he approved of the new levies. "Very well," said he, "for the short course; but what I fear, is the long race.[15] Since however late the war may last, the city has neither money, ships, nor soldiers, but these." And the event justified his prognostics. At first all things appeared fair and promising. Leosthenes gained great reputation by worsting the Bœotians[16] in battle, and driving Antipater within the walls of Lamia, and the citizens were so transported with the first successes, that they kept solemn festivities for them, and offered public sacrifices to the gods. So that some, thinking Phocion must now be convinced of his error, asked him whether he would not willingly have been author of these successful actions. "Yes," said he, "most gladly, but also of the former counsel." And when one express after

---

[15] The *stadium,* or short foot-race, one course, say of two hundred yards, contrasted with the *dolichos,* which would be at least of five or six miles.

[16] The Bœotian towns whose local independence had been secured to them by the fall of Thebes, took in this war the side of the Macedonians.

another came from the camp, confirming and magnifying the victories, "When," said he, "will the end of them come?"

Leosthenes, soon after, was killed, and now those who feared lest if Phocion obtained the command, he would put an end to the war, arranged with an obscure person in the assembly, who should stand up and profess himself to be a friend and old confidant [17] of Phocion's, and persuade the people to spare him at this time, and reserve him (with whom none could compare) for a more pressing occasion, and now to give Antiphilus the command of the army. This pleased the generality, but Phocion made it appear he was so far from having any friendship with him of old standing, that he had not so much as the least familiarity with him; "Yet now, sir," says he, "give me leave to put you down among the number of my friends and well-wishers, as you have given a piece of advice so much to my advantage."

And when the people were eager to make an expedition against the Bœotians, he at first opposed it; and on his friends telling him the people would kill him, for always running counter to them, "That will be unjust of them," he said, "if I give them honest advice, if not, it will be just of them." But when he found them persisting and shouting to him to lead them out, he commanded the crier to make proclamation, that all the Athenians under sixty should instantly provide themselves with five days' provision, and follow him from the assembly.

---

[17] *A friend and old confidant* should be *a friend and old school-fellow*. Phocion in like manner replied, that they *had not ever been at school together, nor had ever been acquainted or familiar with each other.*

This caused a great tumult. Those in years were startled, and clamored against the order; he demanded wherein he injured them, "For I," says he, "am now fourscore, and am ready to lead you." This succeeded in pacifying them for the present.

But when Micion, with a large force of Macedonians and mercenaries, began to pillage the seacoast, having made a descent upon Rhamnus, and overrun the neighboring country, Phocion led out the Athenians to attack him. And when sundry private persons came, intermeddling with his dispositions, and telling him that he ought to occupy such or such a hill, detach the cavalry in this or that direction, engage the enemy on this point or that, "O Hercules," said he, "how many generals have we here, and how few soldiers!" Afterwards, having formed the battle, one who wished to show his bravery, advanced out of his post before the rest, but on the enemy's approaching, lost heart, and retired back into his rank. "Young man," said Phocion, "are you not ashamed twice in one day to desert your station, first that on which I had placed you, and secondly, that on which you had placed yourself?" However, he entirely routed the enemy, killing Micion and many more on the spot. The Grecian army, also, in Thessaly, after Leonnatus and the Macedonians who came with him out of Asia, had arrived and joined Antipater, fought and beat them in a battle. Leonnatus was killed in the fight, Antiphilus commanding the foot, and Menon, the Thessalian, the horse.

But not long after, Craterus crossed from Asia with numerous forces; a pitched battle was fought at Cranon; the Greeks were beaten; though not indeed, in a signal defeat, nor with any great loss of men. But what with their want of obedience to their commanders, who were young and over-indulgent with them, and what with Antipater's tampering and treating with their separate cities, one by one, the end of it was that the army was dissolved, and the Greeks shamefully surrendered the liberty of their country.

Upon the news of Antipater's now advancing at once against Athens with all his force, Demosthenes and Hyperides deserted the city, and Demades, who was altogether insolvent for any part of the fines that had been laid upon him by the city, for he had been condemned no less than seven times for introducing bills contrary to the laws, and who had been disfranchised, and was no longer competent to vote in the assembly, laid hold of this season of impunity, to bring in a bill for sending ambassadors with plenipotentiary power to Antipater, to treat about a peace. But the people distrusted him, and called upon Phocion to give his opinion, as the person they only and entirely confided in. He told them, "If my former counsels had been prevalent with you, we had not been reduced to deliberate on the question at all." However, the vote passed; and a decree was made, and he with others deputed to go to Antipater, who lay now encamped in the Theban territories, but intended to dislodge immediately, and pass into Attica. Phocion's first request was, that he would make the treaty without moving his camp. And when Craterus declared that it was not fair to ask them to be burdensome to the country of their friends and allies by their stay, when they might rather use that of their enemies for provisions and the support of their army, Antipater taking him by the hand, said, "We must grant this favor to Phocion." For the rest, he bade them return to their principals, and acquaint them that he could only offer them the same terms, namely, to surrender at discretion, which Leosthenes had offered to him when he was shut up in Lamia.

When Phocion had returned to the city, and acquainted them with this answer, they made a virtue of necessity, and complied, since it would be no better. So Phocion returned to Thebes with the other ambassadors, and among the rest, Xenocrates, the philosopher,[18] the reputation of whose virtue and wisdom was so great and famous everywhere that they conceived there could not be any pride, cruelty, or anger arising in the heart of man, which would not at the mere sight of him be subdued into something of reverence and admiration. But the result, as it happened, was the very opposite, Antipater showed such a want of feeling, and such a dislike of goodness. He saluted every one else, but would not so much as notice Xenocrates. Xenocrates, they tell us, observed upon it, that Antipater when meditating such cruelty to

[18] Diogenes Laertius, in his life of *Xenocrates the philosopher,* tells a pleasant story, which appears to belong to this occasion of his going as envoy with Phocion, and yet is quite inconsistent with Plutarch's account of it, and must, in some way or other, be inaccurate. *Antipater,* says Diogenes, *asked him to supper. Xenocrates replied to the invitation by repeating the words in the Odyssey used by Ulysses to Circe, when, showing him hospitality, she placed the table before him, and saw him neither eating or drinking,—*" O Circe, what man of a right mind could let himself touch meat or drink before he had ransomed his companions, and beheld them with his eyes,"—*with which Antipater was so well pleased, that he released them.* Xenocrates *paid* the *alien-tax* at Athens (below, p. 401), being a native of Chalcedon, opposite Constantinople.

Athens, did well to be ashamed of seeing him.[19] When he began to speak, he would not hear him, but broke in and rudely interrupted him, until at last he was obliged to be silent. But when Phocion had declared the purport of their embassy, he replied shortly, that he would make peace with the Athenians on these conditions, and no others; that Demosthenes and Hyperides should be delivered up to him; that they should retain their ancient form of government, the franchise being determined by a property qualification; that they should receive a garrison into Munychia, and pay a certain sum for the cost of the war. As things stood, these terms were judged tolerable by the rest of the ambassadors; Xenocrates only said, that if Antipater considered the Athenians slaves, he was treating them fairly, but if free, severely. Phocion pressed him only to spare them the garrison, and used many arguments and entreaties. Antipater replied, "Phocion, we are ready to do you any favor, which will not bring ruin both on ourselves and on you." Others report it differently; that Antipater asked Phocion, supposing he remitted the garrison to the Athenians, would he, Phocion, stand surety for the city's observing the terms and attempting no revolution? And when he hesitated, and did not at once reply, Callimedon, the Carabus,[20] a hot partisan and professed enemy

---

[19] Antipater, at other times, showed considerable respect to Xenocrates.

[20] So called from the *carabus*, a sort of crab which he was fond of. "The fishmongers," says the comic poet Alexis, "have passed a resolution for erecting a brazen statue of Callimedon in the fish-market, holding a roasted crab in the right hand, in consideration of the benefit he has been to their trade."

of free states, cried out, "And if he should talk so idly, Antipater, will you be so much abused as to believe him and not carry out your own purpose?" So the Athenians received the garrison, and Menyllus for the governor, a fair-dealing man, and one of Phocion's acquaintance.

But the proceeding seemed sufficiently imperious and arbitrary, indeed rather a spiteful and insulting ostentation of power, than that the possession of the fortress would be of any great importance. The resentment felt upon it was heightened by the time it happened in, for the garrison was brought in on the twentieth of the month of Boedromion, just at the time of the great festival, when they carry forth Iacchus with solemn pomp from the city to Eleusis; so that the solemnity being disturbed, many began to call to mind instances, both ancient and modern, of divine interventions and intimations. For in old time, upon the occasions of their happiest successes, the presence of the shapes and voices [21] of the mystic ceremonies had been vouchsafed to them, striking terror and amazement into their enemies; but now, at the very season of their celebration, the gods themselves stood witnesses of the saddest oppression of Greece, the most holy time being profaned, and their greatest jubilee made the unlucky date of their most extreme calamity. Not many years before, they had a warning from the oracle at Dodona, that they should carefully

---

[21] He alludes particularly to the appearances noticed at the battle of Salamis. See the Life of Themistocles, Vol. I., p. 244. The 20th of Boedromion was the great day of the feast, on which they carried the image of the mystic Iacchus (Bacchus), son of Demeter (Earth-mother), in solemn procession to Eleusis.

guard the summits of Diana,[22] lest haply strangers should seize them. And about this very time, when they dyed the ribbons and garlands with which they adorn the couches and cars of the procession, instead of a purple, they received only a faint yellow color; and to make the omen yet greater, all the things that were dyed for common use, took the natural color. While a candidate for initiation was washing a young pig in the haven of Cantharus,[23] a shark seized him, bit off all his lower parts up to the belly, and devoured them, by which the god gave them manifestly to understand, that having lost the lower town and the sea-coast, they should keep only the upper city.

Menyllus was sufficient security that the garrison should behave itself inoffensively. But those who were now excluded from the franchise by poverty, amounted to more than twelve thousand; so that both those that remained in the city thought themselves oppressed and shamefully used, and those who on this account left their homes and went away into Thrace, where Antipater offered them a town and some territory to inhabit, regarded themselves only as a colony of slaves and exiles. And when to this was added the deaths of Demosthenes at Calauria, and of Hyperides at Cleonæ, as we have elsewhere related, the citizens began to think with regret of Philip and Alexander, and almost to wish the return of those times. And as, after Antigonus was slain, when those that had taken him off were afflicting and oppressing the

---

[22] To whom Munychia was dedicated.

[23] One of the small basins or recesses (*cantharus* means a cup) of the Piræus. It was part of the preliminaries performed by the mystæ, to wash a young pig in this piece of water.

people, a countryman in Phrygia, digging in the fields, was asked what he was doing, " I am," said he, fetching a deep sigh, " searching for Antigonus;" so said many that remembered those days, and the contests they had with those kings, whose anger, however great, was yet generous and placable; whereas Antipater, with the counterfeit humility of appearing like a private man, in the meanness of his dress [24] and his homely fare, merely belied his real love of that arbitrary power, which he exercised, as a cruel master and despot, to distress those under his command. Yet Phocion had interest with him to recall many from banishment by his intercession, and prevailed also for those who were driven out, that they might not, like others, be hurried beyond Tænarus, and the mountains of Ceraunia, but remain in Greece, and plant themselves in Peloponnesus, of which number was Agnonides, the sycophant. He was no less studious to manage the affairs within the city with equity and moderation, preferring constantly those that were men of worth and good education to the magistracies, and recommending the busy and turbulent talkers, to whom it was a mortal blow to be excluded from office and public debating, to learn to stay at home, and be content to till their land. And observing that Xenocrates paid his alien-tax as a foreigner, he offered him the freedom of the city, which he refused, saying he could not accept a franchise which he had been sent, as an ambassador, to deprecate.

Menyllus wished to give Phocion a considerable present of money, who, thanking him, said, neither

---

[24] He was, said Alexander the Great, scornfully, *holoporphuros,* all over purple, within.

was Menyllus greater than Alexander, nor his own occasions more urgent to receive it now, than when he refused it from him. And on his pressing him to permit his son Phocus to receive it, he replied, "If my son returns to a right mind, his patrimony is sufficient; if not, all supplies will be insufficient." But to Antipater he answered more sharply, who would have him engaged in something dishonorable. "Antipater," said he, "cannot have me both as his friend and his flatterer." And, indeed, Antipater was wont to say, he had two friends at Athens, Phocion and Demades; the one would never suffer him to gratify him at all, the other would never be satisfied. Phocion might well think that poverty a virtue, in which, after having so often been general of the Athenians, and admitted to the friendship of potentates and princes, he had now grown old. Demades, meantime, delighted in lavishing his wealth even in positive transgressions of the law. For there having been an order that no foreigner should be hired to dance in any chorus on the penalty of a fine of one thousand drachmas on the exhibitor, he had the vanity to exhibit an entire chorus of a hundred foreigners, and paid down the penalty of a thousand drachmas a head upon the stage itself. Marrying his son Demeas, he told him with the like vanity, "My son, when I married your mother, it was done so privately it was not known to the next neighbors, but kings and princes give presents at your nuptials."

The garrison in Munychia continued to be felt as a great grievance, and the Athenians did not cease to be importunate upon Phocion, to prevail with Antipater for its removal; but whether he despaired of effecting it, or perhaps observed the people to be more orderly, and public matters more reasonably conducted by the awe that was thus created, he constantly declined the office, and contented himself with obtaining from Antipater the postponement for the present of the payment of the sum of money in which the city was fined. So the people, leaving him off, applied themselves to Demades, who readily undertook the employment, and took along with him his son also into Macedonia; and some superior power, as it seems, so ordering it, he came just at that nick of time, when Antipater was already seized with his sickness, and Cassander, taking upon himself the command, had found a letter of Demades's, formerly written by him to Antigonus in Asia, recommending him to come and possess himself of the empire of Greece and Macedon, now hanging, he said, (a scoff at Antipater,) "by an old and rotten thread." So when Cassander saw him come, he seized him: and first brought out the son and killed him so close before his face, that the blood ran all over his clothes and person, and then, after bitterly taunting and upbraiding him with his ingratitude and treachery, despatched him himself.

Antipater being dead, after nominating Polysperchon general-in-chief, and Cassander commander of the cavalry, Cassander at once set up for himself, and immediately despatched Nicanor to Menyllus, to succeed him in the command of the garrison, commanding him to possess himself of Munychia before the news of Antipater's death should be heard; which being done, and some days after the Athenians hearing the report of it, Phocion was taxed as privy to it before, and censured heavily for dissembling it, out of friendship for Nicanor. But he slighted their talk, and making it his duty to visit and confer continually with Nicanor, he succeeded in procuring his good-will and kindness for the Athenians, and induced him even to put himself to trouble and expense to seek popularity with them, by undertaking the office of presiding at the games.

In the mean time Polysperchon, who was intrusted with the charge of the king,[25] to countermine Cassander, sent a letter to the city, declaring in the name of the king, that he restored them their democracy, and that the whole Athenian people were at liberty to conduct their commonwealth according to their ancient customs and constitutions. The object of these pretences was merely the overthrow of Phocion's influence, as the event manifested. For Polysperchon's design being to possess himself of the city, he despaired altogether of bringing it to pass, whilst Phocion retained his credit; and the most certain way to ruin him, would be again to fill the city with a crowd of disfranchised citizens, and let loose the tongues of the demagogues and common accusers.

With this prospect, the Athenians were all in excitement, and Nicanor, wishing to confer with them on the subject, at a meeting of the Council in Piræus, came himself, trusting for the safety of his person to Phocion. And when Dercyllus, who commanded the guard there, made an attempt to seize him, upon notice of it beforehand, he made his escape, and there was little doubt he would now lose no time in righting himself upon the city for

---

[25] Antipater, for whatever reason, had appointed Polysperchon, not his own son Cassander, to succeed him, as regent, in the charge of the two kings, Arrhidæus Philip, who was imbecile, (who is *the king* here,) and Roxana's child, Alexander Ægus. The rescript was in the name of Arrhidæus, and he is the king who appears further on in the narrative.

the affront; and when Phocion was found fault with for letting him get off and not securing him, he defended himself by saying that he had no mistrust of Nicanor, nor the least reason to expect any mischief from him, but should it prove otherwise, for his part he would have them all know, he would rather receive than do the wrong. And so far as he spoke for himself alone, the answer was honorable and high-minded enough, but he who hazards his country's safety, and that, too, when he is her magistrate and chief commander, can scarcely be acquitted, I fear, of transgressing a higher and more sacred obligation of justice, which he owed to his fellow-citizens. For it will not even do to say, that he dreaded the involving the city in war, by seizing Nicanor, and hoped by professions of confidence and just-dealing, to retain him in the observance of the like; but it was, indeed, his credulity and confidence in him, and an overweening opinion of his sincerity, that imposed upon him. So that notwithstanding the sundry intimations he had of his making preparations to attack Piræus, sending soldiers over into Salamis, and tampering with, and endeavoring to corrupt various residents in Piræus, he would, notwithstanding all this evidence, never be persuaded to believe it. And even when Philomedes of Lampra had got a decree passed, that all the Athenians should stand to their arms, and be ready to follow Phocion their general, he yet sat still and did nothing, until Nicanor actually led his troops out from Munychia, and drew trenches about Piræus; upon which, when Phocion at last would have led out the Athenians, they cried out against him, and slighted his orders.

Alexander, the son of Polysperchon, was at hand with a considerable force, and professed to come to give them succor against Nicanor, but intended nothing less, if possible, than to surprise the city, whilst they were in tumult and divided among themselves. For all that had previously been expelled from the city, now coming back with him, made their way into it, and were joined by a mixed multitude of foreigners and disfranchised persons, and of these a motley and irregular public assembly came together, in which they presently divested Phocion of all power, and chose other generals; and if by chance Alexander had not been spied from the walls, alone in close conference with Nicanor, and had not this, which was often repeated, given the Athenians cause of suspicion, the city had not escaped the snare. The orator Agnonides, however, at once fell foul upon Phocion, and impeached him of treason; Callimedon and Charicles, fearing the worst, consulted their own security by flying from the city; Phocion, with a few of his friends that stayed with him, went over to Polysperchon, and out of respect for him, Solon of Platæa, and Dinarchus of Corinth, who were reputed friends and confidants of Polysperchon, accompanied him. But on account of Dinarchus falling ill, they remained several days in Elatea, during which time, upon the persuasion of Agnonides and on the motion of Archestratus, a decree passed that the people should send delegates thither to accuse Phocion. So both parties reached Polysperchon at the same time, who was going through the country with the king, and was then at a small village of Phocis, Pharygæ, under the mountain now called Galate, but then Acrurium.

There Polysperchon, having set up the golden canopy and seated the king and his company under it, ordered Dinarchus at once to be taken, and tortured, and put to death; and that done, gave audience to the Athenians, who filled the place with noise and tumult, accusing and recriminating on one another, till at last Agnonides came forward, and requested they might all be shut up together in one cage, and conveyed to Athens, there to decide the controversy. At that the king could not forbear smiling, but the company that attended, for their own amusement, Macedonians and strangers, were eager to hear the altercation, and made signs to the delegates to go on with their case at once. But it was no sort of fair hearing. Polysperchon frequently interrupted Phocion, till at last Phocion struck his staff on the ground, and declined to speak further. And when Hegemon said, Polysperchon himself could bear witness to his affection for the people, Polysperchon called out fiercely, "Give over slandering me to the king," and the king starting up was about to have run him through with his javelin, but Polysperchon interposed and hindered him; so that the assembly dissolved.

Phocion, then, and those about him, were seized; those of his friends that were not immediately by him, on seeing this, hid their faces, and saved themselves by flight. The rest Clitus took and brought to Athens, to be submitted to trial; but, in truth, as men already sentenced to die. The manner of conveying them was indeed extremely moving; they were carried in chariots through the Ceramicus, straight to the place of judicature, where Clitus secured them till they had convoked an assembly of the people, which was open to all comers, neither foreigners, nor slaves, nor those who had been punished with disfranchisement, being refused admittance, but all alike, both men and women, being allowed to come into the court, and even upon the place of speaking.

So having read the king's letters, in which he declared he was satisfied himself that these men were traitors, however, they being a free city, he willingly accorded them the grace of trying and judging them according to their own laws, Clitus brought in his prisoners. Every respectable citizen, at the sight of Phocion, covered up his face, and stooped down to conceal his tears. And one of them had the courage to say, that since the king had committed so important a cause to the judgment of the people, it would be well that the strangers, and those of servile condition, should withdraw. But the populace would not endure it, crying out they were oligarchs, and enemies to the liberty of the people, and deserved to be stoned; after which no man durst offer any thing further in Phocion's behalf. He was himself with difficulty heard at all, when he put the question, "Do you wish to put us to death lawfully, or unlawfully?" Some answered, "According to law." He replied, "How can you, except we have a fair hearing?" But when they were deaf to all he said, approaching nearer, "As to myself," said he, "I admit my guilt, and pronounce my public conduct to have deserved sentence of death. But why, O men of Athens, kill others who have offended in nothing?" The rabble cried out, they were his friends, that was enough. Phocion therefore drew back, and said no more.

Then Agnonides read the bill, in accordance with which the people should decide by show of hands whether they judged them guilty, and if so it should be found, the penalty should be death. When this had been read out, some desired it might be added to the sentence that Phocion should be tortured also, and that the rack should be produced with the executioners. But Agnonides perceiving even Clitus to dislike this, and himself thinking it horrid and barbarous, said, "When we catch that slave, Callimedon, men of Athens, we will put him to the rack, but I shall make no motion of the kind in Phocion's case." Upon which one of the better citizens remarked, he was quite right; "If we should torture Phocion, what could we do to you?" So the form of the bill was approved of, and the show of hands called for; upon which, not one man retaining his seat, but all rising up, and some with garlands on their heads, they condemned them all to death.

There were present with Phocion, Nicocles, Thudippus, Hegemon, and Pythocles. Demetrius the Phalerian, Callimedon, Charicles, and some others, were included in the condemnation, being absent.

After the assembly was dismissed, they were carried to the prison; the rest with cries and lamentations, their friends and relatives following and clinging about them, but Phocion looking (as men observed with astonishment at his calmness and magnanimity) just the same as when he had been used to return to his home attended, as general, from the assembly. His enemies ran along by his side, reviling and abusing him. And one of them coming up to him, spat in his face; at which Phocion, turning to the officers, only said, "You should stop this indecency." Thudippus, on their reaching the prison, when he observed the executioner tempering the poison and preparing it for them, gave way to his passion, and began to bemoan his condition and the hard measure he received, thus unjustly to suffer with Phocion. "You cannot be contented," said he, "to die with Phocion?" One of his friends that stood by, asked him if he wished to have any thing said to his son. "Yes, by all means," said he, "bid him bear no grudge against the Athenians." Then Nicocles, the dearest and most faithful of his friends, begged to be allowed to drink the poison first. "My friend," said he, "you ask what I am loath and sorrowful to give, but as I never yet in all my life was so thankless as to refuse you, I must gratify you in this also." After they had all drunk of it, the poison ran short; and the executioner refused to prepare more, except they would pay him twelve drachmas, to defray the cost of the quantity required. Some delay was made, and time spent, when Phocion called one of his friends, and observing that a man could not even die at Athens without paying for it, requested him to give the sum.

It was the nineteenth day of the month Munychion, on which it was the usage to have a solemn procession in the city, in honor of Jupiter. The horsemen, as they passed by, some of them threw away their garlands, others stopped, weeping, and casting sorrowful looks towards the prison doors, and all the citizens whose minds were not absolutely debauched by spite and passion, or who had any humanity left, acknowledged it to have been most impiously done, not, at least, to let that day pass, and the city so be kept pure from death and a public execution at the solemn festival. But as if this triumph had been insufficient, the malice of Phocion's enemies went yet further; his dead body was excluded from burial within the boundaries of the country, and none of the Athenians could light a funeral pile to burn the corpse; neither durst any of his friends venture to concern themselves about it. A certain Conopion, a man who used to do these offices for hire, took the body and carried it beyond Eleusis, and procuring fire from over the frontier of Megara,[26] burned it. Phocion's wife, with her servant-maids, being present and assisting at the solemnity, raised there an empty tomb, and performed the customary libations, and gathering up the bones in her lap, and bringing them home by night, dug a place for them by the fireside in her house, saying, " Blessed hearth, to your custody I commit the remains of a good and brave man; and, I beseech you, protect and restore them to the sepulchre of his fathers, when the Athenians return to their right minds."

And, indeed, a very little time and their own sad experience soon informed them what an excellent governor, and how great an example and guardian of justice and of temperance they had bereft themselves of. And now they decreed him a statue of brass, and his bones to be buried honorably at the public charge; and for his accusers, Agnonides they took themselves, and caused him to be put to death. Epicurus and Demophilus, who fled from the city for fear, his son met with, and took his revenge upon them. This son of his, we are told, was in general of an indifferent character, and once, when enamoured of a slave girl kept by a common harlot merchant, happened to hear Theodorus, the atheist, arguing in the Lyceum, that if it were a good and honorable thing to buy the freedom of a friend in the masculine, why not also of a friend in the feminine, if, for example, a master, why not also a mistress? So putting the good argument and

---

[26] This is in accordance with a corrected reading. According to the usual text it is, " a Megarian woman." Those who were condemned for treason, were burned in the waste ground left between the Athenian and the Megarian territories.

his passion together, he went off and purchased the girl's freedom. The death which was thus suffered by Phocion, revived among the Greeks the memory of that of Socrates, the two cases being so similar, and both equally the sad fault and misfortune of the city.

CATO THE YOUNGER[1]

Translated by Stephen Waller, LL.D.

The family of Cato derived its first lustre from his great-grandfather Cato, whose virtue gained him such great reputation and authority among the Romans, as we have written in his Life.

This Cato was, by the loss of both his parents, left an orphan, together with his brother Cæpio, and his sister Porcia. He had also a half-sister, Servilia, by the mother's side. All these lived together, and were bred up in the house of Livius Drusus, their uncle by the mother, who, at that time, had a great share in the government, being a very eloquent speaker, a man of the greatest temperance, and yielding in dignity to none of the Romans.

It is said of Cato, that even from his infancy, in his speech, his countenance, and all his childish pastimes, he discovered an inflexible temper, unmoved by any passion, and firm in every thing. He was resolute in his purposes, much beyond the strength of his age, to go through with whatever he undertook. He was rough and ungentle toward those that flattered him, and still more unyielding to those who threatened him. It was difficult to excite him to laughter; his countenance seldom relaxed even into a smile; he was not quickly or easily provoked to anger, but if once incensed, he was no less difficult to pacify.

[1] Marcus Porcius Cato was born 95 B.C., and committed suicide at Utica, North Africa, 46 B.C., after spending the greater part of the night reading Plato's Phædo.—Dr. William Smith.

When he began to learn, he proved dull, and slow to apprehend, but of what he once received, his memory was remarkably tenacious. And such, in fact, we find generally to be the course of nature; men of fine genius are readily reminded of things, but those who receive with most pains and difficulty, remember best; every new thing they learn, being, as it were, burnt and branded in on their minds.[2] Cato's natural stubbornness and slowness to be persuaded, may also have made it more difficult for him to be taught. For to learn, is to submit to have something done to one; and persuasion comes soonest to those who have least strength to resist it. Hence young men are sooner persuaded than those that are more in years, and sick men, than those that are well in health. In fine, where there is least previous doubt and difficulty, the new impression is most easily accepted. Yet Cato, they say, was very obedient to his preceptor, and would do whatever he was commanded; but he would also ask the reason, and inquire the cause of every thing. And, indeed, his teacher was a very well-bred man, more ready to instruct, than to beat his scholars. His name was Sarpedon.

When Cato was a child, the allies of the Romans sued to be made free citizens of Rome. Pompæ-

---

[2] The two Greek words employed to express this distinction, are, *anamnestic* and *mnemonic*. Men of genius are anamnestic. Cato was mnemonic. The significance of the first word may perhaps be illustrated by Plato's dictum, that all learning (*mathesis*) is an *anamnesis*, a recollecting; we knew originally, and are now reminded. The man of a retentive memory, the *mnemonicus*, has his facts always at command; the *anamnesticus* requires some hint or suggestion to call up the image. The distinction between a strong and a lively memory is, perhaps nearly equivalent.

dius Silo, one of their deputies, a brave soldier, and a man of great repute, who had contracted a friendship with Drusus, lodged at his house for several days, in which time being grown familiar with the children, "Well," said he to them, "will you entreat your uncle to befriend us in our business?" Cæpio, smiling, assented, but Cato made no answer, only he looked steadfastly and fiercely on the strangers. Then said Pompædius, "And you, young sir, what say you to us? will not you, as well as your brother, intercede with your uncle in our behalf?" And when Cato continued to give no answer, by his silence and his countenance seeming to deny their petition, Pompædius snatched him up to the window as if he would throw him out, and told him to consent, or he would fling him down, and, speaking in a harsher tone, held his body out of the window, and shook him several times. When Cato had suffered this a good while, unmoved and unalarmed, Pompædius setting him down, said in an under-voice to his friend, "What a blessing for Italy, that he is but a child! If he were a man, I believe we should not gain one voice among the people."

Another time, one of his relations, on his birthday, invited Cato and some other children to supper, and some of the company diverted themselves in a separate part of the house, and were at play, the elder and the younger together, their sport being to act the pleadings before the judges, accusing one another, and carrying away the condemned to prison. Among these a very beautiful young child, being bound and carried by a bigger into prison, cried out to Cato, who seeing what was going on, presently ran to the door, and thrusting away those who stood there as a guard, took out the child, and went home in anger, followed by some of his companions.

Cato at length grew so famous among them, that when Sylla designed to exhibit the sacred game of young men riding courses on horseback,[3] which they called Troy, having gotten together the youth of good birth, he appointed two for their leaders. One of them they accepted for his mother's sake, being the son of Metella, the wife of Sylla; but as for the other, Sextus, the nephew of Pompey, they would not be led by him, nor exercise under him. Then Sylla asking, whom they would have, they all cried out, Cato; and Sextus willingly yielded the honor to him, as the more worthy.

Sylla, who was a friend of their family, sent at times for Cato and his brother to see them and talk with them; a favor which he showed to very few, after gaining his great power and authority. Sarpedon, full of the advantage it would be, as well for the honor as the safety of his scholars, would often bring Cato to wait upon Sylla at his house, which, for the multitude of those that were being carried off in custody, and tormented there, looked like a place of execution. Cato was then in his fourteenth year, and seeing the heads of men said to be of great distinction brought thither, and observing the secret sighs of those that were present, he asked his preceptor, "Why does nobody kill this man?" "Because," said he, "they fear him, child, more than they hate him." "Why, then," replied Cato, "did you not give me a sword,

---

[3] The favorite show of boys on horseback, which Virgil takes occasion to describe in the fifth Book of the Æneid, 545-603. *Trojaque nunc, pueri, Trojanum dicitur agmen.*

that I might stab him, and free my country from this slavery?" Sarpedon hearing this, and at the same time seeing his countenance swelling with anger and determination, took care thenceforward to watch him strictly, lest he should hazard any desperate attempt.

While he was yet very young, to some that asked him, whom he loved best, he answered, his brother. And being asked, whom next, he replied, his brother, again. So likewise the third time, and still the same, till they left off to ask any further. As he grew in age, this love to his brother grew yet the stronger. When he was about twenty years old, he never supped, never went out of town, nor into the forum, without Cæpio. But when his brother made use of precious ointments and perfumes, Cato declined them; and he was, in all his habits, very strict and austere, so that when Cæpio was admired for his moderation and temperance, he would acknowledge that indeed he might be accounted such, in comparison with some other men, "but," said he, "when I compare myself with Cato, I find myself scarcely different from Sippius," one at that time notorious for his luxurious and effeminate living.

Cato being made priest of Apollo, went to another house, took his portion of their paternal inheritance, amounting to a hundred and twenty talents, and began to live yet more strictly than before. Having gained the intimate acquaintance of Antipater the Tyrian, the Stoic philosopher, he devoted himself to the study, above every thing, of moral and political doctrine. And though possessed, as it were, by a kind of inspiration for the pursuit of every virtue, yet what most of all virtue and excellence fixed his affection, was that steady and inflexible justice, which is not to be wrought upon by favor or compassion. He learned also the art of speaking and debating in public, thinking that political philosophy, like a great city, should maintain for its security the military and warlike element.[4] But he would never recite his exercises before company, nor was he ever heard to declaim. And to one that told him, men blamed his silence, "But I hope not my life," he replied, "I will begin to speak, when I have that to say which had not better be unsaid."

The great Porcian Hall,[5] as it was called, had been built and dedicated to the public use by the old Cato, when ædile. Here the tribunes of the people used to transact their business, and because one of the pillars was thought to interfere with the convenience of their seats, they deliberated whether it were best to remove it to another place, or to take it away. This occasion first drew Cato, much against his will, into the forum; for he opposed the demand of the tribunes, and in so doing, gave a specimen both of his courage and his powers of speaking, which gained him great admiration. His speech had nothing youthful or refined in it, but was straightforward, full of matter, and rough, at the same time that there was a certain grace about his rough statements which won the attention; and the speaker's character showing itself in all he said, added to his severe language something that excited feelings of natural pleasure and interest. His voice was full and sounding, and sufficient to

[4] There is an allusion, perhaps, to Plato's ideal State or Republic, with its three divisions of the philosophers to govern, the soldiers to protect, and the people to furnish subsistence.

[5] The Porcian basilica; the oldest building of the kind in Rome.

be heard by so great a multitude, and its vigor and capacity of endurance quite indefatigable; for he often would speak a whole day, and never stop.

When he had carried this cause, he betook himself again to study and retirement. He employed himself in inuring his body to labor and violent exercise; and habituated himself to go bareheaded in the hottest and the coldest weather, and to walk on foot at all seasons. When he went on a journey with any of his friends, though they were on horseback and he on foot, yet he would often join now one, then another, and converse with them on the way. In sickness, the patience he showed in supporting, and the abstinence he used for curing his distempers, were admirable. When he had an ague, he would remain alone, and suffer nobody to see him, till he began to recover, and found the fit was over. At supper, when he threw dice for the choice of dishes, and lost, and the company offered him nevertheless his choice, he declined to dispute, as he said, the decision of Venus.[6] At first, he was wont to drink only once after supper, and then go away; but in process of time he grew to drink more, insomuch that oftentimes he would continue till morning. This his friends explained by saying that state affairs and public business took him up all day, and being desirous of knowledge, he liked to pass the night at wine in the conversation of philosophers. Hence, upon one Memmius saying in public, that Cato spent whole nights in drinking, " You should add," replied Cicero, " that he spends whole days in gambling." And in general Cato esteemed the customs and manners of men at that time so corrupt, and a reformation in them so necessary, that he thought it requisite, in many

[6] The highest throw of the dice bore the name of Venus.

things, to go contrary to the ordinary way of the world. Seeing the lightest and gayest purple was then most in fashion, he would always wear that which was nearest black; and he would often go out of doors, after his morning meal, without either shoes or tunic; not that he sought vainglory from such novelties, but he would accustom himself to be ashamed only of what deserves shame, and to despise all other sorts of disgrace.

The estate of one Cato, his cousin, which was worth one hundred talents, falling to him, he turned it all into ready money, which he kept by him for any of his friends that should happen to want, to whom he would lend it without interest. And for some of them, he suffered his own land and his slaves to be mortgaged to the public treasury.

When he thought himself of an age fit to marry, having never before known any woman, he was contracted to Lepida, who had before been contracted to Metellus Scipio, but on Scipio's own withdrawal from it, the contract had been dissolved, and she left at liberty. Yet Scipio afterward repenting himself, did all he could to regain her, before the marriage with Cato was completed, and succeeded in so doing. At which Cato was violently incensed, and resolved at first to go to law about it; but his friends persuaded him to the contrary. However, he was so moved by the heat of youth and passion, that he wrote a quantity of iambic verses against Scipio, in the bitter, sarcastic style of Archilochus, without, however, his license and scurrility. After this, he married Atilia, the daughter of Soranus, the first, but not the only woman he ever knew, less happy thus far than Lælius, the friend of Scipio, who in the whole course of so long a life never knew but the one woman

CATO THE YOUNGER

to whom he was united in his first and only marriage.

In the war of the slaves, which took its name from Spartacus, their ringleader, Gellius was general, and Cato went a volunteer, for the sake of his brother Cæpio, who was a tribune in the army. Cato could find here no opportunity to show his zeal or exercise his valor, on account of the ill conduct of the general. However, amidst the corruption and disorders of that army, he showed such a love of discipline, so much bravery upon occasion, and so much courage and wisdom in every thing, that it appeared he was no way inferior to the old Cato. Gellius offered him great rewards, and would have decreed him the first honors; which, however, he refused, saying, he had done nothing that deserved them. This made him be thought a man of a strange and eccentric temper.

There was a law passed, moreover, that the candidates who stood for any office should not have prompters in their canvass, to tell them the names of the citizens;[7] and Cato, when he sued to be elected tribune, was the only man that obeyed this law. He took great pains to learn by his own knowledge to salute those he had to speak with, and to call them by their names; yet even those who praised

---

[7] *Nomenclatores;* the appearance of knowing the names of their fellow-citizens being, at Rome, one of the commonest arts of candidates for office.

> Mercemur servum qui dictet nomina, lævum
> Qui fodiat latus, et cogat trans pondera dextram
> Porrigere, hic multum in Fabia valet, ille Velina.

The appointment which Cato was seeking was that of tribune in the army.

him for this, did not do so without some envy and jealousy, for the more they considered the excellence of what he did, the more they were grieved at the difficulty they found to do the like.

Being chosen tribune, he was sent into Macedon to join Rubrius, who was general there. It is said that his wife showing much concern, and weeping at his departure, Munatius, one of Cato's friends, said to her, "Do not trouble yourself, Atilia, I will engage to watch over him for you." "By all means," replied Cato; and when they had gone one day's journey together, "Now," said he to Munatius, after they had supped, "that you may be sure to keep your promise to Atilia, you must not leave me day nor night," and from that time, he ordered two beds to be made in his own chamber, that Munatius might lie there. And so he continued to do, Cato making it his jest to see that he was always there. There went with him fifteen slaves, two freedmen, and four of his friends; these rode on horseback, but Cato always went on foot, yet would he keep by them, and talk with each of them in turn, as they went.

When he came to the army, which consisted of several legions, the general gave him the command of one; and as he looked upon it as a small matter, and not worthy a commander, to give evidence of his own single valor, he resolved to make his soldiers, as far as he could, like himself, not, however, in this, relaxing the terrors of his office, but associating reason with his authority. He persuaded and instructed every one in particular, and bestowed rewards or punishments according to desert; and at length his men were so well disciplined, that it was hard to say, whether they were more peaceable,

CATO THE YOUNGER 423

or more warlike, more valiant, or more just; they were alike formidable to their enemies and courteous to their allies, fearful to do wrong, and forward to gain honor. And Cato himself acquired in the fullest measure, what it had been his least desire to seek, glory and good repute; he was highly esteemed by all men, and entirely beloved by the soldiers. Whatever he commanded to be done, he himself took part in the performing; in his apparel, his diet and mode of travelling, he was more like a common soldier than an officer; but in character, high purpose, and wisdom, he far exceeded all that had the names and titles of commanders, and he made himself, without knowing it, the object of general affection. For the true love of virtue is in all men produced by the love and respect they bear to him that teaches it; and those who praise good men, yet do not love them, may respect their reputation, but do not really admire, and will never imitate their virtue.

There dwelt at that time in Pergamus, Athenodorus, surnamed Cordylio, a man of high repute for his knowledge of the stoic philosophy, who was now grown old, and had always steadily refused the friendship and acquaintance of princes and great men. Cato understood this; so that imagining he should not be able to prevail with him by sending or writing, and being by the laws allowed two months' absence from the army, he resolved to go into Asia to see him in person, trusting to his own good qualities not to lose his labor. And when he had conversed with him, and succeeded in persuading him out of his former resolutions, he returned and brought him to the camp, as joyful and as proud of this victory as if he had done some heroic exploit, greater than any of those of Pompey or

Lucullus, who, with their armies, at that time were subduing so many nations and kingdoms.

While Cato was yet in the service, his brother, on a journey towards Asia, fell sick at Ænus in Thrace, letters with intelligence of which were immediately despatched to him. The sea was very rough, and no convenient ship of any size to be had; so Cato getting into a small trading-vessel, with only two of his friends, and three servants, set sail from Thessalonica, and having very narrowly escaped drowning, he arrived at Ænus just as Cæpio expired. Upon this occasion, he was thought to have showed himself more a fond brother than a philosopher, not only in the excess of his grief, bewailing and embracing the dead body, but also in the extravagant expenses of the funeral, the vast quantity of rich perfumes and costly garments which were burnt with the corpse, and the monument of Thasian marble, which he erected at the cost of eight talents, in the public place of the town of Ænus. For there were some who took upon them to cavil at all this, as not consistent with his usual calmness and moderation, not discerning that though he were steadfast, firm, and inflexible to pleasure, fear, or foolish entreaties, yet he was full of natural tenderness and brotherly affection. Divers of the cities and princes of the country, sent him many presents, to honor the funeral of his brother; but he took none of their money, only the perfumes and ornaments he received, and paid for them also. And afterwards, when the inheritance was divided between him and Cæpio's daughter, he did not require any portion of the funeral expenses to be discharged out of it. Notwithstanding this, it has been affirmed that he made his brother's ashes be passed through a sieve, to find the gold that was

CATO THE YOUNGER 425

melted down when burnt with the body. But he who made this statement appears to have anticipated an exemption for his pen, as much as for his sword, from all question and criticism.[8]

The time of Cato's service in the army being expired, he received, at his departure, not only the prayers and praises, but the tears and embraces of the soldiers, who spread their clothes at his feet, and kissed his hand as he passed, an honor which the Romans at that time scarcely paid even to a very few of their generals and commanders-in-chief. Having left the army, he resolved, before he would return home and apply himself to state affairs, to travel in Asia, and observe the manners, the customs, and the strength of every province. He was also unwilling to refuse the kindness of Deiotarus, king of Galatia, who having had great familiarity and friendship with his father, was very desirous to receive a visit from him. Cato's arrangements in his journey were as follows. Early in the morning he sent out his baker and his cook towards the place where he designed to stay the next night; these went soberly and quietly into the town, in which, if there happened to be no friend or acquaintance of Cato or his family, they provided for him in an inn, and gave no disturbance to anybody; but if there were no inn, then and in this case only, they went to the magistrates, and desiring them to help them to lodgings, took without complaint whatever was allotted to them. His servants thus behaving themselves towards the magistrates, without noise and threatening, were often discredited, or neglected by them, so that Cato many times

[8] The allusion is to Julius Cæsar, and the Anti-Cato which he wrote in disparagement of Cato's character.

arrived and found nothing provided for him. And it was all the worse when he appeared himself; still less account was taken of him. When they saw him sitting, without saying any thing, on his baggage, they set him down at once as a person of no consequence, who did not venture to make any demand. Sometimes on such occasions, he would call them to him and tell them, "Foolish people, lay aside this inhospitality. All your visitors will not be Catos. Use your courtesy, to take off the sharp edge of power. There are men enough who desire but a pretence, to take from you by force, what you give with such reluctance."

While he travelled in this manner, a diverting accident befell him in Syria. As he was going into Antioch, he saw a great multitude of people outside the gates, ranged in order on either side the way; here the young men with long cloaks, there the children decently dressed; others wore garlands and white garments, who were the priests and magistrates. Cato, imagining all this could mean nothing but a display in honor of his reception, began to be angry with his servants who had been sent before, for suffering it to be done; then making his friends alight, he walked along with them on foot. As soon as he came near the gate, an elderly man, who seemed to be master of these ceremonies, with a wand and a garland in his hand, came up to Cato, and without saluting him, asked him, where he had left Demetrius, and how soon he thought he would be there. This Demetrius was Pompey's servant, and as at this time the whole world, so to say, had its eyes fixed upon Pompey, this man also was highly honored, on account of his influence with his master. Upon this, Cato's friends fell into such violent laughter, that they could not restrain themselves while they passed through the crowd; and he himself, ashamed and distressed, uttered the words, "Unfortunate city!" and said no more. Afterwards, however, it always made him laugh, when he either told the story or was otherwise reminded of it.

Pompey himself shortly after made the people ashamed of their ignorance and folly in thus neglecting him, for Cato, coming in his journey to Ephesus, went to pay his respects to him, who was the elder man, had gained much honor, and was then general of a great army. Yet Pompey would not receive him sitting, but as soon as he saw him, rose up, and going to meet him, as the more honorable person, gave him his hand, and embraced him with great show of kindness. He said much in commendation of his virtue, both at that time when receiving him, and also yet more, after he had withdrawn. So that now all men began at once to display their respect for Cato, and discovered in the very same things for which they despised him before, an admirable mildness of temper and greatness of spirit. And indeed the civility that Pompey himself showed him, appeared to come from one that rather respected than loved him; and the general opinion was, that while Cato was there, he paid him admiration, but was not sorry when he was gone. For when other young men came to see him, he usually urged and entreated them to continue with him. Now he did not at all invite Cato to stay, but as if his own power were lessened by the other's presence, he very willingly allowed him to take his leave. Yet to Cato alone, of all those who went for Rome, he recommended his children and his wife, who was indeed connected by relationship with Cato.

After this, all the cities through which he

passed, strove and emulated each other in showing him respect and honor. Feasts and entertainments were made for his reception, so that he bade his friends keep strict watch and take care of him, lest he should end by making good what was said by Curio, who though he were his familiar friend, yet disliking the austerity of his temper, asked him one day, if when he left the army, he designed to see Asia, and Cato answering, "Yes, by all means," "You do well," replied Curio, "you will bring back with you a better temper and pleasanter manners;" pretty nearly the very words he used.

Deiotarus being now an old man, had sent for Cato, to recommend his children and family to his protection; and as soon as he came, brought him presents of all sorts of things, which he begged and entreated him to accept. And his importunities displeased Cato so much, that though he came but in the evening, he stayed only that night, and went away early the next morning. After he was gone one day's journey, he found at Pessinus a yet greater quantity of presents provided for him there, and also letters from Deiotarus, entreating him to receive them, or at least to permit his friends to take them, who for his sake deserved some gratification, and could not have much done for them out of Cato's own means. Yet he would not suffer it, though he saw some of them very willing to receive such gifts, and ready to complain of his severity; but he answered, that corruption would never want pretence, and his friends should share with him in whatever he should justly and honestly obtain, and so returned the presents to Deiotarus.

When he took ship for Brundusium, his friends would have persuaded him to put his brother's ashes into another vessel; but he said, he would sooner part with his life than leave them, and so set sail. And as it chanced, he, we are told, had a very dangerous passage, though others at the same time went over safely enough.

After he was returned to Rome, he spent his time for the most part either at home, in conversation with Athenodorus, or at the forum, in the service of his friends. Though it was now the time that he should become quæstor, he would not stand for the place till he had studied the laws relating to it, and by inquiry from persons of experience, had attained a distinct understanding of the duty and authority belonging to it. With this knowledge, as soon as he came into the office, he made a great reformation among the clerks and under-officers of the treasury, people who had long practice and familiarity in all the public records and the laws, and, when new magistrates came in year by year, so ignorant and unskilful as to be in absolute need of others to teach them what to do, did not submit and give way, but kept the power in their own hands, and were in effect the treasurers themselves. Till Cato, applying himself roundly to the work, showed that he possessed not only the title and honor of a quæstor, but the knowledge and understanding and full authority of his office. So that he used the clerks and under-officers like servants, as they were, exposing their corrupt practices, and instructing their ignorance. Being bold impudent fellows, they flattered the other quæstors, his colleagues, and by their means endeavored to maintain an opposition against him. But he convicted the chiefest of them of a breach of trust in the charge of an inheritance, and turned him out of his place. A second he brought to trial for dishonesty, who was defended by Lutatius Catulus, at that time censor, a man very considerable for his office, but yet more for his character, as he was eminent above all the Romans of that age for his reputed wisdom and integrity. He was also intimate with Cato, and much commended his way of living. So perceiving he could not bring off his client, if he stood a fair trial, he openly began to beg him off. Cato objected to his doing this. And when he continued still to be importunate, "It would be shameful, Catulus," he said, "that the censor, the judge of all our lives, should incur the dishonor of removal by our officers."[9] At this expression, Catulus looked as if he would have made some answer; but he said nothing, and either through anger or shame went away silent, and out of countenance. Nevertheless, the man was not found guilty, for the voices that acquitted him were but one in number less than those that condemned him, and Marcus Lollius, one of Cato's colleagues, who was absent by reason of sickness, was sent for by Catulus, and entreated to come and save the man. So Lollius was brought into court in a chair, and gave his voice also for acquitting him. Yet Cato never after made use of that clerk, and never paid him his salary, nor would he make any account of the vote given by Lollius. Having thus humbled the clerks, and brought them to be at command, he made use of the books and registers as he thought fit, and in a little while gained the treasury a higher name than the Senate-house itself; and all men said, Cato had made the office of a quæstor equal to the dignity of a consul. When he found many indebted to the

[9] Cato hinted, (I quote from Mr. Long's note,) "That the officers of the court would turn Catulus out if he continued to act as he did."

state upon old accounts, and the state also in debt to many private persons, he took care that the public might no longer either do or suffer wrong; he strictly and punctually exacted what was due to the treasury, and as freely and speedily paid all those to whom it was indebted. So that the people were filled with sentiments of awe and respect, on seeing those made to pay, who thought to have escaped with their plunder, and others receiving all their due, who despaired of getting any thing. And whereas usually those who brought false bills and pretended orders of the senate, could through favor get them accepted, Cato would never be so imposed upon, and in the case of one particular order, question arising, whether it had passed the senate, he would not believe a great many witnesses that attested it, nor would admit of it, till the consuls came and affirmed it upon oath.

There were at that time a great many whom Sylla had made use of as his agents in the proscription, and to whom he had for their service in putting men to death, given twelve thousand drachmas apiece. These men everybody hated as wicked and polluted wretches, but nobody durst be revenged upon them. Cato called every one to account, as wrongfully possessed of the public money, and exacted it of them, and at the same time sharply reproved them for their unlawful and impious actions. After these proceedings, they were presently accused of murder, and being already in a manner prejudged as guilty, they were easily found so, and accordingly suffered; at which the whole people rejoiced, and thought themselves now to see the old tyranny finally abolished, and Sylla himself, so to say, brought to punishment.

Cato's assiduity also, and indefatigable diligence,

won very much upon the people. He always came
first of any of his colleagues to the treasury, and
went away the last. He never missed any assembly
of the people, or sitting of the senate; being always
anxious and on the watch for those who lightly, or
as a matter of interest, passed votes in favor of this
or that person, for remitting debts or granting away
customs that were owing to the state. And at
length, having kept the exchequer pure and clear
from base informers, and yet having filled it with
treasure, he made it appear the state might be rich,
without oppressing the people. At first he excited
feelings of dislike and irritation in some of his
colleagues, but after a while they were well contented with him, since he was perfectly willing
that they should cast all the odium on him, when
they declined to gratify their friends with the public
money, or to give dishonest judgments in passing
their accounts; and when hard pressed by suitors,
they could readily answer it was impossible to do
any thing, unless Cato would consent. On the last
day of his office, he was honorably attended to his
house by almost all the people; but on the way he
was informed that several powerful friends were in
the treasury with Marcellus, using all their interest
with him to pass a certain debt to the public revenue, as if it had been a gift. Marcellus had been
one of Cato's friends from his childhood, and so
long as Cato was with him, was one of the best of
his colleagues in this office, but when alone, was
unable to resist the importunity of suitors, and
prone to do anybody a kindness. So Cato immediately turned back, and finding that Marcellus had
yielded to pass the thing, he took the book, and
while Marcellus silently stood by and looked on,
struck it out. This done, he brought Marcellus out

of the treasury, and took him home with him; who for all this, neither then, nor ever after, complained of him, but always continued his friendship and familiarity with him.

Cato after he had laid down his office, yet did not cease to keep a watch upon the treasury. He had his servants who continually wrote out the details of the expenditure, and he himself kept always by him certain books, which contained the accounts of the revenue from Sylla's time to his own quæstorship, which he had bought for five talents.

He was always first at the senate, and went out last; and often, while the others were slowly collecting, he would sit and read by himself, holding his gown before his book. He was never once out of town when the senate was to meet. And when afterwards Pompey and his party, finding that he could never be either persuaded or compelled to favor their unjust designs, endeavored to keep him from the senate, by engaging him in business for his friends, to plead their causes, or arbitrate in their differences, or the like, he quickly discovered the trick, and to defeat it, fairly told all his acquaintance that he would never meddle in any private business when the senate was assembled. Since it was not in the hope of gaining honor or riches, nor out of mere impulse, or by chance that he engaged himself in politics, but he undertook the service of the state, as the proper business of an honest man, and therefore he thought himself obliged to be as constant to his public duty, as the bee to the honeycomb. To this end, he took care to have his friends and correspondents everywhere, to send him reports of the edicts, decrees, judgments, and all the important proceedings that passed in any of the provinces. Once when Clodius, the seditious orator, to promote his violent and revolutionary projects, traduced to the people some of the priests and priestesses, (among whom Fabia, sister to Cicero's wife, Terentia, ran great danger,) Cato, having boldly interfered, and having made Clodius appear so infamous that he was forced to leave the town, was addressed, when it was over, by Cicero, who came to thank him for what he had done. "You must thank the commonwealth," said he, for whose sake alone he professed to do every thing. Thus he gained a great and wonderful reputation; so that an advocate in a cause, where there was only one witness against him, told the judges they ought not to rely upon a single witness, though it were Cato himself. And it was a sort of proverb with many people, if any very unlikely and incredible thing were asserted, to say, they would not believe it, though Cato himself should affirm it. One day a debauched and sumptuous liver talking in the senate about frugality and temperance, Amnæus standing up, cried, "Who can endure this, Sir, to have you feast like Crassus, build like Lucullus, and talk like Cato." So likewise those who were vicious and dissolute in their manners, yet affected to be grave and severe in their language, were in derision called Catos.

At first, when his friends would have persuaded him to stand to be tribune of the people, he thought it undesirable; for that the power of so great an office ought to be reserved, as the strongest medicines, for occasions of the last necessity. But afterwards in a vacation time, as he was going, accompanied with his books and philosophers, to Lucania, where he had lands with a pleasant residence, they met by the way a great many horses, carriages, and attendants, of whom they understood, that Metellus

Nepos was going to Rome, to stand to be tribune of the people. Hereupon Cato stopped, and after a little pause, gave orders to return back immediately; at which the company seeming to wonder, "Don't you know," said he, "how dangerous of itself the madness of Metellus is? and now that he comes armed with the support of Pompey, he will fall like lightning on the state, and bring it to utter disorder; therefore this is no time for idleness and diversion, but we must go and prevent this man in his designs, or bravely die in defence of our liberty." Nevertheless, by the persuasion of his friends, he went first to his country-house, where he stayed but a very little time, and then returned to town.

He arrived in the evening, and went straight the next morning to the forum, where he began to solicit for the tribuneship, in opposition to Metellus. The power of this office consists rather in controlling, than performing any business; for though all the rest except any one tribune should be agreed, yet his denial or intercession could put a stop to the whole matter. Cato, at first, had not many that appeared for him; but as soon as his design was known, all the good and distinguished persons of the city quickly came forward to encourage and support him, looking upon him, not as one that desired a favor of them, but one that proposed to do a great favor to his country and all honest men; who had many times refused the same office, when he might have had it without trouble, but now sought it with danger, that he might defend their liberty and their government. It is reported that so great a number flocked about him, that he was like to be stifled amidst the press, and could scarce get through the crowd. He was declared tribune, with several others, among whom was Metellus.

When Cato was chosen into this office, observing that the election of consuls was become a matter of purchase, he sharply rebuked the people for this corruption, and in the conclusion of his speech protested, he would bring to trial whomever he should find giving money, making an exception only in the case of Silanus, on account of their near connection, he having married Servilia, Cato's sister. He therefore did not prosecute him, but accused Lucius Murena, who had been chosen consul by corrupt means with Silanus. There was a law that the party accused might appoint a person to keep watch upon his accuser, that he might know fairly what means he took in preparing the accusation. He that was set upon Cato by Murena, at first followed and observed him strictly, yet never found him dealing any way unfairly or insidiously, but always generously and candidly going on in the just and open methods of proceeding. And he so admired Cato's great spirit, and so entirely trusted to his integrity, that meeting him in the forum, or going to his house, he would ask him, if he designed to do any thing that day in order to the accusation, and if Cato said no, he went away, relying on his word. When the cause was pleaded, Cicero, who was then consul and defended Murena, took occasion to be extremely witty and jocose, in reference to Cato, upon the stoic philosophers, and their paradoxes, as they call them, and so excited great laughter among the judges; upon which Cato, smiling, said to the standers by, "What a pleasant consul we have, my friends." Murena was acquitted, and afterwards showed himself a man of no ill feeling or want of sense; for when he was consul, he always took Cato's advice in the most weighty affairs, and during all the time of his office, paid him much honor and respect.

Of which not only Murena's prudence, but also Cato's own behavior, was the cause; for though he were terrible and severe as to matters of justice, in the senate, and at the bar, yet after the thing was over, his manner to all men was perfectly friendly and humane.

Before he entered on the office of tribune, he assisted Cicero, at that time consul, in many contests that concerned his office, but most especially in his great and noble acts at the time of Catiline's conspiracy; which owed their last successful issue to Cato. Catiline had plotted a dreadful and entire subversion of the Roman state by sedition and open war, but being convicted by Cicero, was forced to fly the city. Yet Lentulus and Cethegus remained with several others, to carry on the same plot; and blaming Catiline, as one that wanted courage, and had been timid and petty in his designs, they themselves resolved to set the whole town on fire, and utterly to overthrow the empire, rousing whole nations to revolt and exciting foreign wars. But the design was discovered by Cicero, (as we have written in his Life,) and the matter brought before the senate. Silanus, who spoke first, delivered his opinion, that the conspirators ought to suffer the last of punishments, and was therein followed by all who spoke after him; till it came to Cæsar, who being an excellent speaker, and looking upon all changes and commotions in the state as materials useful for his own purposes, desired rather to increase than extinguish them; and standing up, he made a very merciful and persuasive speech, that they ought not to suffer death without fair trial according to law, and moved that they might be kept in prison. Thus was the house almost wholly turned by Cæsar, apprehending also the anger of the people; insomuch that even Silanus retracted, and said he did not mean to propose death, but imprisonment, for that was the utmost a Roman could suffer. Upon this they were all inclined to the milder and more merciful opinion, when Cato standing up, began at once with great passion and vehemence to reproach Silanus for his change of opinion, and to attack Cæsar, who would, he said, ruin the commonwealth by soft words and popular speeches, and was endeavoring to frighten the senate, when he himself ought to fear, and be thankful, if he escaped unpunished or unsuspected, who thus openly and boldly dared to protect the enemies of the state, and while finding no compassion for his own native country, brought, with all its glories, so near to utter ruin, could yet be full of pity for those men, who had better never have been born, and whose death must deliver the commonwealth from bloodshed and destruction. This only of all Cato's speeches, it is said, was preserved; for Cicero, the consul, had disposed, in various parts of the senate-house, several of the most expert and rapid writers, whom he had taught to make figures comprising numerous words in a few short strokes; as up to that time they had not used those we call short-hand writers,[10] who then, as it is said, established the first example of the art. Thus Cato carried it, and so turned the house again, that it was decreed the conspirators should be put to death.

Not to omit any small matters that may serve to show Cato's temper, and add something to the portraiture of his mind, it is reported, that while Cæsar and he were in the very heat, and the whole senate regarding them two, a little note was

---

[10] *Short-hand writers;* in the Greek, *semeiographi,* writers by signs; in Latin, *notarii,* which has the same sense.

CATO THE YOUNGER

brought in to Cæsar, which Cato declared to be suspicious, and urging that some seditious act was going on, bade the letter be read. Upon which Cæsar handed the paper to Cato; who discovering it to be a love-letter from his sister Servilia to Cæsar, by whom she had been corrupted, threw it to him again, saying, "Take it, drunkard," and so went on with his discourse. And, indeed, it seems Cato had but ill-fortune in women; for this lady was ill spoken of, for her familiarity with Cæsar, and the other Servilia, Cato's sister also, was yet more ill-conducted; for being married to Lucullus, one of the greatest men in Rome, and having brought him a son, she was afterwards divorced for incontinency. But what was worst of all, Cato's own wife Atilia was not free from the same fault; and after she had borne him two children, he was forced to put her away for her misconduct. After that he married Marcia, the daughter of Philippus, a woman of good reputation, who yet has occasioned much discourse; and the life of Cato, like a dramatic piece, has this one scene or passage full of perplexity and doubtful meaning.[11]

It is thus related by Thrasea, who refers to the authority of Munatius, Cato's friend and constant companion. Among many that loved and admired Cato, some were more remarkable and conspicuous

---

[11] *The life of Cato, like a dramatic piece, has this one scene or passage full of perplexity and doubtful meaning.* Every tragedy, according to Aristotle's remark in the Poetics, consists simply of two portions, one the fastening or complication, the other the undoing or solution of the difficulty or embarrassment in which the plot consists (the *nœud* and the *dénouement* of French criticism); and one particular part, one crisis, will usually bring the complication to its height: the tragic dilemma has first to be in-

than others. Of these was Quintus Hortensius, a man of high repute and approved virtue, who desired not only to live in friendship and familiarity with Cato, but also to unite his whole house and family with him by some sort or other of alliance in marriage. Therefore he set himself to persuade Cato, that his daughter Porcia, who was already married to Bibulus, and had borne him two children, might nevertheless be given to him, as a fair plot of land, to bear fruit also for him. "For," said he, "though this in the opinion of men may seem strange, yet in nature it is honest, and profitable for the public, that a woman in the prime of her youth should not lie useless, and lose the fruit of her womb, nor, on the other side, should burden and impoverish one man, by bringing him too many children. Also by this communication of families among worthy men, virtue would increase, and be diffused through their posterity; and the commonwealth would be united and cemented by their alliances." Yet if Bibulus would not part with his wife altogether, he would restore her as soon as she had brought him a child, whereby he might be united to both their families. Cato answered, that he loved Hortensius very well, and much approved of uniting their houses, but he thought it strange to speak of marrying his daughter, when she was already given to another. Then Hortensius, turning the discourse, did not hesitate to

dicated, then stated in its strongest terms, then one or other alternative taken, or a middle course somehow discovered, and the spectator one way or other relieved of his anxiety. See for the tragic *desis* and *lysis*, Aristotle, Poetics, c. 18. *Thrasea* is the famous Thrasea Pætus, who died by Nero's orders, and who wrote a life of Cato, his Stoic example, just as Arulenus Rusticus wrote one of him.

speak openly and ask for Cato's own wife, for she was young and fruitful, and he had already children enough. Neither can it be thought that Hortensius did this, as imagining Cato did not care for Marcia; for, it is said, she was then with child. Cato, perceiving his earnest desire, did not deny his request, but said that Philippus, the father of Marcia, ought also to be consulted. Philippus, therefore, being sent for, came; and finding they were well agreed, gave his daughter Marcia to Hortensius in the presence of Cato, who himself also assisted at the marriage. This was done at a later time, but since I was speaking of women, I thought it well to mention it now.

Lentulus and the rest of the conspirators were put to death; but Cæsar, finding so much insinuated and charged against him in the senate, betook himself to the people, and proceeded to stir up the most corrupt and dissolute elements of the state to form a party in his support. Cato, apprehensive of what might ensue, persuaded the senate to win over the poor and unprovided-for multitude, by a distribution of corn, the annual charge of which amounted to twelve hundred and fifty talents. This act of humanity and kindness unquestionably dissipated the present danger. But Metellus, coming into his office of tribune, began to hold tumultuous assemblies, and had prepared a decree, that Pompey the Great should presently be called into Italy, with all his forces, to preserve the city from the danger of Catiline's conspiracy. This was the fair pretence; but the true design was, to deliver all into the hands of Pompey, and give him an absolute power. Upon this the senate was assembled, and Cato did not fall sharply upon Metellus, as he often did, but urged his advice in the most reasonable and moderate tone.

At last he descended even to entreaty, and extolled the house of Metellus, as having always taken part with the nobility. At this Metellus grew the more insolent, and despising Cato, as if he yielded and were afraid, let himself proceed to the most audacious menaces, openly threatening to do whatever he pleased in spite of the senate. Upon this Cato changed his countenance, his voice, and his language; and after many sharp expressions, boldly concluded, that while he lived, Pompey should never come armed into the city. The senate thought them both extravagant, and not well in their safe senses; for the design of Metellus seemed to be mere rage and frenzy, out of excess of mischief bringing all things to ruin and confusion, and Cato's virtue looked like a kind of ecstasy of contention in the cause of what was good and just.

But when the day came for the people to give their voices for the passing this decree, and Metellus beforehand occupied the forum with armed men, strangers, gladiators, and slaves, those that in hopes of change followed Pompey, were known to be no small part of the people, and besides, they had great assistance from Cæsar, who was then prætor; and though the best and chiefest men of the city were no less offended at these proceedings than Cato, they seemed rather likely to suffer with him, than able to assist him. In the mean time Cato's whole family were in extreme fear and apprehension for him; some of his friends neither ate not slept all the night, passing the whole time in debating and perplexity; his wife and sisters also bewailed and lamented him. But he himself, void of all fear, and full of assurance, comforted and encouraged them by his own words and conversation with them. After supper he went to rest at his usual hour, and was the next day waked out of a profound sleep by Minucius Thermus, one of his colleagues. So soon as he was up, they two went together into the forum, accompanied by very few, but met by a great many, who bade them have a care of themselves. Cato, therefore, when he saw the temple of Castor and Pollux encompassed with armed men, and the steps guarded by gladiators, and at the top Metellus and Cæsar seated together, turning to his friends, "Behold," said he, "this audacious coward, who has levied a regiment of soldiers against one unarmed naked man;" and so he went on with Thermus. Those who kept the passages, gave way to these two only, and would not let anybody else pass. Yet Cato taking Munatius by the hand, with much difficulty pulled him through along with him. Then going directly to Metellus and Cæsar, he sat himself down between them, to prevent their talking to one another, at which they were both amazed and confounded. And those of the honest party, observing the countenance, and admiring the high spirit and boldness of Cato, went nearer, and cried out to him to have courage, exhorting also one another to stand together, and not betray their liberty, nor the defender of it.

Then the clerk took out the bill, but Cato forbade him to read it, whereupon Metellus took it, and would have read it himself, but Cato snatched away the book. Yet Metellus having the decree by heart, began to recite it without book; but Thermus put his hand to his mouth, and stopped his speech. Metellus seeing them fully bent to withstand him, and the people cowed, and inclining to the better side, sent to his house for armed men. And on their rushing in with great noise and terror, all the rest dispersed and ran away, except Cato, who alone stood still, while the other party threw sticks and stones at him from above, until Murena, whom he had formerly accused, came up to protect him, and holding his gown before him, cried out to them to leave off throwing; and, in fine, persuading and pulling him along, he forced him into the temple of Castor and Pollux. Metellus now seeing the place clear, and all the adverse party fled out of the forum, thought he might easily carry his point; so he commanded the soldiers to retire, and recommencing in an orderly manner, began to proceed to passing the decree. But the other side having recovered themselves, returned very boldly, and with loud shouting, insomuch that Metellus's adherents were seized with a panic, supposing them to be coming with a reinforcement of armed men, and fled every one out of the place. They being thus dispersed, Cato came in again, and confirmed the courage, and commended the resolution of the people; so that now the majority were, by all means, for deposing Metellus from his office. The senate also being assembled, gave orders once more for supporting Cato, and resisting the motion, as of a nature to excite sedition and perhaps civil war in the city.

But Metellus continued still very bold and resolute; and seeing his party stood greatly in fear of Cato, whom they looked upon as invincible, he hurried out of the senate into the forum, and assembled the people, to whom he made a bitter and invidious speech against Cato, crying out, he was forced to fly from his tyranny, and this conspiracy against Pompey; that the city would soon repent their having dishonored so great a man. And from hence he started to go to Asia, with the intention, as would be supposed, of laying before Pompey all the injuries that were done him. Cato was highly extolled for having delivered the state from this dangerous tribuneship, and having in some measure defeated, in the person of Metellus, the power of Pompey; but he was yet more commended when, upon the senate proceeding to disgrace Metellus and depose him from his office, he altogether opposed and at length diverted the design. The common people admired his moderation and humanity, in not trampling wantonly on an enemy whom he had overthrown, and wiser men acknowledged his prudence and policy, in not exasperating Pompey.

Lucullus soon after returned from the war in Asia, the finishing of which, and thereby the glory of the whole, was thus, in all appearance, taken out of his hands by Pompey. And he was also not far from losing his triumph, for Caius Memmius traduced him to the people, and threatened to accuse him; rather, however, out of love to Pompey, than for any particular enmity to him. But Cato, being allied to Lucullus, who had married his sister Servilia, and also thinking it a great injustice, opposed Memmius, thereby exposing himself to much slander and misrepresentation, insomuch that they would have turned him out of his office, pretending that he used his power tyrannically. Yet at length Cato so far prevailed against Memmius, that he was forced to let fall the accusations, and abandon the contest. And Lucullus having thus obtained his triumph, yet more sedulously cultivated Cato's friendship, which he looked upon as a great guard and defence for him against Pompey's power.

And now Pompey also returning with glory from the war, and confiding in the good-will of the people, shown in their splendid reception of him, thought he should be denied nothing, and sent therefore to the senate to put off the assembly for the election of consuls, till he could be present to assist Piso, who stood for that office. To this most of the senators were disposed to yield; Cato, only, not so much thinking that this delay would be of great importance, but, desiring to cut down at once Pompey's high expectations and designs, withstood his request, and so overruled the senate, that it was carried against him. And this not a little disturbed Pompey, who found he should very often fail in his projects, unless he could bring over Cato to his interest. He sent, therefore, for Munatius, his friend; and Cato having two nieces that were marriageable, he offered to marry the eldest himself, and take the youngest for his son. Some say they were not his nieces, but his daughters. Munatius proposed the matter to Cato, in presence of his wife and sisters; the women were full of joy at the prospect of an alliance with so great and important a person. But Cato, without delay or balancing, forming his decision at once, answered, " Go, Munatius, go and tell Pompey, that Cato is not assailable on the side of the women's chamber; I am grateful indeed for the intended kindness, and so long as his actions are upright, I promise him a friendship more sure than any marriage alliance, but I will not give hostages to Pompey's glory, against my country's safety." This answer was very much against the wishes of the women, and to all his friends it seemed somewhat harsh and haughty. But afterwards, when Pompey, endeavoring to get the consulship for one of his friends, gave pay to the people for their votes, and the bribery was notorious, the money being counted out in Pompey's own gardens, Cato then said to the women, they must necessarily have been concerned in the contamination of these misdeeds of Pompey, if they had been allied to his family, and they acknowledged that he

CATO THE YOUNGER 447

did best in refusing it. Yet if we may judge by the event, Cato was much to blame in rejecting that alliance, which thereby fell to Cæsar. And then that match was made, which, uniting his and Pompey's power, had wellnigh ruined the Roman empire, and did destroy the commonwealth. Nothing of which perhaps had come to pass, but that Cato was too apprehensive of Pompey's least faults, and did not consider how he forced him into conferring on another man the opportunity of committing the greatest.

These things, however, were yet to come. Lucullus, meantime, and Pompey, had a great dispute concerning their orders and arrangements in Pontus, each endeavoring that his own ordinances might stand. Cato took part with Lucullus, who was manifestly suffering wrong; and Pompey, finding himself the weaker in the senate, had recourse to the people, and to gain votes, he proposed a law for dividing the lands among the soldiers. Cato opposing him in this also, made the bill be rejected. Upon this he joined himself with Clodius, at that time the most violent of all the demagogues; and entered also into friendship with Cæsar, upon an occasion of which also Cato was the cause. For Cæsar returning from his government in Spain, at the same time sued to be chosen consul, and yet desired not to lose his triumph. Now the law requiring that those who stood for any office should be present, and yet that whoever expected a triumph should continue without the walls, Cæsar requested the senate, that his friends might be permitted to canvass for him in his absence. Many of the senators were willing to consent to it, but Cato opposed it, and perceiving them inclined to favor Cæsar, spent the whole day in speaking, and so prevented the senate from coming to any conclusion. Cæsar, therefore, resolving to let fall his pretensions to the triumph, came into the town, and immediately made a friendship with Pompey, and stood for the consulship. And so soon as he was declared consul elect, he married his daughter Julia to Pompey. And having thus combined themselves together against the commonwealth, the one proposed laws for dividing the lands among the poor people, and the other was present to support the proposals. Lucullus, Cicero, and their friends, joined with Bibulus, the other consul, to hinder their passing, and, foremost of them all, Cato, who already looked upon the friendship and alliance of Pompey and Cæsar as very dangerous, and declared he did not so much dislike the advantage the people should get by this division of the lands, as he feared the reward these men would gain, by thus courting and cozening the people. And in this he gained over the senate to his opinion, as likewise many who were not senators, who were offended at Cæsar's ill conduct, that he, in the office of consul, should thus basely and dishonorably flatter the people; practising, to win their favor, the same means that were wont to be used only by the most rash and rebellious tribunes. Cæsar, therefore, and his party, fearing they should not carry it by fair dealing, fell to open force. First a basket of dung was thrown upon Bibulus as he was going to the forum; then they set upon his lictors and broke their rods; at length several darts were thrown, and many men wounded; so that all that were against those laws, fled out of the forum, the rest with what haste they could, and Cato, last of all, walking out slowly, often turning back and calling down vengeance upon them.

Thus the other party not only carried their point

of dividing the lands, but also ordained, that all the senate should swear to confirm this law, and to defend it against whoever should attempt to alter it, inflicting great penalties on those that should refuse the oath. All the senators seeing the necessity they were in, took the oath, remembering the example of Metellus in old time, who refusing to swear upon the like occasion, was forced to leave Italy. As for Cato, his wife and children with tears besought him, his friends and familiars persuaded and entreated him, to yield and take the oath; but he that principally prevailed with him was Cicero, the orator, who urged upon him that it was perhaps not even right in itself, that a private man should oppose what the public had decreed; that the thing being already past altering, it were folly and madness to throw himself into danger, without the chance of doing his country any good; it would be the greatest of all evils, to embrace, as it were, the opportunity to abandon the commonwealth, for whose sake he did every thing, and to let it fall into the hands of those who designed nothing but its ruin, as if he were glad to be saved from the trouble of defending it. "For," said he, "though Cato have no need of Rome, yet Rome has need of Cato, and so likewise have all his friends." Of whom Cicero professed he himself was the chief, being at that time aimed at by Clodius, who openly threatened to fall upon him, as soon as ever he should get to be tribune. Thus Cato, they say, moved by the entreaties and the arguments of his friends, went unwillingly to take the oath, which he did the last of all, except only Favonius, one of his intimate acquaintance.

Cæsar, exalted with this success, proposed another law, for dividing almost all the country of

Campania among the poor and needy citizens. Nobody durst speak against it but Cato, whom Cæsar therefore pulled from the rostra, and dragged to prison: yet Cato did not even thus remit his freedom of speech, but as he went along, continued to speak against the law, and advised the people to put down all legislators who proposed the like. The senate and the best of the citizens followed him with sad and dejected looks, showing their grief and indignation by their silence, so that Cæsar could not be ignorant how much they were offended; but for contention's sake, he still persisted, expecting Cato should either supplicate him, or make an appeal. But when he saw that he did not so much as think of doing either, ashamed of what he was doing and of what people thought of it, he himself privately bade one of the tribunes interpose and procure his release. However, having won the multitude by these laws and gratifications, they decreed that Cæsar should have the government of Illyricum, and all Gaul, with an army of four legions, for the space of five years, though Cato still cried out they were, by their own vote, placing a tyrant in their citadel. Publius Clodius, who illegally of a patrician became a plebeian, was declared tribune of the people, as he had promised to do all things according to their pleasure, on condition he might banish Cicero. And for consuls, they set up Calpurnius Piso, the father of Cæsar's wife, and Aulus Gabinius, one of Pompey's creatures, as they tell us, who best knew his life and manners.

Yet when they had thus firmly established all things, having mastered one part of the city by favor, and the other by fear, they themselves were still afraid of Cato, and remembered with vexation what pains and trouble their success over him had

CATO THE YOUNGER

cost them, and indeed what shame and disgrace, when at last they were driven to use violence to him. This made Clodius despair of driving Cicero out of Italy while Cato stayed at home. Therefore, having first laid his design, as soon as he came into his office, he sent for Cato, and told him, that he looked upon him as the most incorrupt of all the Romans, and was ready to show he did so. "For whereas," said he, "many have applied to be sent to Cyprus on the commission in the case of Ptolemy, and have solicited to have the appointment, I think you alone are deserving of it, and I desire to give you the favor of the appointment." Cato at once cried out, it was a mere design upon him, and no favor, but an injury. Then Clodius proudly and fiercely answered, "If you will not take it as a kindness, you shall go, though never so unwillingly;" and immediately going into the assembly of the people, he made them pass a decree, that Cato should be sent to Cyprus. But they ordered him neither ship, nor soldier, nor any attendant, except two secretaries; one of whom was a thief and a rascal, and the other a retainer to Clodius. Besides, as if Cyprus and Ptolemy were not work sufficient, he was ordered also to restore the refugees of Byzantium. For Clodius was resolved to keep him far enough off, whilst himself continued tribune.

Cato being in this necessity of going away, advised Cicero, who was next to be set upon, to make no resistance, lest he should throw the state into civil war and confusion, but to give way to the times, and thus become once more the preserver of his country. He himself sent forward Canidius, one of his friends, to Cyprus, to persuade Ptolemy to yield, without being forced; which if he did, he should want neither riches nor honor, for the Romans would give him the priesthood of the goddess at Paphos. He himself stayed at Rhodes, making some preparations, and expecting an answer from Cyprus. In the meantime, Ptolemy, king of Egypt, who had left Alexandria, upon some quarrel between him and his subjects, and was sailing for Rome, in hopes that Pompey and Cæsar would send troops to restore him, in his way thither desired to see Cato, to whom he sent, supposing he would come to him. Cato had taken purging medicine at the time when the messenger came, and made answer, that Ptolemy had better come to him, if he thought fit. And when he came, he neither went forward to meet him, nor so much as rose up to him, but saluting him as an ordinary person, bade him sit down. This at once threw Ptolemy into some confusion, who was surprised to see such stern and haughty manners in one who made so plain and unpretending an appearance; but afterwards, when he began to talk about his affairs, he was no less astonished at the wisdom and freedom of his discourse. For Cato blamed his conduct, and pointed out to him what honor and happiness he was abandoning, and what humiliations and troubles he would run himself into; what bribery he must resort to and what cupidity he would have to satisfy, when he came to the leading men at Rome, whom all Egypt turned into silver would scarcely content. He therefore advised him to return home, and be reconciled to his subjects, offering to go along with him, and assist him in composing the differences. And by this language Ptolemy being brought to himself, as it might be out of a fit of madness or delirium, and discerning the truth and wisdom of what Cato said, resolved to follow his advice; but he was again over-persuaded by his friends to the contrary, and so, according to his first design, went to Rome. When he came there, and was forced to wait at the gate of one of the magistrates, he began to lament his folly, in having rejected, rather, as it seemed to him, the oracle of a god, than the advice merely of a good and wise man.

In the mean time, the other Ptolemy, in Cyprus, very luckily for Cato, poisoned himself. It was reported he had left great riches; therefore Cato designing to go first to Byzantium, sent his nephew Brutus to Cyprus, as he would not wholly trust Canidius. Then, having reconciled the refugees and the people of Byzantium, he left the city in peace and quietness; and so sailed to Cyprus, where he found a royal treasure of plate, tables, precious stones and purple, all which was to be turned into ready money. And being determined to do every thing with the greatest exactness, and to raise the price of every thing to the utmost, to this end he was always present at selling the things, and went carefully into all the accounts. Nor would he trust to the usual customs of the market, but looked doubtfully upon all alike, the officers, criers, purchasers, and even his own friends; and so in fine he himself talked with the buyers, and urged them to bid high, and conducted in this manner the greatest part of the sales.

This mistrustfulness offended others of his friends, and, in particular, Munatius, the most intimate of them all, became almost irreconcilable. And this afforded Cæsar the subject of his severest censures in the book he wrote against Cato. Yet Munatius himself relates, that the quarrel was not so much occasioned by Cato's mistrust, as by his neglect of him, and by his own jealousy of Canidius. For Munatius also wrote a book concerning Cato which is the chief authority followed by Thrasea. Munatius says, that coming to Cyprus after the other, and having a very poor lodging provided for him, he went to Cato's house, but was not admitted, because he was engaged in private with Canidius; of which he afterwards complained in very gentle terms to Cato, but received a very harsh answer, that too much love, according to Theophrastus, often causes hatred; " and you," he said, " because you bear me much love, think you receive too little honor, and presently grow angry. I employ Canidius on account of his industry and his fidelity; he has been with me from the first, and I have found him to be trusted." These things were said in private between them two; but Cato afterwards told Canidius what had passed; on being informed of which, Munatius would no more go to sup with him, and when he was invited to give his counsel, refused to come. Then Cato threatened to seize his goods,[12] as was the custom in the case of those who were disobedient; but Munatius not regarding his threats, returned to Rome, and continued a long

---

[12] *To seize his goods as was the custom.* The magistrate might seize a portion of a man's property, by way of distress, to compel him to the discharge of a public duty. The sum of money brought from Cyprus, *seven thousand talents*, which Cato says (below) was more than Pompey brought home from the ransacked world, seems quite too small; the figure is probably wrong. *Phylargyrus*, just below, should be Philargyrus. *The dock*, a little further on, is the state-arsenal, or *navalia*, high up the river, at the other end of the Campus Martius, so that Cato passed through the whole city, and along a part of the Campus, before he brought his vessel to shore.

time thus discontented. But afterwards, when Cato was come back also, Marcia, who as yet lived with him, contrived to have them both invited to sup together at the house of one Barca; Cato came in last of all, when the rest were laid down, and asked, where he should be. Barca answered him, where he pleased; then looking about, he said, he would be near Munatius, and went and placed himself next to him; yet he showed him no other mark of kindness, all the time they were at table together. But another time, at the entreaty of Marcia, Cato wrote to Munatius, that he desired to speak with him. Munatius went to his house in the morning, and was kept by Marcia till all the company was gone; then Cato came, threw both his arms about him, and embraced him very kindly, and they were reconciled. I have the more fully related this passage, for that I think the manners and tempers of men are more clearly discovered by things of this nature, than by great and conspicuous actions.

Cato got together little less than seven thousand talents of silver; but apprehensive of what might happen in so long a voyage by sea, he provided a great many coffers, that held two talents and five hundred drachmas apiece; to each of these he fastened a long rope, and to the other end of the rope a piece of cork, so that if the ship should miscarry, it might be discovered whereabout the chests lay under water. Thus all the money, except a very little, was safely transported. But he had made two books, in which all the accounts of his commission were carefully written out, and neither of these was preserved. For his freedman Philargyrus, who had the charge of one of them, setting sail from Cenchreæ, was lost, together with the ship and all her freight. And the other Cato himself kept

safe, till he came to Corcyra, but there he set up
his tent in the market-place, and the sailors being
very cold in the night, made a great many fires,
some of which caught the tents, so that they were
burnt, and the book lost. And though he had
brought with him several of Ptolemy's stewards,
who could testify to his integrity, and stop the
mouths of enemies and false accusers, yet the loss
annoyed him, and he was vexed with himself about
the matter, as he had designed them not so much
for a proof of his own fidelity, as for a pattern
of exactness to others.

The news did not fail to reach Rome, that he
was coming up the river. All the magistrates, the
priests, and the whole senate, with great part of the
people, went out to meet him; both the banks of the
Tiber were covered with people; so that his entrance
was in solemnity and honor not inferior to a triumph. But it was thought somewhat strange, and
looked like wilfulness and pride, that when the consuls and prætors appeared, he did not disembark,
nor stay to salute them, but rowed up the stream in
a royal galley of six banks of oars, and stopped not
till he brought his vessels to the dock. However,
when the money was carried through the streets,
the people much wondered at the vast quantity of
it, and the senate being assembled, decreed him in
honorable terms an extraordinary prætorship, and
also the privilege of appearing at the public spectacles in a robe faced with purple. Cato declined
all these honors, but declaring what diligence and
fidelity he had found in Nicias, the steward of
Ptolemy, he requested the senate to give him his
freedom.

Philippus, the father of Marcia, was that year
consul, and the authority and power of the office

rested in a manner in Cato; for the other consul paid him no less regard for his virtue's sake, than Philippus did on account of the connection between them. And Cicero now being returned from his banishment, into which he was driven by Clodius, and having again obtained great credit among the people, went, in the absence of Clodius, and by force took away the records of his tribuneship, which had been laid up in the capitol. Hereupon the senate was assembled, and Clodius complained of Cicero, who answered, that Clodius was never legally tribune, and therefore whatever he had done, was void, and of no authority. But Cato interrupted him while he spoke, and at last standing up said, that indeed he in no way justified or approved of Clodius's proceedings; but if they questioned the validity of what had been done in his tribuneship, they might also question what himself had done at Cyprus, for the expedition was unlawful, if he that sent him had no lawful authority: for himself, he thought Clodius was legally made tribune, who, by permission of the law, was from a patrician adopted into a plebeian family; if he had done ill in his office, he ought to be called to account for it; but the authority of the magistracy ought not to suffer for the faults of the magistrate. Cicero took this ill, and for a long time discontinued his friendship with Cato; but they were afterwards reconciled.

Pompey and Crassus, by agreement with Cæsar, who crossed the Alps to see them, had formed a design, that they two should stand to be chosen consuls a second time, and when they should be in their office, they would continue to Cæsar his government for five years more, and take to themselves the greatest provinces, with armies and money to maintain them. This seemed a plain conspiracy to subvert the constitution and parcel out the empire. Several men of high character had intended to stand to be consuls that year, but upon the appearance of these great competitors, they all desisted, except only Lucius Domitius, who had married Porcia, the sister of Cato, and was by him persuaded to stand it out, and not abandon such an undertaking, which, he said, was not merely to gain the consulship, but to save the liberty of Rome. In the mean time, it was the common topic among the more prudent part of the citizens, that they ought not to suffer the power of Pompey and Crassus to be united, which would then be carried beyond all bounds, and become dangerous to the state; that therefore one of them must be denied. For these reasons they took part with Domitius, whom they exhorted and encouraged to go on, assuring him, that many who feared openly to appear for him, would privately assist him. Pompey's party fearing this, laid wait for Domitius, and set upon him as he was going before daylight, with torches, into the Field. First he that bore the light next before Domitius, was knocked down and killed; then several others being wounded, all the rest fled, except Cato and Domitius, whom Cato held, though himself were wounded in the arm, and crying out, conjured the others to stay, and not while they had any breath, forsake the defence of their liberty against those tyrants, who plainly showed with what moderation they were likely to use the power, which they endeavored to gain by such violence. But at length Domitius also, no longer willing to face the danger, fled to his own house, and so Pompey and Crassus were declared consuls.

Nevertheless, Cato would not give over, but

resolved to stand himself to be prætor that year, which he thought would be some help to him in his design of opposing them; that he might not act as a private man, when he was to contend with public magistrates. Pompey and Crassus apprehended this; and fearing that the office of prætor in the person of Cato might be equal in authority to that of consul, they assembled the senate unexpectedly, without giving any notice to a great many of the senators, and made an order, that those who were chosen prætors, should immediately enter upon their office, without attending the usual time, in which, according to law, they might be accused, if they had corrupted the people with gifts. When by this order they had got leave to bribe freely, without being called to account, they set up their own friends and dependents to stand for the prætorship, giving money, and watching the people as they voted. Yet the virtue and reputation of Cato was like to triumph over all these stratagems; for the people generally felt it to be shameful that a price should be paid for the rejection of Cato, who ought rather to be paid himself to take upon him the office. So he carried it by the voices of the first tribe. Hereupon Pompey immediately framed a lie, crying out, it thundered; and straight broke up the assembly; for the Romans religiously observed this as a bad omen, and never concluded any matter after it had thundered. Before the next time, they had distributed larger bribes, and driving also the best men out of the Field, by these foul means they procured Vatinius to be chosen prætor, instead of Cato. It is said, that those who had thus corruptly and dishonestly given their voices, at once, when it was done, hurried, as if it were in flight, out of the Field. The others staying together, and exclaiming at the event, one of the tribunes continued the assembly, and Cato standing up, as it were by inspiration, foretold all the miseries that afterward befell the state, exhorted them to beware of Pompey and Crassus, who were guilty of such things, and had laid such designs, that they might well fear to have Cato prætor. When he had ended this speech, he was followed to his house by a greater number of people than were all the new prætors elect put together.

Caius Trebonius now proposed the law for allotting provinces to the consuls, one of whom was to have Spain and Africa, the other Egypt and Syria, with full power of making war, and carrying it on both by sea and land, as they should think fit. When this was proposed, all others despaired of putting any stop to it, and neither did nor said any thing against it. But Cato, before the voting began, went up into the place of speaking, and desiring to be heard, was with much difficulty allowed two hours to speak. Having spent that time in informing them and reasoning with them, and in foretelling to them much that was to come, he was not suffered to speak any longer; but as he was going on, a serjeant came and pulled him down; yet when he was down, he still continued speaking in a loud voice, and finding many to listen to him, and join in his indignation. Then the serjeant took him, and forced him out of the forum; but as soon as he got loose, he returned again to the place of speaking, crying out to the people to stand by him. When he had done thus several times, Trebonius grew very angry, and commanded him to be carried to prison; but the multitude followed him, and listened to the speech which he made to them, as he went along; so that Trebonius began to be afraid again, and ordered him to be released. Thus that day was expended, and the business staved off by Cato. But in the days succeeding, many of the citizens being overawed by fears and threats, and others won by gifts and favors, Aquillius, one of the tribunes, they kept by an armed force within the senate-house; Cato, who cried, it thundered, they drove out of the forum; many were wounded, and some slain; and at length by open force they passed the law. At this many were so incensed, that they got together, and were going to throw down the statues of Pompey; but Cato went, and diverted them from that design.

Again, another law was proposed, concerning the provinces and legions for Cæsar. Upon this occasion Cato did not apply himself to the people, but appealed to Pompey himself; and told him, he did not consider now, that he was setting Cæsar upon his own shoulders, who would shortly grow too weighty for him; and at length, not able to lay down the burden, nor yet to bear it any longer, he would precipitate both it and himself with it upon the commonwealth; and then he would remember Cato's advice, which was no less advantageous to him, than just and honest in itself. Thus was Pompey often warned, but still disregarded and slighted it, never mistrusting Cæsar's change, and always confiding in his own power and good fortune.

Cato was made prætor the following year; but, it seems, he did not do more honor and credit to the office by his signal integrity, than he disgraced and diminished it by his strange behavior. For he would often come to the court without his shoes, and sit upon the bench without any under garment, and in this attire would give judgment in capital causes, and upon persons of the highest rank. It is said, also, he used to drink wine after his morning meal, and then transact the business of his office; but this was wrongfully reported of him. The people were at that time extremely corrupted by the gifts of those who sought offices, and most made a constant trade of selling their voices. Cato was eager utterly to root this corruption out of the commonwealth; he therefore persuaded the senate to make an order, that those who were chosen into any office, though nobody should accuse them, should be obliged to come into the court, and give account upon oath of their proceedings in their election. This was extremely obnoxious to those who stood for the offices, and yet more to those vast numbers who took the bribes. Insomuch that one morning, as Cato was going to the tribunal, a great multitude of people flocked together, and with loud cries and maledictions reviled him, and threw stones at him. Those that were about the tribunal presently fled, and Cato himself being forced thence, and jostled about in the throng, very narrowly escaped the stones that were thrown at him, and with much difficulty got hold of the Rostra; where, standing up with a bold and undaunted countenance, he at once mastered the tumult, and silenced the clamor; and addressing them in fit terms for the occasion, was heard with great attention, and perfectly quelled the sedition. Afterwards, on the senate commending him for this, " But I," said he, " do not commend you for abandoning your prætor in danger, and bringing him no assistance."

In the mean time, the candidates were in great perplexity; for every one dreaded to give money himself, and yet feared his competitors should. At length they agreed to lay down one hundred and twenty-five thousand drachmas apiece, and

CATO THE YOUNGER

then all of them to canvass fairly and honestly, on condition, that if any one was found to make use of bribery, he should forfeit the money. Being thus agreed, they chose Cato to keep the stakes, and arbitrate the matter; to him they brought the sum concluded on, and before him subscribed the agreement. The money he did not choose to have paid for them, but took their securities who stood bound for them. Upon the day of election, he placed himself by the tribune who took the votes, and very watchfully observing all that passed, he discovered one who had broken the agreement, and immediately ordered him to pay his money to the rest. They, however, commending his justice highly, remitted the penalty, as thinking the discovery a sufficient punishment. It raised, however, as much envy against Cato as it gained him reputation, and many were offended at his thus taking upon himself the whole authority of the senate, the courts of judicature, and the magistracies. For there is no virtue, the honor and credit for which procures a man more odium than that of justice; and this, because more than any other, it acquires a man power and authority among the common people. For they only honor the valiant and admire the wise, while in addition they also love just men, and put entire trust and confidence in them. They fear the bold man, and mistrust the clever man, and moreover think them rather beholding to their natural complexion, than to any goodness of their will, for these excellences; they look upon valor as a certain natural strength of the mind, and wisdom as a constitutional acuteness; whereas a man has it in his power to be just, if he have but the will to be so, and therefore injustice is thought the most dishonorable, because it is least excusable.

Cato upon this account was opposed by all the great men, who thought themselves reproved by his virtue. Pompey especially looked upon the increase of Cato's credit, as the ruin of his own power, and therefore continually set up men to rail against him. Among these was the seditious Clodius, now again united to Pompey; who declared openly, that Cato had conveyed away a great deal of the treasure that was found in Cyprus; and that he hated Pompey, only because he refused to marry his daughter. Cato answered, that although they had allowed him neither horse nor man, he had brought more treasure from Cyprus alone, than Pompey had, after so many wars and triumphs, from the ransacked world; that he never sought the alliance of Pompey; not that he thought him unworthy of being related to him, but because he differed so much from him, in things that concerned the commonwealth. "For," said he, "I laid down the province that was given me, when I went out of my prætorship; Pompey, on the contrary, retains many provinces for himself, and he bestows many on others; and but now he sent Cæsar a force of six thousand men into Gaul, which Cæsar never asked the people for, nor had Pompey obtained their consent to give. Men, and horse, and arms in any number, are become the mutual gifts of private men to one another; and Pompey keeping the titles of commander and general, hands over the armies and provinces to others to govern, while he himself stays at home to preside at the contests of the canvass, and to stir up tumults at elections; out of the anarchy he thus creates amongst us, seeking, we see well enough, a monarchy for himself." Thus he retorted on Pompey.

He had an intimate friend and admirer of the

name of Marcus Favonius, much the same to Cato as we are told Apollodorus,[13] the Phalerian, was in old time to Socrates, whose words used to throw him into perfect transports and ecstasies, getting into his head, like strong wine, and intoxicating him to a sort of frenzy. This Favonius stood to be chosen ædile, and was like to lose it; but Cato, who was there to assist him, observed that all the votes were written in one hand, and discovering the cheat, appealed to the tribunes, who stopped the election. Favonius was afterward chosen ædile, and Cato, who assisted him in all things that belonged to his office, also undertook the care of the spectacles that were exhibited in the theatre; giving the actors crowns, not of gold, but of wild olive, such as used to be given at the Olympic games; and instead of the magnificent presents that were usually made, he offered to the Greeks beet root, lettuces, radishes, and pears; and to the Romans, earthen pots of wine, pork, figs, cucumbers, and little fagots of wood. Some ridiculed Cato for his economy, others looked with respect on this gentle relaxation of his usual rigor and austerity. In fine, Favonius himself mingled with the crowd, and sitting among the spectators, clapped and applauded Cato, bade him bestow rewards on those who did well, and called on the people to pay their honors to him, as for himself he had placed his whole authority in Cato's hands. At the same time, Curio, the colleague of

---

[13] *Apollodorus the Phalerian is described in Plato's Phædo as shedding tears all through the previous conversation, and, when Socrates took the hemlock, bursting into a passion of distress and horror. Xenophon, in the Memorabilia, calls him an ardent admirer of Socrates, but otherwise rather a silly person. He is also characterized at the beginning of Plato's Symposium.*

Favonius, gave very magnificent entertainments in another theatre; but the people left his, and went to those of Favonius, which they much applauded, and joined heartily in the diversion, seeing him act the private man, and Cato the master of the shows, who, in fact, did all this in derision of the great expenses that others incurred, and to teach them, that in amusements men ought to seek amusement only, and the display of a decent cheerfulness, not great preparations and costly magnificence, demanding the expenditure of endless care and trouble about things of little concern.

After this Scipio, Hypsæus, and Milo, stood to be consuls, and that not only with the usual and now recognized disorders of bribery and corruption, but with arms and slaughter, and every appearance of carrying their audacity and desperation to the length of actual civil war. Whereupon it was proposed, that Pompey might be empowered to preside over that election. This Cato at first opposed, saying that the laws ought not to seek protection from Pompey, but Pompey from the laws. Yet the confusion lasting a long time, the forum continually, as it were, besieged with three armies, and no possibility appearing of a stop being put to these disorders, Cato at length agreed, that rather than fall into the last extremity, the senate should freely confer all on Pompey; since it was necessary to make use of a lesser illegality as a remedy against the greatest of all, and better to set up a monarchy themselves, than to suffer a sedition to continue, that must certainly end in one. Bibulus, therefore, a friend of Cato's, moved the senate to create Pompey sole consul; for that either he would reëstablish the lawful government, or they should serve under the best master. Cato stood up, and, contrary to all expectation, seconded this motion, concluding, that any government was better than mere confusion, and that he did not question but Pompey would deal honorably, and take care of the commonwealth, thus committed to his charge. Pompey being hereupon declared consul, invited Cato to see him in the suburbs. When he came, he saluted and embraced him very kindly, acknowledged the favor he had done him, and desired his counsel and assistance, in the management of this office. Cato made answer, that what he had spoken on any former occasion was not out of hate to Pompey, nor what he had now done, out of love to him, but all for the good of the commonwealth; that in private, if he asked him, he would freely give his advice; and in public, though he asked him not, he would always speak his opinion. And he did accordingly. For first, when Pompey made severe laws for punishing and laying great fines on those who had corrupted the people with gifts, Cato advised him to let alone what was already passed, and to provide for the future; for if he should look up past misdemeanors, it would be difficult to know where to stop; and if he would ordain new penalties, it would be unreasonable to punish men by a law, which at that time they had not the opportunity of breaking. Afterwards, when many considerable men, and some of Pompey's own relations were accused, and he grew remiss, and disinclined to the prosecution, Cato sharply reproved him, and urged him to proceed. Pompey had made a law, also, to forbid the custom of making commendatory orations in behalf of those that were accused; yet he himself wrote one for Munatius Plancus, and sent it while the cause was pleading; upon which Cato, who was sitting as one of the judges, stopped his ears with his hands, and would not hear it read. Whereupon Plancus, before sentence was given, excepted against him, but was condemned notwithstanding. And indeed Cato was a great trouble and perplexity to almost all that were accused of any thing, as they feared to have him one of their judges, yet did not dare to demand his exclusion. And many had been condemned, because by refusing him, they seemed to show that they could not trust their own innocence; and it was a reproach thrown in the teeth of some by their enemies, that they had not accepted Cato for their judge.

In the mean while, Cæsar kept close with his forces in Gaul, and continued in arms; and at the same time employed his gifts, his riches, and his friends above all things, to increase his power in the city. And now Cato's old admonitions began to rouse Pompey out of the negligent security in which he lay, into a sort of imagination of danger at hand; but seeing him slow and unwilling, and timorous to undertake any measures of prevention against Cæsar, Cato resolved himself to stand for the consulship, and presently force Cæsar either to lay down his arms or discover his intentions. Both Cato's competitors were persons of good position; Sulpicius, who was one, owed much to Cato's credit and authority in the city, and it was thought unhandsome and ungratefully done, to stand against him; not that Cato himself took it ill, "For it is no wonder," said he, "if a man will not yield to another, in that which he esteems the greatest good." He had persuaded the senate to make an order, that those who stood for offices, should themselves ask the people for their votes, and not solicit by others, nor take others about with them, to speak for them, in their canvass. And this made the common people very hostile to him, if they were to lose not only the means of receiving money, but also the opportunity of obliging several persons, and so to become by his means both poor and less regarded. Besides this, Cato himself was by nature altogether unfit for the business of canvassing, as he was more anxious to sustain the dignity of his life and character, than to obtain the office. Thus by following his own way of soliciting, and not suffering his friends to do those things which take with the multitude, he was rejected, and lost the consulship.

But whereas, upon such occasions, not only those who missed the office, but even their friends and relations, used to feel themselves disgraced and humiliated, and observed a sort of mourning for several days after, Cato took it so unconcernedly, that he anointed himself, and played at ball in the Field, and after breakfasting, went into the forum, as he used to do, without his shoes or his tunic, and there walked about with his acquaintance. Cicero blames him, for that when affairs required such a consul, he would not take more pains, nor condescend to pay some court to the people, as also because that he afterwards neglected to try again; whereas he had stood a second time to be chosen prætor. Cato answered, that he lost the prætorship the first time, not by the voice of the people, but by the violence and corrupt dealing of his adversaries; whereas in the election of consuls, there had been no foul play. So that he plainly saw the people did not like his manners, which an honest man ought not to alter for their sake; nor yet would a wise man attempt the same thing again, while liable to the same prejudices.

Cæsar was at this time engaged with many

warlike nations, and was subduing them at great hazards. Among the rest, it was believed he had set upon the Germans, in a time of truce, and had thus slain three hundred thousand of them. Upon which, some of his friends moved the senate for a public thanksgiving; but Cato declared, they ought to deliver Cæsar into the hands of those who had been thus unjustly treated, and so expiate the offence and not bring a curse upon the city; "Yet we have reason," said he, "to thank the gods, for that they spared the commonwealth, and did not take vengeance upon the army, for the madness and folly of the general." Hereupon Cæsar wrote a letter to the senate, which was read openly, and was full of reproachful language and accusations against Cato; who, standing up, seemed not at all concerned, and without any heat or passion, but in a calm and, as it were, premeditated discourse, made all Cæsar's charges against him show like mere common scolding and abuse, and in fact a sort of pleasantry and play on Cæsar's part; and proceeding then to go into all Cæsar's political courses, and to explain and reveal (as though he had been not his constant opponent, but his fellow-conspirator,) his whole conduct and purpose from its commencement, he concluded by telling the senate, it was not the sons of the Britons or the Gauls they need fear, but Cæsar himself, if they were wise. And this discourse so moved and awakened the senate, that Cæsar's friends repented they had had a letter read, which had given Cato an opportunity of saying so many reasonable things, and such severe truths against him. However, nothing was then decided upon; it was merely said, that it would be well to send him a successor. Upon that Cæsar's friends required, that Pompey also should lay down his arms, and resign his provinces, or else that Cæsar might not be obliged to either. Then Cato cried out, what he had foretold was come to pass; now it was manifest he was using his forces to compel their judgment, and was turning against the state those armies he had got from it by imposture and trickery. But out of the Senate-house Cato could do but little, as the people were ever ready to magnify Cæsar; and the senate, though convinced by Cato, were afraid of the people.

But when the news was brought that Cæsar had seized Ariminum, and was marching with his army toward Rome, then all men, even Pompey, and the common people too, cast their eyes on Cato, who had alone foreseen and first clearly declared Cæsar's intentions. He, therefore, told them, "If you had believed me, or regarded my advice, you would not now have been reduced to stand in fear of one man, or to put all your hopes in one alone." Pompey acknowledged, that Cato indeed had spoken most like a prophet, while he himself had acted too much like a friend. And Cato advised the senate to put all into the hands of Pompey; "For those who can raise up great evils," said he, "can best allay them."

Pompey, finding he had not sufficient forces, and that those he could raise, were not very resolute, forsook the city. Cato, resolving to follow Pompey into exile, sent his younger son to Munatius, who was then in the country of Bruttium, and took his oldest with him; but wanting somebody to keep his house and take care of his daughters, he took Marcia again, who was now a rich widow, Hortensius being dead, and having left her all his estate. Cæsar afterward made use of this action also, to reproach him with covetousness, and a mercenary design in his marriage. "For," said he, "if he had need of a wife, why did he part with her? And if he had not, why did he take her again? Unless he gave her only as a bait to Hortensius; and lent her when she was young, to have her again when she was rich." But in answer to this, we might fairly apply the saying of Euripides,—

> To speak of mysteries—the chief of these
> Surely were cowardice in Hercules.[14]

For it is much the same thing to reproach Hercules for cowardice, and to accuse Cato of covetousness; though otherwise, whether he did altogether right in this marriage, might be disputed. As soon, however, as he had again taken Marcia, he committed his house and his daughters to her, and himself followed Pompey. And it is said, that from that day he never cut his hair, nor shaved his beard, nor wore a garland, but was always full of sadness, grief and dejectedness for the calamities of his country, and continually showed the same feeling to the last, whatever party had misfortune or success.

The government of Sicily being allotted to him, he passed over to Syracuse; where understanding that Asinius Pollio was arrived at Messena, with forces from the enemy, Cato sent to him, to know the reason of his coming thither: Pollio, on the other side, called upon him to show reason for the present convulsions. And being at the same time informed how Pompey had quite abandoned Italy, and lay encamped at Dyrrhachium, he spoke of the strange-

---

[14] The verses are from the Hercules Furens (174); an answer to a charge of cowardice brought against Hercules.

ness and incomprehensibility of the divine government of things; "Pompey, when he did nothing wisely nor honestly, was always successful; and now that he would preserve his country, and defend her liberty, he is altogether unfortunate." As for Asinius, he said, he could drive him out of Sicily, but as there were larger forces coming to his assistance, he would not engage the island in a war. He therefore advised the Syracusans to join the conquering party and provide for their own safety; and so set sail from thence.

When he came to Pompey, he uniformly gave advice to protract the war; as he always hoped to compose matters, and was by no means desirous that they should come to action; for the commonwealth would suffer extremely, and be the certain cause of its own ruin, whoever were conqueror by the sword. In like manner, he persuaded Pompey and the council to ordain, that no city should be sacked that was subject to the people of Rome; and that no Roman should be killed, but in the heat of battle; and hereby he got himself great honor, and brought over many to Pompey's party, whom his moderation and humanity attracted. Afterwards being sent into Asia, to assist those who were raising men, and preparing ships in those parts, he took with him his sister Servilia, and a little boy whom she had by Lucullus. For since her widowhood, she had lived with her brother, and much recovered her reputation, having put herself under his care, followed him in his voyages, and complied with his severe way of living. Yet Cæsar did not fail to asperse him upon her account also.

Pompey's officers in Asia, it seems, had no great need of Cato; but he brought over the people of Rhodes by his persuasions, and leaving his sister

Servilia and her child there, he returned to Pompey, who had now collected very great forces both by sea and land. And here Pompey, more than in any other act, betrayed his intentions. For at first he designed to give Cato the command of the navy, which consisted of no less than five hundred ships of war, besides a vast number of light galleys, scouts, and open boats. But presently bethinking himself, or put in mind by his friends, that Cato's principal and only aim being to free his country from all usurpation, if he were master of such great forces, as soon as ever Cæsar should be conquered, he would certainly call upon Pompey, also, to lay down his arms, and be subject to the laws, he changed his mind, and though he had already mentioned it to Cato, nevertheless made Bibulus admiral. Notwithstanding this, he had no reason to suppose that Cato's zeal in the cause was in any way diminished. For before one of the battles at Dyrrhachium, when Pompey himself, we are told, made an address to the soldiers and bade the officers do the like, the men listened to them but coldly, and with silence, until Cato, last of all, came forward, and in the language of philosophy, spoke to them, as the occasion required, concerning liberty, manly virtue, death, and a good name; upon all which he delivered himself with strong natural passion, and concluded with calling in the aid of the gods, to whom he directed his speech, as if they were present to behold them fight for their country. And at this the army gave such a shout and showed such excitement, that their officers led them on full of hope and confidence to the danger. Cæsar's party were routed, and put to flight; but his presiding fortune used the advantage of Pompey's cautiousness and diffidence, to render the victory incomplete. But of this we have spoken in the life of Pompey. While, however, all the rest rejoiced, and magnified their success, Cato alone bewailed his country, and cursed that fatal ambition, which made so many brave Romans murder one another.

After this, Pompey following Cæsar into Thessaly, left at Dyrrhachium a quantity of munitions, money, and stores, and many of his domestics [15] and relations; the charge of all which he gave to Cato, with the command only of fifteen cohorts. For though he trusted him much, yet he was afraid of him too, knowing full well, that if he had bad success, Cato would be the last to forsake him, but if he conquered, would never let him use his victory at his pleasure. There were, likewise, many persons of high rank that staid with Cato at Dyrrhachium. When they heard of the overthrow at Pharsalia, Cato resolved with himself, that if Pompey were slain, he would conduct those that were with him into Italy, and then retire as far from the tyranny of Cæsar as he could, and live in exile; but if Pompey were safe, he would keep the army together for him. With this resolution he passed over to Corcyra, where the navy lay; there he would have resigned his command to Cicero, because he had been consul, and himself only a prætor: but Cicero refused it, and was going for Italy. At which Pompey's son being incensed, would rashly and in heat have punished all those who were going away, and in the first place have laid hands on Cicero; but

---

[15] The word *domestics,* used by the old translator, should have been altered; it is simply taken from the Latin word for the original Greek, which means, belonging to his house or family, and is not at all limited, as the word *domestics* is with us, to servants.

Cato spoke with him in private, and diverted him from that design. And thus he clearly saved the life of Cicero, and rescued several others also from ill-treatment.

Conjecturing that Pompey the Great was fled towards Egypt or Africa, Cato resolved to hasten after him; and having taken all his men aboard, he set sail; but first to those who were not zealous to continue the contest, he gave free liberty to depart. When they came to the coast of Africa, they met with Sextus, Pompey's younger son, who told them of the death of his father in Egypt; at which they were all exceedingly grieved, and declared that after Pompey they would follow no other leader but Cato. Out of compassion therefore to so many worthy persons, who had given such testimonies of their fidelity, and whom he could not for shame leave in a desert country, amidst so many difficulties, he took upon him the command, and marched toward the city of Cyrene, which presently received him, though not long before they had shut their gates against Labienus. Here he was informed that Scipio, Pompey's father-in-law, was received by king Juba, and that Attius Varus, whom Pompey had made governor of Africa, had joined them with his forces. Cato therefore resolved to march toward them by land, it being now winter; and got together a number of asses to carry water, and furnished himself likewise with plenty of all other provision, and a number of carriages. He took also with him some of those they call Psylli, who cure the biting of serpents, by sucking out the poison with their mouths, and have likewise certain charms, by which they stupefy and lay asleep the serpents.

Thus they marched seven days together, Cato all the time going on foot at the head of his men, and never making use of any horse or chariot. Ever since the battle of Pharsalia, he used to sit at table,[16] and added this to his other ways of mourning, that he never lay down but to sleep.

Having passed the winter in Africa, Cato drew out his army, which amounted to little less than ten thousand. The affairs of Scipio and Varus went very ill, by reason of their dissensions and quarrels among themselves, and their submissions and flatteries to king Juba, who was insupportable for his vanity, and the pride he took in his strength and riches. The first time he came to a conference with Cato, he had ordered his own seat to be placed in the middle, between Scipio and Cato; which Cato observing, took up his chair, and set himself on the other side of Scipio, to whom he thus gave the honor of sitting in the middle, though he were his enemy, and had formerly published some scandalous writing against him. There are people who speak as if this were quite an insignificant matter, and who nevertheless find fault with Cato, because in Sicily, walking one day with Philostratus, he gave him the middle place, to show his respect for philosophy. However, he now succeeded both in humbling the pride of Juba, who was treating Scipio and Varus much like a pair of satraps under his orders, and also in reconciling them to each other. All the troops desired him to be their leader; Scipio, likewise, and Varus gave way to it, and offered him the command; but he said, he would not break those laws, which he sought to defend, and he, being but proprætor, ought not to command in the presence of a proconsul, (for Scipio had been created pro-

[16] Instead of lying down to his meal according to the usual custom.

consul,) besides that people took it as a good omen, to see a Scipio command in Africa, and the very name inspired the soldiers with hopes of success.

Scipio, having taken upon him the command, presently resolved, at the instigation of Juba, to put all the inhabitants of Utica to the sword, and to raze the city, for having, as they professed, taken part with Cæsar. Cato would by no means suffer this; but invoking the gods, exclaiming and protesting against it in the council of war, he with much difficulty delivered the poor people from this cruelty. And afterwards, upon the entreaty of the inhabitants, and at the instance of Scipio, Cato took upon himself the government of Utica, lest, one way or other, it should fall into Cæsar's hands; for it was a strong place, and very advantageous for either party. And it was yet better provided and more strongly fortified by Cato, who brought in great store of corn, repaired the walls, erected towers, and made deep trenches and palisades around the town. The young men of Utica he lodged among these works, having first taken their arms from them; the rest of the inhabitants he kept within the town, and took the greatest care, that no injury should be done nor affront offered them by the Romans. From hence he sent great quantity of arms, money, and provision to the camp, and made this city their chief magazine.

He advised Scipio, as he had before done Pompey, by no means to hazard a battle against a man experienced in war, and formidable in the field, but to use delay; for time would gradually abate the violence of the crisis, which is the strength of usurpation. But Scipio out of pride rejected this counsel, and wrote a letter to Cato, in which he reproached him with cowardice; and that he could not be content to lie secure himself within walls and trenches, but he must hinder others from boldly using their own good-sense to seize the right opportunity. In answer to this, Cato wrote word again, that he would take the horse and foot which he had brought into Africa, and go over into Italy, to make a diversion there, and draw Cæsar off from them. But Scipio derided this proposition also. Then Cato openly let it be seen that he was sorry he had yielded the command to Scipio, who he saw would not carry on the war with any wisdom, and if, contrary to all appearance, he should succeed, he would use his success as unjustly at home. For Cato had then made up his mind, and so he told his friends, that he could have but slender hopes in those generals that had so much boldness, and so little conduct; yet if any thing should happen beyond expectation, and Cæsar should be overthrown, for his part he would not stay at Rome, but would retire from the cruelty and inhumanity of Scipio, who had already uttered fierce and proud threats against many.

But what Cato had looked for, fell out sooner than he expected. Late in the evening came one from the army, whence he had been three days coming, who brought word there had been a great battle near Thapsus; that all was utterly lost; Cæsar had taken the camps, Scipio and Juba were fled with a few only, and all the rest of the army was lost. This news arriving in time of war, and in the night, so alarmed the people, that they were almost out of their wits, and could scarce keep themselves within the walls of the city. But Cato came forward, and meeting the people in this hurry and clamor, did all he could to comfort and encourage them, and somewhat appeased the fear and amazement they were in, telling them that very likely things were not so bad in truth, but much exaggerated in the report. And so he pacified the tumult for the present. The next morning, he sent for the three hundred, whom he used as his council; these were Romans, who were in Africa upon business, in commerce and money-lending; there were also several senators and their sons. They were summoned to meet in the temple of Jupiter. While they were coming together, Cato walked about very quietly and unconcerned, as if nothing new had happened. He had a book in his hand, which he was reading; in this book was an account of what provision he had for war, armor, corn, ammunition, and soldiers.

When they were assembled, he began his discourse; first, as regarded the three hundred themselves, and very much commended the courage and fidelity they had shown, and their having very well served their country with their persons, money, and counsel. Then he entreated them by no means to separate, as if each single man could hope for any safety in forsaking his companions; on the contrary, while they kept together, Cæsar would have less reason to despise them, if they fought against him, and be more forward to pardon them, if they submitted to him. Therefore, he advised them to consult among themselves, nor should he find fault, whichever course they adopted. If they thought fit to submit to fortune, he would impute their change to necessity; but if they resolved to stand firm, and undertake the danger for the sake of liberty, he should not only commend, but admire their courage, and would himself be their leader and companion too, till they had put to the proof the utmost fortune of their country; which was not

Utica or Adrumetum, but Rome, and she had often, by her own greatness, raised herself after worse disasters. Besides, as there were many things that would conduce to their safety, so chiefly this, that they were to fight against one whose affairs urgently claimed his presence in various quarters. Spain was already revolted to the younger Pompey; Rome was unaccustomed to the bridle, and impatient of it, and would therefore be ready to rise in insurrection upon any turn of affairs. As for themselves, they ought not to shrink from the danger; and in this might take example from their enemy, who so freely exposes his life to effect the most unrighteous designs, yet never can hope for so happy a conclusion, as they may promise themselves; for notwithstanding the uncertainty of war, they will be sure of a most happy life, if they succeed, or a most glorious death, if they miscarry. However, he said, they ought to deliberate among themselves, and he joined with them in praying the gods that in recompense of their former courage and goodwill, they would prosper their present determinations. When Cato had thus spoken, many were moved and encouraged by his arguments, but the greatest part were so animated by the sense of his intrepidity, generosity, and goodness, that they forgot the present danger, and as if he were the only invincible leader, and above all fortune, they entreated him to employ their persons, arms, and estates, as he thought fit; for they esteemed it far better to meet death in following his counsel, than to find their safety in betraying one of so great virtue. One of the assembly proposed the making a decree, to set the slaves at liberty; and most of the rest approved the motion. Cato said, that it ought not to be done, for it was neither just nor lawful; but if any of their masters would willingly set them free, those that were fit for service should be received. Many promised so to do; whose names he ordered to be enrolled, and then withdrew.

Presently after this, he received letters from Juba and Scipio. Juba, with some few of his men, was retired to a mountain, where he waited to hear what Cato would resolve upon; and intended to stay there for him, if he thought fit to leave Utica, or to come to his aid with his troops, if he were besieged. Scipio was on shipboard, near a certain promontory, not far from Utica, expecting an answer upon the same account. But Cato thought fit to retain the messengers, till the three hundred should come to some resolution.

As for the senators that were there, they showed great forwardness, and at once set free their slaves, and furnished them with arms. But the three hundred being men occupied in merchandise and money-lending, much of their substance also consisting in slaves, the enthusiasm that Cato's speech had raised in them, did not long continue. As there are substances that easily admit heat, and as suddenly lose it, when the fire is removed, so these men were heated and inflamed, while Cato was present; but when they began to reason among themselves, the fear they had of Cæsar, soon overcame their reverence for Cato and for virtue. "For who are we," said they, "and who is it we refuse to obey? Is it not that Cæsar, who is now invested with all the power of Rome? and which of us is a Scipio, a Pompey, or a Cato? But now that all men make their honor give way to their fear, shall we alone engage for the liberty of Rome, and in Utica declare war against him, before whom Cato and Pompey the Great fled out of Italy? Shall we set free

CATO THE YOUNGER 483

our slaves against Cæsar, who have ourselves no more liberty than he is pleased to allow? No, let us, poor creatures, know ourselves, submit to the victor, and send deputies to implore his mercy." Thus said the most moderate of them; but the greatest part were for seizing the senators, that by securing them, they might appease Cæsar's anger. Cato, though he perceived the change, took no notice of it; but wrote to Juba and Scipio to keep away from Utica, because he mistrusted the three hundred.

A considerable body of horse, which had escaped from the late fight, riding up towards Utica, sent three men before to Cato, who yet did not all bring the same message; for one party was for going to Juba, another for joining with Cato, and some again were afraid to go into Utica. When Cato heard this, he ordered Marcus Rubrius to attend upon the three hundred, and quietly take the names of those who of their own accord set their slaves at liberty, but by no means to force anybody. Then, taking with him the senators, he went out of the town, and met the principal officers of these horsemen, whom he entreated not to abandon so many Roman senators, nor to prefer Juba for their commander before Cato, but consult the common safety, and to come into the city, which was impregnable, and well furnished with corn and other provisions, sufficient for many years. The senators, likewise, with tears besought them to stay. Hereupon the officers went to consult their soldiers, and Cato with the senators sat down upon an embankment, expecting their resolution. In the mean time comes Rubrius in great disorder, crying out, the three hundred were all in commotion, and exciting revolt and tumult in the city. At this all the rest fell into despair, lamenting and bewailing their condition. Cato endeavored to comfort them, and sent to the three hundred, desiring them to have patience. Then the officers of the horse returned with no very reasonable demands. They said, they did not desire to serve Juba, for his pay, nor should they fear Cæsar, while they followed Cato, but they dreaded to be shut up with the Uticans, men of traitorous temper, and Carthaginian blood; for though they were quiet at present, yet as soon as Cæsar should appear, without doubt they would conspire together, and betray the Romans. Therefore, if he expected they should join with him, he must drive out of the town or destroy all the Uticans, that he might receive them into a place clear both of enemies and barbarians. This Cato thought utterly cruel and barbarous; but he mildly answered, he would consult the three hundred.

Then he returned to the city, where he found the men, not framing excuses, or dissembling out of reverence to him, but openly declaring that no one should compel them to make war against Cæsar; which, they said, they were neither able nor willing to do. And some there were who muttered words about retaining the senators till Cæsar's coming; but Cato seemed not to hear this, as indeed he had the excuse of being a little deaf. At the same time came one to him, and told him the horse were going away. And now, fearing lest the three hundred should take some desperate resolution concerning the senators, he presently went out with some of his friends, and seeing they were gone some way, he took horse, and rode after them. They, when they saw him coming, were very glad, and received him very kindly, entreating him to save himself with them. At this time, it is said, Cato shed tears, while entreating them on behalf of the senators, and stretching out his hands in supplication. He turned some of their horses' heads, and laid hold of the men by their armor, till in fine he prevailed with them, out of compassion, to stay only that one day, to procure a safe retreat for the senators. Having thus persuaded them to go along with him, some he placed at the gates of the town, and to others gave the charge of the citadel. The three hundred began to fear they should suffer for their inconstancy, and sent to Cato, entreating him by all means to come to them; but the senators flocking about him, would not suffer him to go, and said they would not trust their guardian and saviour to the hands of perfidious traitors.

For there had never, perhaps, been a time when Cato's virtue appeared more manifestly; and every class of men in Utica could clearly see, with sorrow and admiration, how entirely free was every thing that he was doing from any secret motives or any mixture of self-regard; he, namely, who had long before resolved on his own death, was taking such extreme pains, toil, and care, only for the sake of others, that when he had secured their lives, he might put an end to his own. For it was easily perceived, that he had determined to die, though he did not let it appear.

Therefore, having pacified the senators, he complied with the request of the three hundred, and went to them alone without any attendance. They gave him many thanks, and entreated him to employ and trust them for the future; and if they were not Catos, and could not aspire to his greatness of mind, they begged he would pity their weakness; and told him, they had determined to send to Cæsar and entreat him, chiefly and in the first place, for Cato, and if they could not prevail for him, they would not accept of pardon for themselves, but as long as they had breath, would fight in his defence. Cato commended their good intentions, and advised them to send speedily, for their own safety, but by no means to ask any thing in his behalf; for those who are conquered, entreat, and those who have done wrong, beg pardon; for himself, he did not confess to any defeat in all his life, but rather, so far as he had thought fit, he had got the victory, and had conquered Cæsar in all points of justice and honesty. It was Cæsar that ought to be looked upon as one surprised and vanquished; for he was now convicted and found guilty of those designs against his country, which he had so long practised and so constantly denied. When he had thus spoken, he went out of the assembly, and being informed that Cæsar was coming with his whole army, "Ah," said he, "he expects to find us brave men." Then he went to the senators, and urged them to make no delay, but hasten to be gone, while the horsemen were yet in the city. So ordering all the gates to be shut, except one towards the sea, he assigned their several ships to those that were to depart, and gave money and provision to those that wanted; all which he did with great order and exactness, taking care to suppress all tumults, and that no wrong should be done to the people.

Marcus Octavius, coming with two legions, now encamped near Utica, and sent to Cato, to arrange about the chief command. Cato returned him no answer; but said to his friends, "Can we wonder all has gone ill with us, when our love of office survives even in our very ruin?" In the mean time, word was

CATO THE YOUNGER 487

brought him, that the horse were going away, and were beginning to spoil and plunder the citizens. Cato ran to them, and from the first he met, snatched what they had taken; the rest threw down all they had gotten, and went away silent, and ashamed of what they had done. Then he called together all the people of Utica, and requested them upon the behalf of the three hundred, not to exasperate Cæsar against them, but all to seek their common safety together with them. After that, he went again to the port to see those who were about to embark; and there he embraced and dismissed those of his friends and acquaintance whom he had persuaded to go. As for his son, he did not counsel him to be gone, nor did he think fit to persuade him to forsake his father. But there was one Statyllius, a young man, in the flower of his age, of a brave spirit, and very desirous to imitate the constancy of Cato. Cato entreated him to go away, as he was a noted enemy to Cæsar, but without success. Then Cato looked at Apollonides, the stoic philosopher, and Demetrius, the peripatetic; "It belongs to you," said he, "to cool the fever of this young man's spirit, and to make him know what is good for him." And thus, in settling his friends upon their way, and in despatching the business of any that applied to him, he spent that night, and the greatest part of the next day.

Lucius Cæsar, a kinsman of Cæsar's, being appointed to go deputy for the three hundred, came to Cato, and desired he would assist him to prepare a persuasive speech for them; "And as to you yourself," said he, "it will be an honor for me to kiss the hands and fall at the knees of Cæsar, in your behalf." But Cato would by no means permit him to do any such thing; "For as to myself," said he, "if I would be preserved by Cæsar's favor, I should myself go to him; but I would not be beholden to a tyrant, for his acts of tyranny. For it is but usurpation in him to save, as their rightful lord, the lives of men over whom he has no title to reign. But if you please, let us consider what you had best say for the three hundred." And when they had continued some time together, as Lucius was going away, Cato recommended to him his son, and the rest of his friends; and taking him by the hand, bade him farewell.

Then he retired to his house again, and called together his son and his friends, to whom he conversed on various subjects; among the rest, he forbade his son to engage himself in the affairs of state. For to act therein as became him, was now impossible; and to do otherwise, would be dishonorable. Toward evening he went into his bath. As he was bathing, he remembered Statyllius, and called out aloud, "Apollonides, have you tamed the high spirit of Statyllius, and is he gone without bidding us farewell?" "No," said Apollonides, "I have said much to him, but to little purpose; he is still resolute and unalterable, and declares he is determined to follow your example." At this, it is said, Cato smiled, and answered, "That will soon be tried."

After he had bathed, he went to supper, with a great deal of company; at which he sat up, as he had always used to do ever since the battle of Pharsalia; for since that time he never lay down, but when he went to sleep. . There supped with him all his own friends and the magistrates of Utica.

After supper, the wine produced a great deal of lively and agreeable discourse, and a whole series of philosophical questions was discussed. At length they came to the strange dogmas of the stoics, called their Paradoxes; and to this in particular, That the good man only is free, and that all wicked men are slaves. The peripatetic, as was to be expected, opposing this, Cato fell upon him very warmly; and somewhat raising his voice, he argued the matter at great length, and urged the point with such vehemence, that it was apparent to everybody, he was resolved to put an end to his life, and set himself at liberty. And so, when he had done speaking, there was a great silence, and evident dejection. Cato, therefore, to divert them from any suspicion of his design, turned the conversation, and began again to talk of matters of present interest and expectation, showing great concern for those that were at sea, as also for the others, who, travelling by land, were to pass through a dry and barbarous desert.

When the company was broke up, he walked with his friends, as he used to do after supper, gave the necessary orders to the officers of the watch, and going into his chamber, he embraced his son and every one of his friends with more than usual warmth, which again renewed their suspicion of his design. Then laying himself down, he took into his hand Plato's dialogue concerning the soul. Having read more than half the book, he looked up, and missing his sword, which his son had taken away while he was at supper, he called his servant, and asked, who had taken away his sword. The servant making no answer, he fell to reading again; and a little after, not seeming importunate, or hasty for it, but as if he would only know what was become of it, he bade it be brought. But having waited some time, when he had read through the book, and still nobody brought the sword, he called up all his servants, and in a louder tone demanded his sword. To one of them he gave such a blow in the mouth, that he hurt his own hand; and now grew more angry, exclaiming that he was betrayed and delivered naked to the enemy by his son and his servants. Then his son, with the rest of his friends, came running into the room, and falling at his feet, began to lament and beseech him. But Cato raising up himself, and looking fiercely, "When," said he, "and how did I become deranged, and out of my senses, that thus no one tries to persuade me by reason, or show me what is better, if I am supposed to be ill-advised? Must I be disarmed, and hindered from using my own reason? And you, young man, why do not you bind your father's hands behind him, that when Cæsar comes, he may find me unable to defend myself? To despatch myself I want no sword; I need but hold my breath awhile, or strike my head against the wall."

When he had thus spoken, his son went weeping out of the chamber, and with him all the rest, except Demetrius and Apollonides, to whom, being left alone with him, he began to speak more calmly. "And you," said he, "do you also think to keep a man of my age alive by force, and to sit here and silently watch me? Or do you bring me some reasons to prove, that it will not be base and unworthy for Cato, when he can find his safety no other way, to seek it from his enemy? If so, adduce your arguments, and show cause why we should now unlearn what we formerly were taught, in order that rejecting all the convictions in which we lived, we may now by Cæsar's help grow wiser, and be yet more obliged to him, than for life only.

Not that I have determined aught concerning myself, but I would have it in my power to perform what I shall think fit to resolve; and I shall not fail to take you as my advisers, in holding counsel, as I shall do, with the doctrines which your philosophy teaches; in the mean time, do not trouble yourselves; but go tell my son, that he should not compel his father to what he cannot persuade him to." They made him no answer, but went weeping out of the chamber. Then the sword being brought in by a little boy, Cato took it, drew it out, and looked at it; and when he saw the point was good, "Now," said he, "I am master of myself;" and laying down the sword, he took his book again, which, it is related, he read [17] twice over. After this he slept so soundly, that he was heard to snore by those that were without.

About midnight, he called up two of his freedmen, Cleanthes, his physician, and Butas, whom he chiefly employed in public business. Him he sent to the port, to see if all his friends had sailed; to the physician he gave his hand to be dressed, as it was swollen with the blow he had struck one of his servants. At this they all rejoiced, hoping that now he designed to live.

Butas, after a while, returned, and brought word they were all gone except Crassus, who had stayed about some business, but was just ready to depart; he said, also, that the wind was high, and the sea very rough. Cato, on hearing this, sighed, out of compassion to those who were at sea, and sent

---

[17] Cato could scarcely have *read* the Dialogue on the Soul (the Phædo of Plato, see National Library Edition, Vol. III., p. 185), *twice over* in so short a time, and it is rather strange that he should have been said to have done so.

Butas again, to see if any of them should happen to return for any thing they wanted, and to acquaint him therewith.

Now the birds began to sing, and he again fell into a little slumber. At length Butas came back, and told him, all was quiet in the port. Then Cato, laying himself down, as if he would sleep out the rest of the night, bade him shut the door after him. But as soon as Butas was gone out, he took his sword, and stabbed it into his breast; yet not being able to use his hand so well, on account of the swelling, he did not immediately die of the wound; but struggling, fell off the bed, and throwing down a little mathematical table that stood by, made such a noise, that the servants, hearing it, cried out. And immediately his son and all his friends came into the chamber, where seeing him lie weltering in his blood, great part of his bowels out of his body, but himself still alive and able to look at them, they all stood in horror. The physician went to him, and would have put in his bowels, which were not pierced, and sewed up the wound; but Cato, recovering himself, and understanding the intention, thrust away the physician, plucked out his own bowels, and tearing open the wound, immediately expired.

In less time than one would think his own family could have known this accident, all the three hundred were at the door. And a little after, the people of Utica flocked thither, crying out with one voice, he was their benefactor and their saviour, the only free and only undefeated man. At the very same time, they had news that Cæsar was coming; yet neither fear of the present danger, nor desire to flatter the conqueror, nor the commotions and discord among themselves, could divert them from doing honor to Cato. For they sumptuously set out his body, made him a magnificent funeral, and buried him by the seaside, where now stands his statue, holding a sword. And only when this had been done, they returned to consider of preserving themselves and their city.

Cæsar had been informed that Cato stayed at Utica, and did not seek to fly; that he had sent away the rest of the Romans, but himself, with his son and a few of his friends, continued there very unconcernedly, so that he could not imagine what might be his design. But having a great consideration for the man, he hastened thither with his army. When he heard of his death, it is related he said these words, " Cato, I grudge you your death, as you have grudged me the preservation of your life." And, indeed, if Cato would have suffered himself to owe his life to Cæsar, he would not so much have impaired his own honor, as augmented the other's glory. What would have been done, of course we cannot know, but from Cæsar's usual clemency, we may guess what was most likely.

Cato was forty-eight years old when he died. His son suffered no injury from Cæsar; but, it is said, he grew idle, and was thought to be dissipated among women. In Cappadocia, he stayed at the house of Marphadates, one of the royal family there, who had a very handsome wife; and continuing his visit longer than was suitable, he made himself the subject of various epigrams; such as, for example,

> To-morrow, (being the thirtieth day),
> Cato, 't is thought, will go away;

> Porcius and Marphadates, friends so true,
> One *Soul*, they say, suffices for the two,

that being the name of the woman,[18] and so again,

> To Cato's greatness every one confesses,
> A royal Soul he certainly possesses.

But all these stains were entirely wiped off by the bravery of his death. For in the battle of Philippi, where he fought for his country's liberty against Cæsar and Antony, when the ranks were breaking, he, scorning to fly, or to escape unknown, called out to the enemy, showed himself to them in the front, and encouraged those of his party who stayed; and at length fell, and left his enemies full of admiration of his valor.

Nor was the daughter of Cato inferior to the rest of her family, for sober-living and greatness of spirit. She was married to Brutus, who killed Cæsar; was acquainted with the conspiracy, and ended her life as became one of her birth and virtue. All which is related in the life of Brutus.

Statyllius, who said he would imitate Cato, was at that time hindered by the philosophers, when he would have put an end to his life. He afterward followed Brutus, to whom he was very faithful and very serviceable, and died in the field of Philippi.

[18] Psyche.

AGIS [1]

TRANSLATED BY SIR ROBERT THOROLD, BART.

THE fable of Ixion, who, embracing a cloud instead of Juno, begot the Centaurs, has been ingeniously enough supposed to have been invented to represent to us ambitious men, whose minds, doting on glory, which is a mere image of virtue, produce nothing that is genuine or uniform, but only, as might be expected of such a conjunction, misshapen and unnatural actions. Running after their emulations and passions, and carried away by the impulses of the moment, they may say with the herdsmen, in the tragedy of Sophocles,

> We follow these, though born their rightful lords,
> And they command us, though they speak no words.[2]

For this is indeed the true condition of men in public life, who, to gain the vain title of being the people's leaders and governors, are content to make themselves the slaves and followers of all the people's humors and caprices. For as the look-

---

[1] Son of Eudamidas II., king of Sparta, reigned 240-244 B.C. He attempted to re-establish the institutions of Lycurgus and to effect a thorough reform in the Spartan state, but was resisted by his colleague Leonidas II., the wealthy, and was thrown into prison and put to death.—DR. WILLIAM SMITH.

[2] *We follow these, though born their rightful lords,* said by the herdsmen of their flocks, is a fragment conjectured to belong to the lost play of the Herdsmen, in which, apparently, the death of Protesilaus by the hand of Hector was the great event, the chorus being a company of herdsmen. It is No. 447 in Dindorf's fragments.

out men at the ship's prow, though they see what is ahead before the men at the helm, yet constantly look back to the pilots there, and obey the orders they give; so these men, steered, as I may say, by popular applause, though they bear the name of governors, are in reality the mere underlings of the multitude. The man who is completely wise and virtuous, has no need at all of glory, except so far as it disposes and eases his way to action by the greater trust that it procures him. A young man, I grant, may be permitted, while yet eager for distinction, to pride himself a little in his good deeds; for (as Theophrastus says) his virtues, which are yet tender and, as it were, in the blade, cherished and supported by praises, grow stronger, and take the deeper root. But when this passion is exorbitant, it is dangerous in all men, and in those who govern a commonwealth, utterly destructive. For in the possession of large power and authority, it transports men to a degree of madness; so that now they no more think what is good, glorious, but will have those actions only esteemed good that are glorious. As Phocion, therefore, answered king Antipater, who sought his approbation of some unworthy action, "I cannot be your flatterer, and your friend," so these men should answer the people, "I cannot govern, and obey you." For it may happen to the commonwealth, as to the serpent in the fable, whose tail, rising in rebellion against the head, complained, as of a great grievance, that it was always forced to follow, and required that it should be permitted by turns to lead the way. And taking the command accordingly, it soon inflicted by its senseless courses mischiefs in abundance upon itself, while the head was torn and lacerated with following, contrary to nature, a guide that was deaf and blind. And such we see to have been the lot of many, who, submitting to be guided by the inclinations of an uninformed and unreasoning multitude, could neither stop, nor recover themselves out of the confusion.

This is what has occurred to us to say, of that glory which depends on the voice of large numbers, considering the sad effects of it in the misfortunes of Caius and Tiberius Gracchus, men of noble nature, and whose generous natural dispositions were improved by the best of educations, and who came to the administration of affairs with the most laudable intentions; yet they were ruined, I cannot say by an immoderate desire of glory, but by a more excusable fear of disgrace. For being excessively beloved and favored by the people, they thought it a discredit to them not to make full repayment, endeavoring by new public acts to outdo the honors they had received, and again, because of these new kindnesses, incurring yet further distinctions; till the people and they mutually inflamed, and vying thus with each other in honors and benefits, brought things at last to such a pass, that they might say that to engage so far was indeed a folly, but to retreat would now be a shame.

This the reader will easily gather from the story. I will now compare with them two Lacedæmonian popular leaders, the kings Agis and Cleomenes. For they, being desirous also to raise the people, and to restore the noble and just form of government, now long fallen into disuse, incurred the hatred of the rich and powerful, who could not endure to be deprived of the selfish enjoyments to which they were accustomed. These were not indeed brothers by nature, as the two Romans, but they had a kind of brotherly resemblance in their actions and designs, which took a rise from such beginnings and occasions as I am now about to relate.

When the love of gold and silver had once gained admittance into the Lacedæmonian commonwealth, it was quickly followed by avarice and baseness of spirit in the pursuit of it, and by luxury, effeminacy, and prodigality in the use. Then Sparta fell from almost all her former virtue and repute, and so continued till the days of Agis and Leonidas, who both together were kings of the Lacedæmonians.

Agis was of the royal family of Eurypon, son of Eudamidas, and the sixth in descent from Agesilaus, who made the expedition into Asia, and was the greatest man of his time in Greece. Agesilaus left behind him a son called Archidamus, the same who was slain at Mandonium,[3] in Italy, by the Messapians, and who was then succeeded by his oldest son Agis. He being killed by Antipater near Megalopolis, and leaving no issue, was succeeded by his brother Eudamidas; he, by a son called Archidamus; and Archidamus, by another Eudamidas, the father of this Agis of whom we now treat.

Leonidas, son of Cleonymus, was of the other royal house of the Agiadæ, and the eighth in descent from Pausanias, who defeated Mardonius in the battle of Platæa. Pausanias was succeeded by a son called Plistoanax; and he, by another Pausanias, who was banished, and lived as a private man at Tegea; while his eldest son Agesipolis

---

[3] Mandyrium, or Manduria, according to the more correct writing, was the name of the place where this battle was fought, on the same day as that of Chæronea.

reigned in his place. He, dying without issue, was succeeded by a younger brother, called Cleombrotus, who left two sons; the elder was Agesipolis, who reigned but a short time, and died without issue; the younger, who then became king, was called Cleomenes, and had also two sons, Acrotatus and Cleonymus. The first died before his father, but left a son called Areus, who succeeded, and being slain at Corinth, left the kingdom to his son Acrotatus. This Acrotatus was defeated, and slain near Megalopolis, in a battle against the tyrant Aristodemus; he left his wife big with child, and on her being delivered of a son, Leonidas, son of the above-named Cleonymus, was made his guardian, and as the young king died before becoming a man, he succeeded in the kingdom.

Leonidas was a king not particularly suitable to his people. For though there were at that time at Sparta a general decline in manners, yet a greater revolt from the old habits appeared in him than in others. For having lived a long time among the great lords of Persia, and been a follower of king Seleucus, he unadvisedly thought to imitate, among Greek institutions and in a lawful government, the pride and assumption usual in those courts. Agis, on the contrary, in fineness of nature and elevation of mind, not only far excelled Leonidas, but in a manner all the kings that had reigned since the great Agesilaus. For though he had been bred very tenderly, in abundance and even in luxury, by his mother Agesistrata and his grandmother Archidamia, who were the wealthiest of the Lacedæmonians, yet before the age of twenty, he renounced all indulgence in pleasures. Withdrawing himself as far as possible from the gaiety and ornament which seemed becoming to the grace of his person, he made it his pride to appear in the coarse Spartan coat. In his meals, his bathings, and in all his exercises, he followed the old Laconian usage, and was often heard to say, he had no desire for the place of king, if he did not hope by means of that authority to restore their ancient laws and discipline.

The Lacedæmonians might date the beginning of their corruption from their conquest of Athens, and the influx of gold and silver among them that thence ensued. Yet, nevertheless, the number of houses which Lycurgus appointed being still maintained, and the law remaining in force by which every one was obliged to leave his lot or portion of land entirely to his son, a kind of order and equality was thereby preserved, which still in some degree sustained the state amidst its errors in other respects. But one Epitadeus happening to be ephor, a man of great influence, and of a wilful, violent spirit, on some occasion of a quarrel with his son, proposed a decree, that all men should have liberty to dispose of their land by gift in their lifetime, or by their last will and testament. This being promoted by him to satisfy a passion of revenge, and through covetousness consented to by others, and thus enacted for a law, was the ruin of the best state of the commonwealth. For the rich men without scruple drew the estates into their own hands, excluding the rightful heirs from their succession; and all the wealth being centered upon a few, the generality were poor and miserable. Honorable pursuits, for which there was no longer leisure, were neglected; and the state was filled with sordid business, and with hatred and envy of the rich. There did not remain above seven hundred of the old Spartan families, of which perhaps one hundred might have estates in land, the rest were destitute alike of wealth and of honor, were tardy and unperforming in the defence of their country against its enemies abroad, and eagerly watched the opportunity for change and revolution at home.

Agis, therefore, believing it a glorious action, as in truth it was, to equalize and repeople the state, began to sound the inclinations of the citizens. He found the young men disposed beyond his expectation; they were eager to enter with him upon the contest in the cause of virtue, and to fling aside, for freedom's sake, their old manner of life, as readily as the wrestler does his garment. But the old men, habituated and more confirmed in their vices, were most of them as alarmed at the very name of Lycurgus, as a fugitive slave to be brought back before his offended master. These men could not endure to hear Agis continually deploring the present state of Sparta, and wishing she might be restored to her ancient glory. But on the other side, Lysander, the son of Libys, Mandroclidas, the son of Ecphanes, together with Agesilaus, not only approved his design, but assisted and confirmed him in it. Lysander had a great authority and credit with the people; Mandroclidas was esteemed the ablest Greek of his time to manage an affair and put it in train, and, joined with skill and cunning, had a great degree of boldness. Agesilaus was the king's uncle, by the mother's side; an eloquent man, but covetous and voluptuous, who was not moved by considerations of public good, but rather seemed to be persuaded to it by his son Hippomedon, whose courage and signal actions in war had gained him a high esteem and great influence among the young men of Sparta, though indeed the true motive was, that he had many debts, and hoped by this means to be freed from them.

As soon as Agis had prevailed with his uncle, he endeavored by his mediation to gain his mother also, who had many friends and followers, and a number of persons in her debt in the city, and took a considerable part in public affairs. At the first proposal, she was very averse, and strongly advised her son not to engage in so difficult and so unprofitable an enterprise. But Agesilaus endeavored to possess her, that the thing was not so difficult as she imagined, and that it might, in all likelihood, redound to the advantage of her family; while the king, her son, besought her not for money's sake to decline assisting his hopes of glory. He told her, he could not pretend to equal other kings in riches, the very followers and menials of the satraps and stewards of Seleucus or Ptolemy abounding more in wealth than all the Spartan kings put together; but if by contempt of wealth and pleasure, by simplicity and magnanimity, he could surpass their luxury and abundance, if he could restore their former equality to the Spartans, then he should be a great king indeed. In conclusion, the mother and the grandmother also were so taken, so carried away with the inspiration, as it were, of the young man's noble and generous ambition, that they not only consented, but were ready on all occasions to spur him on to a perseverance, and not only sent to speak on his behalf with the men with whom they had an interest, but addressed the other women also, knowing well that the Lacedæmonian wives had always a great power with their husbands, who used to impart to them their state affairs with greater freedom than the women would communicate with the men in the private business of their families. Which was indeed one of the greatest obstacles to this design; for the money of Sparta being most of it in the women's hands, it was their interest to oppose it, not only as depriving them of those superfluous trifles, in which through want of better knowledge and experience, they placed their chief felicity, but also because they knew their riches were the main support of their power and credit.

Those, therefore, who were of this faction, had recourse to Leonidas, representing to him, how it was his part, as the elder and more experienced, to put a stop to the ill-advised projects of a rash young man. Leonidas, though of himself sufficiently inclined to oppose Agis, durst not openly, for fear of the people, who were manifestly desirous of this change; but underhand he did all he could to discredit and thwart the project, and to prejudice the chief magistrates against him, and on all occasions craftily insinuated, that it was as the price of letting him usurp arbitrary power, that Agis thus proposed to divide the property of the rich among the poor, and that the object of these measures for cancelling debts and dividing the lands, was not to furnish Sparta with citizens, but purchase him a tyrant's body-guard.

Agis, nevertheless, little regarding these rumors, procured Lysander's election as ephor; and then took the first occasion of proposing through him his Rhetra to the council, the chief articles of which were these: That every one should be free from their debts; all the lands to be divided into equal portions, those that lay betwixt the watercourse near Pellene and Mount Taygetus, and as far as the cities of Malea and Sellasia, into four thousand five hundred lots, the remainder into fifteen thousand; these last to be shared out among those of the country people [4] who were fit for service as heavy-armed soldiers, the first among the natural born Spartans; and their number also should be supplied from any among the country people or strangers who had received the proper breeding of freemen, and were of vigorous body and of age for military service. All these were to be divided into fifteen companies, some of four hundred, and some of two,[5] with a diet and discipline agreeable to the laws of Lycurgus.

This decree being proposed in the council of

[4] The periœci, or subject Laconians.

[5] In the phrase *fifteen companies, some of four hundred, some of two*, the word *companies* is properly *messes*, or *dining-companies, phiditia*, which, as described in the life of Lycurgus, consisted each of fifteen. There would seem to be some corruption in the text. A fragment of Diodorus gives a verse of an oracular warning to Lycurgus, *Love of wealth, and that only, shall be the ruin of Sparta;* which is probably referred to in the passage below about "*the oracles in old time.*" Cassandra, the daughter of Priam, was worshipped in Laconia under the name of Alexandra; there were temples dedicated to her in Amyclæ and Leuctra. Cicero, in his dialogues on Divination (*I.*, 43), mentions the custom observed by the Lacedæmonian magistrates *of sleeping, for the object of having dreams, in the temple of Pasiphae, in a country spot, near the city.* But Thalamæ, named in this passage as the seat of the temple, is at some distance, on the coast, near the Messenian frontier; and here, on the way from Œtylus to Thalamæ, Pausanias says, stood a temple and an oracle of Ino or Paphia, pretty certainly a misreading for Pasiphae, in which inquiry was made after the manner described by Cicero. "People consult it," he says, "by sleeping; and of what they desire to know, the goddess sends them dreams." An Ephor has a dream in the temple of Pasiphae, in the Life of Cleomenes, below.

Elders, met there with opposition; so that Lysander
immediately convoked the great assembly of the
people, to whom he, Mandroclidas, and Agesilaus
made orations, exhorting them that they would not
suffer the majesty of Sparta to remain abandoned
to contempt, to gratify a few rich men, who lorded
it over them; but that they should call to mind
the oracles in old time which had forewarned them
to beware of the love of money, as the great danger
and probable ruin of Sparta, and, moreover,
those recently brought from the temple of Pasiphae.
This was a famous temple and oracle at Thalamæ;
and this Pasiphae, some say, was one of the daughters
of Atlas, who had by Jupiter a son called
Ammon; others are of opinion it was Cassandra,
the daughter of king Priam, who, dying in this
place, was called Pasiphae, as the *revealer* of oracles
to all men.[6] Phylarchus says, that this was Daphne,
the daughter of Amyclas, who, flying from Apollo,
was transformed into a laurel and honored by that
god with the gift of prophecy. But be it as it will,
it is certain the people were made to apprehend,
that this oracle had commanded them to return to
their former state of equality settled by Lycurgus.
As soon as these had done speaking, Agis stood
up, and after a few words, told them he would
make the best contribution in his power to the new
legislation, which was proposed for their advantage.
In the first place, he would divide among them all
his patrimony, which was of large extent in tillage
and pasture; he would also give six hundred talents
in ready money, and his mother, grandmother, and
his other friends and relations, who were the richest

[6] Pasiphae, who *pasi phaei; phaein,* to show or reveal, *pasi,* to all.

of the Lacedæmonians, were ready to follow his example.

The people were transported with admiration of the young man's generosity, and with joy, that after three hundred years' interval, at last there had appeared a king worthy of Sparta. But, on the other side, Leonidas was now more than ever averse, being sensible that he and his friends would be obliged to contribute with their riches, and yet all the honor and obligation would redound to Agis. He asked him then before them all, whether Lycurgus were not in his opinion a wise man, and a lover of his country. Agis answering he was, "And when did Lycurgus," replied Leonidas, "cancel debts, or admit strangers to citizenship,—he who thought the commonwealth not secure unless from time to time the city was cleared of all strangers?"[7] To this Agis replied, "It is no wonder that Leonidas, who was brought up and married abroad, and has children by a wife taken out of a Persian court, should know little of Lycurgus or his laws. Lycurgus took away both debts and loans, by taking away money; and objected indeed to the presence of men who were foreign to the manners and customs of the country, not in any case from an ill-will to their persons, but lest the example of their lives and conduct should infect the city with the love of riches, and of delicate and luxurious habits. For it is well known that he himself gladly kept Terpander, Thales, and Pherecydes, though they were strangers, because he perceived they were in their poems and in their philosophy of the same mind with him. And you that are wont to praise

---

[7] By what were called the *xenelasiai,* or occasional orders for all foreigners to quit Sparta.

AGIS

Ecprepes, who, being ephor, cut with his hatchet two of the nine strings from the instrument of Phrynis, the musician, and to commend those who afterwards imitated him, in cutting the strings of Timotheus's harp, with what face can you blame us, for designing to cut off superfluity and luxury and display from the commonwealth? Do you think those men were so concerned only about a lute-string, or intended any thing else than to check in music that same excess and extravagance which rule in our present lives and manners, and have disturbed and destroyed all the harmony and order of our city?"

From this time forward, as the common people followed Agis, so the rich men adhered to Leonidas. They besought him not to forsake their cause; and with persuasions and entreaties so far prevailed with the council of Elders, whose power consisted in preparing all laws before they were proposed to the people, that the designed Rhetra was rejected, though but by only one vote. Whereupon Lysander, who was still ephor, resolving to be revenged on Leonidas, drew up an information against him, grounded on two old laws: the one forbids any of the blood of Hercules to raise up children by a foreign woman, and the other makes it capital for a Lacedæmonian to leave his country to settle among foreigners. Whilst he set others on to manage this accusation, he with his colleagues went *to observe the sign,* which was a custom they had, and performed in this manner. Every ninth year, the ephors, choosing a starlight night, when there is neither cloud nor moon, sit down together in quiet and silence, and watch the sky. And if they chance to see the shooting of a star, they presently pronounce their king guilty of some offence against the gods, and thereupon he is immediately suspended from all exercise of regal power, till he is relieved by an oracle from Delphi or Olympia.

Lysander, therefore, assured the people, he had seen a star shoot, and at the same time Leonidas was cited to answer for himself. Witnesses were produced to testify he had married an Asian woman, bestowed on him by one of king Seleucus's lieutenants; that he had two children by her, but she so disliked and hated him, that, against his wishes, flying from her, he was in a manner forced to return to Sparta, where, his predecessor dying without issue, he took upon him the government. Lysander, not content with this, persuaded also Cleombrotus to lay claim to the kingdom. He was of the royal family, and son-in-law to Leonidas; who, fearing now the event of this process, fled as a suppliant to the temple of Minerva of the Brazen House, together with his daughter, the wife of Cleombrotus; for she in this occasion resolved to leave her husband, and to follow her father. Leonidas being again cited, and not appearing, they pronounced a sentence of deposition against him, and made Cleombrotus king in his place.

Soon after this revolution, Lysander, his year expiring, went out of his office, and new ephors were chosen, who gave Leonidas assurance of safety, and cited Lysander and Mandroclidas to answer for having, contrary to law, cancelled debts, and designed a new division of lands. They, seeing themselves in danger, had recourse to the two kings, and represented to them, how necessary it was for their interest and safety to act with united authority, and bid defiance to the ephors. For, indeed, the power of the ephors, they said, was only grounded on the dissensions of the kings, it being their privilege, when the kings differed in opinion, to add their suffrage to whichever they judged to have given the best advice; but when the two kings were unanimous, none ought or durst resist their authority, the magistrate, whose office it was to stand as umpire when they were at variance, had no call to interfere when they were of one mind. Agis and Cleombrotus, thus persuaded, went together with their friends into the market-place, where, removing the ephors from their seats, they placed others in their room, of whom Agesilaus was one; proceeding then to arm a company of young men, and releasing many out of prison; so that those of the contrary faction began to be in great fear of their lives; but there was no blood spilt. On the contrary, Agis, having notice that Agesilaus had ordered a company of soldiers to lie in wait for Leonidas, to kill him as he fled to Tegea, immediately sent some of his followers to defend him, and to convey him safely into that city.

Thus far all things proceeded prosperously, none daring to oppose; but through the sordid weakness of one man, these promising beginnings were blasted, and a most noble and truly Spartan purpose overthrown and ruined, by the love of money. Agesilaus, as we said, was much in debt, though in possession of one of the largest and best estates in land; and while he gladly joined in their design to be quit of his debts, he was not at all willing to part with his land. Therefore he persuaded Agis, that if both these things should be put in execution at the same time, so great and so sudden an alteration might cause some dangerous commotion; but if debts were in the first place cancelled, the rich men would afterwards more easily be prevailed with to part with their land. Lysander, also, was of the same opinion, being deceived in like manner by the craft of Agesilaus; so that all men were presently commanded to bring in their bonds, or deeds of obligation, by the Lacedæmonians called *Claria,* into the market-place, where being laid together in a heap, they set fire to them. The wealthy, money-lending people, one may easily imagine, beheld it with a heavy heart; but Agesilaus told them scoffingly, his eyes had never seen so bright and so pure a flame.

And now the people pressed earnestly for an immediate division of lands; the kings also had ordered it should be done; but Agesilaus, sometimes pretending one difficulty, and sometimes another, delayed the execution, till an occasion happened to call Agis to the wars. The Achæans, in virtue of a defensive treaty of alliance, sent to demand succors, as they expected every day that the Ætolians would attempt to enter Peloponnesus, from the territory of Megara. They had sent Aratus, their general, to collect forces to hinder this incursion. Aratus wrote to the ephors, who immediately gave order that Agis should hasten to their assistance with the Lacedæmonian auxiliaries. Agis was extremely pleased to see the zeal and bravery of those who went with him upon this expedition. They were for the most part young men, and poor; and being just released from their debts and set at liberty, and hoping on their return to receive each man his lot of land, they followed their king with wonderful alacrity. The cities through which they passed, were in admiration to see how they marched from one end of Peloponnesus to the other, without the least disorder, and, in a manner, without being heard. It gave the Greeks occasion to discourse with one another, how great might be the temperance and modesty of a Laconian army in old time, under their famous captains Agesilaus, Lysander, or Leonidas, since they saw such discipline and exact obedience under a leader who perhaps was the youngest man in all the army. They saw also how he was himself content to fare hardly, ready to undergo any labors, and not to be distinguished by pomp or richness of habit or arms from the meanest of his soldiers; and to people in general it was an object of regard and admiration. But rich men viewed the innovation with dislike and alarm, lest haply the example might spread, and work changes to their prejudice in their own countries as well.

Agis joined Aratus near the city of Corinth, where it was still a matter of debate whether or no it were expedient to give the enemy battle. Agis, on this occasion, showed great forwardness and resolution, yet without temerity or presumption. He declared it was his opinion they ought to fight, thereby to hinder the enemy from passing the gates of Peloponnesus, but, nevertheless, he would submit to the judgment of Aratus, not only as the elder and more experienced captain, but as he was general of the Achæans, whose forces he would not pretend to command, but was only come thither to assist them. I am not ignorant that Baton of Sinope, relates it in another manner; he says, Aratus would have fought, and that Agis was against it; but it is certain he was mistaken, not having read what Aratus himself wrote in his own justification, that knowing the people had wellnigh got in their harvest, he thought it much better to let the enemy pass, than put all to the hazard of a battle. And therefore, giving thanks to the confederates for their readiness, he dismissed them. And Agis, not without having gained a great deal of honor, returned to Sparta, where he found the people in disorder, and a new revolution imminent, owing to the ill government of Agesilaus.

For he, being now one of the ephors, and freed from the fear which formerly kept him in some restraint, forbore no kind of oppression which might bring in gain. Among other things, he exacted a thirteenth month's tax, whereas the usual cycle required at this time no such addition to the year. For these and other reasons fearing those whom he injured, and knowing how he was hated by the people, he thought it necessary to maintain a guard, which always accompanied him to the magistrate's office. And presuming now on his power, he was grown so insolent, that of the two kings, the one he openly contemned, and if he showed any respect towards Agis, would have it thought rather an effect of his near relationship, than any duty or submission to the royal authority. He gave it out also, that he was to continue ephor the ensuing year.

His enemies, therefore, alarmed by this report, lost no time in risking an attempt against him; and openly bringing back Leonidas from Tegea, reëstablished him in the kingdom, to which even the people, highly incensed for having been defrauded in the promised division of lands, willingly consented. Agesilaus himself would hardly have escaped their fury, if his son, Hippomedon, whose manly virtues made him dear to all, had not saved him out of their hands, and then privately conveyed him from the city.

During this commotion, the two kings fled, Agis to the temple of the Brazen House, and

Cleombrotus to that of Neptune. For Leonidas was more incensed against his son-in-law; and leaving Agis alone, went with his soldiers to Cleombrotus's sanctuary, and there with great passion reproached him for having, though he was his son-in-law, conspired with his enemies, usurped his throne, and forced him from his country. Cleombrotus, having little to say for himself, sat silent. His wife, Chilonis, the daughter of Leonidas, had chosen to follow her father in his sufferings; for when Cleombrotus usurped the kingdom, she forsook him, and wholly devoted herself to comfort her father in his affliction; whilst he still remained in Sparta, she remained also, as a suppliant, with him, and when he fled, she fled with him, bewailing his misfortune, and extremely displeased with Cleombrotus. But now, upon this turn of fortune, she changed in like manner, and was seen sitting now, as a suppliant with her husband, embracing him with her arms, and having her two little children beside her. All men were full of wonder at the piety and tender affection of the young woman, who, pointing to her robes and her hair, both alike neglected and unattended to, said to Leonidas, "I am not brought, my father, to this condition you see me in, on account of the present misfortunes of Cleombrotus; my mourning habit is long since familiar to me. It was put on to condole with you in your banishment; and now you are restored to your country, and to your kingdom, must I still remain in grief and misery? Or would you have me attired in my royal ornaments, that I may rejoice with you, when you have killed, within my arms, the man to whom you gave me for a wife? Either Cleombrotus must appease you by mine and my children's tears, or he must suffer a punishment greater than you propose for his faults, and shall see me, whom he loves so well, die before him. To what end should I live, or how shall I appear among the Spartan women, when it shall so manifestly be seen, that I have not been able to move to compassion either a husband or a father? I was born, it seems, to participate in the ill fortune and in the disgrace, both as a wife and a daughter, of those nearest and dearest to me. As for Cleombrotus, I sufficiently surrendered any honorable plea on his behalf, when I forsook him to follow you; but you yourself offer the fairest excuse for his proceedings, by showing to the world that for the sake of a kingdom, it is just to kill a son-in-law, and be regardless of a daughter." Chilonis, having ended this lamentation, rested her face on her husband's head, and looked round with her weeping and wo-begone eyes upon those who stood before her.

Leonidas, touched with compassion, withdrew a while to advise with his friends; then returning, bade Cleombrotus leave the sanctuary and go into banishment; Chilonis, he said, ought to stay with him, it not being just she should forsake a father whose affection had granted to her intercession the life of her husband. But all he could say would not prevail. She rose up immediately, and taking one of her children in her arms, gave the other to her husband; and making her reverence to the altar of the goddess,[8] went out and followed him. So that, in a word, if Cleombrotus were not

---

[8] It should be "the god." The sanctuary was stated above to be that of Neptune, very likely the famous temple at Tænarus. It may be Plutarch's own forgetfulness.

utterly blinded by ambition he must surely choose to be banished with so excellent a woman rather than without her to possess a kingdom.

Cleombrotus thus removed, Leonidas proceeded also to displace the ephors, and to choose others in their room; then he began to consider how he might entrap Agis. At first, he endeavored by fair means to persuade him to leave the sanctuary, and partake with him in the kingdom. The people, he said, would easily pardon the errors of a young man, ambitious of glory, and deceived by the craft of Agesilaus. But finding Agis was suspicious, and not to be prevailed with to quit his sanctuary, he gave up that design; yet what could not then be effected by the dissimulation of an enemy, was soon after brought to pass by the treachery of friends.

Amphares, Damochares, and Arcesilaus often visited Agis, and he was so confident of their fidelity that after a while he was prevailed with to accompany them to the baths, which were not far distant, they constantly returning to see him safe again in the temple. They were all three his familiars; and Amphares had borrowed a great deal of plate and rich household stuff from Agesistrata, and hoped if he could destroy her and the whole family, he might peaceably enjoy those goods. And he, it is said, was the readiest of all to serve the purposes of Leonidas, and being one of the ephors, did all he could to incense the rest of his colleagues against Agis. These men, therefore, finding that Agis would not quit his sanctuary, but on occasion would venture from it to go to the bath, resolved to seize him on the opportunity thus given them. And one day as he was returning, they met and saluted him as formerly, conversing pleasantly by the way, and jesting, as youthful friends might, till coming to the turning of a street which led to the prison, Amphares, by virtue of his office, laid his hand on Agis, and told him, "You must go with me, Agis, before the other ephors, to answer for your misdemeanors." At the same time, Damochares, who was a tall, strong man, drew his cloak tight round his neck, and dragged him after by it, whilst the others went behind to thrust him on. So that none of Agis's friends being near to assist him, nor any one by, they easily got him into the prison, where Leonidas was already arrived, with a company of soldiers, who strongly guarded all the avenues; the ephors also came in, with as many of the Elders as they knew to be true to their party, being desirous to proceed with some resemblance of justice. And thus they bade him give an account of his actions. To which Agis, smiling at their dissimulation, answered not a word. Amphares told him, it was more seasonable to weep, for now the time was come in which he should be punished for his presumption. Another of the ephors, as though he would be more favorable, and offering as it were an excuse, asked him whether he was not forced to what he did by Agesilaus and Lysander. But Agis answered, he had not been constrained by any man, nor had any other intent in what he did, but only to follow the example of Lycurgus, and to govern conformably to his laws. The same ephor asked him, whether now at least he did not repent his rashness. To which the young man answered, that though he were to suffer the extremest penalty for it, yet he could never repent of so just and so glorious a design. Upon this they passed sentence of death on him, and bade the officers carry him to the Dechas,[9] as it is called, a place in the prison where they strangle malefactors. And when the officers would not venture to lay hands on him, and the very mercenary soldiers declined it, believing it an illegal and a wicked act to lay violent hands on a king, Damochares, threatening and reviling them for it, himself thrust him into the room.

For by this time the news of his being seized had reached many parts of the city, and there was a concourse of people with lights and torches about the prison gates, and in the midst of them the mother and the grandmother of Agis, crying out with a loud voice, that their king ought to appear and to be heard and judged by the people. But this clamor, instead of preventing, hastened his death; his enemies fearing, if the tumult should increase, he might be rescued during the night out of their hands.

Agis, being now at the point to die, perceived one of the officers bitterly bewailing his misfortune; "Weep not, friend," said he, "for me, who die innocent, by the lawless act of wicked men. My condition is much better than theirs." As soon as he had spoken these words, not showing the least sign of fear, he offered his neck to the noose.

Immediately after he was dead, Amphares went out of the prison gate, where he found Agesistrata, who, believing him still the same friend as before, threw herself at his feet. He gently raised her up,

---

[9] Of this execution-chamber, the *Dechas, as it is called,* or *Dekhas,* there appears to be no mention found elsewhere. The Ceadas, or Keadas, the pit in the rocks, into which the bodies of malefactors were thrown, out of which Aristomenes, the Messenian hero, made his escape, is well known, but cannot very well have any thing to do with it.

and assured her, she need not fear any further violence or danger of death for her son, and that if she pleased, she might go in and see him. She begged her mother might also have the favor to be admitted, and he replied, nobody should hinder it. When they were entered, he commanded the gate should again be locked, and Archidamia, the grandmother, to be first introduced; she was now grown very old, and had lived all her days in the highest repute among her fellows. As soon as Amphares thought she was despatched, he told Agesistrata she might now go in if she pleased. She entered, and beholding her son's body stretched on the ground, and her mother hanging by the neck, the first thing she did was, with her own hands, to assist the officers in taking down the body; then covering it decently, she laid it out by her son's, whom then embracing, and kissing his cheeks, "O my son," said she, "it was thy too great mercy and goodness which brought thee and us to ruin." Amphares, who stood watching behind the door, on hearing this, broke in, and said angrily to her, "Since you approve so well of your son's actions, it is fit you should partake in his reward." She, rising up to offer herself to the noose, said only, "I pray that it may redound to the good of Sparta."

And now the three bodies being exposed to view, and the fact divulged, no fear was strong enough to hinder the people from expressing their abhorrence of what was done, and their detestation of Leonidas and Amphares, the contrivers of it. So wicked and barbarous an act had never been committed in Sparta, since first the Dorians inhabited Peloponnesus; the very enemies in war, they said, were always cautious of spilling the blood of a

Lacedæmonian king, insomuch that in any combat they would decline, and endeavor to avoid them, from feelings of respect and reverence for their station. And certainly we see that in the many battles fought betwixt the Lacedæmonians and the other Greeks, up to the time of Philip of Macedon, not one of their kings was ever killed, except Cleombrotus, by a javelin-wound, at the battle of Leuctra. I am not ignorant that the Messenians affirm, Theopompus was also slain by their Aristomenes; but the Lacedæmonians deny it, and say he was only wounded.

Be it as it will, it is certain at least that Agis was the first king put to death in Lacedæmon by the ephors, for having undertaken a design noble in itself and worthy of his country, at a time of life when men's errors usually meet with an easy pardon. And if errors he did commit, his enemies certainly had less reason to blame him, than had his friends for that gentle and compassionate temper which made him save the life of Leonidas, and believe in other men's professions.

CLEOMENES[1]

TRANSLATED BY THE REV. MR. CREECH, FELLOW OF ALL-SOULS COLLEGE, OXFORD. THE TRANSLATOR OF LUCRETIUS, WHOSE NAME HAS APPEARED BEFORE IN VOLS. I. AND II. AS OF WADHAM COLLEGE. HE BECAME FELLOW OF ALL-SOULS AFTERWARDS

THUS fell Agis. His brother Archidamus was too quick for Leonidas, and saved himself by a timely retreat. But his wife, then mother of a young child, he forced from her own house, and compelled Agiatis, for that was her name, to marry his son Cleomenes, though at that time too young for a wife, because he was unwilling that any one else should have her, being heiress to her father Gylippus's great estate; in person the most youthful and beautiful woman in all Greece, and well-conducted in her habits of life. And therefore, they say, she did all she could that she might not be compelled to this new marriage. But being thus united to Cleomenes, she indeed hated Leonidas, but to the youth showed herself a kind and obliging wife. He, as soon as they came together, began to love her very much, and the constant kindness that she still retained for the memory of Agis, wrought somewhat of the like feeling in the young man for him, so that he would often inquire of

---

[1] King of Sparta, son of Leonidas II., reigned 236-222 B.C. He was endowed with a noble mind, strengthened and purified by philosophy, and possessed great energy of purpose. He was at length defeated at the battle of Sellasia (222), fled to Egypt and killed himself 210 B.C.—DR. WILLIAM SMITH.

her concerning what had passed, and attentively listen to the story of Agis's purpose and design. Now Cleomenes had a generous and great soul; he was as temperate and moderate in his pleasures as Agis, but not so scrupulous, circumspect, and gentle. There was something of heat and passion always goading him on, and an impetuosity and violence in his eagerness to pursue any thing which he thought good and just. To have men obey him of their own freewill, he conceived to be the best discipline; but, likewise, to subdue resistance, and force them to the better course, was, in his opinion, commendable and brave.

This disposition made him dislike the management of the city. The citizens lay dissolved in supine idleness and pleasures; the king let every thing take its own way, thankful if nobody gave him any disturbance, nor called him away from the enjoyment of his wealth and luxury. The public interest was neglected, and each man intent upon his private gain. It was dangerous, now Agis was killed, so much as to name such a thing as the exercising and training of their youth; and to speak of the ancient temperance, endurance, and equality, was a sort of treason against the state. It is said also that Cleomenes, whilst a boy, studied philosophy under Sphærus, the Borysthenite,[2] who

[2] *Sphærus the Borysthenite* came from the distant Greek colony of Borysthenis, or Olbia, on the north coast of the Black Sea, having the former name from the neighboring and larger river, the Dnieper, the ancient Borysthenes, but more correctly called Olbia (*Wealthy*), and actually situated on the Hypanis, the present Boug, not far from the Russian arsenal of Nicholaieff. Olbia was visited by Herodotus, and still flourished in the days of Plutarch. It seems to have been a sort of Greek Odessa. *Zeno the*

crossed over to Sparta, and spent some time and trouble in instructing the youth. Sphærus was one of the first of Zeno the Citiean's scholars, and it is likely enough that he admired the manly temper of Cleomenes, and inflamed his generous ambition. The ancient Leonidas, as story tells, being asked what manner of poet he thought Tyrtæus, replied, "Good to whet young men's courage;" for being filled with a divine fury by his poems, they rushed into any danger. And so the stoic philosophy is a dangerous incentive to strong and fiery dispositions, but where it combines with a grave and gentle temper, is most successful in leading it to its proper good.

Upon the death of his father Leonidas, he succeeded, and observing the citizens of all sorts to be debauched, the rich neglecting the public good, and intent on their private gain and pleasure, and the poor distressed in their own homes, and therefore without either spirit for war or ambition to be trained up as Spartans, that he had only the name of king, and the ephors all the power, he was resolved to change the present posture of affairs. He had a friend whose name was Xenares, his lover, (such an affection the Spartans express by the term, being *inspired,* or *imbreathed* with); him he sounded, and of him he would commonly inquire what manner of king Agis was, by what means and by what assistance he began and pursued his designs. Xenares, at first, willingly complied with

Citiean, of Citium in Cyprus, is Zeno the founder of the Stoic philosophy. Sphærus was a philosopher of considerable reputation; in the list of his works given by Diogenes Laertius, there is a book On the Spartan Polity, and another On Lycurgus and Socrates.

his request, and told him the whole story, with all the particular circumstances of the actions. But when he observed Cleomenes to be extremely affected at the relation, and more than ordinarily taken with Agis's new model of the government, and begging a repetition of the story, he at first severely chid him, told him he was frantic, and at last left off all sort of familiarity and intercourse with him, yet he never told any man the cause of their disagreement, but would only say, Cleomenes knew very well. Cleomenes, finding Xenares averse to his designs, and thinking all others to be of the same disposition, consulted with none, but contrived the whole business by himself. And considering that it would be easier to bring about an alteration when the city was at war, than when in peace, he engaged the commonwealth in a quarrel with the Achæans, who had given them fair occasions to complain. For Aratus, a man of the greatest power amongst all the Achæans, designed from the very beginning to bring all the Peloponnesians into one common body. And to effect this was the one object of all his many commanderships and his long political course; as he thought this the only means to make them a match for their foreign enemies. Pretty nearly all the rest agreed to his proposals, only the Lacedæmonians, the Eleans, and as many of the Arcadians as inclined to the Spartan interest, remained unpersuaded. And so as soon as Leonidas was dead, he began to attack the Arcadians, and wasted those especially that bordered on Achæa; by this means designing to try the inclinations of the Spartans, and despising Cleomenes as a youth, and of no experience in affairs of state or war. Upon this, the ephors sent Cleomenes to surprise the Athenæum, near Belbina, which is a pass commanding an entrance into Laconia and was then the subject of litigation with the Megalopolitans. Cleomenes possessed himself of the place, and fortified it, at which action Aratus showed no public resentment, but marched by night to surprise Tegea and Orchomenus. The design failed, for those that were to betray the cities into his hands, turned afraid; so Aratus retreated, imagining that his design had been undiscovered. But Cleomenes wrote a sarcastic letter to him, and desired to know, as from a friend, whither he intended to march at night; and Aratus answering, that having heard of his design to fortify Belbina, he meant to march thither to oppose him, Cleomenes rejoined, that he did not dispute it, but begged to be informed, if he might be allowed to ask the question, why he carried those torches and ladders with him.

Aratus laughing at the jest, and asking what manner of youth this was, Damocrates, a Spartan exile, replied, "If you have any designs upon the Lacedæmonians, begin before this young eagle's talons are grown." Presently after this, Cleomenes, encamping in Arcadia with a few horse and three hundred foot, received orders from the ephors, who feared to engage in the war, commanding him home; but when upon his retreat Aratus took Caphyæ, they commissioned him again. In this expedition he took Methydrium, and overran the country of the Argives; and the Achæans, to oppose him, came out with an army of twenty thousand foot and one thousand horse, under the command of Aristomachus. Cleomenes faced them at Pallantium, and offered battle, but Aratus being cowed by his bravery, would not suffer the general to engage, but retreated, amidst the reproaches of the Achæans, and the derision and scorn of the Spartans, who were not above five thousand. Cleomenes, encouraged by this success, began to speak boldly among the citizens, and reminding them of a sentence of one of their ancient kings, said, it was in vain now that the Spartans asked not how many their enemies were, but where they were.[3] After this, marching to the assistance of the Eleans, whom the Achæans were attacking, falling upon the enemy in their retreat near the Lycæum, he put their whole army to flight, taking a great number of captives, and leaving many dead upon the place; so that it was commonly reported amongst the Greeks that Aratus was slain. But Aratus, making the best advantage of the opportunity, immediately after the defeat marched to Mantinea, and before anybody suspected it, took the city, and put a garrison into it. Upon this, the Lacedæmonians being quite discouraged, and opposing Cleomenes's designs of carrying on the war, he now exerted himself to have Archidamus, the brother of Agis, sent for from Messene, as he, of the other family, had a right to the kingdom; and besides, Cleomenes thought that the power of the ephors would be reduced, when the kingly state was thus filled up, and raised to its proper position. But those that were concerned in the murder of Agis, perceiving the design, and fearing that upon Archidamus's return they should be called to an account, received him on his coming privately into town, and joined in bringing him home, and presently after murdered him. Whether Cleomenes was against it, as Phylarchus thinks, or whether

[3] Agis, their king in old times, had said, the Spartans were not used to ask how many their enemies were, but where they were. Cleomenes says that now it is no use asking even where they are.

he was persuaded by his friends, or let him fall into their hands, is uncertain; however, they were most blamed, as having forced his consent.

He, still resolving to new model the state, bribed the ephors to send him out to war; and won the affections of many others by means of his mother Cratesiclea, who spared no cost and was very zealous to promote her son's ambition; and though of herself she had no inclination to marry, yet for his sake, she accepted, as her husband, one of the chiefest citizens for wealth and power. Cleomenes, marching forth with the army now under his command, took Leuctra, a place belonging to Megalopolis; and the Achæans quickly coming up to resist him with a good body of men commanded by Aratus, in a battle under the very walls of the city some part of his army was routed. But whereas Aratus had commanded the Achæans not to pass a deep watercourse, and thus put a stop to the pursuit, Lydiadas, the Megalopolitan, fretting at the orders, and encouraging the horse which he led, and following the routed enemy, got into a place full of vines, hedges, and ditches; and being forced to break his ranks, began to retire in disorder. Cleomenes, observing the advantage, commanded the Tarentines and Cretans to engage him, by whom, after a brave defence, he was routed and slain. The Lacedæmonians, thus encouraged, fell with a great shout upon the Achæans, and routed their whole army. Of the slain, who were very many, the rest Cleomenes delivered up, when the enemy petitioned for them; but the body of Lydiadas he commanded to be brought to him; and then putting on it a purple robe, and a crown upon its head, sent a convoy with it to the gates of Megalopolis. This is that Lydiadas who resigned his power as tyrant, restored liberty to the citizens, and joined the city to the Achæan interest.

Cleomenes, being very much elated by this success, and persuaded that if matters were wholly at his disposal, he should soon be too hard for the Achæans, persuaded Megistonus, his mother's husband, that it was expedient for the state to shake off the power of the ephors, and to put all their wealth into one common stock for the whole body; thus Sparta, being restored to its old equality, might aspire again to the command of all Greece. Megistonus liked the design, and engaged two or three more of his friends. About that time, one of the ephors, sleeping in Pasiphae's temple, dreamed a very surprising dream; for he thought he saw the four chairs removed out of the place where the ephors used to sit and do the business of their office, and one only set there; and whilst he wondered, he heard a voice out of the temple, saying, " This is best for Sparta." The person telling Cleomenes this dream, he was a little troubled at first, fearing that he used this as a trick to sift him, upon some suspicion of his design, but when he was satisfied that the relater spoke truth, he took heart again. And carrying with him those whom he thought would be most against his project, he took Heræa and Alsæa,[4] two towns in league with the Achæans, furnished Orchomenus with provisions, encamped before Mantinea, and with long marches up and down so harassed the Lacedæmonians, that many of them at their own request were left behind in Arcadia, while he with the mercenaries went on toward Sparta, and by the way communicated his design to those whom he thought fittest for his

[4] Alea or Asea more probably.

purpose, and marched slowly, that he might catch the ephors at supper.

When he was come near the city, he sent Euryclidas to the public table, where the ephors supped, under pretence of carrying some message from him from the army; Therycion, Phœbis, and two of those who had been bred up with Cleomenes, whom they call *mothaces*,[5] followed with a few soldiers; and whilst Euryclidas was delivering his message to the ephors, they ran upon them with their drawn swords, and slew them. The first of them, Agylæus, on receiving the blow, fell and lay as dead; but in a little time quietly raising himself, and drawing himself out of the room, he crept, without being discovered, into a little building, which was dedicated to Fear, and which always used to be shut, but then by chance was open, and being got in, he shut the door, and lay close. The other four were killed, and above ten more that came to their assistance; to those that were quiet they did no harm, stopped none that fled from the city, and spared Agylæus, when he came out of the temple the next day.

The Lacedæmonians have not only sacred places dedicated to Fear, but also to Death, Laughter, and the like Passions. Now they worship Fear, not as they do supernatural powers which they dread, esteeming it hurtful, but thinking their polity is chiefly kept up by fear. And therefore, the

---

[5] The *Mothăces* or *Mothōnes* were young helots, who were admitted, as the associates of some particular young Spartan, to the Spartan training, were brought up with him, and were free, but were not admitted to the full rights of citizenship. There is a statement, but not a very trustworthy one, that Lysander, Callicratidas, and Gylippus all sprang from this class.

ephors, Aristotle is my author, when they entered upon their government, made proclamation to the people, that they should shave their moustaches, and be obedient to the laws, that the laws might not be hard upon them, making, I suppose, this trivial injunction, to accustom their youth to obedience even in the smallest matters. And the ancients, I think, did not imagine bravery to be plain fearlessness, but a cautious fear of blame and disgrace. For those that show most timidity towards the laws, are most bold against their enemies; and those are least afraid of any danger who are most afraid of a just reproach. Therefore it was well said that

> A reverence still attends on fear;[6]

[6] *A reverence still attends on fear.* This is the end of a fragment quoted in Plato's Euthyphro, and said by the scholiast on the passage there to be taken from the Cypria or Cyprian Epics, attributed to the poet Stasinus, at one time thought to be Homer's. The Cypria contained the whole tale of Troy antecedent to the Iliad, as the Little Iliad, the Æthiopid, the Sack of Ilium, and other epic pieces, did the sequel. The two lines which Socrates uses to Euthyphro in the Dialogue are: " But Zeus who did it, and was the sower of it all, you are not willing to name; for *where fear is, there also is reverence,*" or shame. *Feared shall you be, dear father, and revered,* are the words with which Helen when she comes to the walls of the city in the third Iliad returns Priam's salutation and inquiry as to the names of the Greek warriors, whom they see: " I approach you with shame, dear father-in-law, and with trembling. Would that an evil death had met me on the way when I came hither with your son, leaving my marriage chamber and friends, my little daughter, and pleasant companions! . . . But this of whom you ask me is the son of Atreus, Agamemnon with large dominions, brother-in-law, if indeed I may say so, of me the dishonored," (*Iliad, III.,* 172). *In silence fear-*

and by Homer,

> Feared you shall be, dear father, and revered;

and again,

> In silence fearing those that bore the sway;

for the generality of men are most ready to reverence those whom they fear. And, therefore, the Lacedæmonians placed the temple of Fear by the Syssitium of the ephors, having raised that magistracy to almost royal authority.

The next day, Cleomenes proscribed eighty of the citizens, whom he thought necessary to banish, and removed all the seats of the ephors, except one, in which he himself designed to sit and give audience; and calling the citizens together, he made an apology for his proceedings, saying, that by Lycurgus the council of Elders was joined to the

---

ing those that bore the sway is from the description of the steady advance of the Greek line of battle in the fourth Iliad (431). The word translated *reverence* (*aidōs*) is the same which in other places is *shame* or *modesty* (more generally the fear of doing what is disgraceful than the shame of having done it), but it is continually and perhaps most properly used for the feeling of respect for persons and fear of behaving amiss to our betters. Diomede, out of *aidōs* or respect, would not answer Agamemnon's rebuke to him. I felt *aidōs* to do so in their presence, I could not for *aidōs* refuse or contradict him, are current expressions. The distinction between courage or bravery, and a mere absence of fear or being afraid of nothing, is enforced by Aristotle. Some things every one ought to be afraid of. And hence we come, with Plato, to perceive that courage is only another form of knowledge of the truth, knowing what is truly to be feared and avoided, and what is so only in appearance. The Virtues, he said, were all Knowledges.

kings, and that that model of government had continued a long time, and no other sort of magistrates had been wanted. But afterwards, in the long war with the Messenians, when the kings, having to command the army, found no time to administer justice, they chose some of their friends, and left them to determine the suits of the citizens in their stead. These were called ephors, and at first behaved themselves as servants to the kings; but afterwards, by degrees, they appropriated the power to themselves, and erected a distinct magistracy. An evidence of the truth of this was the custom still observed by the kings, who, when the ephors send for them, refuse, upon the first and the second summons, to go, but upon the third, rise up and attend them. And Asteropus, the first that raised the ephors to that height of power, lived a great many years after their institution. So long, therefore, he continued, as they contained themselves within their own proper sphere, it had been better to bear with them than to make a disturbance. But that an upstart introduced power should so far subvert the ancient form of government as to banish some kings, murder others, without hearing their defence, and threaten those who desired to see the best and most divine constitution restored in Sparta, was not to be borne. Therefore, if it had been possible for him, without bloodshed, to free Lacedæmon from those foreign plagues, luxury, sumptuosity, debts, and usury, and from those yet more ancient evils, poverty and riches, he should have thought himself the happiest king in the world, to have succeeded, like an expert physician, in curing the diseases of his country without pain. But now, in this necessity, Lycurgus's example favored his proceedings, who being neither king nor magistrate, but a private man, and aiming at the kingdom, came armed into the market-place, so that king Charillus fled in alarm to the altar. He, being a good man, and a lover of his country, readily concurred in Lycurgus's designs, and admitted the revolution in the state. But, by his own actions, Lycurgus had nevertheless borne witness that it was difficult to change the government without force and fear, in the use of which he himself, he said, had been so moderate as to do no more than put out of the way those who opposed themselves to Sparta's happiness and safety. For the rest of the nation, he told them, the whole land was now their common property; debtors should be cleared of their debts, and examination made of those who were not citizens, that the bravest men might thus be made free Spartans, and give aid in arms to save the city, and "We," he said, "may no longer see Laconia, for want of men to defend it, wasted by the Ætolians and Illyrians."

Then he himself first, with his step father, Megistonus, and his friends, gave up all their wealth into one public stock, and all the other citizens followed the example. The land was divided, and every one that he had banished, had a share assigned him; for he promised to restore all, as soon as things were settled and in quiet. And completing the number of citizens out of the best and most promising of the country people, he raised a body of four thousand men; and instead of a spear, taught them to use a *sarissa*, with both hands, and to carry their shields by a band, and not by a handle,[7] as

---

[7] By an *okhăne*, instead of a *porpax*, the precise distinction between which it is hard to determine. Evidently the former allowed the soldier to use the left hand more freely than the latter; the

CLEOMENES

before. After this, he began to consult about the education of the youth, and the Discipline, as they call it; most of the particulars of which, Sphærus, being then at Sparta, assisted in arranging; and, in a short time, the schools of exercise and the common tables recovered their ancient decency and order, a few out of necessity, but the most voluntarily, returning to that generous and Laconic way of living. And, that the name of monarch might give them no jealousy, he made Euclidas, his brother, partner in the throne; and that was the only time that Sparta had two kings of the same family.

Then, understanding that the Achæans and Aratus imagined that this change had disturbed and shaken his affairs, and that he would not venture out of Sparta and leave the city now unsettled in the midst of so great an alteration, he thought it great and serviceable to his designs, to show his enemies the zeal and forwardness of his troops. And, therefore, making an incursion into the territories of Megalopolis, he wasted the country far and wide, and collected a considerable booty. And, at last, taking a company of actors, as they were travelling from Messene, and building a theatre in the enemy's country, and offering a prize of forty minæ in value, he sat spectator a whole day; not that he either desired or needed such amusement, but wishing to show his disregard for his enemies, and by a display of his contempt, to prove the extent of his superiority to them. For his alone, of all the Greek or royal armies, had no stage-players, no jugglers, no dancing or singing women attending it, but was free from all sorts of looseness, wantonness, and

object of the change was to have both hands hold the long Macedonian spear.

festivity; the young men being for the most part at their exercises, and the old men giving them lessons, or, at leisure times, diverting themselves with their native jests, and quick Laconian answers; the good results of which we have noticed in the life of Lycurgus.

He himself instructed all by his example; he was a living pattern of temperance before every man's eyes; and his course of living was neither more stately, nor more expensive, nor in any way more pretentious, than that of any of his people. And this was a considerable advantage to him in his designs on Greece. For men when they waited upon other kings, did not so much admire their wealth, costly furniture, and numerous attendance, as they hated their pride and state, their difficulty of access, and imperious answers to their addresses. But when they came to Cleomenes, who was both really a king, and bore that title, and saw no purple, no robes of state upon him, no couches and litters about him for his ease, and that he did not receive requests and return answers after a long delay and difficulty, through a number of messengers and doorkeepers, or by memorials, but that he rose and came forward in any dress he might happen to be wearing, to meet those that came to wait upon him, stayed, talked freely and affably with all that had business, they were extremely taken, and won to his service, and professed that he alone was the true son of Hercules. His common every day's meal was in an ordinary room, very sparing, and after the Laconic manner; and when he entertained ambassadors or strangers, two more couches were added, and a little better dinner provided by his servants, but no savoring sauces or sweetmeats; only the dishes were larger, and the wine more

CLEOMENES

plentiful.[8] For he reproved one of his friends for entertaining some strangers with nothing but barley bread and black broth, such diet as they usually had in their *phiditia;* saying, that upon such occasions, and when they entertained strangers, it was not well to be too exact Laconians. After the table was removed, a stand was brought in, with a brass vessel full of wine, two silver bowls, which held about a pint apiece, a few silver cups, of which he that pleased might drink, but wine was not urged on any of the guests. There was no music, nor was any required; for he entertained the company himself, sometimes asking questions, sometimes telling stories; and his conversation was neither too grave or disagreeably serious, nor yet in any way rude or ungraceful in its pleasantry. For he thought those ways of entrapping men by gifts and presents, which other kings use, dishonest and artificial; and it seemed to him to be the most noble method, and most suitable to a king, to win the affections of those that came near him, by personal intercourse and agreeable conversation, since between a friend and a mercenary the only distinction is, that we gain the one by one's character and conversation, the other by one's money.

The Mantineans were the first that requested his aid; and when he entered their city by night, they aided him to expel the Achæan garrison, and put

---

[8] *The wine more plentiful* is perhaps incorrect; it is more exactly, *the wine less ascetic* (literally more *humane,* more *philanthrōpon*), and he means, in quality, not in quantity. The passage, which he followed in Phylarchus the admiring historian of Cleomenes, is quoted in Athenæus, "When he had company, the wine was a little better." It is part of a long extract about Cleomenes and his habits. (*Athenæus, p.* 142.)

themselves under his protection. He restored them their polity and laws, and the same day marched to Tegea; and a little while after, fetching a compass through Arcadia, he made a descent upon Pheræ, in Achæa, intending to force Aratus to a battle, or bring him into disrepute, for refusing to engage, and suffering him to waste the country. Hyperbatas at that time was general, but Aratus had all the power amongst the Achæans. The Achæans, marching forth with their whole strength, and encamping in Dymæ, near the Hecatombæum, Cleomenes came up, and thinking it not advisable to pitch between Dymæ, a city of the enemies, and the camp of the Achæans, he boldly dared the Achæans, and forced them to a battle, and routing their phalanx, slew a great many in the fight, and took many prisoners, and thence marching to Langon, and driving out the Achæan garrison, he restored the city to the Eleans.

The affairs of the Achæans being in this unfortunate condition, Aratus, who was wont to take office every other year, refused the command, though they entreated and urged him to accept it. And this was ill done, when the storm was high, to put the power out of his own hand, and set another to the helm. Cleomenes at first proposed fair and easy conditions by his ambassadors to the Achæans, but afterward he sent others, and required the chief command to be settled upon him; in other matters offering to agree to reasonable terms, and to restore their captives and their country. The Achæans were willing to come to an agreement upon those terms, and invited Cleomenes to Lerna, where an assembly was to be held; but it happened that Cleomenes, hastily marching on, and drinking water at a wrong time, brought up a quantity of blood, and lost his voice; therefore being unable to continue his journey, he sent the chiefest of the captives to the Achæans, and, putting off the meeting for some time, retired to Lacedæmon.

This ruined the affairs of Greece, which was just beginning in some sort to recover from its disasters, and to show some capability of delivering itself from the insolence and rapacity of the Macedonians. For Aratus, (whether fearing or distrusting Cleomenes, or envying his unlooked-for success, or thinking it a disgrace for him who had commanded thirty-three years, to have a young man succeed to all his glory and his power, and be head of that government which he had been raising and settling so many years,) first endeavored to keep the Achæans from closing with Cleomenes; but when they would not hearken to him, fearing Cleomenes's daring spirit and thinking the Lacedæmonians' proposals to be very reasonable, who designed only to reduce Peloponnesus to its old model, upon this he took his last refuge in an action which was unbecoming any of the Greeks, most dishonorable to him, and most unworthy his former bravery and exploits. For he called Antigonus into Greece, and filled Peloponnesus with Macedonians, whom he himself, when a youth, having beaten their garrison out of the castle of Corinth, had driven from the same country. And there had been constant suspicion and variance between him and all the kings, and of Antigonus, in particular, he has said a thousand dishonorable things in the commentaries he has left behind him. And though he declares himself how he suffered considerable losses, and underwent great dangers, that he might free Athens from the garrison of the Macedonians, yet, afterwards, he brought the very same men armed into his own country, and his own house, even to the women's apartments.⁹ He would not endure that one of the family of Hercules, and king of Sparta, and one that had reformed the polity of his country, as it were, from a disordered harmony, and retuned it to the plain Doric measure and rule of life of Lycurgus, should be styled head of the Tritæans and Sicyonians; and whilst he fled the barley-cake and coarse coat, and, which were his chief accusations against Cleomenes, the extirpation of wealth and reformation of poverty, he basely subjected himself, together with Achæa, to the diadem and purple, to the imperious commands of the Macedonians and their satraps. That he might not seem to be under Cleomenes, he offered sacrifices, called Antigonea, in honor of Antigonus, and sang pæans himself, with a garland on his head, to the praise of a wasted, consumptive Macedonian. I write this not out of any design to disgrace Aratus, for in many things he showed himself a true lover of Greece, and a great man, but not out of pity to the weakness of human nature, which, in characters like this, so worthy and in so many ways disposed to virtue, cannot maintain its honors unblemished by some envious fault.

The Achæans meeting again in assembly at Argos, and Cleomenes having come from Tegea, there were great hopes that all differences would be composed. But Aratus, Antigonus and he having already agreed upon the chief articles of their league, fearing that Cleomenes would carry all before him, and either win or force the multitude to

---

⁹ *Even to the women's apartments* is an allusion to what is told in the Life of Aratus of the conduct of Philip, the young king of Macedon, to the wife of Aratus's son.

comply with his demands, proposed, that having three hundred hostages put into his hands, he should come alone into the town, or bring his army to the place of exercise, called the Cyllarabium,[10] outside the city, and treat there.

Cleomenes hearing this, said, that he was unjustly dealt with; for they ought to have told him so plainly at first, and not now he was come even to their doors, show their jealousy, and deny him admission. And writing a letter to the Achæans about the same subject, the greatest part of which was an accusation of Aratus, while Aratus, on the other side, spoke violently against him to the assembly, he hastily dislodged, and sent a trumpeter to denounce war against the Achæans, not to Argos, but to Ægium, as Aratus writes, that he might not give them notice enough to make provision for their defence. There had also been a movement among the Achæans themselves, and the cities were eager for revolt; the common people expecting a division of the land, and a release from their debts, and the chief men being in many places ill-disposed to Aratus, and some of them angry and indignant with him, for having brought the Macedonians into Peloponnesus. Encouraged by these misunderstandings, Cleomenes invaded Achæa, and first took Pellene by surprise, and beat out the Achæan garrison, and afterwards brought over Pheneus and Penteleum to his side. Now the Achæans, suspecting some treacherous designs at Corinth and Sicyon,

---

[10] For the gymnasium of Cyllaribis, Cylarabis, or Cylarabes, see the Life of Pyrrhus, Vol. III., p. 1. The Aspis, also, the Shield, one of the two citadels of the town, so called from a shield that was hung up there as an ensign, is mentioned in the same place.

sent their horse and mercenaries out of Argos, to have an eye upon those cities, and they themselves went to Argos, to celebrate the Nemean games. Cleomenes, advertised of this march, and hoping, as it afterward fell out, that upon an unexpected advance to the city, now busied in the solemnity of the games, and thronged with numerous spectators, he should raise a considerable terror and confusion amongst them, by night marched with his army to the walls, and taking the quarter of the town called Aspis, which lies above the theatre, well fortified, and hard to be approached, he so terrified them that none offered to resist, but they agreed to accept a garrison, to give twenty citizens for hostages, and to assist the Lacedæmonians, and that he should have the chief command.

This action considerably increased his reputation and his power; for the ancient Spartan kings, though they many ways endeavored to effect it, could never bring Argos to be permanently theirs. And Pyrrhus, the most experienced captain, though he entered the city by force, could not keep possession, but was slain himself, with a considerable part of his army. Therefore they admired the despatch and contrivance of Cleomenes; and those that before derided him, for imitating, as they said, Solon and Lycurgus, in releasing the people from their debts, and in equalizing the property of the citizens, were now fain to admit that this was the cause of the change in the Spartans. For before they were very low in the world, and so unable to secure their own, that the Ætolians, invading Laconia, brought away fifty thousand slaves; so that one of the elder Spartans is reported to have said, that they had done Laconia a kindness by unburdening it; and yet a little while after, by merely recurring once

CLEOMENES

again to their native customs, and reëntering the track of the ancient discipline, they were able to give, as though it had been under the eyes and conduct of Lycurgus himself, the most signal instances of courage and obedience, raising Sparta to her ancient place as the commanding state of Greece, and recovering all Peloponnesus.

When Argos was captured, and Cleonæ and Phlius came over, as they did at once, to Cleomenes, Aratus was at Corinth, searching after some who were reported to favor the Spartan interest. The news, being brought to him, disturbed him very much; for he perceived the city inclining to Cleomenes, and willing to be rid of the Achæans. Therefore he summoned the citizens to meet in the Council Hall, and slipping away without being observed to the gate, he mounted his horse that had been brought for him thither, and fled to Sicyon. And the Corinthians made such haste to Cleomenes at Argos, that, as Aratus says, striving who should be first there, they spoiled all their horses; he adds that Cleomenes was very angry with the Corinthians for letting him escape; and that Megistonus came from Cleomenes to him, desiring him to deliver up the castle at Corinth, which was then garrisoned by the Achæans, and offered him a considerable sum of money, and that he answered, that matters were not now in his power, but he in theirs. Thus Aratus himself writes. But Cleomenes, marching from Argos, and taking in the Trœzenians, Epidaurians, and Hermioneans, came to Corinth, and blocked up the castle, which the Achæans would not surrender; and sending for Aratus's friends and stewards, committed his house and estate to their care and management; and sent

Tritymallus, the Messenian,[11] to him a second time, desiring that the castle might be equally garrisoned by the Spartans and Achæans, and promising to Aratus himself double the pension that he received from king Ptolemy. But Aratus, refusing the conditions, and sending his own son with the other hostages to Antigonus, and persuading the Achæans to make a decree for delivering the castle into Antigonus's hands, upon this Cleomenes invaded the territory of the Sicyonians, and by a decree of the Corinthians, accepted Aratus's estate as a gift.

In the mean time, Antigonus, with a great army, was passing Geranea; and Cleomenes, thinking it more advisable to fortify and garrison, not the isthmus, but the mountains called Onea, and by a war of posts and positions to weary the Macedonians, rather than to venture a set battle with the highly disciplined phalanx, put his design in execution, and very much distressed Antigonus. For he had not brought victuals sufficient for his army; nor was it easy to force a way through, whilst Cleomenes guarded the pass. He attempted by night to pass through Lechæum, but failed, and lost some men; so that Cleomenes and his army were mightily encouraged, and so flushed with the victory, that they went merrily to supper; and Antigonus was very much dejected, being driven, by the necessity he was in, to most unpromising attempts. He was proposing to march to the promontory of Heræum, and thence transport his army in boats to Sicyon, which would take up a great deal of time, and require much preparation and means. But when it

[11] *Tritymallus the Messenian* is in the Life of Aratus called Tripylus.

was now evening, some of Aratus's friends came from Argos by sea, and invited him to return, for the Argives would revolt from Cleomenes. Aristoteles was the man that wrought the revolt, and he had no hard task to persuade the common people; for they were all angry with Cleomenes for not releasing them from their debts as they expected. Accordingly, obtaining fifteen hundred of Antigonus's soldiers, Aratus sailed to Epidaurus; but Aristoteles, not staying for his coming, drew out the citizens, and fought against the garrison of the castle; and Timoxenus, with the Achæans from Sicyon, came to his assistance.

Cleomenes heard the news about the second watch of the night, and sending for Megistonus, angrily commanded him to go and set things right at Argos. Megistonus had passed his word for the Argives' loyalty, and had persuaded him not to banish the suspected. Therefore, despatching him with two thousand soldiers, he himself kept watch upon Antigonus, and encouraged the Corinthians, pretending that there was no great matter in the commotions at Argos, but only a little disturbance raised by a few inconsiderable persons. But when Megistonus, entering Argos, was slain, and the garrison could scarce hold out, and frequent messengers came to Cleomenes for succors, he, fearing lest the enemy, having taken Argos, should shut up the passes, and securely waste Laconia, and besiege Sparta itself, which he had left without forces, dislodged from Corinth, and immediately lost that city; for Antigonus entered it, and garrisoned the town. He turned aside from his direct march, and assaulting the walls of Argos, endeavored to carry it by a sudden attack; and then, having collected his forces from their march, breaking into the Aspis, he joined the garrison, which still held out against the Achæans; some parts of the city he scaled and took, and his Cretan archers cleared the streets. But when he saw Antigonus with his phalanx descending from the mountains into the plain, and the horse on all sides entering the city, he thought it impossible to maintain his post, and, gathering together all his men, came safely down, and made his retreat under the walls, having in so short a time possessed himself of great power, and in one journey, so to say, having made himself master of almost all Peloponnesus, and now lost all again in as short a time. For some of his allies at once withdrew and forsook him, and others not long after put their cities under Antigonus's protection. His hopes thus defeated, as he was leading back the relics of his forces, messengers from Lacedæmon met him in the evening at Tegea, and brought him news of as great a misfortune as that which he had lately suffered, and this was the death of his wife; to whom he was so attached, and thought so much of her, that even in his most successful expeditions, when he was most prosperous, he could not refrain but would every now and then come home to Sparta, to visit Agiatis.

This news afflicted him extremely, and he grieved, as a young man would do, for the loss of a very beautiful and excellent wife; yet he did not let his passion disgrace him, or impair the greatness of his mind, but keeping his usual voice, his countenance, and his habit, he gave necessary orders to his captains, and took the precautions required for the safety of Tegea. Next morning he came to Sparta, and having at home with his mother and children bewailed the loss, and finished his mourning, he at once devoted himself to the public affairs of the state.

Now Ptolemy, the king of Egypt, promised him assistance, but demanded his mother and children for hostages. This, for some considerable time, he was ashamed to discover to his mother; and though he often went to her on purpose, and was just upon the discourse, yet he still refrained, and kept it to himself; so that she began to suspect, and asked his friends, whether Cleomenes had something to say to her, which he was afraid to speak. At last, Cleomenes venturing to tell her, she laughed aloud, and said, "Was this the thing that you had so often a mind to tell me, and were afraid? Make haste and put me on shipboard, and send this carcass where it may be most serviceable to Sparta, before age destroys it unprofitably here." Therefore, all things being provided for the voyage, they went by land to Tænarus, and the army waited on them. Cratesiclea, when she was ready to go on board, took Cleomenes aside into Neptune's temple, and embracing him, who was much dejected, and extremely discomposed, she said, "Go to, king of Sparta; when we come forth at the door, let none see us weep, or show any passion that is unworthy of Sparta, for that alone is in our own power; as for success or disappointment, those wait on us as the deity decrees." Having thus said, and composed her countenance, she went to the ship with her little grandson, and bade the pilot put at once out to sea. When she came to Egypt, and understood that Ptolemy entertained proposals and overtures of peace from Antigonus, and that Cleomenes, though the Achæans invited and urged him to an agreement, was afraid, for her sake, to come to any, without Ptolemy's consent, she wrote to him, advising him to do that which was most becoming and most profitable for Sparta, and not, for the sake of an old woman and a little child, stand always in fear of Ptolemy. This character she maintained in her misfortunes.

Antigonus, having taken Tegea, and plundered Orchomenus and Mantinea, Cleomenes was shut up within the narrow bounds of Laconia; and making such of the helots as could pay five Attic pounds,[12] free of Sparta, and, by that means, getting together five hundred talents, and arming two thousand after the Macedonian fashion, that he might make a body fit to oppose Antigonus's Leucaspides,[13] he undertook a great and unexpected enterprise. Megalopolis was at that time a city of itself as great and as powerful as Sparta, and had the forces of the Achæans and of Antigonus encamping beside it; and it was chiefly the Megalopolitans' doing, that Antigonus had been called in to assist the Achæans. Cleomenes, resolving to snatch the city (no other word so well suits so rapid and so surprising an action), ordered his men to take five days' provision, and marched to Sellasia, as if he intended to ravage the country of the Argives; but from thence making a descent into the territories of Megalopolis, and refreshing his army about Rhœteum,[14] he suddenly took the road by Helicus, and advanced directly upon the city. When he was not far off the town, he sent Panteus, with two regiments, to surprise a portion of the wall between two towers, which he

---

[12] Attic minæ.
[13] White-shields.
[14] *Rhœteum* and *Helicus* are unknown. Possibly the right names are Zœtium and Helisson, which are Arcadian towns in Pausanias.

learnt to be the most unguarded quarter of the Megalopolitans' fortifications, and with the rest of his forces he followed leisurely. Panteus not only succeeded at that point, but finding a great part of the wall without guards, he at once proceeded to pull it down in some places, and make openings through it in others, and killed all the defenders that he found. Whilst he was thus busied, Cleomenes came up to him, and was got with his army within the city, before the Megalopolitans knew of the surprise. When, after some time, they learned their misfortune, some left the town immediately, taking with them what property they could; others armed, and engaged the enemy; and though they were not able to beat them out, yet they gave their citizens time and opportunity safely to retire, so that there were not above one thousand persons taken in the town, all the rest flying, with their wives and children, and escaping to Messene. The greater number, also, of those that armed and fought the enemy, were saved, and very few taken, amongst whom were Lysandridas and Thearidas, two men of great power and reputation amongst the Megalopolitans; and therefore the soldiers, as soon as they were taken, brought them to Cleomenes. And Lysandridas, as soon as he saw Cleomenes afar off, cried out, "Now, king of Sparta, it is in your power, by doing a most kingly and a nobler action than you have already performed, to purchase the greatest glory." And Cleomenes, guessing at his meaning, replied, "What, Lysandridas, you will not surely advise me to restore your city to you again?" "It is that which I mean," Lysandridas replied, "and I advise you not to ruin so brave a city, but to fill it with faithful and steadfast friends and allies, by restoring their country to the Megalopolitans, and being the saviour of so considerable a people." Cleomenes paused a while, and then said, "It is very hard to trust so far in these matters; but with us let profit always yield to glory." Having said this, he sent the two men to Messene with a herald from himself, offering the Megalopolitans their city again, if they would forsake the Achæan interest, and be on his side. But though Cleomenes made these generous and humane proposals, Philopœmen would not suffer them to break their league with the Achæans; and accusing Cleomenes to the people, as if his design was not to restore the city, but to take the citizens too, he forced Thearidas and Lysandridas to leave Messene.

This was that Philopœmen who was afterward chief of the Achæans and a man of the greatest reputation amongst the Greeks, as I have related in his own Life. This news coming to Cleomenes, though he had before taken strict care that the city should not be plundered, yet then, being in anger, and out of all patience, he despoiled the place of all the valuables, and sent the statues and pictures to Sparta; and demolishing a great part of the city, he marched away for fear of Antigonus and the Achæans; but they never stirred, for they were at Ægium, at a council of war. There Aratus mounted the speaker's place, and wept a long while, holding his mantle before his face; and at last, the company being amazed, and commanding him to speak, he said, "Megalopolis is destroyed by Cleomenes." The assembly instantly dissolved, the Achæans being astounded at the suddenness and greatness of the loss; and Antigonus, intending to send speedy succors, when he found his forces gather very slowly out of their winter-quarters, sent them orders to continue there still; and he himself

marched to Argos with a small body of men. And
now the second enterprise of Cleomenes, though it
had the look of a desperate and frantic adventure,
yet in Polybius's [15] opinion, was done with mature
deliberation and great foresight. For knowing very
well that the Macedonians were dispersed into their
winter-quarters, and that Antigonus with his friends
and a few mercenaries about him wintered in Argos,
upon these considerations he invaded the country
of the Argives, hoping to shame Antigonus to a
battle upon unequal terms, or else, if he did not
dare to fight, to bring him into disrepute with the
Achæans. And this accordingly happened. For
Cleomenes wasting, plundering, and spoiling the
whole country, the Argives, in grief and anger at
the loss, gathered in crowds at the king's gates,
crying out that he should either fight, or surrender
his command to better and braver men. But Antigonus, as became an experienced captain, accounting it rather dishonorable foolishly to hazard his
army and quit his security, than merely to be railed
at by other people, would not march out against
Cleomenes, but stood firm to his convictions. Cleomenes, in the mean time, brought his army up to
the very walls, and having without opposition
spoiled the country, and insulted over his enemies,
drew off again.

A little while after, being informed that Antigonus designed a new advance to Tegea, and thence
to invade Laconia, he rapidly took his soldiers, and
marching by a side road, appeared early in the
morning before Argos, and wasted the fields about
it. The corn he did not cut down, as is usual, with

[15] Polybius, in his second book, is Plutarch's authority for much of the history; the passage referred to here is II., 64, 2.

reaping hooks and knives, but beat it down with great wooden staves made like broadswords, as if, in mere contempt and wanton scorn, while travelling on his way, without any effort or trouble, he spoiled and destroyed their harvest. Yet when his soldiers would have set Cyllabaris, the exercise ground, on fire, he stopped the attempt, as if he felt, that the mischief he had done at Megalopolis had been the effects of his passion rather than his wisdom. And when Antigonus, first of all, came hastily back to Argos, and then occupied the mountains and passes with his posts, he professed to disregard and despise it all; and sent heralds to ask for the keys of the temple of Juno, as though he proposed to offer sacrifice there and then return. And with this scornful pleasantry upon Antigonus, having sacrificed to the goddess under the walls of the temple, which was shut, he went to Phlius; and from thence driving out those that garrisoned Oligyrtus, he marched down to Orchomenus. And these enterprises not only encouraged the citizens, but made him appear to the very enemies to be a man worthy of high command, and capable of great things. For with the strength of one city, not only to fight the power of the Macedonians and all the Peloponnesians, supported by all the royal treasures, not only to preserve Laconia from being spoiled, but to waste the enemy's country, and to take so many and such considerable cities, was an argument of no common skill and genius for command.

But he that first said that money was the sinews of affairs, seems especially in that saying to refer to war. Demades, when the Athenians had voted that their galleys should be launched and equipped for action, but could produce no money, told them, " The baker was wanted first, and the pilot after." [16] And the old Archidamus, in the beginning of the Peloponnesian war, when the allies desired that the amount of their contributions should be determined, is reported to have answered, that war cannot be fed upon so much a day. For as wrestlers, who have thoroughly trained and disciplined their bodies, in time tire down and exhaust the most agile and most skilful combatant, so Antigonus, coming to the war with great resources to spend from, wore out Cleomenes, whose poverty made it difficult for him to provide the merest sufficiency of pay for the mercenaries, or of provisions for the citizens. For, in all other respects, time favored Cleomenes; for Antigonus's affairs at home began to be disturbed. For the barbarians wasted and overran Macedonia whilst he was absent, and at that particular time a vast army of Illyrians had entered the country; to be freed from whose devastations, the Macedonians sent for Antigonus, and the letters had almost been brought to him before the battle was fought; upon the receipt of which he would at once have marched away home, and left the Achæans to look to themselves. But Fortune, that loves to determine the greatest affairs by a minute, in this conjuncture showed such an exact niceness of time, that immediately after the battle

[16] *The baker was wanted first, and the pilot after,* is literally in the Greek *the kneader comes before the look-out man,* or *kneading before acting as look-out man,* which seems too poor a saying to be the right one. By no very violent alteration it might be brought to the sense, *they must knead before they baked* (*artopteusai* for *prorapteusai,* a conjecture of Hermann's). The copyist had been misled by the mention of the ships just before, and changed the word into one that seemed to suit them. But there are several other conjectures.

in Sellasia was over, and Cleomenes had lost his
army and his city, the messengers came up and
called for Antigonus. And this above every thing
made Cleomenes's misfortune to be pitied; for if
he had gone on retreating and had forborne fighting two days longer, there had been no need of
hazarding a battle; since upon the departure of the
Macedonians, he might have had what conditions
he pleased from the Achæans. But now, as was
said before, for want of money, being necessitated
to trust every thing to arms, he was forced with
twenty thousand (such is Polybius's account) to
engage thirty thousand. And approving himself an
admirable commander in this difficulty, his citizens
showing an extraordinary courage, and his mercenaries bravery enough, he was overborne by the
different way of fighting, and the weight of the
heavy-armed phalanx. Phylarchus also affirms,
that the treachery of some about him was the chief
cause of Cleomenes's ruin.

For Antigonus gave orders, that the Illyrians
and Acarnanians should march round by a secret
way, and encompass the other wing, which Euclidas,
Cleomenes's brother, commanded; and then drew
out the rest of his forces to the battle. And Cleomenes, from a convenient rising, viewing his order,
and not seeing any of the Illyrians and Acarnanians,
began to suspect that Antigonus had sent them upon
some such design; and calling for Damoteles, who
was at the head of those specially appointed to such
ambush duty, he bade him carefully to look after
and discover the enemy's designs upon his rear.
But Damoteles, for some say Antigonus had bribed
him, telling him that he should not be solicitous
about that matter, for all was well enough, but mind
and fight those that met him in the front, he was

satisfied, and advanced against Antigonus; and by the vigorous charge of his Spartans, made the Macedonian phalanx give ground, and pressed upon them with great advantage about half a mile; but then making a stand, and seeing the danger which the surrounded wing, commanded by his brother Euclidas, was in, he cried out, " Thou art lost, dear brother, thou art lost, thou brave example to our Spartan youth, and theme of our matrons' songs." And Euclidas's wing being cut in pieces, and the conquerors from that part falling upon him, he perceived his soldiers to be disordered, and unable to maintain the fight, and therefore provided for his own safety. There fell, we are told, in the battle, besides many of the mercenary soldiers, all the Spartans, six thousand in number, except two hundred.

When Cleomenes came into the city, he advised those citizens that he met to receive Antigonus; and as for himself, he said, which should appear most advantageous to Sparta, whether his life or death, that he would choose. Seeing the women running out to those that had fled with him, taking their arms, and bringing drink to them, he entered into his own house, and his servant, who was a free-born woman, taken from Megalopolis after his wife's death, offering, as usual, to do the service he needed on returning from war, though he was very thirsty, he refused to drink, and though very weary, to sit down; but in his corselet as he was, he laid his arm sideway against a pillar, and leaning his forehead upon his elbow, he rested his body a little while, and ran over in his thoughts all the courses he could take; and then with his friends set on at once for Gythium; where finding ships which had been got ready for this very purpose, they embarked. Antigonus, taking the city, treated the Lacedæmonians courteously, and in no way offering any insult or offence to the dignity of Sparta, but permitting them to enjoy their own laws and polity, and sacrificing to the gods, dislodged the third day. For he heard that there was a great war in Macedonia, and that the country was devastated by the barbarians. Besides, his malady had now thoroughly settled into a consumption and continual catarrh. Yet he still kept up, and managed to return and deliver his country, and meet there a more glorious death in a great defeat and vast slaughter of the barbarians. As Phylarchus says, and as is probable in itself, he broke a bloodvessel by shouting in the battle itself. In the schools we used to be told, that after the victory was won, he cried out for joy, "O glorious day!" and presently bringing up a quantity of blood, fell into a fever, which never left him till his death. And thus much concerning Antigonus.

Cleomenes, sailing from Cythera, touched at another island called Ægialia, whence as he was about to depart for Cyrene, one of his friends, Therycion by name, a man of a noble spirit in all enterprises, and bold and lofty in his talk, came privately to him, and said thus: "Sir, death in battle, which is the most glorious, we have let go; though all heard us say that Antigonus should never tread over the king of Sparta, unless dead. And now that course which is next in honor and virtue, is presented to us. Whither do we madly sail, flying the evil which is near, to seek that which is at a distance? For if it is not dishonorable for the race of Hercules to serve the successors of Philip and Alexander, we shall save a long voyage by delivering ourselves up to Antigonus, who, probably, is as much better than Ptolemy, as the Macedonians are better than the

Egyptians; but if we think it mean to submit to those whose arms have conquered us, why should we choose him for our master, by whom we have not yet been beaten? Is it to acknowledge two superiors instead of one, whilst we run away from Antigonus, and flatter Ptolemy? Or, is it for your mother's sake that you retreat to Egypt? It will indeed be a very fine and very desirable sight for her, to show her son to Ptolemy's women, now changed from a prince into an exile and a slave. Are we not still masters of our own swords? And whilst we have Laconia in view, shall we not here free ourselves from this disgraceful misery, and clear ourselves to those who at Sellasia died for the honor and defence of Sparta? Or, shall we sit lazily in Egypt, inquiring what news from Sparta, and whom Antigonus hath been pleased to make governor of Lacedæmon?" Thus spoke Therycion; and this was Cleomenes's reply: "By seeking death, you coward, the most easy and most ready refuge, you fancy that you shall appear courageous and brave, though this flight is baser than the former. Better men than we have given way to their enemies, having been betrayed by fortune, or oppressed by multitude; but he that gives way under labor or distresses, under the ill opinions or reports of men, yields the victory to his own effeminacy. For a voluntary death ought not to be chosen as a relief from action, but as an exemplary action itself; and it is base either to live or to die only to ourselves. That death to which you now invite us, is proposed only as a release from our present miseries, but carries nothing of nobleness or profit in it. And I think it becomes both me and you not to despair of our country; but when there are no hopes of that left, those that have an inclination may quickly die." To this Therycion returned no answer; but as soon as he had an opportunity of leaving Cleomenes's company, went aside on the sea-shore, and ran himself through.

But Cleomenes sailed from Ægialia, landed in Libya, and being honorably conducted through the king's country, came to Alexandria. When he was first brought to Ptolemy, no more than common civilities and usual attentions were paid him; but when, upon trial, he found him a man of deep sense and great reason, and that his plain Laconic way of conversation carried with it a noble and becoming grace, that he did nothing unbecoming his birth, nor bent under fortune, and was evidently a more faithful counsellor than those who made it their business to please and flatter, he was ashamed, and repented that he had neglected so great a man, and suffered Antigonus to get so much power and reputation by ruining him. He now offered him many marks of respect and kindness, and gave him hopes that he would furnish him with ships and money to return to Greece, and would reinstate him in his kingdom. He granted him a yearly pension of four and twenty talents; a little part of which sum supplied his and his friends' thrifty temperance; and the rest was employed in doing good offices to, and in relieving the necessities of the refugees that had fled from Greece, and retired into Egypt.

But the elder Ptolemy dying before Cleomenes's affairs had received a full despatch, and the successor being a loose, voluptuous, and effeminate prince, under the power of his pleasures and his women, his business was neglected. For the king was so besotted with his women and his wine, that the employments of his most busy and serious hours consisted at the utmost in celebrating religious feasts in his palace, carrying a timbrel, and taking part in the show; while the greatest affairs of state were managed by Agathoclea, the king's mistress, her mother, and the pimp Œnanthes. At the first, indeed, they seemed to stand in need of Cleomenes; for Ptolemy, being afraid of his brother Magas, who by his mother's means had a great interest amongst the soldiers, gave Cleomenes a place in his secret councils, and acquainted him with the design of taking off his brother. He, though all were for it, declared his opinion to the contrary, saying, " The king, if it were possible, should have more brothers for the better security and stability of his affairs." And Sosibius, the greatest favorite, replying, that they were not secure of the mercenaries whilst Magas was alive, Cleomenes returned, that he need not trouble himself about that matter; for amongst the mercenaries there were above three thousand Peloponnesians, who were his fast friends, and whom he could command at any time with a nod. This discourse made Cleomenes for the present to be looked upon as a man of great influence and assured fidelity; but afterwards, Ptolemy's weakness increasing his fear, and he, as it usually happens, where there is no judgment and wisdom, placing his security in general distrust and suspicion, it rendered Cleomenes suspected to the courtiers, as having too much interest with the mercenaries; and many had this saying in their mouths, that he was a lion amidst a flock of sheep. For, in fact, such he seemed to be in the court, quietly watching and keeping his eye upon all that went on.

He, therefore, gave up all thought of asking for ships and soldiers from the king. But receiving news that Antigonus was dead, that the Achæans were engaged in a war with the Ætolians, and that the affairs of Peloponnesus, being now in very great distraction and disorder, required and invited his assistance, he desired leave to depart only with his friends, but could not obtain that, the king not so much as hearing his petition, being shut up amongst his women, and wasting his hours in bacchanalian rites and drinking parties. But Sosibius, the chief minister and counsellor of state, thought that Cleomenes, being detained against his will, would grow ungovernable and dangerous, and yet that it was not safe to let him go, being an aspiring, daring man, and well acquainted with the diseases and weakness of the kingdom. For neither could presents and gifts conciliate or content him; but even as Apis,[17] while living in all possible plenty and apparent delight, yet desires to live as nature would provide for him, to range at liberty, and bound about the fields, and can scarce endure to be under the priests' keeping, so he could not brook their courtship and soft entertainment, but sat like Achilles,

> and languished far,
> Desiring battle and the shout of war.

His affairs standing in this condition, Nicagoras, the Messenian, came to Alexandria, a man that deeply hated Cleomenes, yet pretended to be his friend; for he had formerly sold Cleomenes a fair estate, but never received the money, because Cleomenes was either unable, as it may be, or else, by reason of his engagement in the wars and other distractions, had no opportunity to pay him. Cleomenes, seeing him landing, for he was then walking

[17] The sacred bull whom the Egyptians worshipped.

CLEOMENES

upon the quay, kindly saluted him, and asked what business brought him to Egypt. Nicagoras returned his compliment, and told him, that he came to bring some excellent war-horses to the king. And Cleomenes, with a smile, subjoined, "I could wish you had rather brought young boys and music-girls; for those now are the king's chief occupation." Nicagoras at the moment smiled at the conceit; but a few days after, he put Cleomenes in mind of the estate that he had bought of him, and desired his money, protesting, that he would not have troubled him, if his merchandise had turned out as profitable as he had thought it would. Cleomenes replied, that he had nothing left of all that had been given him. At which answer, Nicagoras, being nettled, told Sosibius Cleomenes's scoff upon the king. He was delighted to receive the information; but desiring to have some greater reason to excite the king against Cleomenes, persuaded Nicagoras to leave a letter written against Cleomenes, importing that he had a design, if he could have gotten ships and soldiers, to surprise Cyrene. Nicagoras wrote such a letter, and left Egypt. Four days after, Sosibius brought the letter to Ptolemy, pretending it was just then delivered him, and excited the young man's fear and anger; upon which it was agreed, that Cleomenes should be invited into a large house, and treated as formerly, but not suffered to go out again.

This usage was grievous to Cleomenes, and another incident that occurred, made him feel his hopes to be yet more entirely overcast. Ptolemy, the son of Chrysermas, a favorite of the king's, had always shown civility to Cleomenes; there was a considerable intimacy between them, and they had been used to talk freely together about the state.

He, upon Cleomenes's desire, came to him, and spoke to him in fair terms, softening down his suspicions and excusing the king's conduct. But as he went out again, not knowing that Cleomenes followed him to the door, he severely reprimanded the keepers for their carelessness in looking after " so great and so furious a wild beast." This Cleomenes himself heard, and retiring before Ptolemy perceived it, told his friends what had been said. Upon this they cast off all their former hopes, and determined for violent proceedings, resolving to be revenged on Ptolemy for his base and unjust dealing, to have satisfaction for the affronts, to die as it became Spartans, and not stay till, like fatted sacrifices, they were butchered. For it was both grievous and dishonorable for Cleomenes, who had scorned to come to terms with Antigonus, a brave warrior, and a man of action, to wait an effeminate king's leisure, till he should lay aside his timbrel and end his dance, and then kill him.

These courses being resolved on, and Ptolemy happening at the same time to make a progress to Canopus, they first spread abroad a report, that his freedom was ordered by the king, and, it being the custom for the king to send presents and an entertainment to those whom he would free, Cleomenes's friends made that provision, and sent it into the prison, thus imposing upon the keepers, who thought it had been sent by the king. For he sacrificed, and gave them large portions, and with a garland upon his head, feasted and made merry with his friends. It is said that he began the action sooner than he designed, having understood that a servant who was privy to the plot, had gone out to visit a mistress that he loved. This made him afraid of a discovery; and therefore, as soon as it was full noon, and all the keepers sleeping off their wine, he put on his coat, and opening the seam to bare his right shoulder, with his drawn sword in his hand, he issued forth, together with his friends, provided in the same manner, making thirteen in all. One of them, by name Hippitas, was lame, and followed the first onset very well, but when he presently perceived that they were more slow in their advances for his sake, he desired them to run him through, and not ruin their enterprise by staying for an useless, unprofitable man. By chance an Alexandrian was then riding by the door; him they threw off, and setting Hippitas on horseback, ran through the streets, and proclaimed liberty to the people. But they, it seems, had courage enough to praise and admire Cleomenes's daring, but not one had the heart to follow and assist him. Three of them fell on Ptolemy, the son of Chrysermas, as he was coming out of the palace, and killed him. Another Ptolemy, the officer in charge of the city, advancing against them in a chariot, they set upon, dispersed his guards and attendants, and pulling him out of the chariot, killed him upon the place. Then they made toward the castle, designing to break open the prison, release those who were confined, and avail themselves of their numbers; but the keepers were too quick for them, and secured the passages. Being baffled in this attempt, Cleomenes with his company roamed about the city, none joining with him, but all retreating from and flying his approach. Therefore, despairing of success, and saying to his friends, that it was no wonder that women ruled over men that were afraid of liberty, he bade them all die as bravely as became his followers and their own past actions. This said, Hippitas was first, as he desired, run through by one of the younger men, and then each of them readily and resolutely fell upon his own sword, except Panteus, the same who first surprised Megalopolis. This man, being of a very handsome person, and a great lover of the Spartan discipline, the king had made his dearest friend; and he now bade him, when he had seen him and the rest fallen, die by their example. Panteus walked over them as they lay, and pricked every one with his dagger, to try whether any was alive, when he pricked Cleomenes in the ancle, and saw him turn upon his back, he kissed him, sat down by him, and when he was quite dead, covered up the body, and then killed himself over it.

Thus fell Cleomenes, after the life which we have narrated, having been king of Sparta sixteen years. The news of their fall being noised through the city, Cratesiclea, though a woman of a great spirit, could not bear up against the weight of this affliction; but embracing Cleomenes's children, broke out into lamentations. But the eldest boy, none suspecting such a spirit in a child, threw himself headlong from the top of the house. He was bruised very much, but not killed by the fall, and was taken up crying, and expressing his resentment for not being permitted to destroy himself. Ptolemy, as soon as an account of the action was brought him, gave order that Cleomenes's body should be flayed and hung up,[18] and that his children, mother, and the

---

[18] *Cleomenes's body should be flayed and hung up.* Flayed is not the correct term; it was one way of insulting a dead body to sew it into the skin of a brute animal and hang it up. Thus a case is quoted from Polybius where a man first has his extremities cut off, then is beheaded, and his trunk then stitched into an ass's skin and hung on a cross. The strange theory of dead oxen generating

women that were with her, should be killed. Amongst these was Panteus's wife, a beautiful and noble-looking woman, who had been but lately married, and suffered these disasters in the height of her love. Her parents would not have her embark with Panteus, so shortly after they were married, though she eagerly desired it, but shut her up, and kept her forcibly at home. But a few days after, she procured a horse and a little money, and escaping by night, made speed to Tænarus, where she embarked for Egypt, came to her husband, and with him cheerfully endured to live in a foreign country. She gave her hand to Cratesiclea, as she was going with the soldiers to execution, held up her robe, and begged her to be courageous; who of herself was not in the least afraid of death, and desired nothing else but only to be killed before the children. When they were come to the place of execution, the children were first killed before Cratesiclea's eyes, and afterward she herself, with only these words in her mouth, "O children, whither are you gone?" But Panteus's wife, fastening her dress close about her, and being a strong woman, in silence and perfect composure, looked after every one that was slain, and laid them decently out as far as circumstances would permit; and after all were killed, rearraying her dress, and drawing her clothes close about her, and suffering none to come near or be an eye-witness of her fall, besides the

---

bees, dead horses wasps, and dead men snakes, seems to have been very prevalent. Ovid, in the last book of the Metamorphoses, mentions all the three supposed phenomena (*XV.*, 365, 368, 379). Virgil has made the first well known by the story of Aristæus and his bees in the fourth Georgic, and Pliny speaks of the third as a received tradition (*Hist. Nat.*, X., 66).

executioner, she courageously submitted to the stroke, and wanted nobody to look after her or wind her up after she was dead. Thus in her death the modesty of her mind appeared, and set that guard upon her body which she always kept when alive. And she, in the declining age of the Spartans, shewed that women were no unequal rivals of the men, and was an instance of a courage superior to the affronts of fortune.

A few days after, those that watched the hanging body of Cleomenes, saw a large snake winding about his head, and covering his face, so that no bird of prey would fly at it. This made the king superstitiously afraid, and set the women upon several expiations, as if he had been some extraordinary being, and one beloved by the gods, that had been slain. And the Alexandrians made processions to the place, and gave Cleomenes the title of hero, and son of the gods, till the philosophers satisfied them by saying, that as oxen breed bees, putrifying horses breed wasps, and beetles rise from the carcasses of dead asses, so the humors and juices of the marrow of a man's body, coagulating, produce serpents. And this the ancients observing, appropriated a serpent, rather than any other creature, to heroes.

TIBERIUS AND CAIUS GRACCHUS[1]

TRANSLATED BY JOHN WARREN, FELLOW
OF CATHERINE HALL, CAMBRIDGE

HAVING completed the first two narratives, we now may proceed to take a view of misfortunes, not less remarkable, in the Roman couple, and with the lives of Agis and Cleomenes, compare these of Tiberius and Caius. They were the sons of Tiberius Gracchus, who, though he had been once censor, twice consul, and twice had triumphed, yet was more renowned and esteemed for his virtue than his honors. Upon this account, after the death of Scipio who overthrew Hannibal, he was thought worthy to match with his daughter Cornelia, though there had been no friendship or familiarity between Scipio and him, but rather the contrary. There is a story told, that he once found in his bed-chamber a couple of snakes,[2] and that the soothsayers, being consulted concerning the prodigy, advised, that he should neither kill them both nor let them both escape; adding, that if the male serpent was killed, Tiberius should die, and if the female,

---

[1] Tiberius Sempronius Gracchus was present under his brother-in-law P. Scipio Africanus, at the destruction of Carthage 146 B.C. He was inferior to his brother in talent, but surpassed him in amiability of nature and purity of motives. His assassination occurred about 133 B.C.—DR. WILLIAM SMITH.

[2] The story of the two snakes is told by Cicero (*de Divinatione I.,* 18, *II.,* 29), who says it was left on record by Caius Gracchus in a letter written to Marcus Pomponius.

Cornelia. And that, therefore, Tiberius, who extremely loved his wife, and thought, besides, that it was much more his part, who was an old man, to die, than it was hers, who as yet was but a young woman, killed the male serpent, and let the female escape; and soon after himself died, leaving behind him twelve children borne to him by Cornelia.

Cornelia, taking upon herself all the care of the household and the education of her children, approved herself so discreet a matron, so affectionate a mother, and so constant and noble-spirited a widow, that Tiberius seemed to all men to have done nothing unreasonable, in choosing to die for such a woman; who, when king Ptolemy himself proffered her his crown, and would have married her, refused it, and chose rather to live a widow. In this state she continued, and lost all her children, except one daughter, who was married to Scipio the younger, and two sons, Tiberius and Caius, whose lives we are now writing.

These she brought up with such care, that though they were without dispute in natural endowments and dispositions the first among the Romans of their time, yet they seemed to owe their virtues even more to their education than to their birth. And as, in the statues and pictures made of Castor and Pollux, though the brothers resemble one another, yet there is a difference to be perceived in their countenances, between the one, who delighted in the cestus, and the other, that was famous in the course, so between these two noble youths, though there was a strong general likeness in their common love of fortitude and temperance, in their liberality, their eloquence, and their greatness of mind, yet in their actions and administrations of public affairs, a considerable variation showed itself. It will not be amiss, before we proceed, to mark the difference between them.

Tiberius, in the form and expression of his countenance, and in his gesture and motion, was gentle and composed; but Caius, earnest and vehement. And so, in their public speeches to the people, the one spoke in a quiet orderly manner, standing throughout on the same spot; the other would walk about on the hustings, and in the heat of his orations, pull his gown off his shoulders, and was the first of all the Romans that used such gestures; as Cleon is said to have been the first orator among the Athenians that pulled off his cloak and smote his thigh, when addressing the people. Caius's oratory was impetuous and passionate, making every thing tell to the utmost, whereas Tiberius was gentle, rather, and persuasive, awakening emotions of pity. His diction was pure, and carefully correct, while that of Caius was vehement and rich. So likewise in their way of living, and at their tables, Tiberius was frugal and plain, Caius, compared with other men temperate and even austere, but contrasting with his brother in a fondness for new fashions and rarities, as appears in Drusus's charge against him, that he had bought some silver dolphins,[3] to the value of twelve hundred and fifty drachmas for every pound weight.

The same difference that appeared in their diction, was observable also in their tempers. The one was mild and reasonable, the other rough and passionate, and to that degree, that often, in the midst of speaking, he was so hurried away by his

[3] Dolphins, *delphinas,* is changed by some critics to *delphicas,* tables of Delphian make.

passion, against his judgment, that his voice lost its tone, and he began to pass into mere abusive talking, spoiling his whole speech. As a remedy to this excess, he made use of an ingenious servant of his, one Licinius, who stood constantly behind him with a sort of pitchpipe, or instrument to regulate the voice by, and whenever he perceived his master's tone alter, and break with anger, he struck a soft note with his pipe, on hearing which, Caius immediately checked the vehemence of his passion and his voice, grew quieter, and allowed himself to be recalled to temper. Such are the differences between the two brothers; but their valor in war against their country's enemies, their justice in the government of its subjects, their care and industry in office, and their self-command in all that regarded their pleasures were equally remarkable in both.

Tiberius was the elder by nine years; owing to which their actions as public men were divided by the difference of the times in which those of the one and those of the other were performed. And one of the principal causes of the failure of their enterprises was this interval between their careers, and the want of combination of their efforts. The power they would have exercised, had they flourished both together, could scarcely have failed to overcome all resistance. We must therefore give an account of each of them singly, and first of the eldest.

Tiberius, immediately on his attaining manhood, had such a reputation, that he was admitted into the college of the augurs, and that in consideration more of his early virtue than of his noble birth. This appeared by what Appius Claudius did, who, though he had been consul and censor, and was now the head of the Roman senate, and had the highest sense of his own place and merit, at a public feast of the augurs, addressed himself openly to Tiberius, and with great expressions of kindness, offered him his daughter in marriage. And when Tiberius gladly accepted, and the agreement had thus been completed, Appius, returning home, no sooner had reached his door, but he called to his wife and cried out in a loud voice, " O Antistia, I have contracted our daughter Claudia to a husband." She, being amazed, answered, " But why so suddenly, or what means this haste? Unless you have provided Tiberius Gracchus for her husband." I am not ignorant that some apply this story to Tiberius, the father of the Gracchi, and Scipio Africanus; but most relate it as we have done. And Polybius writes, that after the death of Scipio Africanus, the nearest relations of Cornelia, preferring Tiberius to all other competitors, gave her to him in marriage, not having been engaged or promised to any one by her father.

This young Tiberius, accordingly, serving in Africa under the younger Scipio, who had married his sister, and living there under the same tent with him, soon learned to estimate the noble spirit of his commander, which was so fit to inspire strong feelings of emulation in virtue and desire to prove merit in action, and in a short time he excelled all the young men of the army in obedience and courage; and he was the first that mounted the enemy's wall, as Fannius[4] says, who writes, that he him-

---

[4] *Fannius* is quoted by Cicero as the author of a history, in which the times of the Gracchi were included. He was the son-in-law of Lælius, and is one of the speakers in Cicero's dialogue, de Amicitia.

self climbed up with him, and was partaker in the achievement. He was regarded, while he continued with the army, with great affection; and left behind him on his departure a strong desire for his return.

After that expedition, being chosen paymaster, it was his fortune to serve in the war against the Numantines, under the command of Caius Mancinus, the consul, a person of no bad character, but the most unfortunate of all the Roman generals. Notwithstanding, amidst the greatest misfortunes, and in the most unsuccessful enterprises, not only the discretion and valor of Tiberius, but also, which was still more to be admired, the great respect and honor which he showed for his general, were most eminently remarkable; though the general himself, when reduced to straits, forgot his own dignity and office. For being beaten in various great battles, he endeavored to dislodge by night, and leave his camp; which the Numantines perceiving, immediately possessed themselves of his camp, and pursuing that part of the forces which was in flight, slew those that were in the rear, hedged the whole army in on every side, and forced them into difficult ground, whence there could be no possibility of an escape. Mancinus, despairing to make his way through by force, sent a messenger to desire a truce, and conditions of peace. But they refused to give their confidence to any one except Tiberius, and required that he should be sent to treat with them. This was not only in regard to the young man's own character, for he had a great reputation amongst the soldiers, but also in remembrance of his father Tiberius, who, in his command against the Spaniards, had reduced great numbers of them to subjection, but

TIBERIUS AND CAIUS GRACCHUS

granted a peace to the Numantines, and prevailed upon the Romans to keep it punctually and inviolably.

Tiberius was accordingly despatched to the enemy, whom he persuaded to accept of several conditions, and he himself complied with others; and by this means it is beyond a question, that he saved twenty thousand of the Roman citizens, besides attendants and camp followers. However, the Numantines retained possession of all the property they had found and plundered in the encampment; and amongst other things were Tiberius's books of accounts, containing the whole transactions of his quæstorship, which he was extremely anxious to recover. And therefore, when the army were already upon their march, he returned to Numantia, accompanied with only three or four of his friends; and making his application to the officers of the Numantines, he entreated that they would return him his books, lest his enemies should have it in their power to reproach him with not being able to give an account of the moneys intrusted to him. The Numantines joyfully embraced this opportunity of obliging him, and invited him into the city; as he stood hesitating, they came up and took him by the hands, and begged that he would no longer look upon them as enemies, but believe them to be his friends, and treat them as such. Tiberius thought it well to consent, desirous as he was to have his books returned, and was afraid lest he should disoblige them by showing any distrust. As soon as he entered into the city, they first offered him food, and made every kind of entreaty that he would sit down and eat something in their company. Afterwards they returned his books, and gave him the liberty to take whatever he wished for in the remaining spoils. He, on the other hand, would accept of nothing but some frankincense, which he used in his public sacrifices, and, bidding them farewell with every expression of kindness, departed.

When he returned to Rome, he found the whole transaction censured and reproached, as a proceeding that was base, and scandalous to the Romans. But the relations and friends of the soldiers, forming a large body among the people, came flocking to Tiberius, whom they acknowledged as the preserver of so many citizens, imputing to the general all the miscarriages which had happened. Those who cried out against what had been done, urged for imitation the example of their ancestors, who stripped and handed over to the Samnites not only the generals who had consented to the terms of release, but also all the quæstors, for example, and tribunes, who had in any way implicated themselves in the agreement, laying the guilt of perjury and breach of conditions on their heads. But, in this affair, the populace, showing an extraordinary kindness and affection for Tiberius, indeed voted that the consul should be stripped and put in irons, and so delivered to the Numantines; but for the sake of Tiberius, spared all the other officers. It may be probable, also, that Scipio, who at that time was the greatest and most powerful man among the Romans, contributed to save him, though indeed he was also censured for not protecting Mancinus too, and that he did not exert himself to maintain the observance of the articles of peace which had been agreed upon by his kinsman and friend Tiberius. But it may be presumed that the difference between them was for the most part due to ambitious feelings, and to the friends and reasoners who urged on Tiberius,[5] and, as it was, it never amounted to any thing that might not have been remedied, or that was really bad. Nor can I think that Tiberius would ever have met with his misfortunes, if Scipio had been concerned in dealing with his measures; but he was away fighting at Numantia, when Tiberius, upon the following occasion, first came forward as a legislator.

Of the land which the Romans gained by conquest from their neighbors, part they sold publicly, and turned the remainder into common; this common land they assigned to such of the citizens as were poor and indigent, for which they were to pay only a small acknowledgment into the public treasury. But when the wealthy men began to offer larger rents, and drive the poorer people out, it was enacted by law, that no person whatever should enjoy more than five hundred acres of ground. This act for some time checked the avarice of the richer, and was of great assistance to the poorer people, who retained under it their

[5] *The friends and reasoners who urged on Tiberius.* The original word for reasoners is *sophistæ;* perhaps it would be better to translate it *friends and philosophical teachers,* or *teachers of philosophy and rhetoric.* Diophanes and Blossius are meant, who are described two pages beyond. *The workhouses full of foreign born slaves* are what the Romans called their *ergastula.* The Latin word *Sapiens* has, he says, below, the two meanings of *Wise* and of *Prudent;* the two original words for which are *sophos* and *phronimos,* famous in Greek philosophy, *sophia* and *phronesis* being the two forms of intellectual virtue or excellence, *sophia,* the knowledge of the truth as it is, *phronesis,* the knowledge of its practical application. What the *sophos* sees by the light of reason, the *phronimos* converts into immediate precepts for action; *sophos* is the epithet of the philosopher, *phronimos*

respective proportions of ground, as they had been formerly rented by them. Afterwards the rich men of the neighborhood contrived to get these lands again into their possession, under other people's names, and at last would not stick to claim most of them publicly in their own. The poor, who were thus deprived of their farms, were no longer either ready, as they had formerly been, to serve in war, or careful in the education of their children; insomuch that in a short time there were comparatively few freemen remaining in all Italy, which swarmed with workhouses full of foreign-born slaves. These the rich men employed in cultivating their ground, of which they dispossessed the citizens. Caius Lælius, the intimate friend of Scipio, undertook to reform this abuse; but meeting with opposition from men of authority, and fearing a disturbance, he soon desisted, and received the name of the Wise or the Prudent, both which meanings belong to the Latin word *Sapiens*.

of the statesman; the first and supreme principles of morality are discerned by the *sophos*, the rules of life and conduct are supplied by the *phronimos*. No two English words exactly express a distinction which is scarcely recognized in English modes of thought. Wisdom is with us rather the practical habit, *phronesis* than *sophia*; yet speculative is a term which it is a disparagement to apply to *sophia*, the perceptions of which are of an absolute certainty: the word science would be better, as implying this, but the range of scientific knowledge must be extended (to make it commensurate with the claims of Greek intellect) to include subjects to which, in modern use, such an expression would never be applied. What geometry is to magnitudes, such is another, not less exact science to the highest phenomena of the world and of human nature, and in the knowledge of this consists the proper exercise of sophia.

But Tiberius, being elected tribune of the people, entered upon that design without delay, at the instigation, as is most commonly stated, of Diophanes, the rhetorician, and Blossius, the philosopher. Diophanes was a refugee from Mitylene, the other was an Italian, of the city of Cuma, and was educated there under Antipater of Tarsus, who afterwards did him the honor to dedicate some of his philosophical lectures to him. Some have also charged Cornelia, the mother of Tiberius, with contributing towards it, because she frequently upbraided her sons, that the Romans as yet rather called her the daughter of Scipio, than the mother of the Gracchi. Others again say Spurius Postumius was the chief occasion. He was a man of the same age with Tiberius, and his rival for reputation as a public speaker; and when Tiberius, at his return from the campaign, found him to have got far beyond him in fame and influence, and to be much looked up to, he thought to outdo him, by attempting a popular enterprise of this difficulty, and of such great consequence. But his brother Caius has left it us in writing, that when Tiberius went through Tuscany to Numantia, and found the country almost depopulated, there being hardly any free husbandmen or shepherds, but for the most part only barbarian, imported slaves, he then first conceived the course of policy which in the sequel proved so fatal to his family. Though it is also most certain that the people themselves chiefly excited his zeal and determination in the prosecution of it, by setting up writings upon the porches, walls, and monuments, calling upon him to reinstate the poor citizens in their former possessions.

However, he did not draw up his law without the advice and assistance of those citizens that were then most eminent for their virtue and authority; amongst whom were Crassus, the high-priest, Mucius Scævola, the lawyer, who at that time was consul, and Claudius Appius, his father-in-law. Never did any law appear more moderate and gentle, especially being enacted against such great oppression and avarice. For they who ought to have been severely punished for transgressing the former laws, and should at least have lost all their titles to such lands which they had unjustly usurped, were notwithstanding to receive a price for quitting their unlawful claims, and giving up their lands to those fit owners who stood in need of help. But though this reformation was managed with so much tenderness, that, all the former transactions being passed over, the people were only thankful to prevent abuses of the like nature for the future, yet, on the other hand, the moneyed men, and those of great estates, were exasperated, through their covetous feelings against the law itself, and against the law giver, through anger and party spirit. They therefore endeavored to seduce the people, declaring that Tiberius was designing a general redivision of lands, to overthrow the government, and put all things into confusion.

But they had no success. For Tiberius, maintaining an honorable and just cause, and possessed of eloquence sufficient to have made a less creditable action appear plausible, was no safe or easy antagonist, when, with the people crowding around the hustings, he took his place, and spoke in behalf of the poor. "The savage beasts," said he, "in Italy, have their particular dens, they have their places of repose and refuge; but the men who bear arms, and expose their lives for the safety of their country, enjoy in the mean time nothing more in it but the air and

TIBERIUS AND CAIUS GRACCHUS 577

light; and having no houses or settlements of their own, are constrained to wander from place to place with their wives and children." He told them that the commanders were guilty of a ridiculous error, when, at the head of their armies, they exhorted the common soldiers to fight for their sepulchres and altars; when not any amongst so many Romans is possessed of either altar or monument, neither have they any houses of their own, or hearths of their ancestors to defend. They fought indeed, and were slain, but it was to maintain the luxury and the wealth of other men. They were styled the masters of the world, but in the mean time had not one foot of ground which they could call their own. An harangue of this nature, spoken to an enthusiastic and sympathizing audience, by a person of commanding spirit and genuine feeling, no adversaries at that time were competent to oppose. Forbearing, therefore, all discussion and debate, they addressed themselves to Marcus Octavius, his fellow-tribune, who, being a young man of a steady, orderly character, and an intimate friend of Tiberius, upon this account declined at first the task of opposing him; but at length, over persuaded with the repeated importunities of numerous considerable persons, he was prevailed upon to do so, and hindered the passing of the law; it being the rule that any tribune has a power to hinder an act, and that all the rest can effect nothing, if only one of them dissents. Tiberius, irritated at these proceedings, presently laid aside this milder bill, but at the same time preferred another; which, as it was more grateful to the common people, so it was much more severe against the wrongdoers, commanding them to make an immediate surrender of all lands which, contrary to former laws, had come into their possession.

Hence there arose daily contentions between him and Octavius in their orations. However, though they expressed themselves with the utmost heat and determination, they yet were never known to descend to any personal reproaches, or in their passion to let slip any indecent expressions, so as to derogate from one another.

For not alone

> In revellings and Bacchic play,[6]

but also in contentions and political animosities, a noble nature and a temperate education stay and compose the mind. Observing, however, that Octavius himself was an offender against this law, and detained a great quantity of ground from the commonalty, Tiberius desired him to forbear opposing him any further, and proffered, for the public good, though he himself had but an indifferent estate, to pay a price for Octavius's share at his own cost and charges. But upon the refusal of this proffer by Octavius, he then interposed an edict, prohibiting all magistrates to exercise their respective functions,

---

[6] The words *in revellings and Bacchic play* are from the Bacchæ of Euripides (317). Tiresias, defending the Bacchic rites to Pentheus, who forbids them, says that

> Even in revellings and Bacchic play,
> She that is modest, modest still will stay.

There is a story told of a banquet in Sicily where Dionysius bade all the company get up, each one in his turn, put on a purple gown, and perform a dance; Plato declined, quoting the words of Pentheus (*Bacchæ*, 835), "I cannot go into a woman's robes;" Aristippus complied, and quoted Tiresias, in the same play, as above.

TIBERIUS AND CAIUS GRACCHUS 579

till such time as the law was either ratified or rejected by public votes. He further sealed up the gates of Saturn's temple, so that the treasurer could neither take any money out from thence, or put any in. He threatened to impose a severe fine upon those of the prætors who presumed to disobey his commands, insomuch that all the officers, for fear of this penalty, intermitted the exercise of their several jurisdictions. Upon this, the rich proprietors put themselves into mourning, went up and down melancholy and dejected; they entered also into a conspiracy against Tiberius, and procured men to murder him; so that he also, with all men's knowledge, whenever he went abroad, took with him a sword-staff, such as robbers use, called in Latin a *dolo*.

When the day appointed was come, and the people summoned to give their votes, the rich men seized upon the voting urns, and carried them away by force; thus all things were in confusion. But when Tiberius's party appeared strong enough to oppose the contrary faction, and drew together in a body, with the resolution to do so, Manlius and Fulvius, two of the consular quality, threw themselves before Tiberius, took him by the hand, and with tears in their eyes, begged of him to desist. Tiberius, considering the mischiefs that were all but now occurring, and having a great respect for two such eminent persons, demanded of them what they would advise him to do. They acknowledged themselves unfit to advise in a matter of so great importance, but earnestly entreated him to leave it to the determination of the senate. But when the senate assembled, and could not bring the business to any result, through the prevalence of the rich faction, he then was driven to a course neither legal nor fair, and proposed to deprive Octavius of his tribuneship, it being impossible for him in any other way to get the law brought to the vote. At first he addressed him publicly, with entreaties couched in the kindest terms, and taking him by his hands, besought him, that now, in the presence of all the people, he would take this opportunity to oblige them, in granting only that request which was in itself so just and reasonable, being but a small recompense in regard of those many dangers and hardships which they had undergone for the public safety. Octavius, however, would by no means be persuaded to compliance; upon which Tiberius declared openly, that seeing they two were united in the same office, and of equal authority, it would be a difficult matter to compose their difference on so weighty a matter without a civil war; and that the only remedy which he knew, must be the deposing one of them from their office. He desired, therefore, that Octavius would summon the people to pass their verdict upon him first, averring that he would willingly relinquish his authority if the citizens desired it. Octavius refused; and Tiberius then said he would himself put to the people the question of Octavius's deposition, if upon mature deliberation he did not alter his mind; and after this declaration, he adjourned the assembly till the next day.

When the people were met together again, Tiberius placed himself in the rostra, and endeavored a second time to persuade Octavius. But all being to no purpose, he referred the whole matter to the people, calling on them to vote at once, whether Octavius should be deposed or not; and when seventeen of the thirty-five tribes had already voted against him, and there wanted only the votes of one tribe more for his final deprivation, Tiberius put a short stop to the proceedings, and once more renewed his importunities; he embraced and kissed him before all the assembly, begging, with all the earnestness imaginable, that he would neither suffer himself to incur the dishonor, nor him to be reputed the author and promoter of so odious a measure. Octavius, we are told, did seem a little softened and moved with these entreaties; his eyes filled with tears, and he continued silent for a considerable time. But presently looking towards the rich men and proprietors of estates, who stood gathered in a body together, partly for shame, and partly for fear of disgracing himself with them, he boldly bade Tiberius use any severity he pleased. The law for his deprivation being thus voted, Tiberius ordered one of his servants, whom he had made a freeman, to remove Octavius from the rostra, employing his own domestic freed servants in the stead of the public officers. And it made the action seem all the sadder, that Octavius was dragged out in such an ignominious manner. The people immediately assaulted him, whilst the rich men ran in to his assistance. Octavius, with some difficulty, was snatched away, and safely conveyed out of the crowd; though a trusty servant of his, who had placed himself in front of his master that he might assist his escape, in keeping off the multitude, had his eyes struck out, much to the displeasure of Tiberius, who ran with all haste, when he perceived the disturbance, to appease the rioters.

This being done, the law concerning the lands was ratified and confirmed, and three commissioners were appointed, to make a survey of the grounds and see the same equally divided. These were Tiberius himself, Claudius Appius, his father-in-law, and his brother, Caius Gracchus, who at this time was not at Rome, but in the army under the command of Scipio Africanus before Numantia. These things were transacted by Tiberius without any disturbance, none daring to offer any resistance to him; besides which, he gave the appointment as tribune in Octavius's place, not to any person of distinction, but to a certain Mucius, one of his own clients. The great men of the city were therefore utterly offended, and, fearing lest he should grow yet more popular, they took all opportunities of affronting him publicly in the senate house. For when he requested, as was usual, to have a tent provided at the public charge for his use, while dividing the lands, though it was a favor commonly granted to persons employed in business of much less importance, it was peremptorily refused to him; and the allowance made him for his daily expenses was fixed to nine obols only. The chief promoter of these affronts was Publius Nasica, who openly abandoned himself to his feelings of hatred against Tiberius, being a large holder of the public lands, and not a little resenting now to be turned out of them by force. The people, on the other hand, were still more and more excited, insomuch that a little after this, it happening that one of Tiberius's friends died suddenly, and his body being marked with malignant-looking spots, they ran, in a tumultuous manner, to his funeral, crying aloud that the man was poisoned. They took the bier upon their shoulders, and stood over it, while it was placed on the pile, and really seemed to have fair grounds for their suspicion of foul play. For the body burst open, and such a quantity of corrupt humors issued out, that the funeral fire was extinguished, and when it was

TIBERIUS AND CAIUS GRACCHUS

again kindled, the wood still would not burn; insomuch that they were constrained to carry the corpse to another place, where with much difficulty it took fire. Besides this, Tiberius, that he might incense the people yet more, put himself into mourning, brought his children amongst the crowd, and entreated the people to provide for them and their mother, as if he now despaired of his own security.

About this time, king Attalus, surnamed Philometor, died, and Eudemus, a Pergamenian, brought his last will to Rome, by which he had made the Roman people his heirs. Tiberius, to please the people, immediately proposed making a law, that all the money which Attalus left, should be distributed amongst such poor citizens as were to be sharers of the public lands, for the better enabling them to proceed in stocking and cultivating their ground; and as for the cities that were in the territories of Attalus, he declared that the disposal of them did not at all belong to the senate, but to the people, and that he himself would ask their pleasure herein. By this he offended the senate more than ever he had done before, and Pompeius stood up, and acquainted them that he was the next neighbor to Tiberius, and so had the opportunity of knowing that Eudemus, the Pergamenian, had presented Tiberius with a royal diadem and a purple robe, as before long he was to be king of Rome. Quintus Metellus also upbraided him, saying, that when his father was censor, the Romans, whenever he happened to be going home from a supper, used to put out all their lights, lest they should be seen to have indulged themselves in feasting and drinking at unseasonable hours, whereas now, the most indigent and audacious of the people were found with their torches at night, following Tiberius home. Titus Annius, a man of no great repute for either justice or temperance, but famous for his skill in putting and answering questions, challenged Tiberius to the proof by wager, declaring him to have deposed a magistrate who by law was sacred and inviolable. Loud clamor ensued, and Tiberius, quitting the senate hastily, called together the people, and summoning Annius to appear, was proceeding to accuse him. But Annius, being no great speaker, nor of any repute compared to him, sheltered himself in his own particular art, and desired that he might propose one or two questions to Tiberius, before he entered upon the chief argument. This liberty being granted, and silence proclaimed, Annius proposed his question. "If you," said he, "had a design to disgrace and defame me, and I should apply myself to one of your colleagues for redress, and he should come forward to my assistance, would you for that reason fall into a passion, and depose him?" Tiberius, they say, was so much disconcerted at this question, that, though at other times his assurance as well as his readiness of speech was always remarkable, yet now he was silent and made no reply.

For the present he dismissed the assembly. But beginning to understand that the course he had taken with Octavius had created offence even among the populace as well as the nobility, because the dignity of the tribunes seemed to be violated, which had always continued till that day sacred and honorable, he made a speech to the people in justification of himself; out of which it may not be improper to collect some particulars, to give an impression of his force and persuasiveness in speaking. "A tribune," he said, "of the people, is sacred indeed, and ought to be inviolable, because in a manner consecrated to be the guardian and protector of them; but if he degenerate so far as to oppress the people, abridge their powers, and take away their liberty of voting, he stands deprived by his own act of his honors and immunities, by the neglect of the duty, for which the honor was bestowed upon him. Otherwise we should be under the obligation to let a tribune do his pleasure, though he should proceed to destroy the capitol or set fire to the arsenal. He who should make these attempts, would be a bad tribune. He who assails the power of the people, is no longer a tribune at all. Is it not inconceivable, that a tribune should have power to imprison a consul, and the people have no authority to degrade him when he uses that honor which he received from them, to their detriment? For the tribunes, as well as the consuls, hold office by the people's votes. The kingly government, which comprehends all sorts of authority in itself alone, is moreover elevated by the greatest and most religious solemnity imaginable into a condition of sanctity. But the citizens, notwithstanding this, deposed Tarquin, when he acted wrongfully; and for the crime of one single man, the ancient government under which Rome was built, was abolished for ever. What is there in all Rome so sacred and venerable as the vestal virgins, to whose care alone the preservation of the eternal fire is committed? yet if one of these transgress, she is buried alive; the sanctity which for the gods' sakes is allowed them, is forfeited when they offend against the gods. So likewise a tribune retains not his inviolability, which for the people's sake was accorded to him, when he offends against the people, and attacks the foundations of that authority from whence he derived his own. We esteem him to be legally chosen tribune who is elected only by the majority of votes; and is not therefore the same person much more lawfully degraded, when by a general consent of them all, they agree to depose him? Nothing is so sacred as religious offerings; yet the people were never prohibited to make use of them, but suffered to remove and carry them wherever they pleased; so likewise, as it were some sacred present, they have lawful power to transfer the tribuneship from one man's hands to another's. Nor can that authority be thought inviolable and irremovable which many of those who have held it, have of their own act surrendered, and desired to be discharged from."

These were the principal heads of Tiberius's apology. But his friends, apprehending the dangers which seemed to threaten him, and the conspiracy that was gathering head against him, were of opinion, that the safest way would be for him to petition that he might be continued tribune for the year ensuing. Upon this consideration, he again endeavored to secure the people's good-will with fresh laws, making the years of serving in the war fewer than formerly, granting liberty of appeal from the judges to the people, and joining to the senators, who were judges at that time, an equal number of citizens of the horsemen's degree, endeavoring as much as in him lay to lessen the power of the senate, rather from passion and partisanship than from any rational regard to equity and the public good. And when it came to the question, whether these laws should be passed, and they perceived that the opposite party were strongest, the people as yet being not got together in a full body, they began first of all to gain time by speeches in accusation of some of their fellow-magistrates, and at length adjourned the assembly till the day following.

Tiberius then went down into the market-place amongst the people, and made his addresses to them humbly and with tears in his eyes; and told them, he had just reason to suspect, that his adversaries would attempt in the night time to break open his house, and murder him. This worked so strongly with the multitude, that several of them pitched tents round about his house, and kept guard all night for the security of his person. By break of day came one of the soothsayers, who prognosticate good or bad success by the pecking of fowls, and threw them something to eat. The soothsayer used his utmost endeavors to fright the fowls out of their coop; but none of them except one would venture out, which fluttered with its left wing, and stretched out its leg, and ran back again into the coop, without eating any thing. This put Tiberius in mind of another ill omen which had formerly happened to him. He had a very costly headpiece, which he made use of when he engaged in any battle, and into this piece of armor two serpents crawled, laid eggs, and brought forth young ones. The remembrance of which made Tiberius more concerned now, than otherwise he would have been. However, he went towards the capitol, as soon as he understood that the people were assembled there; but before he got out of the house, he stumbled upon the threshold with such violence, that he broke the nail of his great toe, insomuch that blood gushed out of his shoe. He was not gone very far before he saw two ravens fighting on the top of a house which stood on his left hand as he passed along; and though he was surrounded with a number of people, a stone, struck from its place by one of the ravens, fell just at his foot. This even the boldest men about him felt as a check. But Blossius of Cuma, who was present, told him, that it would be a shame, and an ignominious thing, for Tiberius, who was the son of Gracchus, the grandson of Scipio Africanus, and the protector of the Roman people, to refuse, for fear of a silly bird, to answer, when his countrymen called to him; and that his adversaries would represent it not as a mere matter for their ridicule, but would declaim about it to the people as the mark of a tyrannical temper, which felt a pride in taking liberties with the people. At the same time several messengers came also from his friends, to desire his presence at the capitol, saying that all things went there according to expectation. And indeed Tiberius's first entrance there was in every way successful; as soon as ever he appeared, the people welcomed him with loud acclamations, and as he went up to his place, they repeated their expressions of joy, and gathered in a body around him, so that no one who was not well known to be his friend, might approach. Mucius then began to put the business again to the vote; but nothing could be performed in the usual course and order, because of the disturbance caused by those who were on the outside of the crowd, where there was a struggle going on with those of the opposite party, who were pushing on and trying to force their way in and establish themselves among them.

Whilst things were in this confusion, Flavius Flaccus,[7] a senator, standing in a place where he could be seen, but at such a distance from Tiberius that he could not make him hear, signified to him

---

[7] Flavius should, in accordance with Roman usage, be Fulvius.

by motions of his hand, that he wished to impart something of consequence to him in private. Tiberius ordered the multitude to make way for him, by which means, though not without some difficulty, Flavius got to him, and informed him, that the rich men, in a sitting of the senate, seeing they could not prevail upon the consul to espouse their quarrel, had come to a final determination amongst themselves, that he should be assassinated, and to that purpose had a great number of their friends and servants ready armed to accomplish it. Tiberius no sooner communicated this confederacy to those about him, but they immediately tucked up their gowns, broke the halberts which the officers used to keep the crowd off into pieces, and distributed them among themselves, resolving to resist the attack with these. Those who stood at a distance wondered, and asked what was the occasion; Tiberius, knowing that they could not hear him at that distance, lifted his hand to his head, wishing to intimate the great danger which he apprehended himself to be in. His adversaries, taking notice of that action, ran off at once to the senate house, and declared, that Tiberius desired the people to bestow a crown upon him, as if this were the meaning of his touching his head. This news created general confusion in the senators, and Nasica at once called upon the consul to punish this tyrant, and defend the government. The consul mildly replied, that he would not be the first to do any violence; and as he would not suffer any freeman to be put to death, before sentence had lawfully passed upon him, so neither would he allow any measure to be carried into effect, if by persuasion or compulsion on the part of Tiberius the people had been induced to pass any unlawful vote. But Nasica, rising from his seat, "Since the consul," said he, "regards not the safety of the commonwealth, let every one who will defend the laws, follow me." He, then, casting the skirt of his gown over his head, hastened to the capitol; those who bore him company, wrapped their gowns also about their arms, and forced their way after him. And as they were persons of the greatest authority in the city, the common people did not venture to obstruct their passing, but were rather so eager to clear the way for them, that they tumbled over one another in haste. The attendants they brought with them, had furnished themselves with clubs and staves from their houses, and they themselves picked up the feet and other fragments of stools and chairs, which were broken by the hasty flight of the common people. Thus armed, they made towards Tiberius, knocking down those whom they found in front of him, and those were soon wholly dispersed, and many of them slain. Tiberius tried to save himself by flight. As he was running he was stopped by one who caught hold of him by the gown; but he threw it off, and fled in his under-garments only. And stumbling over those who before had been knocked down, as he was endeavoring to get up again, Publius Satureius, a tribune, one of his colleagues, was observed to give him the first fatal stroke, by hitting him upon the head with the foot of a stool. The second blow was claimed, as though it had been a deed to be proud of, by Lucius Rufus. And of the rest there fell above three hundred, killed by clubs and staves only, none by an iron weapon.

This, we are told, was the first sedition amongst the Romans, since the abrogation of kingly government, that ended in the effusion of blood. All

TIBERIUS AND CAIUS GRACCHUS

former quarrels which were neither small nor about trivial matters, were always amicably composed, by mutual concessions on either side, the senate yielding for fear of the commons, and the commons out of respect to the senate. And it is probable indeed that Tiberius himself might then have been easily induced, by mere persuasion, to give way, and certainly, if attacked at all, must have yielded without any recourse to violence and bloodshed, as he had not at that time above three thousand men to support him. But it is evident, that this conspiracy was fomented against him, more out of the hatred and malice which the rich men had to his person, than for the reasons which they commonly pretended against him. In testimony of which, we may adduce the cruelty and unnatural insults which they used to his dead body. For they would not suffer his own brother, though he earnestly begged the favor, to bury him in the night, but threw him, together with the other corpses, into the river. Neither did their animosity stop here; for they banished some of his friends without legal process, and slew as many of the others as they could lay their hands on; amongst whom Diophanes, the orator, was slain, and one Caius Villius cruelly murdered [8] by being shut up in a large tun with

[8] This punishment, by which *Caius Villius* was *cruelly murdered*, is that usually said to have been reserved for parricides, except that the tun, as Plutarch calls it, should be a sack. The parricide was sewn up in a leather sack (*insutus in culeum*) with a dog, an ape, a viper, and a cock, and thrown into the sea. Thus Juvenal, VIII., 214,

> Cujus supplicio non debuit una parari
> Simia, nec serpens unus, nec culeus unus.

vipers and serpents. Blossius of Cuma, indeed, was carried before the consuls, and examined touching what had happened, and freely confessed, that he had done, without scruple, whatever Tiberius bade him. "What," replied Nasica, "then if Tiberius had bidden you burn the capitol, would you have burnt it?" His first answer was, that Tiberius never would have ordered any such thing; but being pressed with the same question by several others, he declared, "If Tiberius had commanded it, it would have been right for me to do it; for he never would have commanded it, if it had not been for the people's good." Blossius [9] at this time was pardoned, and afterwards went away to Aristonicus in Asia, and when Aristonicus was overthrown and ruined, killed himself.

The senate, to soothe the people after these transactions, did not oppose the division of the public lands, and permitted them to choose another commissioner in the room of Tiberius. So they elected Publius Crassus, who was Gracchus's near connection, as his daughter Licinia was married to Caius Gracchus; although Cornelius Nepos says, that it was not Crassus's daughter whom Caius married, but Brutus's, who triumphed for his victories over the Lusitanians; but most writers state it as we have done. The people, however, showed evident marks of their anger at Tiberius's death; and were clearly waiting only for the opportunity

---

[9] The story of Blossius is told by Cicero in the dialogue on Friendship (*de Amicitia*, 11). *The verse out of Homer* in the following page is from the first book of the Odyssey (47). Minerva says so to Jupiter, who has spoken of Orestes killing Ægisthus; *he has died the death he deserved;* "so perish any one else that does as he has been doing."

to be revenged, and Nasica was already threatened with an impeachment. The senate, therefore, fearing lest some mischief should befall him, sent him ambassador into Asia, though there was no occasion for his going thither. For the people did not conceal their indignation, even in the open streets, but railed at him, whenever they met him abroad, calling him a murderer and a tyrant, one who had polluted the most holy and religious spot in Rome with the blood of a sacred and inviolable magistrate. And so Nasica left Italy, although he was bound, being the chief priest, to officiate in all principal sacrifices. Thus wandering wretchedly and ignominiously from one place to another, he died in a short time after, not far from Pergamus. It is no wonder that the people had such an aversion to Nasica, when even Scipio Africanus, though so much and so deservedly beloved by the Romans, was in danger of quite losing the good opinion which the people had of him, only for repeating, when the news of Tiberius's death was first brought to Numantia, the verse out of Homer

Even so perish all who do the same.

And afterwards, being asked by Caius and Fulvius, in a great assembly, what he thought of Tiberius's death, he gave an answer adverse to Tiberius's public actions. Upon which account, the people thenceforth used to interrupt him when he spoke, which, until that time, they had never done, and he, on the other hand, was induced to speak ill of the people. But of this the particulars are given in the Life of Scipio.

CAIUS GRACCHUS[1]

Translated by John Warren, Fellow of Catherine Hall, Cambridge

Caius Gracchus, at first, either for fear of his brother's enemies, or designing to render them more odious to the people, absented himself from the public assemblies, and lived quietly in his own house, as if he were not only reduced for the present to live unambitiously, but was disposed in general to pass his life in inaction. And some, indeed, went so far as to say that he disliked his brother's measures, and had wholly abandoned the defence of them. However, he was now but very young, being not so old as Tiberius by nine years; and he was not yet thirty when he was slain.

In some little time, however, he quietly let his temper appear, which was one of an utter antipathy to a lazy retirement and effeminacy, and not the least likely to be contented with a life of eating, drinking, and money getting. He gave great pains to the study of eloquence, as wings upon which he might aspire to public business; and it was very apparent that he did not intend to pass his days in obscurity. When Vettius, a friend of his, was on his trial, he defended his cause, and the people were in an ecstasy, and transported with joy, finding him master of such eloquence that the other orators seemed like children in comparison, and jealousies and fears on the other hand began to

[1] Caius Sempronius Gracchus was killed at Rome about 121 B.C. It is impossible to allow to him that freedom from personal motives which ennobled his brother Tiberius.—Dr. William Smith.

CAIUS GRACCHUS

be felt by the powerful citizens; and it was generally spoken of amongst them that they must hinder Caius from being made tribune.

But soon after, it happened that he was elected quæstor, and obliged to attend Orestes, the consul, into Sardinia. This, as it pleased his enemies, so it was not ungrateful to him, being naturally of a warlike character, and as well trained in the art of war as in that of pleading. And, besides, as yet he very much dreaded meddling with state affairs, and appearing publicly in the rostra, which, because of the importunity of the people and his friends, he could no otherwise avoid, than by taking this journey. He was therefore most thankful for the opportunity of absenting himself. Notwithstanding which, it is the prevailing opinion that Caius was a far more thorough demagogue, and more ambitious than ever Tiberius had been, of popular applause; yet it is certain that he was borne rather by a sort of necessity than by any purpose of his own into public business. And Cicero,[2] the orator, relates, that when he declined all such concerns, and would have lived privately, his brother appeared to him in a dream, and calling him by his name, said, "why do you tarry, Caius? There is no escape; one life and one death is appointed for us both, to spend the one and to meet the other, in the service of the people."

[2] *Cicero relates* the story of Caius's dream in the dialogue on Divination I., 26: " quam vellet, cunctaretur; tamen eodem sibi leto quo ipse interisset, esse pereundum." Caius had the dream when he was a candidate for the quæstorship, and had related it, some time before he was elected tribune, to many persons, and amongst others to Cælius the historian, from whom Cicero took the statement.

Caius was no sooner arrived in Sardinia, but he gave exemplary proofs of his high merit; he not only excelled all the young men of his age in his actions against his enemies, in doing justice to his inferiors, and in showing all obedience and respect to his superior officer; but likewise in temperance, frugality, and industry, he surpassed even those who were much older than himself. It happened to be a sharp and sickly winter in Sardinia, insomuch that the general was forced to lay an imposition upon several towns to supply the soldiers with necessary clothes. The cities sent to Rome, petitioning to be excused from that burden; the senate found their request reasonable, and ordered the general to find some other way of new clothing the army. While he was at a loss what course to take in this affair, the soldiers were reduced to great distress; but Caius went from one city to another, and by his mere representations, he prevailed with them, that of their own accord they clothed the Roman army. This again being reported to Rome, and seeming to be only an intimation of what was to be expected of him as a popular leader hereafter, raised new jealousies amongst the senators. And, besides, there came ambassadors out of Africa from king Micipsa, to acquaint the senate, that their master, out of respect to Caius Gracchus, had sent a considerable quantity of corn to the general in Sardinia; at which the senators were so much offended, that they turned the ambassadors out of the senate house, and made an order that the soldiers should be relieved by sending others in their room; but that Orestes should continue at his post, with whom Caius, also, as they presumed, being his quæstor, would remain. But he, finding how things were carried, immediately in anger took ship for Rome, where his unexpected appearance obtained him the censure not only of his enemies, but also of the people; who thought it strange that a quæstor should leave before his commander. Nevertheless, when some accusation upon this ground was made against him to the censors, he desired leave to defend himself, and did it so effectually, that, when he ended, he was regarded as one who had been very much injured. He made it then appear, that he had served twelve years in the army, whereas others are obliged to serve only ten; that he had continued quæstor to the general three years,[3] whereas he might by law have returned at the end of one year; and alone of all who went on the expedition, he had carried out a full, and had brought home an empty purse, while others, after drinking up the wine they had carried out with them, brought back the wine-jars filled again with gold and silver from the war.

After this, they brought other accusations and writs against him, for exciting insurrection amongst the allies, and being engaged in the conspiracy that was discovered about Fregellæ. But having cleared himself of every suspicion, and proved his entire innocence, he now at once came forward to ask for the tribuneship; in which, though he was uni-

---

[3] Two years is the correct amount, if not the true reading. "Biennium fui in provincia," are the original words as quoted by Aulus Gellius, Noctes Atticæ, XV. 12, where there are some remarkable extracts given from Caius's speech; amongst them, the passage which Plutarch refers to below. "Itaque, Quirites, quum Romam profectus sum, zonas quas plenas argenti extuli, eas ex provincia inanes retuli: alii vini amphoras quas plenas tulerunt, eas argento plenas domum reportaverunt."

versally opposed by all persons of distinction, yet there came such infinite numbers of people from all parts of Italy to vote for Caius, that lodgings for them could not be supplied in the city; and the Field being not large enough to contain the assembly, there were numbers who climbed upon the roofs and the tilings of the houses to use their voices in his favor. However, the nobility so far forced the people to their pleasure and disappointed Caius's hope, that, he was not returned the first, as was expected, but the fourth tribune. But when he came to the execution of his office, it was seen presently who was really first tribune, as he was a better orator than any of his contemporaries, and the passion with which he still lamented his brother's death, made him the bolder in speaking. He used on all occasions to remind the people of what had happened in that tumult, and laid before them the examples of their ancestors, how they declared war against the Faliscans, only for giving scurrilous language to one Genucius, a tribune of the people; and sentenced Caius Veturius to death for refusing to give way in the forum to a tribune; "Whereas," said he, "these men did, in the presence of you all, murder Tiberius with clubs, and dragged the slaughtered body through the middle of the city, to be cast into the river. Even his friends, as many as could be taken, were put to death immediately, without any trial, notwithstanding that just and ancient custom, which has always been observed in our city, that whenever any one is accused of a capital crime, and does not make his personal appearance in court, a trumpeter is sent in the morning to his lodging, to summon him by sound of trumpet to appear; and before this ceremony is performed, the judges do not proceed to the vote; so cautious and reserved were our ancestors about business of life and death."

Having moved the people's passion with such addresses (and his voice was of the loudest and strongest), he proposed two laws. The first was, that whoever was turned out of any public office by the people, should be thereby rendered incapable of bearing any office afterwards; the second, that if any magistrate condemn a Roman to be banished, without legal trial, the people be authorized to take cognizance thereof.

One of these laws was manifestly levelled at Marcus Octavius, who, at the instigation of Tiberius, had been deprived of his tribuneship. The other touched Popilius, who, in his prætorship, had banished all Tiberius's friends; whereupon Popilius, being unwilling to stand the hazard of a trial, fled out of Italy. As for the former law, it was withdrawn by Caius himself, who said he yielded in the case of Octavius, at the request of his mother Cornelia. This was very acceptable and pleasing to the people, who had a great veneration for Cornelia, not more for the sake of her father than for that of her children; and they afterwards erected a statue of brass in honor of her, with this inscription, *Cornelia, the mother of the Gracchi.* There are several expressions recorded, in which he used her name perhaps with too much rhetoric, and too little self-respect, in his attacks upon his adversaries. "How," said he, "dare you presume to reflect upon Cornelia, the mother of Tiberius?" And because the person who made the reflections had been suspected of effeminate courses, "With what face," said he, "can you compare Cornelia with yourself? Have you brought forth children as she has done? And yet all Rome knows, that she has refrained from the conversation of men longer than you yourself have done." Such was the bitterness he used in his language; and numerous similar expressions might be adduced from his written remains.

Of the laws which he now proposed, with the object of gratifying the people and abridging the power of the senate, the first was concerning the public lands, which were to be divided amongst the poor citizens; another was concerning the common soldiers, that they should be clothed at the public charge, without any diminution of their pay, and that none should be obliged to serve in the army who was not full seventeen years old; another gave the same right to all the Italians in general, of voting at elections, as was enjoyed by the citizens of Rome; a fourth related to the price of corn, which was to be sold at a lower rate than formerly to the poor; and a fifth regulated the courts of justice, greatly reducing the power of the senators. For hitherto, in all causes senators only sat as judges, and were therefore much dreaded by the Roman knights and the people. But Caius joined three hundred ordinary citizens of equestrian rank with the senators, who were three hundred likewise in number, and ordained that the judicial authority should be equally invested in the six hundred. While he was arguing for the ratification of this law, his behavior was observed to show in many respects unusual earnestness, and whereas other popular leaders had always hitherto, when speaking, turned their faces towards the senate house, and the place called the comitium, he, on the contrary, was the first man that in his harangue to the people turned himself the other way, towards them, and continued after that time to do so.

An insignificant movement and change of posture, yet it marked no small revolution in state affairs, the conversion, in a manner, of the whole government from an aristocracy to a democracy; his action intimating that public speakers should address themselves to the people, not the senate.

When the commonalty ratified this law, and gave him power to select those of the knights whom he approved of, to be judges, he was invested with a sort of kingly power, and the senate itself submitted to receive his advice in matters of difficulty; nor did he advise anything that might derogate from the honor of that body. As, for example, his resolution about the corn which Fabius the proprætor sent from Spain, was very just and honorable; for he persuaded the senate to sell the corn, and return the money to the same provinces which had furnished them with it; and also that Fabius should be censured for rendering the Roman government odious and insupportable. This got him extraordinary respect and favor among the provinces. Besides all this, he proposed measures for the colonization of several cities, for making roads, and for building public granaries; of all which works he himself undertook the management and superintendence, and was never wanting to give necessary orders for the despatch of all these different and great undertakings; and that with such wonderful expedition and diligence, as if he had been but engaged upon one of them; insomuch that all persons, even those who hated or feared him, stood amazed to see what a capacity he had for effecting and completing all he undertook. As for the people themselves, they were transported at the very sight, when they saw him surrounded with a crowd of contractors, artificers, public deputies, military officers, soldiers, and scholars. All these he treated with an easy familiarity, yet without abandoning his dignity in his gentleness; and so accommodated his nature to the wants and occasions of every one who addressed him, that those were looked upon as no better than envious detractors, who had represented him as a terrible, assuming, and violent character. He was even a greater master of the popular leader's art in his common talk and his actions, than he was in his public addresses.

His most especial exertions were given to constructing the roads, which he was careful to make beautiful and pleasant, as well as convenient. They were drawn by his directions through the fields, exactly in a straight line, partly paved with hewn stone, and partly laid with solid masses of gravel. When he met with any valleys or deep watercourses crossing the line, he either caused them to be filled up with rubbish, or bridges to be built over them, so well levelled, that all being of an equal height on both sides, the work presented one uniform and beautiful prospect. Besides this, he caused the roads to be all divided into miles (each mile containing little less than eight furlongs), and erected pillars of stone to signify the distance from one place to another. He likewise placed other stones at small distances from one another, on both sides of the way, by the help of which travellers might get easily on horseback without wanting a groom.

For these reasons, the people highly extolled him, and were ready upon all occasions to express their affection towards him. One day, in an oration to them, he declared that he had only one favor to request, which if they granted, he should think the greatest obligation in the world; yet if it were denied, he would never blame them for the refusal. This expression made the world believe that his ambition was to be consul; and it was generally expected that he wished to be both consul and tribune at the same time. When the day for election of consuls was at hand, and all in great expectation, he appeared in the Field with Caius Fannius,[4] canvassing together with his friends for his election. This was of great effect in Fannius's favor. He was chosen consul, and Caius elected tribune the second time, without his own seeking or petitioning for it, but at the voluntary motion of the people. But when he understood that the senators were his declared enemies, and that Fannius himself was none of the most zealous of friends, he began again to rouse the people with other new laws. He proposed that a colony of Roman citizens might be sent to re-people Tarentum and Capua, and that the Latins should enjoy the same privileges with the citizens of Rome. But the senate, apprehending that he would at last grow too powerful and dangerous, took a new and unusual course to alienate the people's affections from him, by playing the demagogue in opposition to him, and offering favors contrary to all good policy. Livius Drusus was fellow-tribune with Caius, a person of as good a family and as well educated as any amongst the Romans, and noways inferior to those who for their eloquence and riches were the most honored and most powerful men of that time. To him, therefore, the chief senators made their application, exhorting him to attack Caius, and

[4] This *Caius Fannius* is not Lælius's son-in-law, who is quoted in the Life of Tiberius, but a different person, Caius Fannius Strabo.

join in their confederacy against him; which they designed to carry on, not by using any force, or opposing the common people, but by gratifying and obliging them with such unreasonable things as otherwise they would have felt it honorable for them to incur the greatest unpopularity in resisting.

Livius offered to serve the senate with his authority in this business; and proceeded accordingly to bring forward such laws as were in reality neither honorable nor advantageous for the public; his whole design being to outdo Caius in pleasing and cajoling the populace (as if it had been in some comedy), with obsequious flattery and every kind of gratifications; the senate thus letting it be seen plainly, that they were not angry with Caius's public measures, but only desirous to ruin him utterly, or at least to lessen his reputation. For when Caius proposed the settlement of only two colonies, and mentioned the better class of citizens for that purpose, they accused him of abusing the people; and yet, on the contrary, were pleased with Drusus, when he proposed the sending out of twelve colonies, each to consist of three thousand persons, and those, too, the most needy that he could find. When Caius divided the public land amongst the poor citizens, and charged them with a small rent, annually, to be paid into the exchequer, they were angry at him, as one who sought to gratify the people only for his own interest; yet afterwards they commended Livius, though he exempted them from paying even that little acknowledgment. They were displeased with Caius, for offering the Latins an equal right with the Romans of voting at the election of magistrates; but when Livius proposed that it might not be lawful for a Roman captain to scourge a Latin soldier, they promoted the passing of that law. And Livius, in all his speeches to the people, always told them, that he proposed no laws but such as were agreeable to the senate, who had a particular regard to the people's advantage. And this truly was the only point in all his proceedings which was of any real service, as it created more kindly feelings towards the senate in the people; and whereas they formerly suspected and hated the principal senators, Livius appeased and mitigated this perverseness and animosity, by his profession that he had done nothing in favor and for the benefit of the commons, without their advice and approbation.

But the greatest credit which Drusus got for kindness and justice towards the people was, that he never seemed to propose any law for his own sake, or his own advantage; he committed the charge of seeing the colonies rightly settled to other commissioners; neither did he ever concern himself with the distribution of the moneys; whereas Caius always took the principal part in any important transactions of this kind. Rubrius, another tribune of the people, had proposed to have Carthage again inhabited, which had been demolished by Scipio, and it fell to Caius's lot to see this performed, and for that purpose he sailed to Africa. Drusus took this opportunity of his absence to insinuate himself still more into the people's affections, which he did chiefly by accusing Fulvius, who was a particular friend to Caius, and was appointed a commissioner with him for the division of the lands. Fulvius was a man of a turbulent spirit, and notoriously hated by the senate; and besides, he was suspected by others to have fomented the differences between the citizens and their confederates, and underhand to be inciting the Italians to rebel; though there was little other evidence of the truth of these accusations, than his being an unsettled character, and of a well-known seditious temper. This was one principal cause of Caius's ruin; for part of the envy which fell upon Fulvius, was extended to him. And when Scipio Africanus died suddenly, and no cause of such an unexpected death could be assigned, only some marks of blows upon his body seemed to intimate that he had suffered violence, as is related in the history of his life, the greatest part of the odium attached to Fulvius, because he was his enemy, and that very day had reflected upon Scipio in a public address to the people. Nor was Caius himself clear from suspicion. However, this great outrage, committed too upon the person of the greatest and most considerable man in Rome, was never either punished or inquired into thoroughly, for the populace opposed and hindered any judicial investigation, for fear that Caius should be implicated in the charge if proceedings were carried on. This, however, had happened some time before.

But in Africa, where at present Caius was engaged in the repeopling of Carthage, which he named Junonia, many ominous appearances, which presaged mischief, are reported to have been sent from the gods. For a sudden gust of wind falling upon the first standard, and the standard-bearer holding it fast, the staff broke; another sudden storm blew away the sacrifices, which were laid upon the altars, and carried them beyond the bounds laid out for the city; and the wolves came and carried away the very marks that were set up to show the boundary. Caius, notwithstanding all this, ordered and despatched the whole business in

CAIUS GRACCHUS

the space of seventy days, and then returned to Rome, understanding how Fulvius was prosecuted by Drusus, and that the present juncture of affairs would not suffer him to be absent. For Lucius Opimius, one who sided with the nobility, and was of no small authority in the senate, who had formerly sued to be consul, but was repulsed by Caius's interest, at the time when Fannius was elected, was in a fair way now of being chosen consul, having a numerous company of supporters. And it was generally believed, if he did obtain it, that he would wholly ruin Caius, whose power was already in a declining condition; and the people were not so apt to admire his actions as formerly, because there were so many others who every day contrived new ways to please them, with which the senate readily complied.

After his return to Rome, he quitted his house on the Palatine Mount, and went to live near the market-place, endeavoring to make himself more popular in those parts, where most of the humbler and poorer citizens lived. He then brought forward the remainder of his proposed laws, as intending to have them ratified by the popular vote; to support which a vast number of people collected from all quarters. But the senate persuaded Fannius, the consul, to command all persons who were not born Romans, to depart the city. A new and unusual proclamation was thereupon made, prohibiting any of the Allies or Confederates to appear at Rome during that time. Caius, on the contrary, published an edict, accusing the consul for what he had done, and setting forth to the Confederates, that if they would continue upon the place, they might be assured of his assistance and protection. However, he was not so good

as his word; for though he saw one of his own
familiar friends and companions dragged to prison
by Fannius's officers, he notwithstanding passed
by, without assisting him; either because he was
afraid to stand the test of his power, which was
already decreased, or because, as he himself reported, he was unwilling to give his enemies an
opportunity, which they very much desired, of
coming to actual violence and fighting. About
that time there happened likewise a difference between him and his fellow-officers upon this occasion. A show of gladiators was to be exhibited
before the people in the market-place, and most of
the magistrates erected scaffolds round about, with
an intention of letting them for advantage. Caius
commanded them to take down their scaffolds, that
the poor people might see the sport without paying
any thing. But nobody obeying these orders of
his, he gathered together a body of laborers, who
worked for him, and overthrew all the scaffolds,
the very night before the contest was to take
place. So that by the next morning the market-
place was cleared, and the common people had an
opportunity of seeing the pastime. In this, the
populace thought he had acted the part of a man;
but he much disobliged the tribunes, his colleagues,
who regarded it as a piece of violent and presumptuous interference.

This was thought to be the chief reason that he
failed of being a third time elected tribune; not
but that he had the most votes, but because his colleagues out of revenge caused false returns to be
made. But as to this matter there was a controversy. Certain it is, he very much resented this
repulse, and behaved with unusual arrogance towards some of his adversaries who were joyful at

his defeat, telling them, that all this was but a false, sardonic mirth,[5] as they little knew how much his actions threw them into obscurity.

As soon as Opimius also was chosen consul, they presently cancelled several of Caius's laws, and especially called in question his proceedings at Carthage, omitting nothing that was likely to irritate him, that from some effect of his passion they might find out a colorable pretence to put him to death. Caius at first bore these things very patiently; but afterwards, at the instigation of his friends, especially Fulvius, he resolved to put himself at the head of a body of supporters, to oppose the consul by force. They say also that on this occasion his mother, Cornelia, joined in the sedition, and assisted him by sending privately several strangers into Rome, under pretence as if they came to be hired there for harvest-men; for that intimations of this are given in her letters to him. However, it is confidently affirmed by others, that Cornelia did not in the least approve of these actions.

When the day came in which Opimius designed to abrogate the laws of Caius, both parties met very early at the capitol; and the consul having performed all the rites usual in their sacrifices, one Quintus Antyllius, an attendant on the consul, carrying out the entrails of the victim, spoke to Fulvius, and his friends who stood about him, " Ye factious citizens, make way for honest men." Some

---

[5] The Sardonic, or Sardonian laugh, is an expression as old as the Odyssey, the origin of which is not precisely known, and the meaning not always very clear. A forced, unnatural laugh, such as would be occasioned by tasting a bitter herb, which grew, it is said, in Sardinia, is the usual explanation.

report, that besides this provoking language, he extended his naked arm towards them, as a piece of scorn and contempt. Upon this he was presently killed with the strong stiles [6] which are commonly used in writing, though some say that on this occasion they had been manufactured for this purpose only. This murder caused a sudden consternation in the whole assembly, and the heads of each faction had their different sentiments about it. As for Caius he was much grieved, and severely reprimanded his own party, because they had given their adversaries a reasonable pretence to proceed against them, which they had so long hoped for. Opimius, immediately seizing the occasion thus offered, was in great delight, and urged the people to revenge; but there happening a great shower of rain on a sudden, it put an end to the business of that day.

Early the next morning, the consul summoned the senate, and whilst he advised with the senators in the senate-house, the corpse of Antyllius was laid upon a bier, and brought through the market-place, being there exposed to open view, just before the senate-house, with a great deal of crying and lamentation. Opimius was not at all ignorant that this was designed to be done; however, he seemed to be surprised, and wondered what the meaning of it should be; the senators, therefore, presently went out to know the occasion of it, and, standing about the corpse, uttered exclamations against the inhuman and barbarous act. The people meantime could not but feel resentment and

---

[6] The writing *stilus* or *stylus* (whence our word style) was a formidable piece of metal, flat at one end, and sharp at the other.

hatred for the senators, remembering how they themselves had not only assassinated Tiberius Gracchus, as he was executing his office in the very capitol, but had also thrown his mangled body into the river; yet now they could honor with their presence and their public lamentations in the forum the corpse of an ordinary hired attendant, (who, though he might perhaps die wrongfully, was, however, in a great measure the occasion of it himself,) by these means hoping to undermine him who was the only remaining defender and safeguard of the people.

The senators, after some time, withdrew, and presently ordered that Opimius, the consul, should be invested with extraordinary power to protect the commonwealth and suppress all tyrants. This being decreed, he presently commanded the senators to arm themselves, and the Roman knights to be in readiness very early the next morning, and every one of them to be attended with two servants well armed. Fulvius, on the other side, made his preparations and collected the populace. Caius at that time returning from the market-place, made a stop just before his father's statue, and fixing his eyes for some time upon it, remained in a deep contemplation; at length he sighed, shed tears, and departed. This made no small impression upon those who saw it, and they began to upbraid themselves, that they should desert and betray so worthy a man as Caius. They therefore went directly to his house, remaining there as a guard about it all night, though in a different manner from those who were a guard to Fulvius; for they passed away the night with shouting and drinking, and Fulvius himself, being the first to get drunk, spoke and acted many things very unbecoming a man of his age and character. On the other side, the party which guarded Caius, were quiet and diligent, relieving one another by turns, and forecasting, as in a public calamity, what the issue of things might be. As soon as daylight appeared, they roused Fulvius, who had not yet slept off the effects of his drinking; and having armed themselves with the weapons hung up in his house, that were formerly taken from the Gauls, whom he conquered in the time of his consulship, they presently, with threats and loud acclamations, made their way towards the Aventine Mount.

Caius could not be persuaded to arm himself, but put on his own gown, as if he had been going to the assembly of the people, only with this difference, that under it he had then a short dagger by his side. As he was going out, his wife came running to him at the gate, holding him with one hand, and with her other a young child of his. She thus bespoke him: "Alas, Caius, I do not now part with you to let you address the people, either as a tribune or a lawgiver, nor as if you were going to some honorable war, when though you might perhaps have encountered that fate which all must some time or other submit to, yet you had left me this mitigation of my sorrow, that my mourning was respected and honored. You go now to expose your person to the murderers of Tiberius, unarmed, indeed, and rightly so, choosing rather to suffer the worst of injuries, than do the least yourself. But even your very death at this time will not be serviceable to the public good. Faction prevails; power and arms are now the only measures of justice. Had your brother fallen before Numantia, the enemy would have given back what then had remained of Tiberius; but such is my hard fate, that I probably must be an humble suppliant to the floods or the waves, that they would somewhere restore to me your relics; for since Tiberius was not spared, what trust can we place either on the laws, or in the gods?" Licinia, thus bewailing, Caius, by degrees getting loose from her embraces, silently withdrew himself, being accompanied by his friends; she, endeavoring to catch him by the gown, fell prostrate upon the earth, lying there for some time speechless. Her servants took her up for dead, and conveyed her to her brother Crassus.

Fulvius, when the people were gathered together in a full body, by the advice of Caius, sent his youngest son into the market-place, with a herald's rod in his hand. He, being a very handsome youth, and modestly addressing himself, with tears in his eyes and a becoming bashfulness, offered proposals of agreement to the consul and the whole senate. The greatest part of the assembly were inclinable to accept of the proposals; but Opimius said, that it did not become them to send messengers and capitulate with the senate, but to surrender at discretion to the laws, like loyal citizens, and endeavor to merit their pardon by submission. He commanded the youth not to return, unless they would comply with these conditions. Caius, as it is reported, was very forward to go and clear himself before the senate; but none of his friends consenting to it, Fulvius sent his son a second time to intercede for them, as before. But Opimius, who was resolved that a battle should ensue, caused the youth to be apprehended, and committed into custody; and then, with a company of his foot-soldiers and some Cretan archers, set upon the party under Fulvius. These archers did such execution, and inflicted so many wounds, that a rout and flight quickly ensued. Fulvius fled into an obscure bathing-house; but shortly after being discovered, he and his eldest son were slain together. Caius was not observed to use any violence against any one; but, extremely disliking all these outrages, retired to Diana's temple. There he attempted to kill himself, but was hindered by his faithful friends, Pomponius and Licinius; they took his sword away from him, and were very urgent that he would endeavor to make his escape. It is reported, that falling upon his knee and lifting up his hands, he prayed the goddess that the Roman people, as a punishment for their ingratitude and treachery, might always remain in slavery. For as soon as a proclamation was made of a pardon, the greater part openly deserted him.

Caius, therefore, endeavored now to make his escape, but was pursued so close by his enemies, as far as the wooden bridge, that from thence he narrowly escaped. There his two trusty friends begged of him to preserve his own person by flight, whilst they in the mean time would keep their post, and maintain the passage; neither could their enemies, until they were both slain, pass the bridge. Caius had no other companion in his flight but one Philocrates, a servant of his. As he ran along, everybody encouraged him, and wished him success, as standers-by may do to those who are engaged in a race, but nobody either lent him any assistance, or would furnish him with a horse, though he asked for one; for his enemies had gained ground, and got very near him. However, he had still time enough to hide himself in a little grove, consecrated to the Furies.[7] In that place, his servant Philocrates hav-

---

[7] The *grove consecrated to the Furies* is probably the grove of Furina, *lucus Furinæ*, a goddess whom Cicero (*de Natura*

ing first slain him, presently afterwards killed himself also, and fell dead upon his master. Though some affirm it for a truth, that they were both taken alive by their enemies, and that Philocrates embraced his master so close, that they could not wound Caius until his servant was slain.

They say that when Caius's head was cut off, and carried away by one of his murderers, Septimuleius, Opimius's friend, met him, and forced it from him; because, before the battle began, they had made proclamation, that whoever should bring the head either of Caius or Fulvius, should, as a reward, receive its weight in gold. Septimuleius, therefore, having fixed Caius's head upon the top of his spear, came and presented it to Opimius. They presently brought the scales, and it was found to weigh above seventeen pounds. But in this affair, Septimuleius gave as great signs of his knavery, as he had done before of his cruelty; for having taken out the brains, he had filled the skull with lead. There were others who brought the head of Fulvius too, but, being mean, inconsiderable persons, were turned

Deorum, III., 8) connects with the Greek Eumenides or Erinnyes, so that it would not be absolutely a mistake in Plutarch; and Aurelius Victor expressly says, *by the help of his friend Pomponius, who turned to withstand the pursuers at the gate Trigemina and of Publius Lætorius who did so on the Sublician bridge, he reached the lucus Furinæ.* This obscure divinity, whether a Fury or a patron goddess of theft, nevertheless had had a high priest of her own, a *flamen Furinalis,* and a yearly festival, the *Furinalia,* facts in the time of Cicero and Varro scarcely known to a few antiquarians. The passages showing the route taken by Caius in his flight are of some interest in the topography of Rome, as they appear to prove that the Old Bridge, the Sublician, was outside the walls.

away without the promised reward. The bodies of these two persons, as well as of the rest who were slain, to the number of three thousand men, were all thrown into the river; their goods were confiscated, and their widows forbidden to put themselves into mourning. They dealt even more severely with Licinia, Caius's wife, and deprived her even of her jointure; and as an addition still to all their inhumanity, they barbarously murdered Fulvius's youngest son; his only crime being, not that he took up arms against them, or that he was present in the battle, but merely that he had come with articles of agreement; for this he was first imprisoned, then slain.

But that which angered the common people beyond all these things was, because at this time, in memory of his success, Opimius built the temple of Concord, as if he gloried and triumphed in the slaughter of so many citizens. Somebody in the night time, under the inscription of the temple, added this verse:—

Folly and Discord Concord's temple built.

Yet this Opimius, the first who, being consul, presumed to usurp the power of a dictator, condemning, without any trial, with three thousand other citizens, Caius Gracchus and Fulvius Flaccus, one of whom had triumphed, and been consul, the other far excelled all his contemporaries in virtue and honor, afterwards was found incapable of keeping his hands from thieving; and when he was sent ambassador to Jugurtha, king of Numidia, he was there corrupted by presents, and at his return being shamefully convicted of it, lost all his honors, and grew old amidst the hatred and the insults of the people; who, though humbled, and affrighted at the time, did not fail before long to let everybody see what respect and veneration they had for the memory of the Gracchi. They ordered their statues to be made and set up in public view; they consecrated the places where they were slain, and thither brought the first-fruits of every thing, according to the season of the year, to make their offerings. Many came likewise thither to their devotions, and daily worshipped there, as at the temples of the gods.

It is reported, that as Cornelia, their mother, bore the loss of her two sons with a noble and undaunted spirit, so, in reference to the holy places in which they were slain, she said, their dead bodies were well worthy of such sepulchres. She removed afterwards, and dwelt near the place called Misenum, not at all altering her former way of living. She had many friends, and hospitably received many strangers at her house; many Greeks and learned men were continually about her; nor was there any foreign prince but received gifts from her and presented her again. Those who were conversant with her, were much interested, when she pleased to entertain them with her recollections of her father Scipio Africanus, and of his habits and way of living. But it was most admirable to hear her make mention of her sons, without any tears or sign of grief, and give the full account of all their deeds and misfortunes, as if she had been relating the history of some ancient heroes. This made some imagine, that age, or the greatness of her afflictions, had made her senseless and devoid of natural feelings. But they who so thought, were themselves more truly insensible, not to see how much a noble nature and education avail to conquer any affliction;

and though fortune may often be more successful, and may defeat the efforts of virtue to avert misfortunes, it cannot, when we incur them, prevent our bearing them reasonably.

COMPARISON OF TIBERIUS AND CAIUS GRACCHUS

WITH

AGIS AND CLEOMENES

HAVING given an account severally of these persons, it remains only that we should take a view of them in comparison with one another.

As for the Gracchi, the greatest detractors and their worst enemies could not but allow, that they had a genius to virtue beyond all other Romans, which was improved also by a generous education. Agis and Cleomenes may be supposed to have had stronger natural gifts, since, though they wanted all the advantages of good education, and were bred up in those very customs, manners, and habits of living, which had for a long time corrupted others, yet they were public examples of temperance and frugality. Besides, the Gracchi, happening to live when Rome had her greatest repute for honor and virtuous actions, might justly have been ashamed, if they had not also left to the next generation the noble inheritance of the virtues of their ancestors. Whereas the other two had parents of different morals; and though they found their country in a sinking condition, and debauched, yet that did not quench their forward zeal to what was just and honorable.

The integrity of the two Romans, and their superiority to money, was chiefly remarkable in this; that in office and the administration of public affairs, they kept themselves from the imputation of unjust gain; whereas Agis might justly be offended, if he had only that mean commendation given him, that he took nothing wrongfully from any man, seeing he distributed his own fortunes, which, in ready money only, amounted to the value of six hundred talents, amongst his fellow-citizens. Extortion would have appeared a crime of a strange nature to him, who esteemed it a piece of covetousness to possess, though never so justly gotten, greater riches than his neighbors.

Their political actions, also, and the state revolutions they attempted, were very different in magnitude. The chief things in general that the two Romans commonly aimed at, were the settlement of cities and mending of highways; and, in particular, the boldest design which Tiberius is famed for, was the recovery of the public lands; and Caius gained his greatest reputation by the addition, for the exercise of judicial powers, of three hundred of the order of knights to the same number of senators. Whereas the alteration which Agis and Cleomenes made, was in a quite different kind. They did not set about removing partial evils and curing petty incidents[1] of disease, which would have been (as Plato says), like cutting off one of the Hydra's heads, the very means to increase the number; but they instituted a thorough reformation, such as

[1] The ordinary small legislation about petty cases of theft and breach of contract and the like is compared by Plato in the Republic (National Library Edition, Vol. II., p. 144) to *cutting the Hydra* (*quid leges sine moribus Vanæ proficiunt?*)—a fundamental change of principle is needed in the training, education, and discipline of mankind; in a commonwealth where this exists all minor observances will follow as a matter of course, and where it does not, these complex regulations are worse than useless.

would free the country at once from all its grievances, or rather, to speak more truly, they reversed that former change which had been the cause of all their calamities, and so restored their city to its ancient state.

However, this must be confessed in the behalf of the Gracchi, that their undertakings were always opposed by men of the greatest influence. On the other side, those things which were first attempted by Agis, and afterwards consummated by Cleomenes, were supported by the great and glorious precedent of those ancient laws concerning frugality and levelling which they had themselves received upon the authority of Lycurgus, and he had instituted on that of Apollo. It is also further observable, that from the actions of the Gracchi, Rome received no additions to her former greatness; whereas, under the conduct of Cleomenes, Greece presently saw Sparta exert her sovereign power over all Peloponnesus, and contest the supreme command with the most powerful princes of the time; success in which would have freed Greece from Illyrian and Gaulish violence, and placed her once again under the orderly rule of the sons of Hercules.

From the circumstances of their deaths, also, we may infer some difference in the quality of their courage. The Gracchi, fighting with their fellow-citizens, were both slain, as they endeavored to make their escape; Agis willingly submitted to his fate, rather than any citizen should be in danger of his life. Cleomenes, being shamefully and unjustly treated, made an effort toward revenge, but failing of that, generously fell by his own hand.

On the other side it must be said, that Agis never did a great action worthy a commander, being prevented by an untimely death. And as for those heroic actions of Cleomenes, we may justly compare with them that of Tiberius, when he was the first who attempted to scale the walls of Carthage, which was no mean exploit. We may add the peace which he concluded with the Numantines, by which he saved the lives of twenty thousand Romans, who otherwise had certainly been cut off. And Caius, not only at home, but in war in Sardinia, displayed distinguished courage. So that their early actions were no small argument, that afterwards they might have rivalled the best of the Roman commanders, if they had not died so young.

In civil life, Agis showed a lack of determination; he let himself be baffled by the craft of Agesilaus, disappointed the expectations of the citizens as to the division of the lands, and generally left all the designs which he had deliberately formed and publicly announced, unperformed and unfulfilled, through a young man's want of resolution. Cleomenes, on the other hand, proceeded to effect the revolution with only too much boldness and violence, and unjustly slew the Ephors, whom he might, by superiority in arms, have gained over to his party, or else might easily have banished, as he did several others of the city. For to use the knife, unless in the extremest necessity, is neither good surgery nor wise policy, but in both cases mere unskilfulness; and in the latter, unjust as well as unfeeling. Of the Gracchi, neither the one nor the other was the first to shed the blood of his fellow-citizens; and Caius is reported to have avoided all manner of resistance, even when his life was aimed at, showing himself always valiant against a foreign enemy, but wholly inactive in a sedition. This was the reason that he went from his own house unarmed, and withdrew when the battle began, and in all respects showed himself anxious rather not to do any harm to others, than not to suffer any himself. Even the very flight of the Gracchi must not be looked upon as an argument of their mean spirit, but an honorable retreat from endangering of others. For if they had staid, they must either have yielded to those who assailed them, or else have fought them in their own defence.

The greatest crime that can be laid to Tiberius's charge, was the deposing of his fellow tribune, and seeking afterwards a second tribuneship for himself. As for the death of Antyllius, it is falsely and unjustly attributed to Caius, for he was slain unknown to him, and much to his grief. On the contrary, Cleomenes (not to mention the murder of the Ephors) set all the slaves at liberty, and governed by himself alone in reality, having a partner only for show; having made choice of his brother Euclidas, who was one of the same family. He prevailed upon Archidamus, who was the right heir to the kingdom of the other line, to venture to return home from Messene; but after his being slain, by not doing any thing to revenge his death, confirmed the suspicion that he was privy to it himself. Lycurgus, whose example he professed to imitate, after he had voluntarily settled his kingdom upon Charillus, his brother's son, fearing lest, if the youth should chance to die by accident, he might be suspected for it, travelled a long time, and would not return again to Sparta until Charillus had a son, and an heir to his kingdom. But we have indeed no other Grecian who is worthy to be compared with Lycurgus, and it is clear enough that in the public measures of Cleomenes various acts of considerable audacity and lawlessness may be found.

Those, therefore, who incline to blame their characters, may observe, that the two Grecians were disturbers even from their youth, lovers of contest, and aspirants to despotic power; that Tiberius and Caius by nature had an excessive desire after glory and honors. Beyond this, their enemies could find nothing to bring against them; but as soon as the contention began with their adversaries, their heat and passions would so far prevail beyond their natural temper, that by them, as by ill winds, they were driven afterwards to all their rash undertakings. What could be more just and honorable than their first design, had not the power and the faction of the rich, by endeavoring to abrogate that law, engaged them both in those fatal quarrels, the one, for his own preservation, the other, to revenge his brother's death, who was murdered without any law or justice?

From the account, therefore, which has been given, you yourself may perceive the difference; which if it were to be pronounced of every one singly, I should affirm Tiberius to have excelled them all in virtue; that young Agis had been guilty of the fewest misdeeds; and that in action and boldness Caius came far short of Cleomenes.

www.ingramcontent.com/pod-product-compliance
Lightning Source LLC
Chambersburg PA
CBHW020629230426
43665CB00008B/92